CCNA
Cloud Complete
Study Guide
Exam 210-451 and Exam 210-455

Todd Montgomery

Stephen Olson

SYBEX®
A Wiley Brand

Senior Acquisitions Editor: Kenyon Brown
Development Editor: David Clark
Technical Editor: Jon Buhagair
Copy Editor: Kim Wimpsett
Editorial Manager: Pete Gaughan
Production Manager: Kathleen Wisor
Executive Editor: Jim Minatel
Proofreader: Nancy Carrasco
Indexer: Jack Lewis
Project Coordinator, Cover: Brent Savage
Cover Designer: Wiley
Cover Image: @Jeremy Woodhouse/Getty Images, Inc.

To my awesome son, William, and incredible daughter, Allison: This book is dedicated to both of you.
—Todd Montgomery

To my extremely patient wife, Melissa, who gives up countless nights to my working and writing. Thank you for being the true provider in our house.
—Stephen Olson

About the Authors

Todd Montgomery has been in the networking industry for more than 35 years and holds many certifications from Cisco, CompTIA, Juniper, VMware, and other companies. He is Cisco CCNA Security, route/switch, data center, and CCNP/CCDP route/switch certified.

Todd has spent most of his career out in the field working on-site in data centers throughout North America and around the world. He has worked for equipment manufacturers, systems integrators, and end users of data center equipment in the public, service provider, and government sectors. He is currently working as a writer and technical editor and is involved in network automation projects.

Todd lives in Austin, Texas, and in his free time enjoys auto racing, general aviation, and Austin's live music venues. He can be reached at toddmont@thegateway.net.

Steve Olson has been in the networking industry for almost 15 years and holds many certifications including Cisco's CCIE #21910, the Cisco CCNA and CCNP amongst others. Steve has spent the majority of his career working in large enterprise as well as consulting for service providers around the world in the cloud, wan, and data center segments. He is currently working on SDN projects in the wan and data center spaces as well as overall cloud networking for the enterprise. He currently resides in Austin, Texas with his wife and two children. Steve enjoys music and guitar in his free time. Steve can be reached at stephenjolson@gmail.com.

Acknowledgments

There are many people who work to put a book together, and although as authors we dedicate an enormous amount of time to writing the book, it would never be published without the dedicated, hard work of the whole team at Wiley. They are truly a fantastic group to work with, and without the Wiley team this book would have never been possible.

First, we'd like to thank Kenyon Brown, our senior acquisitions editor, who offered us support and guidance through the writing process. Ken was always there to answer questions and point us in the right direction. Without Ken as a mentor, we could never have pulled this one off.

We also can never thank our development editor David Clark too many times; David is a true professional who stayed on top of the schedule and professionally reminded us of the next upcoming deadline we were working to meet. Without David's help putting this book together, it would have been much more difficult than it was. David has the ability to take the raw text from the authors, who are primarily engineers, and manage to turn it into presentable copy. Thanks again, David!

Jon Buhagiar offered excellent input as our technical editor. He gave us invaluable feedback on how to make the technical concepts more understandable to the readers and pointed out where we needed to modify our technical content for accuracy. It was great that Jon was able to be on this project with us.

A big thank-you to Katie Wisor, the production editor for this book. Kim Wimpsett worked her markup magic in the background as the copy editor. The authors are both amazed at how Katie and Kim along with their team of professionals could take our work and transform it into such a presentable book. We're sure there is a whole staff at Wiley lurking in the background, and we will never know how much they helped, but to everyone at Wiley, a big thank-you! You made the late nights and long weekends of writing and putting this book together all worthwhile.

Contents

Introduction

Welcome to the exciting world of cloud computing and Cisco certifications! If you picked up this book because you want to improve yourself with a secure and rewarding job in the new and fast-growing cloud computing space, you have come to the right place. Whether you are striving to enter the thriving, dynamic IT sector or seeking to enhance your skills in the emerging cloud computing field, being Cisco CCNA Cloud certified can seriously stack the odds in your favor of success.

Cisco certifications are powerful instruments of success that will most certainly improve your knowledge of cloud computing. As you progress through this book, you'll gain a broad and deep understanding of cloud computing operations that offers unprecedented exposure to this dynamic and fast-growing field. The knowledge and expertise you will gain are essential for your success in all areas of the cloud computing field.

By deciding to become a Cisco CCNA Cloud certified professional, you're proudly announcing to the world that you want to become an unrivaled cloud computing expert, a goal that this book will get you well on your way to achieving. Congratulations in advance on the beginning of your brilliant future!

> For up-to-the-minute updates covering additions or modifications to the Cisco certification exams, as well as additional study tools, videos, practice questions, and bonus material, be sure to visit the Sybex website and forum at www.sybex.com.

Why Should You Become Certified in Cisco Cloud Technologies?

Cisco is the world's leading networking equipment vendor. It plays a key role in cloud computing operations, from the networking, computing, and storage equipment in the data center to the wide area networks, security hardware and software, and applications that enable cloud computing.

Cisco certifications are recognized and respected worldwide for their quality and rigorous standards. Cisco offers a broad range of certifications on a wide variety of networking topics. When you become CCNA Cloud certified, you have validated your skills and expertise in the implementation and ongoing support of cloud-based services. Becoming a CCNA Cloud certified professional validates that you have the knowledge to be a successful cloud engineer.

In fact, Cisco certifications are some of the most sought-after certifications in the market today. Studying for and passing the two CCNA Cloud exams gives engineers a set of skills to succeed in the fast-growing field of cloud computing.

Rest assured that when you pass the CCNA cloud exams, you're headed down a path to certain success!

What Does This Book Cover?

This book follows the official Cisco exam blueprints for the two exams required to become cloud certified at the CCNA level.

The first exam is CLDFND 210-451, which covers the fundamentals of cloud computing and offers the big picture of cloud architectures, models, and terminology. We will take you from little or no knowledge of cloud computing to a level that gives you a broad background and overview of modern cloud operations. You will also learn about the underlying technologies used to enable cloud computing such as networking, compute, storage, automation, and security.

The second part of this book will prepare you for the CLDADM 210-455 exam, which focuses on cloud administration, deployment, and management applications in the Cisco cloud product portfolio.

You will learn the following information in this book:

Chapter 1: Fundamentals of Cloud Computing   The book starts out investigating the most common cloud models and characteristics. Then it moves into more detail with an introduction to the components of on-demand computing, resource pooling, elasticity, metering of cloud services, how the cloud provides ubiquitous access, and the concept of multitenancy.

Chapter 2: Defining Cloud Service Models   In this chapter, you'll learn about cloud service models including Infrastructure as a Service, Platform as a Service, and Software as a Service, and you'll learn about the use cases for each type.

Chapter 3: Understanding Cloud Deployment Models   Chapter 3 covers cloud deployment modes and goes into detail on the four most common models: private, public, community, and hybrid clouds.

Chapter 4: Introducing the Cisco Intercloud Solution   Chapter 4 builds on your cloud knowledge by explaining the Cisco Intercloud Fabric application suite and goes into detail on the various fabric services offered with this product family.

Chapter 5: The Cisco Unified Computing System   This chapter covers Cisco-specific cloud hardware and software products that will be covered on the exam including the UCS family of servers. The chapter also covers the UCS Manager application used to configure, monitor, and manage the UCS family of products.

Chapter 6: Cisco Data Center Products and Technologies   This extensive chapter covers Cisco's data center product lines including the Nexus product line. You will also learn about network architectures in the cloud data center, Cisco's unified switching fabric, software-defined networking, data center spine and leaf designs, and the APIC controller. This chapter covers a lot of core material and is important to understand before taking the exam.

Chapter 7: Server Virtualization in the Cloud   You'll now delve deeper into the underlying infrastructure of the cloud data center. Virtualization is the technology that enables cloud computing; this chapter will focus on server virtualization.

Chapter 8: Infrastructure Virtualization   Infrastructure virtualization includes the software abstraction of data center core networking technologies such as Ethernet switching, routing, and other networking services. Also covered in this chapter are container services.

Chapter 9: Cloud Storage   Chapter 9 starts exploring the storage objects outlined in the 210-451 exam. This is an introductory storage chapter that covers the provisioning and pooling of storage resources.

Chapter 10: Storage Area Networking   Chapter 10 delves deeper into cloud storage by covering the networking aspects of storage systems. You will learn about storage access technologies, network-attached storage systems, and storage area networking.

Chapter 11: Cisco Storage Product Families and Offerings   Chapter 11 continues the investigation into cloud storage by covering the Cisco hardware products in its storage lineup. These include the core SAN products in the MDS family, the storage network capabilities in the Nexus switching family, and the Invicta products.

Chapter 12: Integrated Cloud Infrastructure Offerings   There are several reference designs that are central to Cisco cloud and data center implementations. This chapter covers integrated infrastructure designs from Network Appliance, VCE, EMS, and Red Hat.

Chapter 12 ends the coverage of the objectives required to complete the CLDFND 210-451 exam.

Chapter 13: Configuring Roles and Profiles   This chapter begins the study for the CLDADM 210-455 cloud administration exam. The cloud administration exam focuses on Cisco applications and management applications for the cloud. For the rest of the book, we will focus primarily on the Cisco ONE Enterprise Cloud suite of applications since the CLDADM 210-455 exam tests you on the applications that make up the Cisco ONE product family. In this chapter, you will learn how to configure user roles and how to create groups, roles, and profiles.

Chapter 14: Virtual Machine Operations   Chapter 14 covers cloud virtual machine topics such as migrations, editing, and snapshots.

Chapter 15: Virtual Application Containers   Virtual application containers are the focus of this chapter and explain how to create and manage and troubleshoot containers using Cisco cloud management applications.

Chapter 16: Intercloud Chargeback Model   The Intercloud Chargeback model covers billing reports, chargeback model and features, budget policies, and cost models.

Chapter 17: Cloud Reporting Systems   Cloud reports are a key part of the Cisco cloud family of applications. Report generation for virtual, physical, billing, system utilization, and snapshots are covered in this chapter.

Chapter 18: UCS Director Service Catalogs   Service catalogs are integrated into the Cisco UCS Director suite of cloud management applications. Service catalogs allow for the ordering and provisioning of predefined services. You will learn about the Prime Service Catalog in this chapter.

Chapter 19: Cisco Prime Service Catalog Templates and Provisioning   Chapter 19 continues exploring the Prime Service Catalog for provisioning, template formations, verification, end-user ordering using the catalog, deploying VMs, and applications with the catalog.

Chapter 20: Cisco Prime Service Catalog Components   This chapter covers the storefront ordering, Stack Designer, and heat orchestration of the Cisco Prime Service Catalog. We also provide more detail into the UCS Director by introducing management, monitoring, and orchestration, the Bare Metal Agent, and the portal. Finally, UCS Performance Manager and Cisco Intelligent Automation for Cloud are discussed.

Chapter 21: Cloud Monitoring and Remediation   The final chapter for the CLDADM 210-455 exam covers fault and performance provisioning and monitoring, dashboards, triggers, and logging. We will finish the chapter with coverage of backing up the monitoring applications.

Appendix A: Answers to Review Questions   This appendix contains the answers to the book's review questions.

Appendix B: Answers to Written Lab   This appendix contains the answers to the book's written labs.

Interactive Online Learning Environment and Test Bank

We've put together some great online tools to help you pass the two CCNA cloud exams. The free interactive online learning environment that accompanies this CCNA Cloud exam certification guide provides a test bank and study tools to help you prepare for the exam. By using these tools, you can dramatically increase your chances of passing the exam on your first try.

The online section includes the following:

Sample Tests   Many sample tests are provided throughout this book and online, including the assessment test (which you'll find at the end of this Introduction) and the review questions at the end of each chapter. In addition, there is an *exclusive* online practice exam for each of the two CCNA Cloud exams that are included at no charge. Use these questions to test your knowledge of the study guide material. The online test bank runs on multiple devices.

Flashcards   The online text banks include 100 flashcards for each exam that are designed and specifically written to hit you hard, so don't get discouraged if you don't ace your way through them at first! They're there to ensure that you're ready for the exam. And no worries—armed with the review questions, practice exams, and flashcards, you'll be more than prepared when exam day comes. The questions are provided in digital flashcard format (a question followed by a single correct answer). You can use the flashcards to reinforce your learning and provide last-minute test prep before the exam.

Other Study Tools   A glossary of key terms from this book and their definitions is available as a fully searchable PDF.

 Go to www.wiley.com/go/sybextestprep to register and gain access to this interactive online learning environment and test bank with study tools.

How to Use This Book

If you want a solid foundation for the serious effort of preparing for the two Cisco CCNA Cloud exams, then look no further. We've spent hundreds of hours putting together this book with the sole intention of helping you to pass the exam as well as learn about the exciting field of cloud computing!

This book is loaded with valuable information, and you will get the most out of your study time if you understand why the book is organized the way it is.

So, to maximize your benefit from this book, we recommend the following study method:

1. Take the assessment test that's provided at the end of this Introduction. (The answers are at the end of the test.) It's okay if you don't know any of the answers; that's why you bought this book! Carefully read over the explanations for any question you get wrong and note the chapters in which the material relevant to them is covered. This information should help you plan your study strategy.

2. Study each chapter carefully, making sure you fully understand the information and the test objectives listed at the beginning of each one. Pay extra-close attention to any chapters that include material covered in questions you missed.

3. Answer all the review questions related to each chapter. Many of the questions are presented in a scenario format to emulate real-world tasks that you may encounter. (The answers appear in Appendix A.) Note the questions that confuse you, and study the topics they cover again until the concepts are crystal clear. And again—do not just skim these questions! Make sure you fully comprehend the reason for each correct answer. Remember that these will not be the exact questions you will find on the exam, but they're written to help you understand the chapter material and ultimately pass the exam.

4. Each chapter also concludes with a fill-in-the-blank type of written exam that is designed to improve your memory and comprehension of key items that were presented in the chapter. These are great for test preparation; we suggest going over these questions until you are able to consistently answer them error free. (The answers appear in Appendix B.)

5. Try your hand at the practice questions that are exclusive to this book. The questions can be found at www.wiley.com/go/sybextestprep.

Remember, this book covers both the CLDFND 210-451 and CLDADM 210-455 exams. We suggest you study and take the 210-451 exam first and then move on to the 210-455 exam because the second exam builds on the material in the first exam.

To learn every bit of the material covered in this book, you'll have to apply yourself regularly and with discipline. Try to set aside the same time period every day to study, and select a comfortable and quiet place to do so. We're confident that if you work hard, you'll be surprised at how quickly you learn this material.

If you follow these steps and study in addition to using the written and review questions, the practice exams, and the electronic flashcards, it would actually be hard to fail the two Cisco exams. But understand that studying for the Cisco CCNA Cloud exams is a lot like getting in shape—if you do not go to the gym every day, it's not going to happen!

According to the Cisco certification website, the CCNA Cloud exam details are as follows:

CLDFND 210-451 Understanding Cisco Cloud Fundamentals

- **Exam description:** CLDFN covers basic cloud computing terms, deployment models, and Cisco cloud infrastructure, Intercloud, the Unified Computing System that includes server, storage, networking, and unified fabric and cloud management applications.

- **Number of questions:** 55–65

- **Type of questions:** Multiple choice

- **Length of test:** 90 minutes

- **Language:** English

- **Testing center:** Pearson VUE

CLDADM 210-455 Understanding Cisco Cloud Administration

- **Exam description:** CLDADM covers administration of the Cisco Cloud suite of products including provisioning systems, catalogs, management, monitoring, reporting, charge-back, and problem remediation.

- **Number of questions:** 55–65

- **Type of questions:** Multiple choice

- **Length of test:** 90 minutes

- **Language:** English

- **Testing center:** Pearson VUE

Suggested Experience

We suggest that you have at least 24–36 months of work experience in IT networking, network storage, or data center administration. A familiarity with any major hypervisor technologies for server virtualization is useful in understanding the core virtualization concepts discussed.

Knowledge of the definitions of the cloud service models (IaaS, PaaS, SaaS) and common cloud deployment models (private, public, hybrid) is helpful in understanding the concepts presented in this book.

Hands-on experience with at least one public cloud IaaS platform is helpful.

If you do not meet these suggestions, do not worry! They are only suggestions and not absolute requirements. We offer these so you know what to expect, but you can gain knowledge by becoming familiar with the objectives covered in this book.

How Do You Go About Taking the Exam?

Cisco testing is provided by its global testing partner, Pearson VUE. You can locate your closest testing center at https://home.pearsonvue.com/test-taker.aspx.

This website enables you to locate your nearest testing center and schedule your exam. In the search area, enter **Cisco Systems** and click Available Exams on the right side of the screen. Enter the exam number (either **210-451** or **210-455**). Select Schedule This Exam and log into the site. If you do not have an account with Pearson VUE, it will ask you to create one. Follow the steps to schedule and pay for the exam. You will be prompted to accept the Cisco terms and conditions as well as the confidentiality agreement before proceeding. The next step is to locate a testing center near you; enter your address to have the site list all centers in your area. After selecting the testing center you prefer, select the date and time you want to sit for the exam. Then all you need to do is to make your payment and you are ready to go!

After you have registered for the Cloud certification exams, you will receive a confirmation e-mail that supplies you with all the information you will need to take the exam. Remember to take a printout of the confirmation e-mail and two forms of ID (one with a photograph) with you to the testing center.

Tips for Taking Your Cloud Exams

The Cisco CCNA Cloud exams contain 55–65 multiple-choice questions and must be completed in 90 minutes or less. This information may change over time, and we advise you to check www.cisco.com for the latest updates.

Many questions on the exam offer answer choices that at first glance look identical, especially the syntax questions. So, remember to read through the choices carefully because close just doesn't cut it. If you get information in the wrong order or forget one measly character, you may get the question wrong. Many of the questions will be presented in a scenario format that can be a long involved statement that is designed to confuse or misdirect you. Read these questions carefully and make sure you completely understand what is being asked. It is important to filter out irrelevant statements in scenario questions and focus on what they are asking you to identify as the correct answer. So, to practice, do the exams and hands-on exercises from this book's chapters over and over again until they feel natural to you. Do the online sample tests and flashcards until you can consistently answer all the questions correctly. Relax, read the question over until you are 100 percent clear on what it is asking, and then eliminate a few of the obviously wrong answers.

Here are some general tips for exam success:

- Arrive early at the exam center so you can relax and review your study materials.

- Read the questions carefully. Don't jump to conclusions. Make sure you're clear about exactly what each question asks. "Read twice, answer once!" Scenario questions can be long and contain information that is not relevant to the answer; take your time and understand what they are *really* asking you.

- Ask for a piece of paper and pencil if it is offered so you can jot down notes and make sketches during the exam.

- When answering multiple-choice questions that you're not sure about, use the process of elimination to get rid of the obviously incorrect answers first. Doing this greatly improves your odds if you need to make an educated guess.

After you complete an exam, you'll get immediate, online notification of your pass or fail status, a printed examination score report that indicates your pass or fail status, and your exam results by section. (The test administrator will give you the printed score report.) Test scores are automatically forwarded to Cisco after the test is completed, so you don't need to send your score to them. If you pass the certification, you'll receive confirmation from Cisco and a package in the mail with a nice document suitable for framing showing that you are now a Cisco CCNA Cloud certified professional!

CCNA Cloud Certification Renewals

The CCNA Cloud certification is good for three years from the date of achieving the certification. You can keep your certification up-to-date by taking other CCNA or CCNP exams before the certification expires. See the Cisco website for the latest recertification policies.

CLDFND 210-451 Exam Objectives

The following topics are Cisco's general guidelines for the content likely to be included on the exam. Since this is a general guideline, you may find that other topics will appear on the exams that are not included in the listed objectives. Cisco reserves the right to change the exam at any time.

The following lists the technical areas covered in the certification and the extent to which they are represented:

Domain	Percentage of examination
1.0 Cloud Characteristics and Models	14%
2.0 Cloud Deployment	16%
3.0 Basic Knowledge of Cloud Compute	24%
4.0 Basic Knowledge of Cloud Networking	22%
5.0 Basic Knowledge of Cloud Storage	24%
Total	100%

1.0 210-451 Cloud Characteristics and Models

Exam Objective	Chapter
1.1 Describe common cloud characteristics	1
1.1.a On-demand self service	1
1.1.b Elasticity	1
1.1.c Resource pooling	1
1.1.d Metered service	1
1.1.e Ubiquitous network access (smartphone, tablet, mobility)	1
1.1.f Multi-tenancy	1

2.0 210-451 Cloud Deployment

3.0 210-451 Basic Knowledge of Cloud Compute

4.0 210-451 Basic Knowledge of Cloud Networking

5.0 210-451 Basic Knowledge of Cloud Storage

Exam objectives are subject to change at any time without prior notice and at Cisco's sole discretion. Please visit Cisco's certification website (https://learningnetwork.cisco.com/community/certifications/ccna-cloud/overview) for the latest information on the CCNA Cloud exams.

Understanding Cisco Cloud Fundamentals (210-451) Assessment Exam

1. Which of the following is a primary component of cloud computing?

    A. Interexchange services

    B. Shared application software

    C. Virtualization

    D. On-demand self-service

2. What are three NIST service models found in the cloud?

    A. IaaS, SaaS, PaaS

    B. Public, private, hybrid

    C. CaaS, PaaS, DRaaS

    D. Public, community, shared

3. Which deployment model is usually accessed by a large and diverse group of companies?

    A. Hybrid

    B. Private

    C. Community

    D. Public

4. What does Intercloud Director provide the end user?

    A. Security configuration utility to enable encrypted cloud interconnections

    B. A single management portal for hybrid clouds

    C. Scale-up and scale-out elasticity

    D. vPath as a virtual machine

5. Which Cisco UCS application manages a cluster of domains?

    A. XML

    B. UCSM

    C. UCS Central

    D. Java

6. The Cisco three-tier design model consists of which layers? (Choose three.)

    A. Access

    B. Unified fabric

    C. ACL

    D. Core

    E. Switch block

    F. Aggregation

    G. UCSM

7. What software enables a server to be logically abstracted and appear to the operating system running on it as if it is running directly on the server hardware itself?

    A. Virtualization

    B. Hypervisor

    C. IaaS

    D. Virtual machine

8. Which Cisco-developed protocol steers traffic to or from a VM to a services node via forwarding policies?

    A. WCCP

    B. VSG

    C. vPath

    D. LACP

9. Which storage implementation in the cloud supports the failure of two disks simultaneously without losing data?

    A. DAS

    B. RAID 5

    C. NAS

    D. RAID 6

    E. Fibre Channel

10. Which two storage protocols encapsulate storage requests and data that can be transported over an Ethernet LAN? (Choose two.)

    A. iSCSI

    B. Ethernet

    C. SCSI

    D. Fibre Channel

    E. FCoE

11. Which chassis-based Cisco switch is used for core and aggregation switching in large cloud and data center deployments?

    A. 3124SA

    B. 5696

    C. 9513

    D. 7010

12. Which of the following are NIST-defined cloud service models that can host a service provider database?

   A. Software as a Service

   B. Security as a Service

   C. Platform as a Service

   D. Applications as a Service

   E. Communications as a Service

   F. Infrastructure as a Service

13. A cloud service provider will provide which services in the IaaS service model? (Choose three.)

   A. Linux or Windows OS

   B. Storage

   C. CPU

   D. DNS

   E. Memory

   F. Object brokers

14. What virtualization technology is used in the public cloud to react in almost real time to increases or decreases of the application processing requirements?

   A. Load balancing

   B. Service chaining

   C. Resource pooling

   D. Elasticity

15. Which of the following statements are true about Cisco Intercloud? (Choose two.)

   A. Operates with specific hypervisors

   B. Centralized management portal

   C. Interconnects community clouds to the Internet

   D. Service provider and business application components

16. The UCS family of products includes which base technologies? (Choose three.)

   A. Storage

   B. Firewall security

   C. Intrusion detection

   D. Servers

   E. Load balancing

   F. Networking

   G. Cloud orchestration

17. What is a Cisco remote line card interconnect technology?

    A. FEX

    B. VDC

    C. VPC

    D. ACI

18. What kind of hypervisor runs directly on the bare-metal server?

    A. Virtualized

    B. Type 1

    C. Type 2

    D. ACI

19. Virtual switching is implemented where in the cloud network?

    A. Virtual machine

    B. Hypervisor

    C. Aggregation

    D. SaaS

    E. Distribution

20. What provisioning model is used by cloud-based orchestration systems to allocate the maximum purchased storage capacity at deployment?

    A. Thick

    B. Thin

    C. Tier 1

    D. Tier 2

21. What storage technology segments a SAN switching fabric into port groupings on the SAN switches with each running a separate FLOGI process and only communicating with themselves?

    A. Zoning

    B. LUN masking

    C. VSAN

    D. ACL

22. What operating system is used in the Nexus line of data center switches?

    A. NX-OS

    B. ISR-OS

    C. IOS

    D. SAN-OS

23. What is the unit of compute and infrastructure that is designed for a specific purpose?

    A. Rack

    B. POD

    C. ROW

    D. Farm

24. Software-defined networks centralize and virtualize which network component?

    A. Forwarding plane

    B. Control plane

    C. Converged fabric

    D. Core layer

25. What server migration type is used when cloning an existing virtual machine and installing it on a cloud provider's hypervisor?

    A. Type 1

    B. P2V

    C. Type 2

    D. V2V

Answers to Understanding Cisco Cloud Fundamentals (210-451) Assessment Exam

1. D. On-demand service provisioning is a key enabler of cloud computing.

2. A. The three primary cloud service models defined by NIST are Infrastructure as a Service (IaaS), Platform as a Service (PaaS), and Software as a Service (SaaS).

3. D. The public cloud is shared by many customers across a wide spectrum of businesses.

4. B. Intercloud Director is a centralized management portal for hybrid cloud deployments.

5. C. UCS Central manages and monitors one or more UCS domains.

6. A, D, F. The Cisco three-tier network model includes the access, aggregation, and core layers.

7. B. The hypervisor is software that allows multiple virtual machines to run on a single server hardware platform.

8. C. vPath directs the flow of traffic to virtual appliances and network services.

9. D. RAID 6 writes two separate parity stripes across the entire array and supports operations when one or two disks in the array fail.

10. A, E. iSCSI and FCoE are LAN protocols that encapsulate storage traffic for transmission over an Ethernet network.

11. D. The Nexus 7000 series of chassis-based switches is designed for data center aggregation and core switching.

12. A. Software as a Service includes cloud-based applications such as databases.

13. B, C, E. Infrastructure is the key word in this question and indicates that hardware, such as memory, storage, and CPUs, is included in the IaaS service model.

14. D. Elasticity is the ability of a cloud service to react to load demands.

15. B, D. Cisco Intercloud includes a centralized management portal, application services, a service catalog, and secure interconnections to public, private, and Cisco partner clouds.

16. A, D, F. The UCS product family integrates compute, networking, and storage technologies into one product family.

17. A. The Cisco Fabric Extender (FEX) technology is used to interconnect and control remote Nexus 2000 series switches.

18. A. A Type 1 hypervisor runs directly on the server hardware.

19. B. Virtual switching operates at the hypervisor level.

20. A. Thick provisioning allows for the allocation of the maximum volume size at deployment time.

21. C. A VSAN segments a Fibre Channel SAN switch into multiple logical storage area networks, with each VSAN providing network services such as login and an initiator to target communications.

22. A. NX-OS is the operating system for the Nexus product line and is derived from the SAN-OS MDS operating system.

23. B. POD is a term that refers to a group of devices or infrastructure designed for a certain requirement, network service, or application.

24. B. SDNs centralize and automate the network control plane.

25. D. A virtual-to-virtual (V2V) migration is when a virtual machine is migrated from one virtualized server environment to another.

CLDADM 210-455 Exam Objectives

The following topics are Cisco's general guidelines for the content likely to be included on the exam. Since this is a general guideline, you may find that other topics will appear on the exams that are not included in the listed objectives. Cisco reserves the right to change the exam at any time.

The following lists the technical areas covered in the certification and the extent to which they are represented:

Domain	Percentage of examination
1.0 Cloud Infrastructure Administration and reporting	21%
2.0 Chargeback and Billing reports	10%
3.0 Cloud Provisioning	26%
4.0 Cloud Systems Management and Monitoring	26%
5.0 Cloud Remediation	17%
Total	100%

1.0 210-455 Cloud Infrastructure Administration and Reporting

Exam Objective	Chapter
1.0 Cloud Infrastructure Administration and Reporting	13
1.1 Configure users/groups and role-based access control in the portal, including basic troubleshooting	13
1.1.a Describe default roles	13
1.1.b Configure new user with single role	13
1.1.c Describe multirole user profiles	13
1.1.d Configure a user profile	13
1.2 Perform virtual machine operations	13
1.2.a Configure live migrations of VMs from host to host	14
1.2.b Edit VM	14

2.0 210-455 Chargeback and Billing Reports

3.0 210-455 Cloud Provisioning

4.0 210-455 Cloud Systems Management and Monitoring

5.0 210-455 Cloud Remediation

Cisco Cloud Administration (210-455) Assessment Exam

1. What role in UCS Director is considered a superuser account?
    A. Systems administrator
    B. Root operator
    C. All access administrators
    D. Web administrator

2. What audience is Prime Service Catalog meant for?
    A. Developers
    B. Managers
    C. End users
    D. Architects

3. In UCS Director, a workflow is made up of a series of what?
    A. Tasks
    B. Services
    C. Service chains
    D. Actions

4. In VACS, which Cisco firewall product can be used?
    A. PIX
    B. ASA 1000
    C. ASAv
    D. IOS ACL

5. From the following list, choose the hypervisor not supported by UCS Director.
    A. VMware
    B. Hyper-V
    C. Xen
    D. Red Hat KVM

6. UCS Central can scale to how many endpoints?
    A. 500
    B. 199
    C. 1000
    D. 10,000

7. What feature belongs to UCS Performance Manager?

   A. Access stats

   B. End-user portal

   C. Capacity management

   D. Shopping cart

8. In Prime Service Catalog, what term refers to the basic unit of organization for services to be put into?

   A. Categories

   B. Showcase

   C. Service container

   D. Containers

9. In the absence of Prime Service Catalog, what feature of UCS Director is meant to take its place?

   A. Integrated portal

   B. Shopping cart

   C. UCSD End-user portal

   D. Showcase

10. Which protocol deals with logging?

   A. Service logging

   B. FTP

   C. Syslog

   D. Service reporting

11. What definition relates to chargeback and how to assign the cost of virtual resources on a value per unit consumed?

   A. Budget model

   B. Cost framework

   C. Cost models

   D. Resourcing

12. What feature of UCS Director controls whether a group goes over their allotted budget for orderable services?

   A. Budget Check

   B. Service Watch

   C. Budget Watch

   D. Service Assurance

13. Cisco's cloud offering allows for logical constructs for private deployment in the public cloud. Which term refers to this offering?

   A. Prime

   B. ACI

   C. VPC

   D. VACS

14. Which product from the Cisco Cloud offering is meant for end-user self-service?

   A. UCS Director

   B. Prime Service Catalog

   C. UCS Central

   D. UCS Manager

15. Which policies must be set up first before you can provision a VM in UCS Director?

   A. Network, compute, system, and storage policies

   B. Virtual storage policies

   C. Bare-metal policies

   D. Service policies

16. The shell in UCS Director is required to do what?

   A. Change a service

   B. Set up NTP

   C. Back up the workflows

   D. Back up the database

17. The Bare Metal Agent makes use of what to boot virtual and physical machines?

   A. PXE

   B. VDC

   C. VNS

   D. DHCP

18. Which feature of CloudSense in UCS Director allows the user to create custom reports?

   A. Report Framework

   B. Report Designer

   C. Report Builder

   D. Reports

19. Bottom-Left is a name given to a location of a front page item in which platform?

    A. UCS Director

    B. UCS Performance Manager

    C. Prime Service Catalog

    D. vSphere

20. Which version of UCS Performance Manager does not include network and storage statistics?

    A. UCS Performance Manager Medium

    B. UCS Performance Manager Small

    C. UCS Performance Manager Express

    D. UCS Performance Manager

21. Which protocol is for sending mail?

    A. IMAP

    B. POP

    C. SMTP

    D. TLS

22. Prime Service Catalog is based on which of the following?

    A. Java

    B. Python

    C. HTML

    D. HTML5

23. The fenced virtual application controller includes a load balancer from what vendor?

    A. A10

    B. F5

    C. Cisco

    D. Citrix

24. Which product can use ACLs?

    A. APIC

    B. UCS Director

    C. Converged Fabric

    D. CSR 1000v

25. What catalog in UCS Director uses custom and predefined workflows?

    A. Advanced Catalog

    B. Standard Catalog

    C. Expert Catalog

    D. Classic Catalog

Answers to Cisco Cloud Administration (210-455) Assessment Exam

1. A. The primary management account in UCS Director is the systems administrator.

2. C. Prime Service Catalog is a catalog meant for end users to shop and order services.

3. A. Workflows are a collection of tasks grouped together to execute. They make up the workflow.

4. C. The virtualized ASA can be used for security and firewall services in VACS.

5. C. Xen is not a currently supported hypervisor.

6. D. UCS Central can scale to 10,000 endpoints and multiple UCS domains.

7. C. The UCS Performance Manager has capacity management features as well as statistics about the environment as a whole for network, storage, and compute.

8. A. Categories are the organizational unit that services are put into and organized.

9. C. The UCSD end-user portal of UCS Director is a small services catalog meant to be used until Prime Service Catalog can be integrated. It is not as full featured as Prime Service Catalog and for this reason can be used as a basic portal.

10. C. Syslog is the standard for local and remote logging.

11. C. Cost models allow you to create resources such as memory and storage and use them as building blocks to create a chargeback policy.

12. C. Budget Watch is the feature in chargeback that would allow UCS Director to monitor the budget of groups.

13. D. Virtual Application Container Segmentation is the offering where three-tier apps, among other applications, can be deployed as containers.

14. B. While it could be argued that UCS Director fits this, UCS Director is more for automation and workflow use. Prime Service Catalog is meant to be an end-user portal for orderable services. It integrates with UCS Director.

15. A. These policies are required to be configured before a VM can be provisioned.

16. D. The shell is required to back up the database. This is because all services need to stop, and this cannot be done from the GUI.

17. A. While DHCP is indeed used, PXE is the correct answer. PXE uses DHCP and other protocols to assist machines in booting and transferring their configuration and OS.

18. C. The Report Builder under CloudSense allows for many custom options.

19. C. Prime Service Catalog has several names and sections for the front page, or showcase, that can be customized to display certain content.

20. C. There are only two versions of Performance Manager:

Express and the default version. Express monitors only compute and offers compute statistics and monitoring.

21. C. The most correct answer is SMTP. SMTP is the standard protocol for sending mail between systems.

22. D. Prime Service Catalog is focused on the GUI experience of customers and as such is written in HTML5 for a universal browser experience.

23. B. The fenced container uses a virtual load balancer offering from F5.

24. D. The CSR is a virtual router offering that has many features from its physical counterparts, including ACLs.

25. A. Even though it is named *advanced*, the Advanced Catalog combines and builds more advanced functionality by pulling from previously built and default workflows.

Chapter 1

Fundamentals of Cloud Computing

THE FOLLOWING UNDERSTANDING CISCO CLOUD FUNDAMENTALS CLDFND (210-451) EXAM OBJECTIVES ARE COVERED IN THIS CHAPTER:

✓ **1.0 Cloud characteristics and models**

- 1.1 Describe common cloud characteristics
    - 1.1.a On-demand self service
    - 1.1.b Elasticity
    - 1.1.c Resource pooling
    - 1.1.d Metered service
    - 1.1.e Ubiquitous network access (smartphone, tablet, mobility)
    - 1.1.f Multi-tenancy

An Introduction to Cloud Computing

You will set out on your journey to the destination of earning a Cisco Certified Networking Associate in cloud computing by taking a look at the big picture of this phenomenon called the *cloud*. You will be introduced to many definitions and concepts that will better enable you to truly understand the finer details of cloud computing as you progress on your certification journey. This book will investigate both the many generic aspects of the cloud and the details and technology pieces of the Cisco cloud service offerings.

How Cloud Computing Is Different from Traditional Computing

Throughout this chapter and book you will be comparing the old with the new, in other words, the traditional data center with the new cloud-based computing model. With cloud computing, you pay for only what you use and do not own the equipment as is usually the case in the traditional world of corporate data centers. Cloud computing allows you to not have to be involved with the day-to-day needs of patching servers, swapping out failed power supplies and disk drives, or doing any of the other myriad of issues you have to deal with when you own and maintain your own equipment.

The cloud allows you to scale up and down on your computing needs very quickly and to pay for only what you use and not for any standby capacity. You can now deploy your applications closer to your customers no matter where they are located in the world. Also, smaller companies can use advanced services that were usually available only with the budgets of the largest corporations in the world.

Cloud computing is also different from the corporate IT models in that the time to spin up new services is greatly reduced. There are no large, up-front financial commitments either; you are renting capacity instead of purchasing it.

Computing as a Utility

In the distant past, each and every factory or town that needed power would be responsible for the generation and distribution of its own electricity. The same was also true for many other services such as water, gas, and telephone services that we take for granted today. The up-front costs, ongoing maintenance, and general headaches of operating a power plant to run your business is unthinkable today, but this was actually commonplace in the past. A manufacturing company, for example, would rather not concentrate on making the power to run its factory but would instead rather focus on their area of expertise and purchase electricity as needed from a utility that specializes in the generation and distribution of electrical power. However, at one time, that was not an option!

There was also the matter of economy of scale; it is much cheaper per unit to generate power with a single large facility than having many small generation plants connected to each individual factory in every town.

The computing industry took a very different track before the cloud. Companies that needed computing resources to effectively run their companies would purchase their own large computer systems. This came with a heavy up-front expense not only for the computer systems and all of the needed peripheral equipment; they also needed to build expensive rooms to put these machines in. Since computers can be temperamental, the data centers needed to be cooled and the heat emitting from the computers needed to be removed from the data center. Computers are also rather finicky on electricity, demanding a steady and stable power source and lots of it! Then there was the staff of engineers (such as your two authors!) who meticulously designed, installed, and maintained these systems. There were programmers and too many axillary products and subsystems to count! Don't worry, we are going to talk about a lot of these systems, but believe us, you need to have an extensive array of support products, software, and personnel to pull all of this off.

What happens when your business fluctuates and you are busy during the holiday season and not so much the rest of the year, as in the case of a retailer? Well, you will need to engineer and scale the data-processing capacity to meet the anticipated heaviest load (with some additional capacity just in case). This, of course, means that there is usually a whole lot of idle capacity the rest of the year. Yes, that's right—that very expensive compute capacity and all the trimmings such as the staff and support equipment in the corporate data center just sits there unused the rest of the year, making your financial staff very upset.

It only gets worse. What happens when you need to add capacity as your company, and with it your data-processing needs, grow?

As you will learn, with the progress of technology and especially with virtualization and automation, the computing world has evolved greatly and can now be offered as a utility service just like electricity, gas, and water. Sure, we had to give it the fancy name of *cloud computing*, but it is the process of running applications on a computer to support your business operations.

However, in the past when new capacity was required, a team of engineers would need to determine the best approach to accomplish the company's goals and determine the equipment and software that would be required. Then the equipment list would go out for bid, or quotes would need to be gathered. There would be time for the purchasing cycle to get the equipment ordered. After some time, it would be delivered at the loading dock, and the fun would really begin. The equipment would need to be unpackaged, racked, cabled, and powered up, and then usually a fair amount of configuration would take place. Then the application teams would install the software, and even more configuration would be needed. After much testing, the application would go live, and all would be good. However, this could take a very long time, and as that equipment aged, a new refresh cycle would begin all over again.

With the utility model of computing, or the *cloud*, there are no long design, purchasing, delivery, setup, and testing cycles. You can go online, order a compute instance, and have everything up and running in literally minutes. Also, the financial staff is very happy as there are no capital expenditures or up-front costs. It is just like electricity—you pay for only what you use!

The Role of Virtualization

The new model of computing has largely been made possible with the widespread deployment of *virtualization* technologies. While the concept of taking one piece of computing hardware and running many virtual computers inside of it goes back decades to the days of mainframe computers, new virtualization software and cheap, powerful hardware has brought virtualization to the mainstream and enabled the ability to do many amazing things in the cloud, as you will explore throughout this study guide.

Now, with a powerful server running on commodity silicon, you can run hundreds of virtual machines on one piece of hardware; in the past, a physical server would often be used for each application.

Many other functions of data center operations have also been virtualized such as load balancers, firewalls, switches, and routers. The more that is virtualized, the more cost-effective cloud services are becoming. Also, the management and automation systems that were developed around the virtualized data center allow for fast implementation of complete solutions from the cloud provider. It is often as simple as logging into a cloud *dashboard* using a common web browser and spinning up multiple servers, network connections, storage, load balances, firewalls, and, of course, applications. This level of automation enabled by virtualization is going to be a focus of the CCNA Cloud certification.

What Cloud Computing Offers That Is New

Is this the same old data center that has been moved to the other side of the Internet, or is this something new and completely different? Well, actually it is a little of each. What is new is that the time to bring new applications online has been greatly reduced as the computing capacity already exists in the cloud data center and is available as an on-demand service. You can now simply order the compute virtual machines and associated storage and services just like you would any utility service.

The cost models are now completely different in that the up-front costs have largely been eliminated, and you pay as you go for only what you are using. Also, if you require additional capacity, even for a short amount of time, you can scale automatically in the cloud and then shut down the added servers when your computing workload decreases.

The Growth of Cloud Computing

Because of the lower total cost of operations and short deployment times, the growth of cloud computing has been nothing short of phenomenal. Cloud companies that are only a few years old are now multibillion-dollar enterprises. The growth rates are in the double digits in this industry and seem to be increasing every year. The business model is just too great for almost any business to ignore.

It can be difficult to get accurate numbers on the size of the cloud market because of company financial reporting not breaking out their cloud financials from other business entities. Also, no one seems to really agree on what cloud computing is in the first place.

What is clear is that the growth of cloud computing is phenomenal and is accelerating every year as more and more companies move their operations to the cloud. It is common to see cloud growth estimates at 25 to 40 percent or even higher every year and accelerating for many years into the future with revenues way north of $100 billion per year.

Migrating to the Cloud

In later chapters, you will investigate what is going to be required to migrate your computing operations from the private data center to the cloud, as shown in Figure 1.1. *Cloud migration* may not be trivial given the nature of many custom applications and systems that have evolved over many years or are running on platform-specific hardware and operating systems. However, as virtualization technology has exploded and you gain more experience in the cloud, there are many tools and utilities that can make life much simpler (well, let's just say less complicated) than doing migrations in the past.

FIGURE 1.1   Migrations from the corporate data center to the cloud

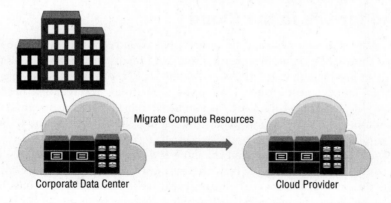

You cannot simply just take an application running on your corporate data centers and file transfer it to the cloud. Life is far from being that simple. The operating systems and applications running directly on a server, such as an e-mail server, will need to be converted to the virtual world and be compatible with the virtualization technologies used by the cloud providers.

The process of migrating to the cloud is actually a very large business in itself, with many professional services teams working throughout the world every day assisting in the great migration to the cloud.

A Look at How the CCNA Role Is Evolving

In the past, the networking professional with a Cisco Certified Network Associate certification could often be found in the network room or wiring closet racking a switch or router and then configuring the VLANs and routing protocols required to make everything work. How is our world changing now that another company, the cloud company, owns the network and the computing systems? Should we all go look for another gig? Don't worry, there will plenty for all of us to do!

As you will learn on your journey to becoming a Cisco Certified Network Associate Cloud professional, the way you do things will certainly be changing, but there will always be a demand for your expertise and knowledge.

The cloud engineer will still be doing configurations and working in consoles; it is just that you will be doing different but related tasks. Your work will be different than the world of IOS commands that you might know and love, but that is a good thing.

You will be doing higher-level work on the cloud deployments and not be concerned with the underlying hardware and systems as much since that will be the responsibility of the cloud service providers. Also, the siloed world between the different groups in the data center, such as networking, storage, security, operating systems, and applications, will now be more integrated than the industry has ever been in the past. You will be concerned with not only the network but with storage, security, and all the other systems that must work together in both corporate and cloud data centers.

Preparing for Life in the Cloud

As a student, there is much to learn to become CCNA Cloud certified. We will cover all the topics that the CCNA Cloud blueprint outlines and that is specific to Cisco's intercloud and the family of products that are used, such as the UCS, the Nexus and MDS products, and the software management products in the Cisco portfolio. You will also need to learn much more than networking. Topics such as storage systems, operating systems, server hardware, and more will require your understanding and knowledge for you to be a cloud engineer.

The cloud marketplace is growing and changing at a breakneck pace, and as such, you will need to be constantly learning the new offerings just to keep up. New services and offerings from the cloud providers are being released weekly, and existing products are constantly being improved and expanded. The learning will never stop!

It is important to learn the terms and structure in the cloud that the CLDFND 210-451 exam covers as a strong knowledge base. From these topics, you can build and expand your knowledge in more specific and detailed topics in cloud computing. You are advised to fully understand the big picture of cloud computing and build on that as you gather knowledge and expertise.

The Evolutionary History of Cloud Computing

In this section, you will step back and look at how the world of computing has evolved over the decades. This will help you get some historical perspective and to see that what was once old can now be new again! Once you have an understanding of the past, we will give you a quick look at where we are today and make a few predictions of where we are headed.

A Brief History of Computing

The history of computing is a rather large topic area, and some of us who have been in the industry for many years can sometimes be nostalgic of the good ol' days. At the same, time we can admit to being shocked when walking through the Smithsonian museum in Washington, DC, and seeing "historical" equipment that we used to work on! In IT, it is not an understatement that the technology and, more specifically, the computing and net-working industry have evolved at a very fast speed. It is also true that the only constant is change and that the change is happening at a faster pace than ever before.

Computing in the Past

Back in the dark ages of computing, the computers were large, expensive, and complicated, and they had limited processing power by today's standards. In fact, today the smartphones we carry in our pockets are more powerful than most of the room-sized computers of the past.

The original architecture of computing was that of large, centralized systems that were accessed with remote systems with limited intelligence and computing power. Over the years, the large *mainframes* gave way to multiple *minicomputers*, as shown in Figure 1.2, which were still housed in climate-controlled computer rooms with dumb terminals using only a keyboard and monitor to access the processing capabilities of the minicomputers.

FIGURE 1.2 Mainframe and minicomputers

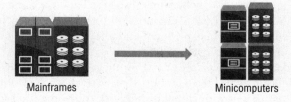

Mainframes → Minicomputers

When the Intel-based servers entered the marketplace and local area networks made their first appearance, there was a fundamental shift in the industry. The power of computing moved out from the "big glass rooms" that computer rooms were called back then and into the departmental areas of the corporations. This new *client-server* architecture was that of distributed computing where a central file server was used to store data and offered printing services to a large number of personal computers; the central file server was the replacement of the dumb terminals used in the mainframe and minicomputer world (see Figure 1.3). This was a huge industry change where the end users of systems gained control over their computing requirements and operations.

FIGURE 1.3   Client-server computing

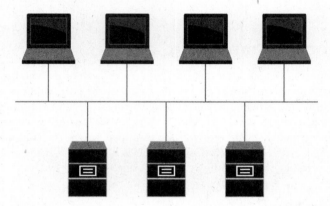

Client-server systems were not without their problems, however. Many islands of computing networks sprung up everywhere, and there were many proprietary protocols that meant most of these systems were not compatible with each other; hence, there was no interoperability. Data was now scattered all over the company with no central control of security, data integrity, or the ability to manage the company's valuable data. Networking these client-server systems across a wide area network was at best expensive and slow and at worst unattainable.

As the industry grew and evolved, it would frequently revert to what was old but cleaned up and presented as something new. One example is how the client-server systems were brought back into the data center, internetworked, and patched, with management and redundancy implemented; most importantly, that valuable data was collected and managed in a central area. Over time that myriad of proprietary, vendor-developed protocols, shown in Figure 1.4, slowly became obsolete. This was a major development in the networking industry as *TCP/IP* (Transmission Control Protocol/Internet Protocol) became the standard communications protocol and allowed the many different computing systems to communicate using a standardized protocol.

During the consolidation era, wide area networking evolved from slow dial-up lines and either analog or subrate digital telco circuits that were all leased from the local phone companies for private use to a now open public network called the Internet with high-speed fiber optic networks widely available.

FIGURE 1.4   Incompatible communications protocols

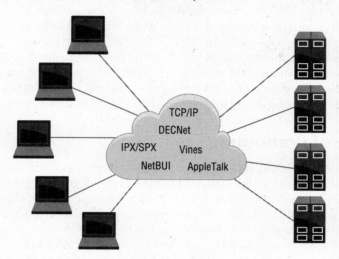

With the opening of the Internet to the world and the emergence of the World Wide Web, the world became interconnected, and the computing industry flourished, with the networking industry exploding right along with it. Now that we have become interconnected, the innovation in applications opened a whole new area of what computing can offer, all leading up to the cloud computing models of today.

Computing in the Present Day

Corporate-owned data center models that provide compute and storage resources for the company are predominate today. These data centers can be either company owned or leased from a hosting facility where many companies install equipment in secure data centers owned by a third party. As we discussed earlier in this chapter, traditional data centers are designed for peak workload conditions, with the servers being unused or lightly used during times of low workloads.

Corporate data centers require a large up-front capital investment in building facilities, backup power, cooling systems, and redundant network connections in addition to the racks of servers, network equipment, and storage systems. Also, because of business continuity needs, there are usually one or more backup data centers that can take the workload should the primary data center go offline for any reason.

In addition to the up-front costs, there are ongoing operational costs such as maintenance and support, power and cooling costs, a large staff of talented engineers to keep it all running, and usually a large number of programmers working on the applications that the companies require to operate their business. There are many other costs such as software licensing that add to the expense of a company operating its own data centers.

This is not to say that modern data center operations are not using much of the same technology as the cloud data centers are using. They are. Server virtualization has been in use for many years, and large centralized storage arrays are found in the private data centers just as they are in the cloud facilities.

With the current marketing hype surrounding cloud computing, many companies have rebranded their internal data centers to be private clouds. This is valid because they have exclusive use of the data center and implement automation and virtualization; many of the cloud technologies and processes are also found in the corporate data centers.

The Future of Computing

Clearly the future of computing is to move to the shared model of service offerings of the cloud. This can be witnessed by the high growth rates of the large cloud providers. The move to the cloud has been nothing less than a massive paradigm shift in the industry to public clouds, as shown in Figure 1.5. The business case and financial models are too great to ignore. There is also the ability of cloud services to be implemented very rapidly and with elastic computing technology that can expand and contract on the fly. Companies can save the large capital expenses of owning and operating their own data centers and focusing on their core business while outsourcing their computing requirements to the cloud.

FIGURE 1.5   Cloud computing model

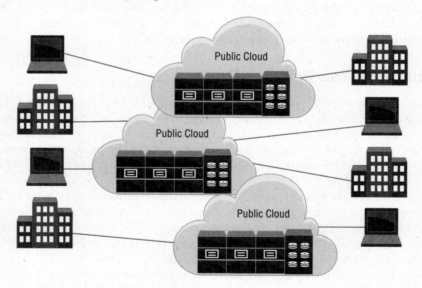

For smaller companies or startups, the low costs and advanced service offerings of the cloud companies are too great not to use cloud services. Also, as is apparent, the time to market or time to get an operation up and running is very fast with cloud services, where advanced services can be implemented in hours or a few short days. Technologies that were available only to large corporations with massive budgets to apply to information technologies are now available to the "little guys."

The Great Cloud Journey: How We Got Here

We are just getting started with widespread cloud technologies and offerings. The great migration to cloud computing has just begun, and we have a long way to go if we look at the recent and projected growth rate of the cloud service providers.

The nature of the network engineer's job is clearly going to change. How much and where it is headed is open for debate. We feel that the days of silos where each engineering discipline, such as networking, application support, storage, and the Linux and Windows teams will all blur together, and we must all become familiar with technologies outside of our core competencies.

As you can see, what is old is now new again because the ability to take a piece of technology and virtualize it into many systems on the same hardware was the great enabler that got us to where we are today. Along the way, some amazing software was developed to implement and manage these new clouds. As you will see on your way to becoming CCNA Cloud certified, Cisco clearly intends to be a big player in this market and has developed a suite of cloud software and services to enable not only a single cloud but a group of clouds, the *intercloud*, to operate. This is a very exciting time for our industry!

What Exactly Is Cloud Computing?

What is cloud computing? Well, that can be a bit complicated and convoluted with all of the marketing hype surrounding this technology area that has such a high growth rate and the attention of the world.

A cynic would note that everything in the past has been relabeled to be "cloud this and cloud that." Anything that was connected to the Internet and offered to the public now seems to be called a cloud service. The cloud marketplace is also very large and growing at a fast pace. Because of this rapid expansion, there are many sections and subsections to this new industry. There are many types of different clouds and services offered. Applications and technologies that have been in place for many years now have cloud attached to their name, while at the same time, the development of new cloud service offerings seems to be a daily event with a constant stream of new product announcements.

Cloud computing is essentially outsourcing *data center* operations, applications, or a section of operations to a provider of computing resources often called a cloud company or cloud *service provider*. The *consumer* of cloud services pays either a monthly charge or by the amount of usage of the service. You will explore many different models and types of cloud computing in this book.

While there may never be agreement on a clear and concise definition, you can turn to the organization that keeps track of these things, the National Institute of Standards and Technologies (*NIST*), as the authoritative source for what you are looking for.

The NIST Definition of the Cloud

NIST SP 800-145 is the main source of cloud computing definitions. NIST defines cloud computing as:

> ...a model for enabling convenient, *on-demand* network access to a shared pool of configurable computing resources (e.g., networks, servers, storage, applications, and services) that can be rapidly provisioned and released with minimal management effort or service provider interaction. This cloud model is composed of five essential characteristics, three service models, and four deployment models.

That seems to the point and accurate, with no spin and just the facts. There seems to be agreement that the cloud is an on-demand self-service computing service and is the most common definition. That is something us as engineers really appreciate. Of course, behind this definition is so much technology it is going to make your head spin and sometimes overwhelm you, but that's the business.

In this book, you will investigate all of the models and characteristics and then dig into the technologies that make all of this work. When you are done, you will be proud to call yourself CCNA Cloud certified!

How Many Definitions Are There?

There are many definitions of cloud computing. Some are accurate, and many are just spins on older, already existing offerings and technologies. It is advised that you understand the big picture of cloud computing and then dig into the finer details and not get caught up in the excitement surrounding cloud computing. It is our job to make it work, not to keep it polished for the whole world to see.

The Many Types of Clouds

While the definition of the cloud can be very generic and broad, you can get granular with the different types of service models and deployment models. These will be explored in detail in the following two chapters. Service models break down and define basic cloud offerings in what is provided by the cloud provider and what you will be responsible for as the cloud customer.

Service Models

For example, there are three main service categories that are defined (and many more that are not in these groups). The three main service models include Infrastructure as a Service (IaaS), Platform as a Service (PaaS), and Software as a Service (SaaS). With Infrastructure as a Service, as shown in Figure 1.6, the cloud provider generally provides all the systems that make up a data center deployment such as the server platform, storage, and network but leaves the operating system and application responsibilities to the customer. This has been the predominate cloud service model until recently and allows the customer complete control and responsibility of the operating system and applications.

FIGURE 1.6   Infrastructure as a Service

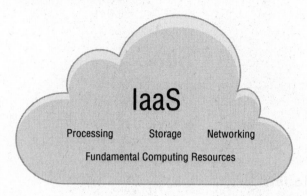

The Platform as a Service model, shown in Figure 1.7, moves one step up the stack, and the cloud provider takes on operating system responsibilities. This is to say that the cloud company owns the responsibility of loading and maintaining either a Microsoft Windows operating system variant or one of the many different releases of Linux. With the Platform as a Service model, the cloud customer is responsible for the applications running in the cloud, and the provider takes care of all the underlying infrastructure and operating systems.

FIGURE 1.7   Platform as a Service

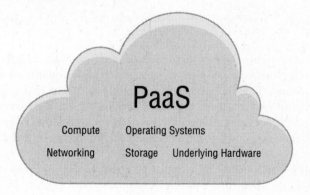

At the top of the stack is the Software as a Service model, as shown in Figure 1.8, which is just like it sounds: The cloud company provides a complete package including the application that can be a wide variety of solutions, such as database, enterprise resource planning, software development applications, or most any mainstream application that is currently running in corporate data centers.

FIGURE 1.8   Software as a Service

Deployment Models

Cloud deployment models define the larger topic of where the cloud is deployed and who is responsible for the operations. There are four main cloud deployment models that include the public cloud, the private cloud, the community cloud, and finally the hybrid cloud, as illustrated in Figure 1.9. You will learn the details of these models in Chapter 3, but you will get an overview in this chapter.

FIGURE 1.9   Cloud deployment models

The public cloud is probably the most widely deployed and discussed, as illustrated in Figure 1.10. The public cloud is usually what we tend to think of when we hear the term *cloud* being tossed around. This includes the cloud companies that make up the intercloud, in other words, the major players in the market, such as Amazon Web Services, Microsoft Azure, and Google Cloud Services, along with many other companies. The public cloud is where a company offers cloud computing services to the public in the utility model covered earlier in the chapter.

The private cloud is predominantly computing services that are privately owned and operated and are not open to the public. Corporate data centers fit into the private cloud definition. Private clouds are owned by a single organization such as a corporation or a third-party provider (see Figure 1.11). Private clouds can be either on-premises or off-site at a remote hosting facility with dedicated hardware for the private cloud.

FIGURE 1.10   Multiple organizations sharing a public cloud service

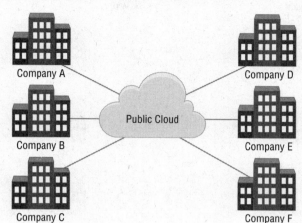

FIGURE 1.11   A single organization accessing a private cloud

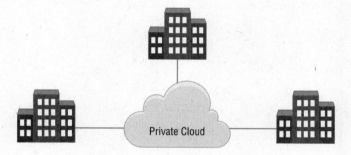

A community cloud, as shown in Figure 1.12, is designed around a community of inter-est and shared by companies with similar requirements. For example, companies in the healthcare or financial services markets will have similar regulatory requirements that have to be adhered to. A public cloud offering can be designed around these requirements and offered to that specific marketplace or industry.

Finally, there is the hybrid cloud model, which is the interconnection of the various cloud models defined earlier, as illustrated in Figure 1.13. If a corporation has its own private cloud but is also connected to the public cloud for additional services, then that would con-stitute a hybrid cloud. A community cloud used for specific requirements and also connected to the public cloud for general processing needs would also be considered a hybrid cloud.

As you will learn, the intercloud technologies from Cisco enable the hybrid cloud model. This will be investigated in detail in the second part of this book that covers the Cisco Cloud Administration (CLDM) 210-455 exam.

FIGURE 1.12   The community cloud based on common interests or requirements

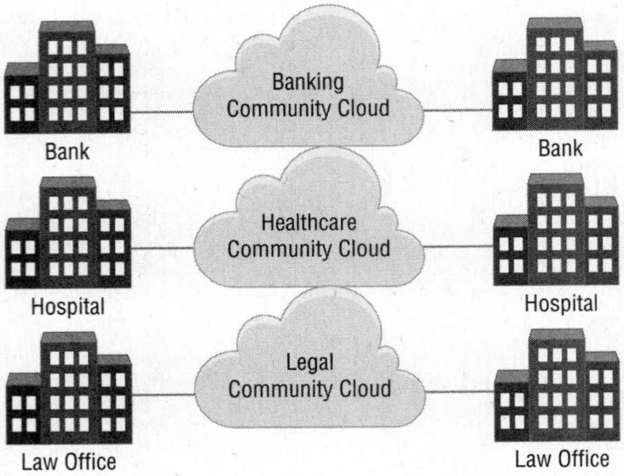

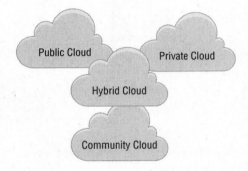

FIGURE 1.13   The hybrid is a combination of clouds.

Introducing the Data Center

This section will provide an overview of the modern *data center* and the business models, deployment models, and support services. The section will also discuss how to design a data center for the anticipated workload. Since the topic of data center design and operations could fill many books, we will not attempt to go into great detail as it is not required for the Understanding Cisco Cloud Fundamentals exam 210-451. However, it is important to understand the layout and basic designs of the modern data center, which is what we will accomplish in this section.

The Modern Data Center

There is a common design structure to the modern data center, no matter if it is a privately owned data center, a hosting facility, or a data center that is owned by a cloud company. They are all data centers, and the structure and design are common between them all.

We will start by taking a closer look at what their basic requirements are. Data centers are going to consume a rather large amount of electrical power and need access to high-speed communications networks. Since they may contain sensitive or critical data, both data security and physical security are requirements. From those fundamental needs, we will look at the various components of the data center to allow you to have a good understanding of all the pieces that come together to make a fully functioning modern data center.

It is a truism that data centers are real power sinks! The servers, storage systems, network gear, and supporting systems all require electricity to operate. Most data centers tend to be quite large to obtain economies of scale that make them more cost effective. This means that being connected to a power grid that has capacity and stability is critical. Also, plans must be made for the eventuality of a power failure. What do you do then? A modern data center can generate its own power if the main power grid from the local utility fails. There may also be massive racks of battery or other stored power systems to power the data center momentarily between the time the power grid fails and the local data generation systems come online.

Data must come and go not only inside the systems in the data center, which is commonly called *east-west* traffic, but also from the outside world, which is referred to as *north-south* data. This will require the ability to connect to high-speed data networks. These fiber networks can be owned and operated by the same company that owns the data center or, more likely, a service provider that specializes in networking services. These networks tend to be almost exclusively fiber-optic, and it is preferable to have more than one entry point into the data center for the fiber to avoid a single point of failure. You will also notice that there will be two or more service providers connected to allow for network connectivity if one of the provider's networks experiences problems and there is a need to fail over to the backup network provider.

With the power and communications addressed, you will find that data centers are located in secure areas with security gates, cameras, and guards protecting the physical building and its grounds.

Inside of the data center you will find distribution systems for power and communications and an operations center that is tasked with monitoring and maintaining operations. The floor for the data center will be raised tiles to allow cable trays for the power and sometimes communications cables to interconnect the racks inside the computer room.

There will be rows of equipment cabinets to house all of the servers, storage systems, switches, routers, load balancers, firewalls, monitoring systems, and a host of other hardware needed for operations.

In addition, all of the electronics in the data center generate a lot of thermal heat. This is not trivial and must be addressed with large cooling systems, or *chillers*, as we like to call them, to get the heat out of the data center to protect the electronics inside the enclosures.

While no two data centers seem to be the same, these basic components are what make up the modern data centers found around the world.

Business Models

Cloud-based business models can be distilled to four basic models that IT channel companies are adopting. While there are, of course, a large variety of companies in the cloud business space, each with their own way of doing business, we will look at the more common models.

The "build it" model is a natural progression in the IT industry to help customers build a private cloud. There are also many companies that have built very large public cloud offerings. The "provide or provision" category providers can either resell or relabel a vendor's cloud offering. They can also operate their own data center and sell homegrown cloud services. Many companies follow the "manage and support" model, which includes ongoing management and support of cloud-based services such as remote monitoring and management and security offerings. With the "enabling or integration model" solution, providers work with customers in a professional services role to assist in the business and technical aspects of their startup and ongoing cloud operations.

Data Center Deployment Models

Data center deployment models encompass subjects such as usable square footage, the density of server and storage systems, and cooling techniques. In the cloud it is common to use a regional deployment model and implement multiple data centers per region into availability zones.

A cloud service provider will offer regions for customers to provide their deployments. For example, there may be USA Central, Brazil, and China East regions that are selected to deploy your cloud applications. Each region will be segmented into multiple availability zones that allow for redundancy. An availability zone is usually a complete and separate data center in the same region. Should one zone fail, cloud providers can fail over to another availability zone for continuity and to alleviate a loss of service.

Data Center Operations

Data center operations concern the workflow and processes conducted in the data center. This includes both compute and noncompute operations specific to the data center; the operations include all the processes needed to maintain the data center.

Infrastructure support includes the ongoing installation, cabling, maintenance, monitoring, patching and updating of servers, storage, and networking systems. Security is an important component to operations, and there are both physical and logical security models. Security includes all security processes, tools, and systems to maintain both physical and logical security. Power and cooling operations maintain sufficient power, and cooling is reliably available in the data center. Of course, there will also be a management component that includes policy development, monitoring, and enforcement.

Designing the Data Center for the Anticipated Workload

The data center must be scaled not only for the present but for the anticipated workload. This can be tricky as there are many unknowns. Server technology is constantly evolving, allowing you to do more processing in less rack space, and the silicon used in the physical devices has become more power efficient as well, enabling more processing per power unit. When designing a data center, items such as square footage, power, cooling, communications, and connections all must be considered.

The Difference Between the Data Center and Cloud Computing Models

In this section, we will contrast and compare what makes the cloud model different from the traditional corporate computing model.

The traditional corporate data center utilizes the approach of purchasing and having available enough additional computing capacity to allow for times when there is a peak workload. This is terribly inefficient as it requires a significant up-front investment in technology that may rarely get used but that needs to be available during the times it is required. Also, the lead times from concept to deployment in the data center can take months or even years to complete.

The differentiation is that, in theory at least, the resources are always available in the cloud and just sitting there waiting to be turned on at the click of an icon with your mouse. The cloud computing model then is that of a utility, as we have discussed. You order only what you need and pay for only what you use. The cloud model has many of the advantages of traditional data centers in that there is a huge, and constantly growing, amount of advanced offerings that would never have been possible to implement for most small and medium-sized businesses, or even large ones in some cases. If you are a business located in the United States but have many customers in Asia, you may want to store your web content in Japan, for example, to provide for faster response times in Asia. In a traditional data center model, this would probably not be practical. With these services offered, your cloud provider may have access points in many Asian countries with your web content locally stored for fast response times since the request no longer has to come all the way to the United States for the data be served out of the local web server and the content returned to Asia. Another advanced and costly service that is out of the realm of possibility for most companies is the cloud feature of availability zones offered in the cloud; for example, if you as the cloud provider have a data center go down, you can automatically shift all of your cloud services to another availability zone, and the people accessing your site in the cloud may not have even noticed what happened.

There are many other examples of the differences between the traditional data center model and the cloud as it is today and as it continues to evolve. We will explore these differences and contrast the advantages of cloud computing in this book as we go along.

Common Cloud Characteristics

In this section, you will learn about the common characteristics that make up a cloud computing operation. We will start with the core principle of the cloud model, which is on-demand computing, and then move on to discuss the ability to automatically expand and contract by discussing the concept of elasticity. We will look at several scaling techniques commonly deployed, including whether to scale up or scale out. The concept of resource pooling will be explored with a look at the various types of pools such as CPUs, memory, storage, and networking.

Metered services will be discussed, and you will learn that with the ability to measure the consumed services, the cloud company can offer many different billing options.

Finally, we will end this section by exploring the different methods commonly utilized to access the cloud remotely.

On-Demand Self-Service

The *on-demand* cloud services allow the customer to access a self-service portal, usually with a web browser or application programmable interface (API), and instantly create additional servers, storage, processing power, or any other services as required.

If the computing workload increases, then additional resources can be created and applied as needed. On-demand allows you to consume cloud services only as needed and scale back when they are no longer required. For example, if your e-commerce site is expecting an increased load during a sales promotion that lasts for several weeks, on-demand services can be used to provision the additional resources of the website only during this time frame, and when the workload goes back to normal, the resources can be removed or scaled back. You can also refer to on-demand self-service as a *just-in-time service* because it allows cloud services to be added as required and removed based on the workload.

On-demand services are entirely controlled by the cloud customer, and with cloud automation systems, the request from the customer will be automatically deployed in a short amount of time.

Elasticity

Elasticity provides for on-demand provisioning of resources in near real time. The ability to add and remove or to increase and decrease computing resources is called *elasticity*. Cloud resources can be storage, CPUs, memory, and even servers. When the cloud user's deployment experiences a shortage of a resource, the cloud automation systems can automatically and dynamically add the needed resources.

Elasticity is done "on the fly" as needed and is different from provisioning servers with added resources that may be required in the future. Elasticity allows cloud consumers to automatically scale up as their workload increases and then have the cloud automation systems remove the services after the workload subsides. With cloud management software, performance and utilization thresholds can be defined, and when these metrics are met, the cloud automation software can automatically add resources to allow the metrics to remain in a defined range. When the workload subsides, the service that was added will be automatically removed or scaled back.

With elastic computing, there is no longer any need to deploy servers and storage systems designed to handle peak loads—servers and systems that may otherwise sit idle during normal operations. Now you can scale the cloud infrastructure to what is the normal load and automatically expand as needed when the occasion arises.

Scaling Up

When additional computing capacity is needed in the cloud, the *scaling up* approach is one in which larger and more power servers are used to replace a smaller system, as shown in Figure 1.14. Instead of adding more and additional servers, for example, the scale-up model will instead replace the smaller with the larger.

FIGURE 1.14   Scaling up increases the capacity of a server.

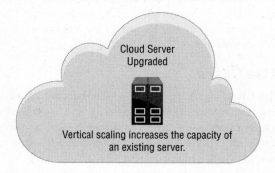

You will learn throughout this book that there is a lot more to cloud capacity than just raw compute power. For example, a system may have more than enough CPU capacity but instead need additional storage read/write bandwidth if it is running a database that needs constant access with fast response times. Another example of scaling up would be a web server that sends large graphics files to remote connections and is constantly saturating its LAN bandwidth and necessitating the need to add more network I/O bandwidth.

Cloud service providers offer many options when selecting services to meet your requirements, and they offer multiple tiers of capacity to allow for growth. For example, there are many different server virtual machine options available in the cloud that offer scalable compute power, with others designed for different storage applications, graphics processing, and network I/O.

Scaling Out

Scaling out is the second, and arguably more common, approach to additional capacity in the cloud, as shown in Figure 1.15. The scaling-out design utilizes additional resources that are incrementally added to your existing cloud operations instead of replacing them with a larger and more powerful system.

FIGURE 1.15   Scaling out by adding additional servers to accommodate increased workloads

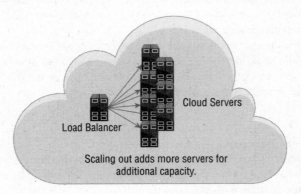

For example, if the cloud web servers are experiencing a heavy load and the CPU utilization exceeds a predefined threshold of say, 85 percent, additional web servers can be added to the existing web servers to share the workload. The use of multiple web servers servicing the same web domain is accomplished with the use of load balancers that spread the connections across multiple web servers.

Cloud Elasticity Use Cases

There are many examples where elasticity can be a valuable cloud feature to implement to save money and maintain performance levels. It is desirable to design the cloud computing resources for your anticipated day-to-day needs and then to add resources as required. A company that needs to process data for business intelligence will often have a large processing job that would take a very long time to run on available servers that would then sit idle until the process repeats. In this case, many servers, sometimes in the hundreds, can be provisioned for the job to run in a timely manner, and when complete, the servers are removed, and the company will no longer be charged for their use.

Many e-commerce retailers experience heavy traffic during the holiday season and then see their web traffic drop significantly for the rest of the year. It makes no sense to pay for the needed web capacity over the holiday season for the rest of the year. This is a prime use case for the value of cloud elasticity. As you are probably noticing, you can either scale up or scale out, and the provisioning can be done automatically or manually through the web configuration portal and using automation.

Resource Pooling

Resource pooling is the term used to define when the cloud service provider allocates resources into a group, or *pool*, and then these pools are made available to a multitenant cloud environment.

The resources that are pooled are then dynamically allocated and reallocated as the demand requires. Resource pooling takes advantage of virtualization technologies to abstract what used to be physical systems into virtual allocations or pools. Resource pooling hides the physical hardware from the virtual machines and allows for many tenants to share the available resources, as shown in Figure 1.16.

FIGURE 1.16   Resource pooling

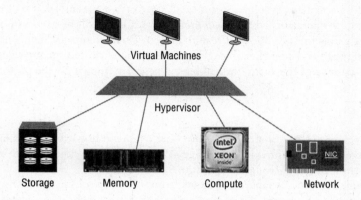

A physical server may have 256 CPU cores and 1,204GB of RAM on the motherboard. The CPU and memory can be broken into pools, and these pools can be allocated to individual groups that are running virtual machines on the server. If a virtual machine needs more memory or CPU resources, with scaling and elasticity, these can be accessed from the pool. Since processing power, storage, network bandwidth, and storage are finite resources, the use of pooling will allow for their more efficient use since they are now being shared in a pool for multiple users to access as required.

CPU

A physical nonvirtualized server running a single operating system uses the processing power of the CPUs installed on its motherboard.

In the case of a virtualized server, it will have tens or even hundreds of virtual machines all operating on the same server at the same time. The virtualization software's job is to allocate the physical or hard resources on the motherboard to the virtual machines running on it. The hypervisor virtualizes the physical CPUs into *virtual CPUs*, and then the VMs running on the hypervisor will be allocated these virtual CPUs for processing. By using virtualized CPUs, VMs can be assigned or allocated CPUs for use that are not physical but rather virtual. The virtualization function is the role of the hypervisor. Pools of CPUs can be created using administrative controls, and these pools are used or consumed by the virtual machines. When a VM is created, resources will be defined that will determine how much CPU, RAM, storage, and LAN capacity it will consume. These allocations can be dynamically expanded up to the hard quota limits based on the cloud provider's offerings.

Memory

Memory virtualization and its allocations to the virtual machines use the same concepts that we discussed in the previous section on virtualizing CPUs. There is a total and finite amount of RAM installed in a bare-metal or physical server. This RAM is then virtualized by the hypervisor software and allocated to the virtual machines. As with the allocation of processing resources, you can assign a base amount of RAM per virtual machine and dynamically increase the memory available to the VM based on the needs and limits configured for the virtual machine.

When the VM's operating system consumes all the available memory, it will begin to utilize storage for its operations. This *swap file*, as it is called, will be used in place of RAM for its operation and is undesirable as it results in poor performance. When configuring a VM, it is important to consider that storage space must be allocated for the swap file and that the storage latency of the swap file will have a negative impact on the performance of the server.

Storage

We will cover storage systems in great detail in later chapters; however, to better understand cloud operations, we will explore storage allocations in the cloud here to gain a more complete understanding of basic cloud operations.

Storage systems are usually separate systems from the actual physical servers in the cloud and in private data centers. These are large storage arrays of disks and controllers that are accessed by the servers over dedicated storage communication networks. As you can imagine, these storage arrays are massive and can store petabytes of data on each system, and there can be tens or even hundreds of these systems in a large data center.

Each physical server will usually not have very many disk drives installed in it for use by the VMs running on that server. Often cloud servers will contain no hard drives at all, and storage will be accessed remotely.

With these large storage systems being external from the servers and connected over a storage area network, the design of the SAN and storage arrays is critical for server and application performance. The systems must be engineered to avoid high read and write latency on the drives or contention over the storage network, for optimal performance.

To alleviate performance issues, cloud providers use enterprise-grade storage systems with high disk RPM rates, fast I/O, sufficient bandwidth to the storage controller, and SAN controller interfaces that are fast enough to handle the storage traffic load across the network. Cloud service providers will offer a wide variety of storage options to meet the requirements of the applications. There can be fast permanent storage all the way to offline backup storage that can take hours or days to retrieve. Storage allocations can also be used temporarily and then deleted when the virtual machine is powered off. By using a multi-tiered storage model, the cloud providers offer storage services priced for the needs of their customers.

One major advantage of designing the cloud storage arrays to be remote from the virtual machines they support is that this allows the cloud management applications to move the VMs from one hypervisor to another both inside a cloud data center or even between data centers. The VM will move and continue to access its storage over the storage network. This can even be accomplished where an application will continue to operate even as it is being moved between physical servers. Centralized storage is an enabler of this technology and is useful for maintenance, cloud bursting, fault tolerance, and disaster recovery purposes.

As with the CPUs discussed in the previous section, storage systems are allocated into virtual pools, and then the pools are allocated for dynamic use by the virtual machines.

Networking

Networking services can be virtualized like CPU cores and storage facilities are. Networking is virtualized in many different aspects, as the Understanding Cisco Cloud Fundamentals exam covers extensively. In this section, we will briefly discuss the virtualization of LAN network interface cards and switches in servers. NICs and switchports are virtualized and then allocated to virtual machines.

A typical server in the cloud data center will be connected to an external physical LAN switch with multiple high-speed Ethernet LAN interfaces. These interfaces are grouped together or aggregated into channel groups for additional throughput and fault tolerance. LAN interfaces in the server are connected to a *virtual switch* running as a software application on the hypervisor. Each VM will have one or more connections to this virtual switch using its *virtual NIC (vNIC)*. The LAN bandwidth and capacity is then allocated to each VM as was done with processing, memory, and storage discussed earlier. By using multiple physical NICs connecting to multiple external switches, the network can be designed to offer a highly fault-tolerant operation. However, since the available amount of LAN bandwidth is a finite resource just like the other resources on the server, it will be shared with all VMs running on the server.

Metered Service

A cloud provider will meter, or measure, the usage of cloud resources with its network monitoring systems. Metering collects the usage data, which is valuable to track system utilization for future growth, and the data allows us to know when to use elasticity to add or remove and to scale up or scale down resources in the day-to-day operation of the cloud.

This *metered service* data is also used for billing and reporting systems that can be viewed in the cloud management portal, or dashboard as it is commonly called.

Metering is frequently used to measure resource usage for billing purposes. Examples are the amount of Internet bandwidth consumed, storage traffic over the SAN, gigabytes of storage consumed, the number of DNS queries received over a period of time, or database queries consumed.

There are many examples and use cases for metering services in the cloud. Many cloud services can be purchased to run for a fixed amount of time; for example, batch jobs can be run overnight and with metered systems, and VMs can be brought online to run these jobs at a certain time and then shut down when the job is completed.

Cloud Access Options

Connections to the cloud provider are generally over the Internet. Since cloud data centers are at remote locations from the users accessing the services, there are multiple methods used to connect to the cloud.

The most common method is to use a secure, encrypted connection over the public Internet. Web browsers can use SSL/TLS connections over TCP port 443, which is commonly known as an HTTPS connection. This allows a web browser to access the cloud services securely from any remote location that has an Internet connection.

If the cloud customer needs to connect many users from a company office or its own data center, a VPN connection is commonly implemented from a router or a firewall to the cloud, and it offers network-to-network connectivity over the encrypted VPN tunnel.

For high-bandwidth requirements, the solution is to connect to an interexchange provider that hosts direct high-speed network connections from the cloud to the exchange provider. The customer can also install a high-speed connection from their facility to the *interexchange provider.* At the exchange data center, a direct interconnection between the cloud provider and the corporate network is made. The direct connect model also supports cloud options such as cloud bursting and hybrid cloud designs where the corporate cloud and public cloud provider's data centers are directly connected.

Exploring the Cloud Multitenancy Model

The ability to take a software package and, by using segmentation, share it to serve multiple tenants or customers is called *multitenancy.*

Multitenancy is a cost-effective approach when the costs of the application, its licenses, and its ongoing support agreements are shared among multiple customers accessing the application hosted in the cloud.

In a multitenant application deployment, a dedicated share of the application is allocated to each customer, and the data is kept private from the other companies accessing the same application. The multi-instance model is a similar approach, with the difference being that each consumer has exclusive access to an instance of the application instead of one single application being shared.

Summary

In this introductory chapter, we explored the history and evolution of computing, from the early days of computing to where we are today and where the industry is headed in the future. We then explored how cloud computing is different from the traditional models with the evolution to the utility model found in cloud computing. Virtualization was introduced, and you learned about the role it plays in the cloud.

You then explored the many definitions of cloud computing, cloud growth, how to migrate operations from traditional data centers to the cloud, and how the role of the CCNA Cloud engineer will fit into working with the cloud models. The basic cloud models of public, private, hybrid, and community were each introduced and discussed.

We then introduced data center business, deployment, and operational models. How to design a data center for anticipated workload was then discussed.

This chapter concluded with a look at the common cloud characteristics, such as on-demand, elasticity, scaling, and pooling. These characteristics are important base concepts that will allow you to have a foundation for further discussions in future chapters.

Keep the concepts covered in this chapter in mind. They provide a structure that you will build on as you progress on your journey to becoming a CCNA Cloud certified professional.

Exam Essentials

Understand the basic terms and concepts of cloud computing service models.   Study the service models of IaaS, PaaS, and SaaS, and understand their differences and what each model includes and excludes.

Understand the basic concepts of virtualization.   Know what virtualization is and how it is a key enabler of cloud computing. We will cover this in greater detail in later chapters.

Know the primary cloud deployment models.   You will also be expected to identify what Public, Private, Community, and Hybrid clouds are; the differences between them; and where they are best used.

Understand the concepts of resource pooling.   Be able to identify the pooled resources in a virtualized cloud that include CPU, memory, storage, and networking. This topic will be covered in greater detail in later chapters.

Identify elasticity and scaling terminology and concepts.   Cloud elasticity is the ability to add and remove resources dynamically in the cloud. Closely related to elasticity is scaling, where you can scale up your computed resources by moving to a larger server or scale out by adding additional servers.

Written Lab

Fill in the blanks for the questions provided in the written lab. You can find the answers to the written labs in Appendix B.

1. Name the three NIST service models of cloud computing.

   1. _____

   2. _____

   3. _____

2. Name the four main cloud deployment models.

    1. _____

    2. _____

    3. _____

    4. _____

3. _____ provides for on-demand provisioning of resources in near real time.

4. _____ _____ is when a cloud provider allocates resources into a group and makes these available to a multitenant environment.

5. The ability to take a software package and, by using segmentation, share it to serve multiple tenants or customers is called _____.

Review Questions

The following questions are designed to test your understanding of this chapter's material. You can find the answers to the questions in Appendix A. For more information on how to obtain additional questions, please see this book's Introduction.

1. What model of computing allows for on-demand access without the need to provide internal systems and purchase technology hardware?

   A. Interexchange

   B. Community

   C. On-demand

   D. Utility

2. When elastic cloud services are required, what model implements larger, more powerful systems in place of smaller virtual machines?

   A. Elasticity

   B. Scale out

   C. On-demand

   D. Scale up

3. Hypervisors and virtual machines implement what networking technologies in software? (Choose two.)

   A. VPN

   B. Switches

   C. SAN

   D. NICs

4. What virtualization technology allocates pools of memory, CPUs, and storage to virtual machines?

   A. Scaling

   B. SAN

   C. Hypervisors

   D. Orchestration

5. What is an essential component of the cloud?

   A. Shared application software

   B. On-demand self-service

   C. Interexchange services

   D. Virtualization

6. What is the ability to segment a software application to serve multiple tenants called?

   A. Scale up

   B. Hybrid cloud

   C. Multitenancy

   D. Elasticity

7. A cloud data center must be designed with what in mind?

   A. Workload

   B. Interexchanges

   C. Virtualization

   D. SAN

8. Memory pooling allows for the dynamic allocation of what resource?

   A. Storage

   B. Disk drives

   C. RAM

   D. SAN

9. Which of the following are considered valid cloud deployment models? (Choose three.)

   A. Public

   B. On demand

   C. Hybrid

   D. Interexchange

   E. Resilient

   F. Private

10. The public cloud provides which of the following? (Choose three.)

   A. Measured usage

   B. Tiered service

   C. Exclusive access

   D. Multitenancy

   E. On-demand usage

11. Which terms are NIST-defined cloud service models? (Choose three.)

   A. Software as a Service

   B. Security as a Service

   C. Platform as a Service

   D. Applications as a Service

   E. Communications as a Service

   F. Infrastructure as a Service

12. What three characteristics are common to the cloud? (Choose three.)

    A. Interconnectivity

    B. Metered service

    C. Virtualization

    D. Elasticity

    E. Resource pooling

    F. Ubiquitous access

13. When additional cloud capacity is required, what model adds virtual machines?

    A. Elasticity

    B. Scale out

    C. On-demand

    D. Scale up

14. Storage systems are interconnected to the virtual servers on the cloud using what communications technology?

    A. LAN

    B. SAN

    C. Fiber optics

    D. VPN

15. Tipofthehat.com is an e-commerce company that hosts its applications in its private cloud. However, during the busy holiday season, because of increased workload, it utilizes external cloud computing capacity to meet demand. What cloud deployment model is Tipofthehat.com using?

    A. Public

    B. On demand

    C. Hybrid

    D. Multitenant

    E. Private

16. What are critical facilities of a modern data center? (Choose all that apply.)

    A. Power

    B. Servers

    C. Physical security

    D. Storage

    E. Virtualization

    F. Cooling

17. What is an example of a private dedicated connection to the cloud?

    A. Interexchange providers

    B. VPN

    C. Fiber optics

    D. SAN

18. What technology was instrumental in the advent of cloud computing?

    A. Mainframes

    B. Elasticity

    C. Virtualization

    D. Scaling

19. Which is not a valid cloud deployment model?

    A. Public

    B. Corporate

    C. Hybrid

    D. Community

    E. Private

20. Cloud service providers offer high availability by using what two data center deployments? (Choose two.)

    A. Regions

    B. Hybrid clouds

    C. Availability zones

    D. Virtual machines

Chapter 2

Defining Cloud Service Models

Introducing the Cloud Computing Service Models

In the previous chapter, we introduced some of the common cloud models. For the CCNA Cloud certification, you'll be expected to know the differences between the models and when you would choose specific ones for deployment. Therefore, this chapter will discuss the cloud *service models* in depth and compare the product offerings from several common *service providers*.

Cloud computing providers are nothing more than evolved service providers. Businesses have outsourced IT needs for years, especially support contracts, application needs that are not easily fulfilled on-site, and certain IT services that are too expensive to provide internally. Common examples of companies offering outsourcing services include traditional Internet service providers, managed service providers, systems integrators, and web hosting providers, among others.

These service providers were the precursor to *cloud computing*. Let's use web hosting as an easy example for comparison. In the early years of the dot-com boom, traditional web hosting fell into several models. One of these models included renting a web server in a hosting service provider's data center. You would use this server to run your website and applications on. While this was a service you can use, it couldn't scale in the current cloud sense. If you rented only one web server, then that's all the processing capabilities you had. If your server got overloaded with traffic, there was little recourse besides asking for help from the service provider to quickly purchase more server capacity. Of course, this was all before server *virtualization* was widely implemented and an explosive growth in the public cloud gave way to the many cloud technologies we know and use today.

The growth of virtualization and rapid provisioning paved the way for the current cloud offerings. Figure 2.1 illustrates a few of the many cloud services. Keep in mind that there are hundreds of services offered, with many more being introduced weekly in this rapidly expanding market.

These services are not limited to but commonly include the following:

Servers   To deliver applications and services to clients

Storage   To store files and data

Networking   To offer interconnectivity between servers, services, exchanges, and, in some cases, network services such as firewalls, load balancers, DNS services, VPNs, and more

Applications   Specialized programs that fulfill the needs of the business or end user

Middleware   Data broker services, single sign-on services with authentication, account management, and more

Databases   A collection of data that can be called upon by the end user or other applications, middleware, and more

Web Services   Web-based applications called upon to provide services to other applications (such as a web-based weather service with an API)

The preceding list is not all-encompassing, and you will find hundreds of other resources that further expand these terms. This is especially true with the thousands of application offerings available. However, these are some of the basic building blocks that cloud consumers are looking for in their deployment requirements. In the following sections, you'll explore how the different cloud service models are defined and subdivided.

FIGURE 2.1   Cloud services

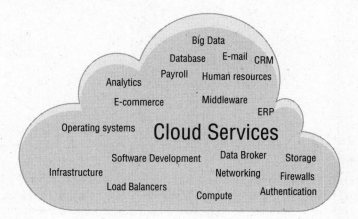

Understanding the Different Cloud Service Models

Cloud services is a general term used to describe the main categories of cloud offerings and products available to consumers. In the context of the CCNA Cloud certification, cloud services are broken into three main categories, sometimes referred to collectively as SPI:

- Software as a Service
- Platform as a Service
- Infrastructure as a Service

In addition to these main service models, there are many other offerings on the market today that range from the general to the specific.

It's important to understand the differences between the three main cloud service models. Your business needs and end-user needs should be considered when choosing any one of these models. In fact, there may be certain business and financial requirements that dictate the use of only one of these models in your organization.

To explain the various cloud service models, we'll use the common framework shown in Figure 2.2 to contrast the differences between them. Online you'll find many similar diagrams—some shorter and some larger—but they all revolve around the same premise.

FIGURE 2.2 Building blocks of a cloud

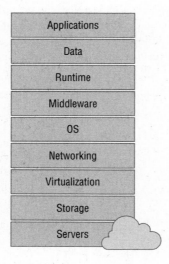

In the following sections, we'll go through the definitions as defined by the National Institute of Standards and Technology (NIST) and how they relate to the model in Figure 2.2. This chapter will explore some of the common use cases seen today and look at several of the well-known providers of these services.

Defining Infrastructure as a Service

Infrastructure as a Service (IaaS) is perhaps the most established model in terms of longevity. IaaS started in the early 2000s and exploded later in the decade with large contributions from Amazon, NASA/Rackspace, Microsoft, and Google.

Before we get too deep into the topic, let's visit NIST again to learn what the established definition of infrastructure as a service is. NIST SP 800-145 defines IaaS as follows:

> The capability provided to the consumer is to provision processing, storage, networks, and other fundamental computing resources where the consumer is able to deploy and run arbitrary software, which can include

operating systems and applications. The consumer does not manage or control the underlying cloud infrastructure but has control over operating systems, storage, and deployed applications; and possibly limited control of select networking components (e.g., host firewalls).

What most cloud customers are looking for in an IaaS solution is that they want the majority of control over their infrastructure for the length of time they determine. This could be networking, operating systems, storage, applications, processing, or any of the additional IaaS services available as options offered by the cloud service provider. IaaS specifically caters to IT administrators who want to rent or follow the pay-as-you-go utility model rather than purchase and operate infrastructure in their own data centers or private clouds. When a company moves its data center operations to the cloud, it is usually following the IaaS model during the transition because the IaaS model is similar to traditional corporate data centers. There are enormous benefits to this, and not all may relate to cost as you might immediately think. Time to deployment is also a contributing factor, as well as the ongoing support of the overall hardware. Traditional on-site information technology operations require a myriad of hardware and software to support. Your company will need the building, power, data center floor space, cooling, and a staff of specialized engineers to support your deployments during their entire life cycle. IaaS swoops in here and makes an easy case for outsourcing some of your infrastructure needs. Not only can you save on capital expenses, but you can deploy IaaS in a few mouse clicks, saving time. Look at Figure 2.3 to see the differences between on-site control and traditional IaaS.

FIGURE 2.3   IaaS: what the consumer controls

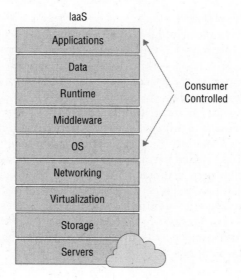

Some of the areas in Figure 2.3 fall into a gray area, especially virtualization. Most cloud providers offer the ability to run physical hardware or virtual hardware, as shown in Figure 2.4, which is abstracted from the physical hardware. This distinction is important because it is in the best interest of the cloud providers to offer a wide range of services, but they need to do this quickly and as efficiently as possible. By virtualizing their offerings and enabling multitenant access, cloud service providers achieve the speed and elasticity they need to spin up instances at lightning speeds. For this reason, most providers will sell you both hardware and virtualized services, or a combination of the two, which you'll explore in later sections.

FIGURE 2.4 IaaS: virtual vs. physical IaaS

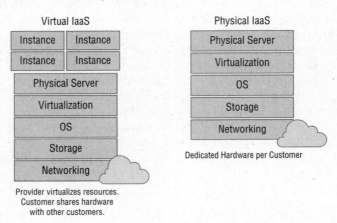

Regardless of which cloud service model you choose, you're still "renting" infrastructure, which is the underlying theme of IaaS. You, the consumer, get to choose the operating system to use, how much and what type of storage, the CPU processing requirements, the amount of memory required, networking features and services, and many other IaaS options. One potential drawback for the consumer could be security. When you're renting a dedicated server, you do not need to worry about who else is on it. It's your server for the length of time you continue to pay for it. That's not the case, however, with the more common IaaS offering of a virtualized infrastructure. You're paying to rent virtual space on shared hardware. You're trusting that the *cloud provider* will maintain separation and that its *hypervisor* separates your virtual machine instances and services correctly. Separation isn't the only factor to be concerned about. With the ever-increasing number of distributed denial of service (DDoS) attacks and security threats, you must understand the immediate effects of this. Any neighbor on the same hardware enduring a long attack would adversely affect your virtual machine instances. Most cloud providers offer security services and models to mitigate some of these concerns. It's for these reasons that cloud providers offer many different types of IaaS options.

Exploring IaaS Examples

One of the most commonly referenced IaaS examples is *Amazon Web Services (AWS)*. It's the often-referenced leader in this space and for years has appeared at the top of the Gartner magic quadrant. In this section, we'll be discussing IaaS examples and terminology, but AWS definitely has offerings in other areas as well. For example, the Elastic Beanstalk service is commonly thought of as PaaS for good reasons that we'll explore later in the chapter.

After you've signed up for a free trial of AWS, at aws.amazon.com you can begin to explore the many services that AWS offers. When you log in, you'll see a similar shortcut page as in Figure 2.5. Notice one of the first links is to launch a virtual machine. This is the most common first step with AWS for beginners and is a virtual instance running shared hardware. However, as it is with IaaS, you're still in control of the CPU and memory as well as the assigned operating system and the applications you install. We'll walk through some of these options later so you can get a feel of how you would launch these services.

FIGURE 2.5 AWS: front page

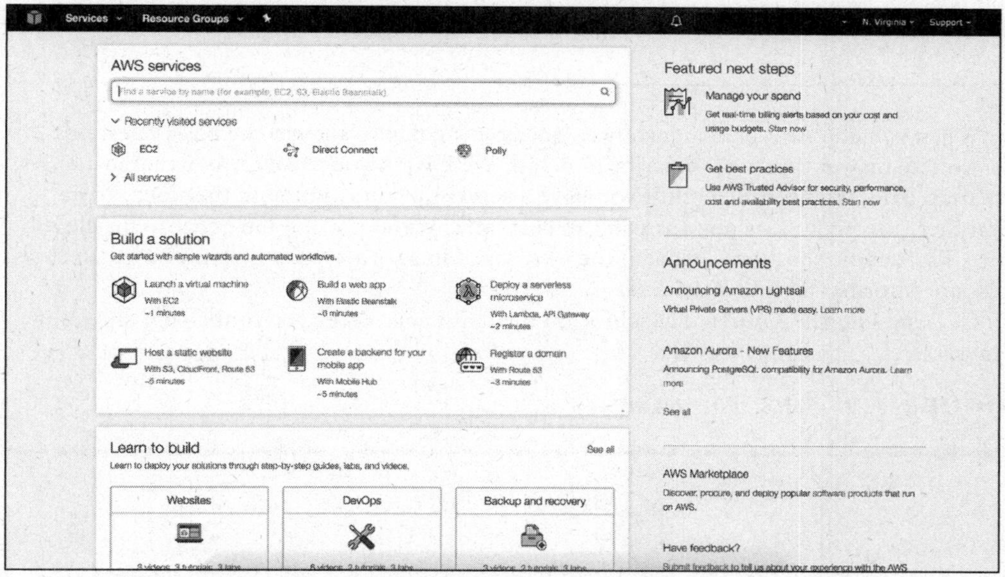

Beyond the AWS main front page, you can delve deeper into the console by clicking All Services and seeing what is offered (see Figure 2.6). We'll be discussing the storage options later in this book as they relate to the exam. It's on this page that you can jump directly into dedicated instance creation by clicking *EC2*. This takes you to an elastic compute cloud, which is the Amazon Web Services definition of a virtual machine instance running on the AWS platform. Then you can jump over to dedicated hosts.

FIGURE 2.6   AWS: services

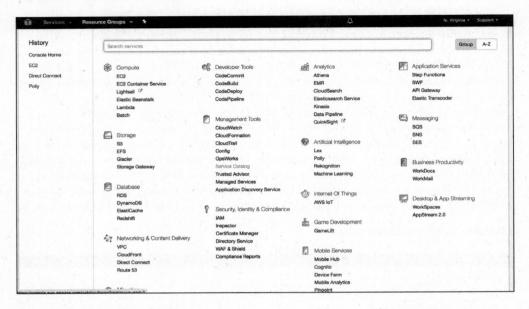

When you choose a launch instance, Amazon is going to show some basic questions for you to answer that we'll describe in detail. We'll walk you through a virtual instance creation from the beginning until you have a server up and running in the cloud. Note that there are a lot more options you can customize without using the quick route shown here. Please note that some items in the next set of images are purposely obscured, such as account information and IP address.

Clicking Launch A Virtual Machine on the main page takes you to the page shown in Figure 2.7.

FIGURE 2.7   AWS: getting started

When you click Get Started, the screen shown in Figure 2.8 will appear, and you can name your instance.

FIGURE 2.8   AWS: naming the VM

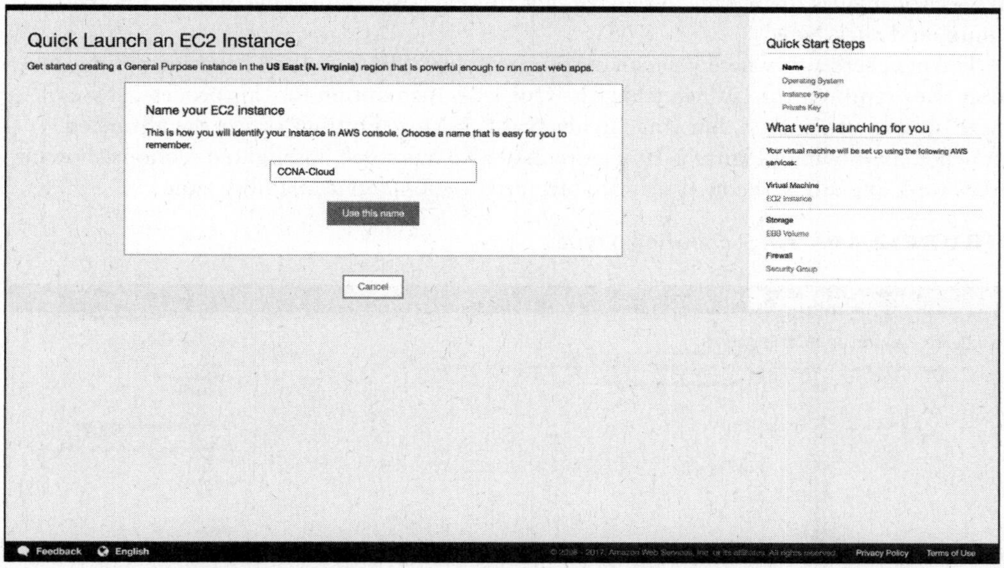

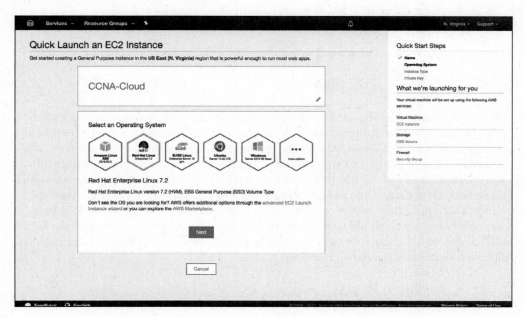

After clicking Use This Name, you get to some interesting options, as shown in Figure 2.9.

FIGURE 2.9   AWS: choosing an OS

It's here where the flexibility of IaaS comes into play for your operating system selections. There are quite a few OS options and even more if you go to the advanced section. If you don't see what you need here, you can find more options in the Amazon Marketplace. There are also many documents online for how to convert and migrate VMware or other hypervisor images to an Amazon image. For this exercise, choose the default, Red Hat Linux, and click Next.

The next screen is where you can customize your CPU, RAM, and storage options to meet your requirements. When using the Quick Launch option for this process, some of these options are limited, but you can always click More Options or use the advanced launcher, as shown in Figure 2.10. Figure 2.10 also has some highlighted sections showing areas we'll explain in the next section, primarily region and availability zone.

FIGURE 2.10   AWS: choosing a type

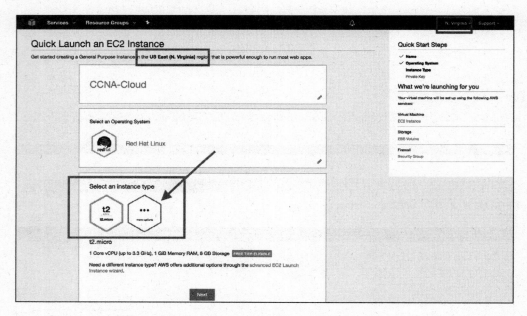

After this, you will be required to name and download a *private key*, which is a public-private key pair used for authentication and encryption. Do not lose this key! Save it in a safe place because if you lose it, you will be permanently locked out of your account. You will need this key to connect to your instance. Amazon defaults to certificate authentication to connect to any of the instances created on AWS, and by default the password option is turned off. Of course, if you use any third-party tools or your own image to create an instance, you'll need to be aware of what options are enabled, especially if the SSH password login is on, which would require the use of a key pair. After you download the key, you'll have to wait a minute for your instance to launch, as shown in Figure 2.11. Then you will see the dashboard, as shown in Figure 2.12.

FIGURE 2.11   AWS: image launching

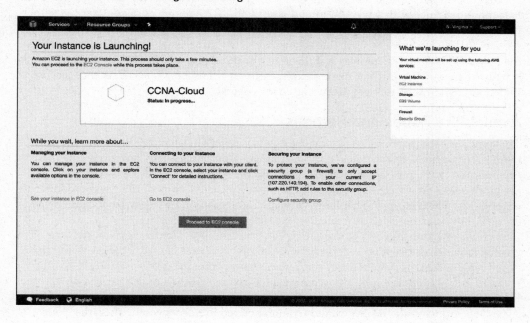

FIGURE 2.12   AWS: the dashboard

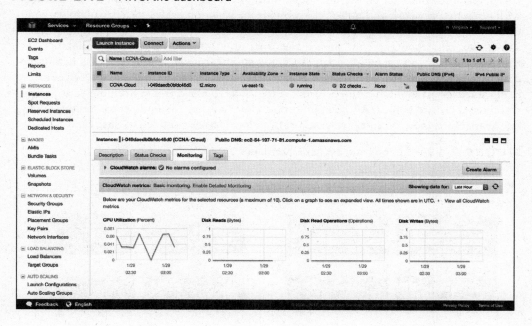

The preceding example took only a few minutes on AWS. You were able to launch a Red Hat Linux instance with a predetermined set of CPU, RAM, and storage. After the launch, you were able to *ssh* (which stands for secure shell and is an encrypted virtual terminal service) to your *instance* or virtual machine (with the private key) and begin configuring the server. This shows the power and flexibility of the cloud, and it was just a simple quick-start use case. AWS is just one example; there are other large IaaS providers such as Cisco Intercloud, Microsoft, Google, IBM, and many others.

Availability Zones and Regions

The previous example didn't touch on *availability zones* (*AZs*) and *regions*, but they are there in the options. In the quick-start version, you don't necessarily have to define these options, and in the previous example, you chose the defaults offered. However, you can manually select your desired regions and availability zones in any of the advanced launcher dashboards. The concepts of availability zones and regions are used by most cloud providers now, but Amazon originally popularized the terms.

Regions are simply geographical areas where a cloud provider has service. A common example in current cloud providers includes the east and west United States with international regions such as Asia and Europe, among many other locations around the world.

Availability zones are typically separate data centers within a region, as shown in Figure 2.13. For example, US East is a popular Amazon region, and it contains multiple AZs. Depending on the resiliency and redundancy requirements you're after, the cloud architecture for your application might designate a need for more than one availability zone in each region. Each availability zone is usually a completely independent data center with separated network and power connections for isolation between the availability zones. Cloud consumers do this to isolate themselves from bad things that happen, such as a local AZ failure, partial outages, and man-made or natural disasters. When one availability zone fails, all services including compute, applications, storage, and networking can immediately fail over to another availability zone in the same region so that cloud services are maintained. Most modern cloud providers offer tools to assist you in deciding your architecture and how to deploy. At the minimum, a cloud consumer should consider more than one availability zone to protect themselves from local issues confined to data centers.

FIGURE 2.13   Regions and availability zones

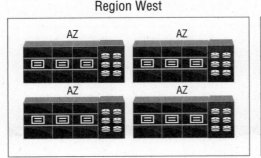
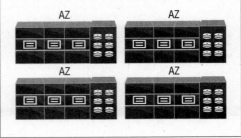

Availability Zones Within Regions

Defining Platform as a Service

Platform as a Service (PaaS) is an alternative to IaaS when the consumer needs to scale out applications without regard to the underlying infrastructure. PaaS has become a popular model for consumer choice, and even AWS, traditionally thought of as an IaaS provider, offers PaaS-like services. In the following sections, we'll discuss the differences of PaaS as it relates to IaaS.

However, first let's check the NIST definition of PaaS to get a good reference point to build on. NIST 800-145 defines PaaS as follows:

> ...the capability provided to the consumer is to deploy onto the cloud infrastructure consumer-created or acquired applications created using programming languages, libraries, services, and tools supported by the provider. The consumer does not manage or control the underlying cloud infrastructure including network, servers, operating systems, or storage, but has control over the deployed applications and possibly configuration settings for the application-hosting environment.

As noted by NIST, the primary difference is consumer control. As illustrated in Figure 2.14, it's all about what the cloud provider manages and what you, the consumer, do not.

FIGURE 2.14   IaaS vs. PaaS

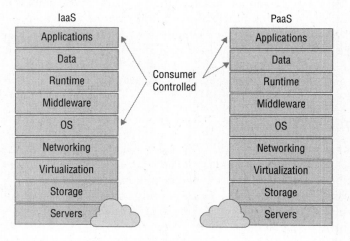

PaaS can be thought of as IaaS with the provider running the IaaS part and, additionally, providing the operating system and possibly other services for you. PaaS can host things such as middleware, applications, portals, and web services—anything you the consumer/developer can code. The cloud provider takes care of the server, operating system, RAM, CPU, network, scalability, on-demand provisioning, and other services, which allows you to focus on the applications you are responsible for. These are all the things you wouldn't need control of if you wanted to just run an application and didn't care about the underlying infrastructure as long as it met the requirements of your application.

Most PaaS provider solutions are custom to their own environment. This leads to a consumer problem, which is mainly intercloud portability in the PaaS ecosphere. It can be difficult, if not impossible, to migrate to another PaaS provider. PaaS providers often have vendor-specific tools and development applications that are used to install your application on their cloud platform. Careful thought needs to be done by the consumer before locking into a PaaS platform natively. There are, of course, third-party tools out there to address these issues and assist with portability.

PaaS environments are also billed differently than IaaS environments, and not all PaaS providers follow the same pricing scheme. In IaaS, the amount of compute used is a fairly easy measurement. In the PaaS case, you're sharing hardware with everyone else who is also running their own applications. Usual charge cases are application requests served, data in/out, runtime, and more. Each provider will treat this differently.

Security and *isolation* are other things to consider in PaaS. Because of the nature of how PaaS works, you will likely have little control over this. The best approach is to be an informed consumer and discern how a PaaS provider deals with isolation and security. NIST 800-146 covers these well, especially as they relate to SaaS and PaaS. One of the more common sharing aspects is *instance isolation*. Essentially the PaaS provider spins up a separate instance of an application and a separate database for each individual consumer. Consumers might be running on the same physical host, but they have separated instances of applications and databases. It's paramount to know the separation is only virtual. Cloud providers might offer separate VMs or physical hosts per tenant, but this can be extremely cost prohibitive. You may find options for the model in your PaaS provider search. Another model is the *shared process*, which gives the cloud provider the most efficiency and the consumer less security. The provider reengineers their framework to share a single database or process with consumers. It's this backend logic that often leads to cloud portability issues, depending on how the PaaS provider approaches this problem.

Exploring PaaS Examples

Google App Engine is a well-known PaaS provider that offers great resources and tutorials to start you on your journey in playing with PaaS. Let's walk through a brief Hello World app in Python. You'll deploy it, access it, and then destroy it.

Navigate to http://cloud.google.com (as of this writing) and sign up for a free account. Then click Products and App Engine to get started. You'll be presented with the screen shown in Figure 2.15.

We chose Python here and then clicked and selected a computing language; you get to choose your region next, as shown in Figure 2.16.

After that, you'll be presented with the launch screen. Note the tutorial area on the right that will guide you through this process.

FIGURE 2.15   Google App Engine

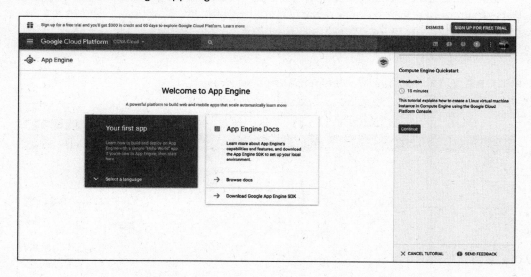

FIGURE 2.16   Google App Engine: selecting a region

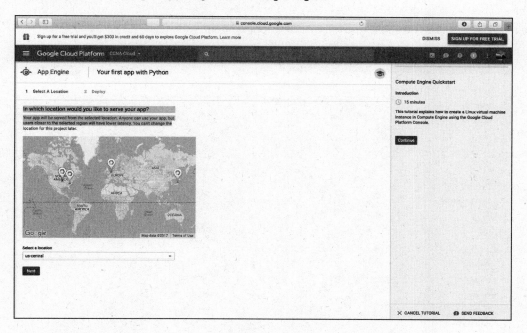

With the backend resources created, as shown in Figure 2.17, the code is ready to be configured, so next you can navigate over to the development section, as shown in Figure 2.18. Then go to the source code, as shown in Figure 2.19. The tutorial guides you on the right with what to look at next.

FIGURE 2.17   Google App Engine: backend services

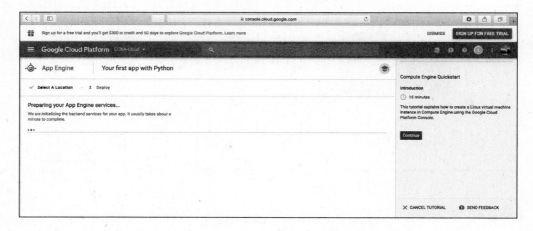

FIGURE 2.18   Google App Engine: Development option

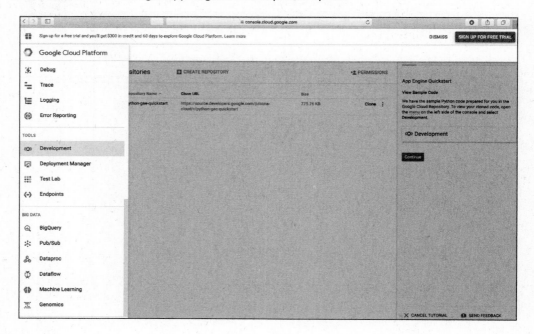

FIGURE 2.19 Google App Engine: Source Code area

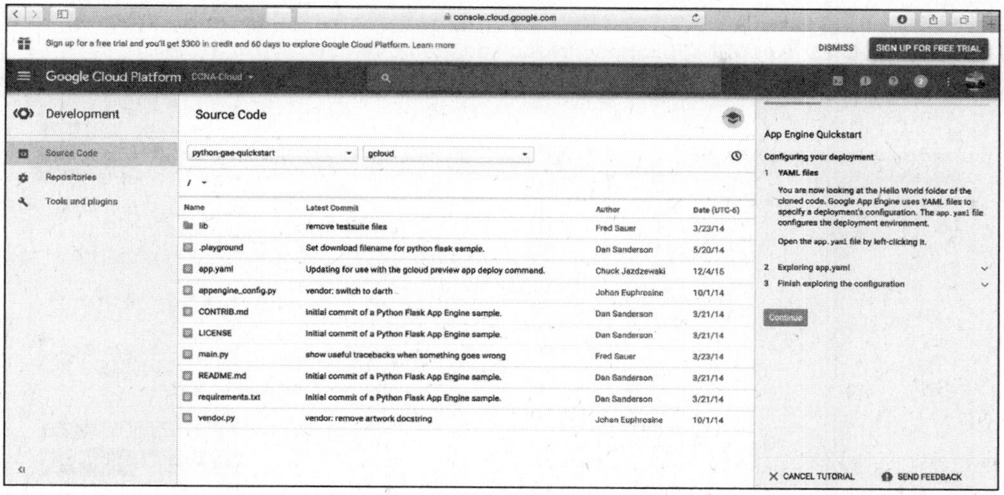

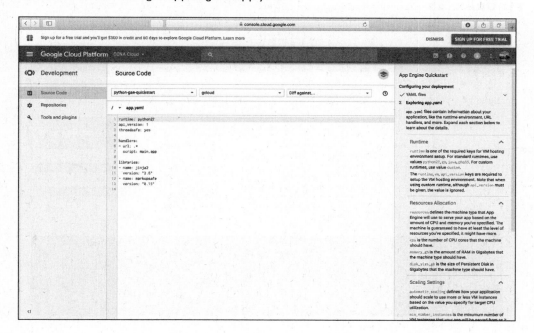

Figure 2.20 shows yaml file and some of the control the cloud PaaS consumer has in this case over various resources such as CPU and memory that a virtual machine instance may require. You can see some of the options on the far right of the screen as it's called out under "App Engine Quickstart". Each PaaS provider is different, and you may have limited control about what instances your application can deploy to.

FIGURE 2.20 Google App Engine: app.yaml

Figures 2.21 and 2.22 show the Google cloud shell and using Git to clone the source code and check it out.

FIGURE 2.21 Google App Engine: cloud shell

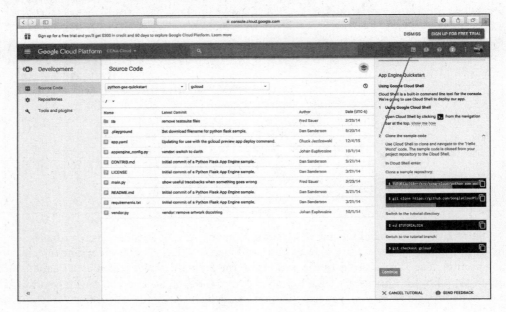

FIGURE 2.22 Google App Engine: using Git

Figure 2.23 shows the deploying of the app, following the tutorial on the right of the screen. From here you can click Web Preview to see your app. After this you'll see the screen that you're ready to go (Figure 2.24). You can then access your app at the URL you used, which may differ from Figure 2.25.

FIGURE 2.23   Google App Engine: deploy

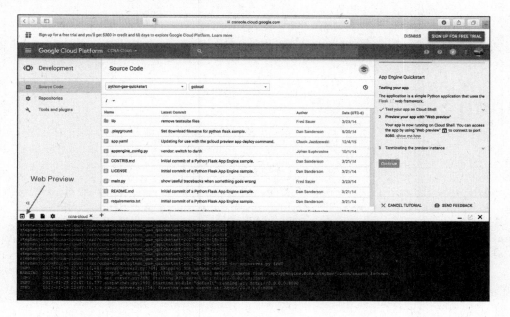

FIGURE 2.24   Google App Engine: finished app

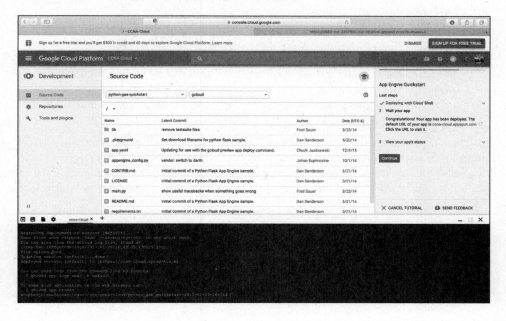

FIGURE 2.25   Google App Engine: web page

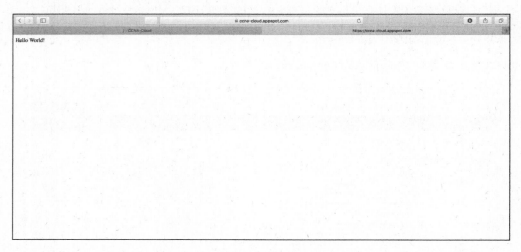

After this, the tutorial on the right guides you to deploy the app. That's all there is to it! While this was a small Hello World example, you can consider the possibilities of your code or application running in Google App Engine. Don't forget to clean up your instances either! After completing this tutorial, you can go ahead and delete these particular examples.

Defining Software as a Service

The last of the three cloud service models is called Software as a Service. NIST 800-145 defines SaaS as follows:

> The capability provided to the consumer is to use the provider's applications running on a cloud infrastructure. The applications are accessible from various client devices through either a thin client interface, such as a web browser (e.g., web-based e-mail), or a program interface. The consumer does not manage or control the underlying cloud infrastructure including network, servers, operating systems, storage, or even individual application capabilities, with the possible exception of limited user-specific application configuration settings.

SaaS has been around for a long while and was available way before everyone started calling it SaaS. SaaS can be understood as PaaS with almost zero control by you. The cloud service provider manages the complete service, up to and including the application. In other words, it's an application you're using, usually web-based, which you have no control over. Take a look at Figure 2.26.

FIGURE 2.26 SaaS vs. PaaS

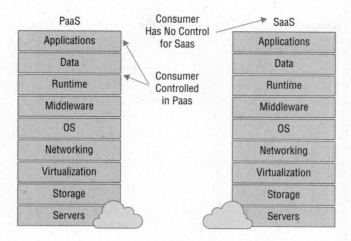

You probably use many SaaS applications and may not realize it. Apple's iCloud service is basically a SaaS service, and Google Docs and Google Gmail are two examples. Microsoft Office 365 is another popular example; it's a SaaS that runs on the Microsoft Azure public cloud. The majority of these are web browser–accessed applications. Both Google Docs and Office 365 host spreadsheet tools, documents, and notes along with storage and e-mail. If the software scales on demand, you pay for it as you go, and the provider manages everything for you, then you're likely using a SaaS.

These categories aren't just limited to documents and e-mail. There are popular SaaS apps for many areas of business. WebEx by Cisco or GoToMeeting from Citrix, for example, are SaaS applications for web conferencing. Other examples might be sales applications like Salesforce.com and HR/finance applications accessed via web browsers.

The same security implications for PaaS apply to SaaS. Since the vendor remains in complete control, you have little recourse in how to combat this. You're assuming that the SaaS provider will cleanly isolate instances and not trade off security for their efficiency and cost. Cloud portability is also an issue here, just like with PaaS. However, in this case it's probably worse since SaaS is often just a paid application with no way to translate into another vendor cleanly. There are, of course, exceptions, and companies do offer migration services. Migrating your documents from Google Docs to a storage provider like Dropbox shouldn't be difficult, but it's likely not a simple button push.

Other "as a Service" Models

It seems that there are many "as a service" models out there. Every year a new term gets defined, and businesses spring up around that term. There are so many models that there are now cloud brokers. A *cloud broker* is a third-party entity to help guide businesses through the many types of services available.

Desktop as a Service (DaaS), *IP telephony as a Service (IPTaaS)*, and *Communications as a Service (CaaS)* are common ones used to deploy simple remote services for corporate or individual use. Using thin clients for access to the services, a corporation could request and use remote desktops and phones for their workers. This model closely relates to help-desk-oriented companies, but that's not the only example. In some cases, these are useful as disaster recovery plans (or *DRaaS*). There are others too such as *VPNaaS* for corporations to use autoscaling VPN services. This list constantly changes, and you'll find more "as a service" models as time goes on. Cisco refers to all these examples as *anything as a service (XaaS)*.

Summary

This chapter covered the three most common cloud service models: IaaS, SaaS, and PaaS. The differences were noted between each, and we talked about the security implications that you might have deploying in any of these models.

We briefly walked you through the examples of IaaS and PaaS using Amazon Web Services and Google Cloud Services, respectively, showing you how easy it is to start a cloud service. Finally, we concluded with some examples of other "as a service" models and how they fit into the larger role of cloud services.

The services model is useful in defining basic categories of offerings and to better understand what services are included by the cloud provider and what is the responsibility of the customer. As we went through the models, we identified the three primary definitions of infrastructure, platform, and software as a service. These are hierarchical from a basic infrastructure through operating system offerings up to a complete solution that includes the application software.

Exam Essentials

Identify the three primary cloud service models.   The three primary services offered in the cloud are defined by NIST as being Infrastructure as a Service, Platform as a Service and Software as a Service.

Define the components of IaaS.   IaaS includes all underlying infrastructure such as CPU, memory, storage, and networking but does not include the operating system or any applications. Know that this is the base offering and was considered to be the first cloud service.

Define the components of PaaS.   Know that the PaaS offering is one level above IaaS and includes the operating systems but no applications.

Define SaaS.   Understand that SaaS is offered as a complete package that includes all the underlying infrastructure (IaaS), the operating systems (PaaS), and the applications such as e-mail, websites, collaboration, development tools, human resource applications, and thousands of other offerings.

Be able to identify other cloud service models in addition to the three well-known models. There are many other types of services in the marketplace beyond just IaaS, PaaS, and SaaS. For example, there are DaaS, IPTaaS, and CaaS. There are offerings for security, disaster recovery, virtual private networks, and many others, with overlapping offerings and high levels of confusion. We like the catchall phrase *Anything as a Service (XaaS)*, as the marketing people have taken over the naming conventions!

Written Lab

Fill in the blanks for the questions provided in the written lab. You can find the answers to the written labs in Appendix B.

1. Name the three primary NIST service models of cloud computing.

    1. _____

    2. _____

    3. _____

2. _____ as a Service provides both infrastructure and the operating system.

3. Name four public cloud service providers.

    1. _____

    2. _____

    3. _____

    4. _____

4. Cloud providers often segment their data centers into two areas called _____ and _____ that you can select for proximity and redundancy.

5. A cloud provider that offers all networking, storage, and compute functionality and allows you to install your preferred operating system and applications is offering the _____ as a Service.

Review Questions

The following questions are designed to test your understanding of this chapter's material. You can find the answers to the questions in Appendix A. For more information on how to obtain additional questions, please see this book's Introduction.

1. Which service model includes the operating system but not the application?

   A. PaaS

   B. IaaS

   C. SaaS

   D. CaaS

2. Which of the following are the three primary NIST service models?

   A. Public, private, hybrid

   B. Public, community, private

   C. IaaS. SaaS, PaaS

   D. CaaS, PaaS, DRaaS

3. What is a geographical area of cloud computing?

   A. Availability zone

   B. Hybrid

   C. Region

   D. Elasticity

4. Which of the following is descriptive of the SaaS model?

   A. A server service that allows for selection of memory, CPU, network, and storage

   B. A platform that allows user access to applications

   C. The service that creates a virtual machine on a hypervisor

   D. An operating system that can have applications installed on it

5. Which data center topology is a facility in a single geographic area that has its own power and communications to allow for failover and resiliency?

   A. Zone

   B. Availability zone

   C. Region

   D. Hybrid cloud

6. A service provider provides which services in the IaaS service model? (Choose three.)

   A. Linux

   B. Memory

   C. Storage

   D. CPU

   E. DNS

   F. Object brokers

7. What does IaaS stand for?

    A. Instances as a Service

    B. Infrastructure as a Service

    C. Internet as a Service

    D. Internetworking as a Service

8. Which NIST service model offers e-mail and big data services?

    A. PaaS

    B. IaaS

    C. SaaS

    D. XaaS

9. What are three common cloud security concepts?

    A. Instance isolation

    B. CRN

    C. VPN tunnels

    D. LDAP

    E. Firewalls

10. A cloud provider offering services under the PaaS models would not include which two of the following services?

    A. ERP

    B. Operating systems

    C. Analytics

    D. Virtualization

    E. Application load balancers

    F. Storage

11. Which NIST service model best describes the offering of cloud hardware to consumers?

    A. PaaS

    B. IaaS

    C. SaaS

    D. XaaS

12. What does PaaS stand for?

    A. Programs as a Service

    B. Processing as a Service

    C. Platform as a Service

    D. Programming as a Service

13. When moving a physical data center's operations to the cloud, which is the most common service model utilized?

    A. Platform as a Service

    B. Software as a Service

    C. Infrastructure as a Service

    D. Computing as a Service

14. What does SaaS stand for?

    A. Security as a Service

    B. Single sign-on as a Service

    C. Software as a Service

    D. Server hardware as a Service

15. Which service model is most commonly deployed by IT systems administrators?

    A. Platform as a Service

    B. Software as a Service

    C. Infrastructure as a Service

    D. Computing as a Service

16. Cloud-hosted collaboration is an example of what type of service?

    A. PaaS

    B. CaaS

    C. SaaS

    D. XaaS

17. Which of the following is an example of a PaaS cloud service provider?

    A. Amazon Web Services

    B. Google App Engine

    C. Rackspace

    D. Cisco WebEx

18. Which services must be provided by the cloud consumer when implementing a PaaS?

    A. Operating systems

    B. Infrastructure

    C. Applications

    D. Virtual servers

19. Which service model is used as a global definition that is not a primary NIST service model?

   A. PaaS

   B. CaaS

   C. SaaS

   D. XaaS

   E. IaaS

20. Which service models are not part of the NIST definitions? (Choose three.)

   A. PaaS

   B. CaaS

   C. SaaS

   D. XaaS

   E. IaaS

   F. DRaaS

Chapter

3

Understanding Cloud Deployment Models

THE FOLLOWING UNDERSTANDING CISCO CLOUD FUNDAMENTALS CLDFND (210-451) EXAM OBJECTIVES ARE COVERED IN THIS CHAPTER:

What Are the Primary Cloud Deployment Models?

In this chapter, we will expand upon the cloud deployment models introduced in Chapter 1. While there are actually a number of independent and combined deployment models, we will focus on the primary deployment models for the CCNA Cloud certification.

The four primary deployment models are public, private, community, and hybrid, as shown in Figure 3.1. This chapter will go over each of these in detail because they are important foundational topics.

FIGURE 3.1   Cloud deployment models

By understanding the deployment models combined with the service models introduced in Chapter 2, you can select a cloud configuration that best meets your needs.

Many organizations that are migrating to the cloud will select a model that allows for an incremental approach to cloud adoption. This could include starting with IaaS and, with a staged implementation, later migrating to either a PaaS service model or a SaaS service model. The same approach works for the deployment models; a corporation may start with a private cloud model and over time migrate to a hybrid or public cloud deployment. Migrations to the cloud can be, and often are, incremental. With a solid understanding of deployment and service models, you can plan and execute a migration strategy that best fits your requirements.

The deployment models are defined around the audience and use case requirements for each unique customer's needs. There are four primary deployment models, and we will cover each in detail in this chapter.

One critical point that we would like to stress is that in the world of cloud computing, there will usually never be a single right or wrong answer for which service or deployment model to use. You will often hear us saying "It depends!" when evaluating cloud architecture and design issues. We suggest you keep an open mind, review the pros and cons offered, and arrive at the best solution for your individual requirements. Also remember that there can be, and often are, combinations of the cloud models that can be implemented to most effectively achieve your own business and computing requirements.

The Public Cloud Model

The public cloud deployment model is the outsourcing of your data center operations to a company that offers cloud services as its primary area of expertise. This allows you as the customer of the public cloud to focus on your core areas of business and outsource your data center operations to the public cloud provider. When you hear the term *cloud* in the media and in conversations, you can usually assume it is in reference to the public cloud. While there are other models, it is clear that the public model is the most prevalent and commonly used of the four models.

Let's start your exploration of the *public cloud* with another visit to the National Institute of Standards and Technology to learn what the established definition of the public cloud deployment model is:

> The cloud infrastructure is provisioned for open use by the general public. It may be owned, managed, and operated by a business, academic, or government organization, or some combination of them. It exists on the premises of the cloud provider.

As shown in Figure 3.2, there are many companies offering public cloud services; some offer basic services, while others are more specialized. They all follow the model of on-demand shared compute resources offered as a service to the public.

FIGURE 3.2   Public cloud deployment model

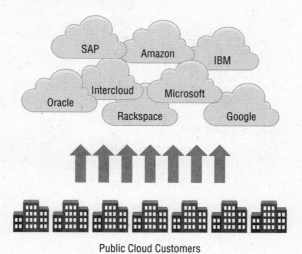

Public Cloud Customers

The public cloud is provisioned for multitenant access to a group or, as they are often called, a *grid* of virtualized services. The compute resources are virtualized in remote data center regions and are shared by the many different customers of the public cloud provider. Public cloud data centers are located all over the globe and are often interconnected with high-speed fiber-optic interconnects and accessed externally over the Internet.

Most of the complexity of the infrastructure is hidden from the customers, who typically interface with the deployment using a web-based front end, or control panel. There are also command-line interfaces and application programmable interfaces (APIs) typically offered for configuration and management.

The public cloud primarily utilizes the pay-as-you-go utilities model introduced in Chapter 1. You are charged only for what services you consume, and there are no up-front hardware and software costs that you as the customer have to assume. While there are many different pricing models offered, most are based on the pay-as-you-go model.

One of the benefits that public cloud computing offers is elasticity, in that the large pooling of resources in the public cloud allows your applications to increase or decrease compute resources as needed and on the fly. With elasticity, the public cloud can react in almost real time to increases or decreases of application processing requirements or demands. This means the compute elasticity resources do not need to be purchased and just sit idle while waiting to become available when the need arises. With the public cloud, you access these resources out of a pool and pay for them as needed and return them to the pool when they are no longer required.

These resource pools can consist of the resources introduced in Chapter 1 and include CPU, memory, storage, and network bandwidth, as shown in Figure 3.3.

FIGURE 3.3   Resource pools

With the utility pricing model offered in the public cloud deployment model, you will have to pay for only what is used and do not have to pay for the computing and data center infrastructure that sits idle that would, in the corporate data center, require a large up-front investment. No hardware acquisition costs are required since all capital expenditures for the needed compute, storage, networking, and all additional cloud data center hardware are the responsibility of the public cloud service provider. Compute cycles do not sit unused in the public cloud because if one customer does not need them, they are returned to the pool for use by other public cloud customers.

While there are many advantages to the public cloud deployment model, there are, as you could probably imagine, some downsides. Probably the biggest concern with many customers when considering a migration of their operations to the public cloud is that they will be giving up control of the data center infrastructure. Public cloud customers have to rely on the provider to perform at an expected level of service that meets each customer's requirements. These expectations are outlined in agreements between the cloud provider and the customer and are referred to as *service level agreements (SLAs)*. The SLA will outline all of the performance metrics the public cloud provider will be contracted to meet. However, if there is an outage, the customer is totally at the mercy of the cloud company to restore services and has no control of that mean time to repair and mean time to restore metrics. The public cloud provider will take total responsibility for all system redundancy and uptime objectives. The public cloud provider also must provide adequate compute, storage, and network performance to the public cloud customers.

Many companies in highly regulated fields, such as finance and healthcare, will have compliance requirements that they are required to conform to. These can include encryption requirements to ensure the security of the data either in flight or at rest; there may also be restrictions on which countries that data can be stored in, and who can access the data and reporting and record-keeping regulations that must be followed. These rules and regulations are often set by governments as a requirement to do business in their countries. If the public cloud provider does not adhere to these regulations, then the public deployment model would not be an appropriate fit.

Another public cloud reality is that the customers lose control over their computing operations having flexible configurations options. The public cloud provider will usually offer a limited and controlled number of infrastructure options such as storage, virtual machines, memory, load balancing, and network performance (to name the most common resources). These resources are offered to meet the basic requirements of the majority of their customer's needs. However, if you have any special or specific needs, you may not be able to find public cloud offerings to meet those needs.

Since many public cloud services are running with proprietary or custom-designed applications, tools, APIs, and automation functions, vendor lock-in may be a customer concern. Once you move your operations to the public cloud, will you be able to easily migrate away at a later time? The ability to migrate later should be investigated up front prior to purchasing public cloud services in order to evaluate the risks of provider lock-in.

Some common public cloud use cases are where company growth or computing needs are hard to predict and to plan for, such as e-commerce sites with holiday traffic load fluctuations or companies that have marketing campaigns that direct traffic to their corporate websites. Web hosting and applications that can be run in parallel are also good candidates for a public cloud deployment mode. Batch processing, encoding of media files, mobile applications, analytics, big data, end-of-month processing, development, and proof of concepts are all good fits for the public cloud model. In the previous examples, the processing requirements may fluctuate greatly, which fits the elastic computing abilities of the public cloud, where you can allocate additional compute resources when required and scale back when the compute capacity is no longer needed.

The Private Cloud Model

The *private cloud* deployment model allows for your organization to have exclusive access to the computing resources, as shown in Figure 3.4. This model prevents sharing cloud operations with other cloud consumers and is, by definition, a single-tenant deployment model. However, the private cloud can be either managed internally or outsourced to a separate organization or entity. With a hosted private cloud, you may still have to follow, and be dependent on, the cloud service provider to provide the data center infrastructure. Remember that these resources are exclusive and not shared.

FIGURE 3.4   Private cloud model

Private Cloud

Let's review the NIST definition of the private cloud:

> The cloud infrastructure is provisioned for exclusive use by a single organization comprising multiple consumers (e.g., business units). It may be owned, managed, and operated by the organization, a third party, or some combination of them, and it may exist on or off premises.

You can see that the private cloud gives you much more control over your operations and will allow you to make changes to your infrastructure to meet any specific hardware requirements you may not have with the public model. Legacy applications can also be more effectively supported in the private cloud as compared to the other deployment models that have more structured offerings that may not allow for any special requirements.

If there are specific regulatory or compliance requirements, the private cloud may be your only option if the other deployment models do not offer specific regulatory support for your data ownership, compliance, and security requirements. Some of the more common regulatory requirements in the United States include Sarbanes–Oxley (SOX), Health Insurance Portability and Accountability Act (HIPAA), The Payment Card Industry Data Security Standard (PCI DSS), and The Federal Risk and Authorization Management Program (FedRAMP).

As is true with all cloud deployment models, there are both positive and negative aspects to each approach. The pro and cons will often depend on your specific requirements, and in some situations a positive aspect of a deployment model for one customer may be considered to be a negative for another.

Some of the primary advantages of cloud computing models are resource pooling, rapid elasticity, and the ability to take advantage of the utility model of pay-as-you-go pricing. Since a private cloud is by definition owned or has exclusive use by one organization, the advantages of pooling, scaling, and cost models are greatly reduced if not eliminated completely. Since there are no other users to share resources with, it becomes difficult to cost-effectively scale up and scale down resources as is often leveraged in the public cloud deployment model. This limitation of a private model increases operational costs since additional resources and capacity must be financed and provided on standby for peak loads. Because the private cloud deployment model requires the up-front costs of resources, regardless if they are being utilized or not, the pay-as-you-go model of computing is difficult to achieve.

The Community Cloud Model

The *community cloud* model is a specialized extension of cloud computing where organizations with similar requirements access a specialized cloud deployment offering. For example, a group of companies or organizations may have similar requirements or needs that can benefit from a shared computing approach. With a community cloud, services are designed around these common needs and offered to the groups of cloud customers that have those requirements.

Here is the NIST definition of the community cloud:

> The cloud infrastructure is provisioned for exclusive use by a specific
> community of consumers from organizations that have shared concerns
> (e.g., mission, security requirements, policy, and compliance considerations).
> It may be owned, managed, and operated by one or more of the organizations
> in the community, a third party, or some combination of them, and it may
> exist on or off premise.

Organizations such as finance, healthcare, governments, education, or those required to meet various regulatory requirements are examples of communities of interest that would benefit from the community model, as shown in Figure 3.5.

A community cloud can exist as a privately owned and operated service restricted to a group of customers with the same needs. Service providers can offer a specialized community cloud model, or large organizations can create a community cloud for operational efficiency of internal departments. Depending on the nature of the requirements, the community cloud may have restricted public access. Public cloud providers may also partition their networks to offer specialized community offerings for specific areas of interest. These partitions will restrict access only to members subscribing to the services offered in the community cloud.

FIGURE 3.5   Community model

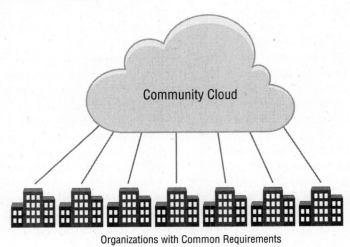

Organizations with Common Requirements

The sharing of resources saves money and operational expenses since the operations and ongoing support are a shared cost between the members of the community.

The Hybrid Cloud Model

Often a combination of cloud deployment models is the best solution. You can leverage the best characteristics of each model and take advantage of the pros and cons of each approach by combining them to achieve what is referred to as the *hybrid cloud* model, as shown in Figure 3.6. In this section, we will expand on the hybrid cloud first introduced in Chapter 1.

For the final time, we will turn to the NIST definition and see how it defines the hybrid cloud:

> The Hybrid cloud infrastructure is a composition of two or more distinct cloud infrastructures (private, community, or public) that remain unique entities, but are bound together by standardized or proprietary technology that enables data and application portability (e.g., cloud bursting for load balancing between clouds).

When you are running more than one of the deployment models (community, public, or private) and they are interconnected, you have a hybrid cloud! This can be as basic as using the public cloud for remote backup storage to as elaborate as a globally interconnected e-commerce site hosted in regions all over the world that link back to a company's private cloud data center and to other cloud-hosted applications for financial transactions and shipping systems.

FIGURE 3.6 Hybrid cloud model

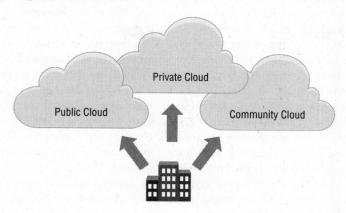

When utilizing the best of each cloud deployment model, it is often most desirable to use the public cloud as your primary platform to take advantage of the benefits of cloud computing rapid elasticity, resource pooling, and the pay-as-you-go pricing model. Then, using the hybrid approach, you can interconnect to the private or community cloud where appropriate for custom applications that may require specialized hardware or to meet regulatory requirements as reviewed earlier with the private cloud deployment model.

Some common use cases for implementing the hybrid cloud is when the public-private combinations are reversed from the public first and private as the secondary hybrid model. In this case, a company may want to perform their primary processing in their private cloud and use the public cloud to augment capacity during periods that require additional computing capacity, which is referred to as *cloud bursting*.

Also, the pubic cloud is useful for noncritical applications. With this in mind, these applications can be hosted in the public cloud, and more company mission-critical applications will remain in the private cloud. The public-private clouds can then be interconnected to create the hybrid cloud. One cloud deployment can be used as your primary data center processing platform such as a private cloud, and then when additional capacity is required, instead of having to purchase the infrastructure to have a standby, you can use the public cloud as needed.

As you will learn as you progress on your CCNA Cloud certification journey, the hybrid cloud requires interoperability and coordination, and the Cisco Intercloud enables the capabilities to make hybrid computing agile, efficient, easy to manage, and cost-effective.

Summary

This chapter described the four primary cloud deployment models. You learned that there are public, private, community, and hybrid deployment models and what each of them provided.

We explained that the public model was the most common and is shared by a large number of public customers in a pay-as-you-go model that allows for economies of scale as all resources are shared. The public cloud resides on the premises of the cloud provider. Both the benefits and limitations of the public model were explained, and examples were given of each.

The private cloud is for the exclusive use of an organization. However, the organization can have many units accessing the private cloud. It may be owned and managed internally or by a third-party company and may be local or remote from the company.

You then learned about the community cloud model and explained that it is for the exclusive use of a group of customers that have common compute needs or concerns such as mission, security, or government regulations and compliance concerns. The community cloud can be owned by the company or by a third-party service provider. A community cloud can reside either on or off the customer's premises.

Finally, the hybrid cloud was introduced, and you learned that it is simply a combination of two of the other cloud deployment models reviewed earlier in the chapter.

Exam Essentials

Know what the four main cloud deployment models are.   The four primary deployment models are public, private, community, and hybrid. The names are very self-descriptive as to what they are used for. These models are used to define the four primary categories of cloud computing offerings and how they are different from each other. The public cloud is the most common of the deployment models.

Understand where the four models are used.   Understand what each model's primary use is in the marketplace. The public cloud is for general applications that do not require any customized hardware and work on basic server platforms. The private model is used where the data may be sensitive or need specialized compute hardware that is not available in a public cloud offering. The community cloud is found where a group of companies, or organizations inside of a company, have similar requirements that can be shared. A hybrid cloud is simply a combination of any two of the other cloud types.

Written Lab

Fill in the blanks for the questions provided in the written lab. You can find the answers to the written labs in Appendix B.

1. Name the four primary cloud deployment models.

    1. _____

    2. _____

    3. _____

    4. _____

2. The _____ model is a combination of two or more deployment models.

3. What is the name of the document that outlines the responsibilities of the cloud provider?

    _____

    _____

    _____

4. Name the model that is hosted by the cloud provider.

    _____

5. The _____ model can be used to meet regulatory compliance requirements.

Review Questions

The following questions are designed to test your understanding of this chapter's material. You can find the answers to the questions in Appendix A. For more information on how to obtain additional questions, please see this book's Introduction.

1. Which deployment model is hosted by the provider?
   A. Public
   B. Private
   C. Community
   D. Hybrid

2. Which deployment model is usually accessed by a single customer?
   A. Public
   B. Private
   C. Community
   D. Hybrid

3. What are the NIST-defined cloud deployment models?
   A. Public, private, hybrid, shared
   B. IaaS, PaaS, CaaS, SaaS
   C. Public, private, community, and hybrid
   D. Public, interexchange, hosted

4. Which deployment model is usually accessed by a large and diverse group of companies?
   A. Public
   B. Private
   C. Community
   D. Hybrid

5. Which deployment models offer exclusivity?
   A. Public
   B. Hybrid
   C. Community
   D. Private

6. What is cloud bursting?
   A. Exceeding the capacity of the cloud infrastructure
   B. Scaling out new servers using load balancers
   C. Utilizing the public cloud when private cloud resources reach a threshold
   D. Utilizing two or more public clouds simultaneously

7. What resources can be grouped together and shared in a virtualized data center? (Choose two.)

   A. Applications

   B. Memory

   C. Storage

   D. Infrastructure

8. Which deployment model offers the most customer control?

   A. Public

   B. Hybrid

   C. Community

   D. Private

9. What is the ability to access compute resources in another cloud facility called?

   A. Resiliency

   B. On-demand

   C. Bursting

   D. Pay-as-you-go

10. Which regulations can be addressed with the use of a community cloud? (Choose three.)

   A. SOX

   B. PCI DSS

   C. SSH

   D. ACE

   E. HIPAA

   F. TRILL

11. Which deployment model offers a large number of companies a pay-as-you-go pricing model?

   A. Public

   B. Hybrid

   C. Community

   D. Private

12. What document outlines the responsibilities of the service provider?

   A. CMDB

   B. Statement of work

   C. SLA

   D. MOC

13. Which deployment model is best suited for non-mission-critical applications?

    A. Public

    B. Hybrid

    C. Community

    D. Private

14. A public-private cloud interconnect is referred to as which of the following?

    A. Community

    B. Inter-exchange

    C. Peering

    D. Hybrid

15. Which two deployment models may exist on or off the premises?

    A. Public

    B. Hybrid

    C. Community

    D. Private

16. An e-commerce company that experiences wide fluctuations in load during the holiday season is well suited for what type of deployment model?

    A. Public

    B. Hybrid

    C. Community

    D. Private

17. What is a potential drawback to using a public cloud?

    A. SLA

    B. Lock-in

    C. Resiliency

    D. Scaling

18. What are common methods to configure and manage a public cloud deployment? (Choose three.)

    A. JSON

    B. APIs

    C. SNMP

    D. CLI

    E. Web GUI

    F. VxCloud

19. What allows the public cloud to react in almost real time to increases or declines of application processing requirements?

   A. Scaling

   B. Elasticity

   C. Load balancing

   D. Resource pooling

20. Utilizing off-site storage from your private corporate data center is an example of utilizing which deployment model?

   A. Public

   B. Private

   C. Community

   D. Hybrid

Chapter 4

Introducing the Cisco Intercloud Solution

THE FOLLOWING UNDERSTANDING CISCO CLOUD FUNDAMENTALS CLDFND (210-451) EXAM OBJECTIVES ARE COVERED IN THIS CHAPTER:

✓ **1.0 The Cisco Intercloud Fabric Solution**

- 1.1 What is Cisco Intercloud Fabric

- 1.2 Exploring Cisco Intercloud Fabric components

  - 1.2.1 Exploring Intercloud Fabric Services

  - 1.2.2 Defining Intercloud Fabric benefits

Introduction to the Cisco Intercloud Fabric Solution

In the previous chapter, we discussed cloud deployment models. One of the most popular and commonly deployed cloud models is the hybrid cloud. As discussed, a hybrid cloud is simply when you use more than one type of interconnected deployment model. The most common use case of a hybrid cloud is having infrastructure in your business's private data center or building *and* having data in the public cloud. The public cloud is directly connected to your data center or private cloud, so by definition you are using a hybrid cloud.

Businesses are doing this for many reasons. Not all companies are ready or able to be completely cloud native. Some organizations might have specific security requirements or data privacy and regulatory requirements, such as PCI for credit transactions or HIPPA for medical records, that may be better suited for the private data center (or private cloud as it is commonly referred to). By interconnecting your private data center operations to the public cloud, you will be able to access the almost limitless computing resources available in public and Cisco business partner clouds. The hybrid model allows for economically bursting resources to accommodate peak loads. These are a few of the reasons that you'll find a lot of organizations implementing a hybrid cloud approach.

Implementing a hybrid deployment model has a unique set of challenges that must be overcome for a successful deployment. There are compatibility requirements and cross-platform issues between providers and your on-site resources. Turning up services in one large cloud provider may be great in the short term, but what happens when your business needs to move to another cloud provider? This isn't necessarily only a cloud provider issue. Interconnecting multiple private cloud offerings into your own business operations and on-premise infrastructure isn't that simple either. The issues that must be addressed when interconnecting multiple clouds into a hybrid cloud are what Cisco Intercloud Fabric was developed to address. VM portability, secure interconnections, a streamlined security policy across all cloud platforms, a services catalog feature to greatly simplify and standardize VM deployments, a monitoring dashboard, firewall services, layer 2 switching, layer 3 routing, and many other features are all included in the Cisco Intercloud Fabric feature set.

There are many different public cloud solutions available on the market that offer a wide variety of specialized services. A company may choose to select the best cloud service that meets their own unique requirements. Also, if your operations require a global reach, a fast response time, and localized services, or must adhere to regulatory issues, you may decide to purchase public cloud services from a number of different providers that offer local cloud connectivity in the international markets you desire to do business in. This can add up to many different cloud deployments that need to be interconnected using a hybrid design that allows seamless interoperation with many clouds.

These scenarios are how and why *Cisco Intercloud Fabric (ICF)* was born. Cisco studied the many different challenges its customers were experiencing with their cloud deployments, as well as the many different rollout scenarios, and found a large portion of their customers wanted to deploy a hybrid cloud model but lacked a centralized management solution to facilitate the requirement. The Cisco Intercloud Fabric solution also provides a self-service portal to manage your hybrid cloud resources, provides a common view of workloads across all locations, provides workload mobility, and includes a secure communications connection from your private cloud to one or more public or Cisco partner clouds. Figure 4.1 illustrates the use of many different discrete and independent cloud providers compared to that of the Cisco Intercloud Fabric solution. ICF seeks to solve the cloud management issue by providing an encrypted network with centralized management and workload mobility.

FIGURE 4.1   Separate providers vs. Cisco Intercloud

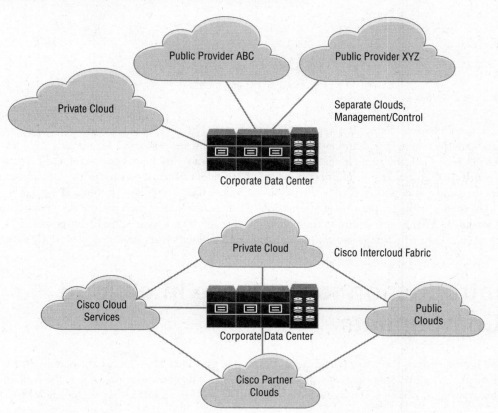

The Cisco Intercloud Fabric solution is a software-only product that comes in two unique application models that are designed to work together as a complete solution. *Cisco Intercloud for Providers* is a Cisco Intercloud application software that is installed and managed by cloud providers that are part of a Cisco Intercloud partner cloud offering. These are your commercial cloud providers that offer consumer services through Cisco Intercloud. *Cisco Intercloud for Business* is the traditional model for end consumers and corporations that want to use Cisco Intercloud. Cisco Intercloud for Business enables enterprise users to interconnect their private cloud to the public cloud and to maintain the same level of control over their operations. This is the model we'll be referring to most, though it is important to understand the difference. See the distinction pointed out in Figure 4.2. The two Cisco Intercloud Fabric versions work together, but the provider and businesses versions have different distinctions. Businesses will consume services via this model, and providers will provide into it.

FIGURE 4.2   Cisco Intercloud Fabric

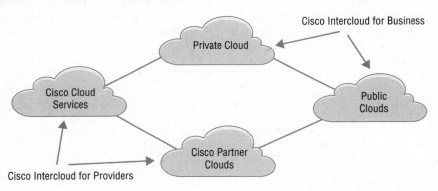

Cisco Intercloud Fabric is a software-only solution. ICF serves as a portal for customers to facilitate the management and movement of on-site resources and services and public cloud resources at the same time. It enables secure workload mobility from end to end and extends the private data center into multiple public cloud providers' infrastructure. This gives customers the choice in how they deploy their cloud services. They aren't locked into a large public cloud vendor or by on-premise virtualized data center offerings. Cisco Intercloud works with Amazon and Microsoft Azure in the public cloud space, along with other Cisco-powered partner clouds. The Intercloud solution aims to make mobility between these solutions easy.

Introduction to the Cisco Intercloud Components

We'll now discuss the main components that make up Cisco Intercloud Fabric and what their use cases are. As previously mentioned, ICF is a software solution and, at the time of this writing, it is supported by several major virtualization technologies, including VMware vCenter, Microsoft Hyper-V, and Linux KVM with both OpenStack and CloudStack. There are several components of ICF.

Cisco Intercloud Fabric Virtual Machine   This is the virtual machine that will contain the *Intercloud Fabric Director (ICFD)* application.

Intercloud Virtual Supervisor Module   *Intercloud Virtual Supervisor Module (VSM)* is the management interface for the cloud extension solution that ICF offers.

Cisco Intercloud Fabric Secure Extender   This extension encompasses the *Intercloud Fabric Extender (ICX)* and the *Intercloud Fabric Switch (ICS)*.

Cisco Intercloud Fabric Router   The *Cisco Intercloud Fabric Router (CSR)* is a software-only router provided to enable routing and other advanced network needs in the cloud. The Intercloud Fabric Router is part of the Cisco Cloud Services Router family of products.

Cisco Virtual Security Gateway   *Cisco Virtual Security Gateway (VSG)* is an edge security gateway and firewall for the ICF fabric to protect VM-to-VM and VM-to-edge security.

Figure 4.3 shows the components working together. In the following chapters, you'll explore the Cisco Intercloud components to gain a better understanding of how they work together.

FIGURE 4.3   Intercloud components

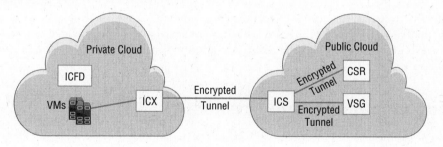

Cisco Intercloud Fabric Director

ICFD is a single point of management for end users and IT administrators of hybrid clouds. This allows users and IT administrators to provision workloads and deal with security policies that they would like to associate to those workloads across multiple public and private clouds. The end users don't necessarily have to use the GUI either; ICFD provides northbound APIs for programmatic access to all available functions. The use of open APIs allows ICFD to interoperate with third-party management platforms for the cloud.

For CCNA cloud administrators, it's important to know some of the use cases the ICFD offers and how you would use the ICFD portal when administering a Cisco Intercloud deployment. The following list is certainly not all the items, but it outlines common services for which you'd use ICFD:

Monitoring   With ICFD being the single pane of glass it is, the primary use case is monitoring your capacity and utilization. This includes both on-premise and public cloud resources that ICFD has provisioned. Capacity reporting and utilization trends are available.

User Management   ICFD is used for user management and enablement across your hybrid cloud scenario. You can add, delete, and edit users from the central console.

Service Catalog   Create and publish your own catalog for your IT end users to manage and deploy their own workloads from server templates you create using ICFD.

Policy Management   Use ICFD to create policies that control where workloads are placed and security policies between them throughout the hybrid cloud model.

VM Management   You can use ICFD for the overall VM management and connections to your VM manager on-site such as vSphere or in the public cloud for templates, image imports, assigning categories, and entitlement options.

Customized Portals   ICFD allows you to customize your own portal.

ICX Management   You can use ICFD to manage and perform the secure Intercloud extender piece of ICF.

ICFD enables a complete cloud deployment solution by offering a single management interface point. Even so, the end consumer is not locked into using only ICFD as their cloud management system of choice; ICFD can be complementary to other third-party management applications. By using ICFD and the software development kit provided with northbound APIs, consumers are not limited to one option for private and public clouds and can build a cooperative system.

Cisco Intercloud Fabric Extender

The Intercloud Secure Extender (ICX) is one of the main Cisco Intercloud components and provides the switching and service capabilities to the Cisco Intercloud Fabric. There are several subcomponents that work together to form the ICF secure extension, and we'll discuss them here.

The Intercloud Secure Extension provides the following features to the ICF solution:

- Secure layer 2 extension from your on-site infrastructure to the provider cloud
- Encryption services for data in motion
- Core switching functionality for applications and servers running both off-site and on-site
- Security and firewall features to protect inter-VM traffic and on-site traffic to public cloud traffic

Figure 4.4 shows the components making up the Intercloud Secure Extension. One of the first components we'll address is the Intercloud Fabric Extender.

FIGURE 4.4   Cisco Intercloud Secure Extension

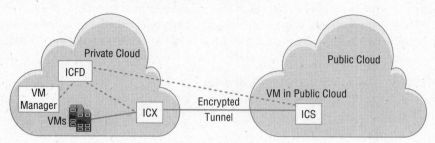

All data between the private and public clouds, as well as the VM-to-VM traffic, is encrypted via the ICX and Intercloud Fabric Switch systems. These are the two components that work together to form the secure extension. The ICX runs in the private cloud and is a VM. It can also be deployed in a high availability fashion if desired. The ICS runs in the public cloud and receives the tunnel from the ICX.

The ICX VM primary functions are as follows:

- Interaction with the private cloud/on-site switch

- Initiator of the secure tunnel to the far-end public ICS

As shown earlier, the ICX is the initiator of the secure tunnel. It encapsulates Ethernet frames into IP packets and uses Datagram Transport Layer Security (DTLS) to ensure confidentiality. Importantly, the ICX must have access to the local VLANs (Virtual Local Area Networks) and switching information on the private network end. This network connection is usually obtained through a virtual switch, such as the Cisco Nexus 1000V virtual switch, which we'll discuss in later chapters. The 1000v is not required for ICX to get local data center VLAN information; it can also work with platform native switches like VMware's distributed vSwitch and other virtual switching options.

The Intercloud Fabric Switch also operates as a virtual machine running in the private cloud. The ICS VM primary functions are as follows:

- Establishment of a secure tunnel from ICX in the private cloud

- Responsible for public cloud VM tunnel establishment

- Monitoring of tunnel status and reporting component failures

The Intercloud Fabric Switch is a software virtual machine running in the provider cloud. As mentioned, it receives the secure tunnel frames from the ICX on-site and delivers the traffic to cloud resources. Not only is it responsible for the delivery of tunnel traffic, but it also monitors and reports statistics on such objects as tunnels and any alarms from component failures. These of course can be seen in the centralized ICFD management console.

The ICS is also responsible for building secure tunnels to the cloud virtual machines. Because of this, no traffic is sent in the clear between private and public VMs, regardless of where they are deployed or if they're managed by the ICF solution. All traffic is encrypted with the ICS and ICX switching traffic between locations and VMs.

The public cloud VMs run an agent referred to as *Intercloud Fabric Agent (ICA)*. This agent provides an overlay in the cloud environment, which tunnels to the ICS for VM-to-VM communication. Overlay statistics are also collected via the agent and used for monitoring. Take a look at Figure 4.5 to get a better view of the components working together.

FIGURE 4.5   VM to VM via ICX, ICS, and ICA

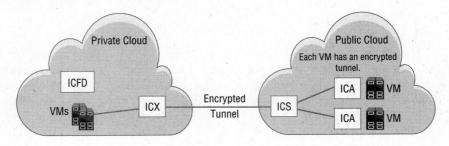

Cisco Intercloud Fabric Services

Cisco Intercloud Fabric Services (CIFS) defines a list of services that are beneficial to a successful deployment for hybrid cloud. We've already discussed some of these, and we'll expand on ones we haven't so you can get a complete understanding of the services available. It is important for CCNA Cloud certified professionals to understand how Cisco defines these services.

Cisco considers the following core fabric services:

Automation   This includes automating workload availability, mobility, and operations. It also includes utilizing APIs for programmatic access to control operations using machine-to-machine intelligence and third-party application and automation vendors' products.

Networking   This includes routing, switching, and other advanced network technologies.

Management and Visibility   This includes being able to monitor the hybrid cloud. An example is the Intercloud Fabric Director.

Cloud Security   This includes securely enforcing communications from the private to public cloud and from VM to VM. Several items work together to provide features, including the Virtual Security Gateway, Intercloud Fabric Director, and Cloud Services Router. The primary feature is the secure tunneling, but don't forget the fabric firewall services and zoning services.

VM Portability   This includes the ability to move VMs between cloud providers and the private cloud. This is the ability to create VMs anywhere along with policy portability and format conversion for different cloud providers. ICFD assists with the format conversion and contributes to this key feature for fabric services.

Cisco Intercloud Firewall Services

In the enterprise data center, either virtualized or physical firewalls can be used to secure traffic between virtual machines. By using a virtual firewall, east-to-west traffic inside the cloud can be secured as well as north-south traffic entering and exiting the clouds. This same concept can be extended to the cloud via Cisco Intercloud services.

Cisco Intercloud Fabric includes a zone-based firewall that can be used for policy enforcement in the public cloud. It is not a requirement but is beneficial to most deployments. The firewall operates as a virtual machine called the Virtual Security Gateway, mentioned previously in the chapter. The VSG uses *Cisco Virtual Path (vPath)* technology from the Nexus 1000v virtual switching product line; vPath is a service that abstracts the forwarding plane and allows inline redirection of traffic for vServices. This allows for traffic redirection, steering, and service chaining. An important note is that the Nexus 1000v is not required for the VSG to operate. The VSG software is a stand-alone VM in Cisco Intercloud. There is, however, a benefit to using Nexus 1000v on the private side of the cloud, which is the site of the enterprise data center. Customers that utilize the Nexus 1000v as their virtual switch can benefit from consistent policies across the entire Intercloud Fabric. Since the VSG in the Nexus 1000v is the same as the ICF version, the policies can be identical and shared across the fabric. VMs that move in and out of the private and public cloud will be subjected to the same policy framework. Figure 4.6 shows the VSG deployed in the public ICF side.

FIGURE 4.6   VSG and firewall services

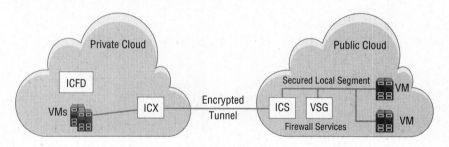

We won't deep dive here into the VSG as the exam does not cover it in any detail. It is important to understand the main features and benefits of the VSG, which can be described as follows:

Zone-Based Firewall Policies   The VSG allows for a zone-based policy definition that can manage the virtual cloud as separate logical security partitions.

Policy Attributes   The VSG allows policy definitions by standard network elements or even machine name and the running operating system.

Performance   Using Cisco vPath, caching of policy decisions can be made after the initial flow lookup, enabling high-performance internetworking.

Cisco Intercloud Routing Services

The Cisco Intercloud Fabric provides a layer 2 extension from the data center to the provider public cloud over a routed layer 3 internetwork such as the Internet. This is facilitated by the Intercloud Fabric Switch and Intercloud Fabric Extender as previously mentioned. You can use ICF in this fashion if you are only extending workloads via layer 2. There are a few cases where this might make sense, but it is our feeling that layer 3 services to the public cloud are far more common. Layer 3 interconnection services have not been left out of the Intercloud Fabric solution, and it is provided by virtual router services. It is included in the Intercloud Fabric and is a virtual machine that runs as the virtual router. The virtual router is based on the carrier-grade Cisco IOS XE networking software family. The Cisco Intercloud routing services can be integrated with the ICF components or run as a separate VM image that is the CSR, as shown in Figure 4.7. The integrated vs. CSR is beyond the scope of the exam and will not be covered in depth here.

FIGURE 4.7   ICF routing services

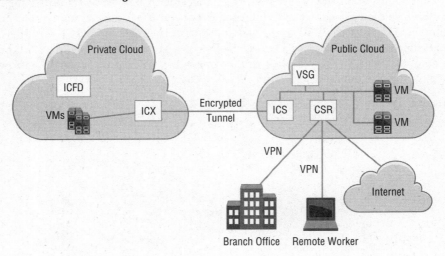

However, the benefits are similar. Here are some of the key capabilities that Cisco defines for the ICF router:

- It offers routing between VLANs in the public cloud. This is highly beneficial and avoids the trombone effect. Without this, some traffic may have to trombone through the enterprise data center to talk to other VMs on different subnets.

- It offers direct network access to virtual machines running in the public cloud.

- It offers NAT functionality, which allows VMs to perform network address translation to reach external networks.

- The router can offer a direct VPN tunnel to branch connections as well as to the data center, extending access to all remote sites.

- It provides the classic edge firewall and security services via access control lists or other basic network security options and is complementary to the VSG that provides network security protection for VM-to-VM traffic.

Cisco Secure Intercloud Fabric Shell

Putting all the Cisco Intercloud components together from the previous sections, you can refer to the complete offering as *Cisco Secure Intercloud Fabric Shell*, or the Secure ICF Shell. The Secure ICF Shell is the high-level grouping of all the previously mentioned technologies working together with virtual machines and their associated cloud profiles. Cloud profiles are designed to be secure and portable among the public cloud providers.

At a high level, a cloud profile includes the following:

Cloud VM Security and Access Control   Cisco ICF facilitates control over how cloud machines are accessed via the tunnel between ICX and ICS, or even directly via the public IP if the CSR is involved.

VM Identity   This is to guarantee that known VMs are only allowed to contact other known VMs. This ensures the extension and cloud VMs can access only what the administrator has defined.

Policies   These are policies that are created by administrators that define what networks can be extended, what type of security policies should be applied, and other network configurations.

Don't let the preceding definitions detour you. The fabric shell is simply all the components provisioned by ICF we previously discussed, working together, as shown in Figure 4.8.

FIGURE 4.8   Secure ICF Shell

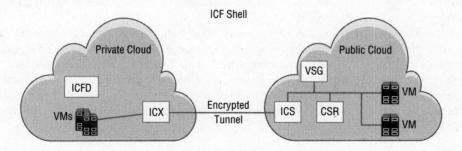

Cisco Intercloud Fabric for Providers

The previous topics we've discussed are related to Cisco Intercloud Fabric for Business. The exam may not make the distinction, but it's important to note that there are two versions if asked. The provider version is for managed service providers that deal with hybrid workloads. These are your regional providers or even large-scale providers. As of this writing, two major providers, Azure and AWS, are the only exceptions to this. Intercloud Fabric interconnects and communicates directly with Azure and AWS via their own APIs. Any other provider or managed service offering would use Intercloud Fabric for Provider to offer services to customers. Cisco Intercloud Fabric for Providers uses the following components:

- Cisco Intercloud Fabric Director
- Cisco Intercloud Secure Fabric
- Cisco Intercloud Fabric Provider Platform

Providers that only want to be a target for workloads can use the provider platform by itself without implementing either Fabric Director or Secure Fabric.

Cisco Intercloud Fabric Benefits

We spent the previous section discussing the many components that make up ICF. We also touched a little on benefits and why you would choose certain features. For the exam, it's important to know the high-level benefits of the Intercloud solution, which we will cover in this section.

Cisco developed ICF to give customers a choice in how they develop and deploy hybrid cloud workloads. A hybrid cloud is a popular deployment model for many reasons and unpopular for others such as vendor lock-in and loss of flexibility. Often customers are forced into a trade-off of requirements or overlook others to land on a public cloud that fits their needs. The lack of service migration flexibility between them often meant the customer was usually stuck with one public cloud provider. Overcoming this limitation and the flexibility it offers hybrid cloud customers are two of the largest benefits that the Cisco ICF solution provides. The ability to deploy a workload to multiple private and public clouds seamlessly enables customer choice and is a huge benefit of hybrid cloud computing that ICF integrates into a single system.

In addition to flexibility, a single management platform offers many other large benefits. Using ICF, customers can deploy heterogeneous environments with a few clicks. Important items such as capacity, security, and compliance can all be managed from the director.

Lastly, an important benefit is the integrated security and tunneling from end to end in the Intercloud Fabric. VM-to-VM traffic and DC-to-cloud traffic is controlled and secured per the administrator policies. Not only is edge security maintained, but the policies can be pushed all the way to the VM itself.

Cisco Intercloud Fabric Use Cases

We haven't formally touched on use cases, but it's likely you've thought of many as you read this chapter. The flexibility of the hybrid cloud leads to many options and solutions that ICF customers can deploy. We won't cover all use cases here, but we'll briefly touch on some common themes you might find online or in your research.

Development and Quality Assurance

Many application developers need compute resources for QA and testing operations. These resources are usually found on-site in the enterprise data center. However, this often leads to several operational and organizational issues that must be addressed. The on-site environment is often heavily locked down with corporate security policies implemented in firewalls in the data center. This means to gain such access to useful development and quality assurance workloads, firewalls and security policies may need to be modified. In most large organizations with detailed change management policies, changing data center configurations to accommodate QA isn't always an immediate change. Application developers or *Cisco Intercloud for Providers*, who need to test quickly, might need to investigate other solutions such as the public cloud offerings.

The cloud is an easy target for testing and quality assurance. With the ease and speed of deployment and a large catalog of choices, it's no wonder developers have flocked to the cloud for this use case alone. Security teams have become increasingly aware of this trend, and the security of both off-site and on-site workloads needs to be controlled and contained. There may also be compliance restrictions that need to be adhered to.

Cisco Intercloud Fabric provides a framework for this to work seamlessly together. Now using the Intercloud Fabric, developers can spin up workloads in the public or private cloud in near real time, and then they can move these workloads back and forth between clouds as well. A developer could spin up QA workloads in the cloud and not affect production systems running in the private cloud. When the application and workloads are perfected using the QA processes, the ICF will facilitate the movement of services to production on-site with a click! This mobility is a large use case for the development and testing aspects of production applications. With the security and encryption aspects built-in, ICF facilitates an easy use case for a hybrid production and testing environment.

Cloud Bursting and Capacity Management

The cloud bursting use case may be the one that enterprises think of most as an advantage to the hybrid cloud deployment that is managed by Intercloud Fabric Services. What does a business do when they need 100 extra web servers? Do they have them sitting around or in stock? Are they in development or laying around in storage? What if none of those scenarios is true? If you said "Buy more!" your vendors likely adore you; however, you are still weeks or maybe even months away from deploying those new web servers.

Traditionally speaking, these problems were resolved with more equipment purchases. There are some obvious problems with this model and line of thinking. If your business is an e-commerce firm that is preparing for heavy data center workloads during holidays, you may consider building out resources to accommodate only a few days of heavy utilization per year. Why would you buy extra capacity when it sits idle for the rest of the year? Many businesses would find they didn't decommission or power off their extra capacity during the slow times that the servers are not needed, necessitating needless power and cooling expenses for servers that are not even being used during most of the year.

The public cloud first hinted at solving this problem. However, the cloud provider lock-in that was discovered was, of course, a major concern to enterprise customers. Without the flexibility of a hybrid cloud, you might solve this problem but be chained to a provider and their proprietary methods and find it difficult to migrate to other solutions in the future if needed. Not only that, but businesses had to worry about mobility between the public and private cloud. Capacity management doesn't help if you can't deploy like-for-like services in both places!

Cisco Intercloud Fabric is a great solution for these concerns. ICF makes hybrid clouds flexible and fast. Businesses can now use this to spin up temporary resources in the public cloud and then spin them down when they are no longer needed. Security policies that follow from the data center to the cloud maintain a consistent posture when dealing with threats and meet network security directives with a unified and consolidated approach. Using ICF in this fashion allows businesses to benefit from all that the cloud has to offer while maintaining control, flexibility, and security.

Shadow IT

Enterprises today are finding that applications and workloads are deployed in the cloud far faster than the slow internal deployment steps that we discussed at the beginning of this study guide. There isn't an issue with this, except that it is often found that internal corporate user groups take it upon themselves to deploy cloud services without notifying, or getting approval from, the company's IT department. When the corporation's internal IT group is bypassed, it is often referred to as *shadow IT*. Organizations are finding workloads running in public clouds that have company assets or connections back to the main data center or office, which can be a huge security hole for the company. The ease of cloud deployments has led to this shadow IT. For example, software developers might cite long internal lead times, excessive paperwork, or a lengthy approval process to get internal compute resources they need, so they turn to the cloud to quickly provision workloads and applications to their needs.

Shadow IT causes an issue for the on-site security team and creates an overall fear about what is being shared and what company property or valuable data is exposed. There may even be regulatory requirements, as you learned about, that are being violated by the shadow IT groups internal to your company. Intercloud Fabric enables an easy model to provision in the hybrid cloud while maintaining control of the organizational assets. Security can be overseen, and data protection can occur through built-in security policies. The internal software developers in this example will get what they want as well, which is fast and easy resource usage when they need it.

While not covered on the test, Intercloud Fabric offers a service to help monitor cloud assets and shadow IT deployed outside the realm of the ICF.

Summary

In this chapter, we covered the Cisco Intercloud Fabric solution, and you learned that it is a family of software products developed by Cisco that is used to integrate and manage hybrid cloud deployments for service providers and corporate customers. We provided a high-level overview of Cisco Intercloud Fabric, the components, and how all of the systems are used to create hybrid cloud models. We then walked you through introductions, explanations, and summaries of each component and explained how they are used in Intercloud Fabric. You also learned some of the benefits and use cases for the Intercloud Fabric.

Cisco Intercloud Fabric includes many separate components that interoperate to provide a complete managed hybrid cloud interconnect solution. The ICF components include the following systems:

- Intercloud Fabric Director operates as a virtual machine in the data center and is used to orchestrate and deploy Intercloud resources such as secure extensions, virtual machine mobility, and security.

- The Intercloud Virtual Supervisor Module is an application used to manage the cloud extensions in the fabric and includes the Intercloud Fabric Extender, which builds a secure tunnel to the public cloud, and the Intercloud Fabric Switch, which terminates the secure tunnel for the fabric extender and provides local switching.

- The Cloud Services Router is an IOS-XE based router running as a virtual machine that provides routing and advanced services to the Intercloud.

For security, the Cisco Intercloud Fabric service uses the Virtual Security Gateway as an edge firewall for VM-to-VM and VM-to-Fabric security. To provide cloud interconnections, the Intercloud Secure Extension provides layer 2 interconnections between cloud sites, core switching, and some security features. The Intercloud Secure Fabric Shell puts all of the components together under one interface that provides VM security, access control, VM identity, and policies.

You learned that there are two main offerings of the Intercloud product, the Intercloud Fabric for Providers and Intercloud for Business.

Exam Essentials

Understand all of the Intercloud components outlined in this chapter and what each is used for.   Know that the Intercloud Fabric Director resides in the private cloud as a virtual machine and is the primary portal. You can expect to be asked questions on the VSM, ICX, ICS, CSR, and VSG products. Understand these acronyms, what they are, and what their role is in the complete Intercloud Fabric solution.

Understand all the Intercloud Fabric services.   They are a family of Cisco products to manage, operate, and deploy a complete, secure, hybrid cloud service that interconnects private, public, and Cisco business partner cloud services. The products that make up the solution operate together to resolve common hybrid cloud issues, such as limited VM mobility, different deployment policies, and security issues.

Identify and explain what is and is not part of the Intercloud solution.   If you know all of the components of ICF, the acronyms, and what each application is used for, you will do fine on this section of the exam. We strongly suggest that you study the written and practice exams until you are able to differentiate all of the components and understand the use cases for each.

Written Lab

The following questions are designed to test your understanding of this chapter's material. You can find the answers to the questions in Appendix B. For more information on how to obtain additional questions, please see this book's Introduction.

1. Employees deploying cloud services independently of the corporate IT organization are commonly referred to as _____ _____.

2. The _____ _____ _____ features access control, VM identity, and policy creation.

3. The networking virtual machine that supports edge security, protects the ICFR fabric, and allows policies for VM-to-VM security is the Cisco _____ _____ _____.

4. Intercloud routing services such as NAT, VPN services, inter-VLAN routing, and direct network access to VMs are provided by the _____ _____ _____.

5. Security services such as firewall functionality and secure Intercloud connections are provided by the _____ _____ _____.

Review Questions

The following questions are designed to test your understanding of this chapter's material. You can find the answers to the questions in Appendix A. For more information on how to obtain additional questions, please see this book's Introduction.

1. Intercloud interconnects which types of cloud deployment models? (Choose three.)
   A. Private
   B. Community
   C. Public
   D. Hybrid
   E. Partner

2. What are benefits of the Cisco Intercloud? (Choose two.)
   A. Self-service management
   B. Integrated SaaS options
   C. Virtualization
   D. Secure interconnects

3. What are the two primary Intercloud applications that are designed to work together as a complete solution? (Choose two.)
   A. Intercloud Fabric Director
   B. Intercloud for Providers
   C. Intercloud Fabric Extender
   D. Intercloud for Business

4. Intercloud supports which of the following cloud platforms?
   A. Microsoft Azure
   B. The Google cloud platform
   C. Amazon AWS
   D. Cisco cloud business partners
   E. None of the above
   F. All of the above

5. The ICFD provides what cloud services? (Choose four.)
   A. Monitoring
   B. VM management
   C. Policy management
   D. DHCP
   E. Site-to-site encryption

F. Portals

G. Peering

6. What two statements about vPath are accurate? (Choose two.)

   A. Is a source agent for site-to-site encrypted tunnel creation

   B. Abstracts the forwarding plane

   C. Implements security policies using zones

   D. Provides inline traffic redirection

7. The Cisco Intercloud solution includes which of the following components? (Choose three.)

   A. Cisco Intercloud Fabric Extender

   B. Cisco Intercloud vCenter

   C. Cisco Intercloud Fabric Director

   D. Cisco Virtual Security Gateway

   E. Cisco Intercloud Hypervisor

8. What does the Intercloud Director offer?

   A. A security configuration utility to enable encrypted cloud interconnections

   B. Implements vPath as a virtual machine

   C. A single management portal for hybrid clouds

   D. Allows for scale-up and scale-out elasticity

9. Which Intercloud solution provides virtual layer 3 services?

   A. IOS-XE 1000 CSR

   B. Intercloud Fabric Director

   C. Intercloud Fabric Extender

   D. Cloud Services Router

10. Which Intercloud application provides virtualized firewall services?

    A. CSR

    B. VSG

    C. ICX

    D. ICFD

11. Which Intercloud application provides virtualized local layer 2 services?

    A. Fabric Extender

    B. Fabric Switch

    C. Fabric Director

    D. Virtual Security Gateway

12. Intercloud layer 2 extensions between data centers are provided by which component?

    A. Fabric Director

    B. Fabric Switch

    C. Intercloud Secure Extension

    D. Virtual Security Gateway

13. What is not considered part of the Intercloud Fabric? (Choose two.)

    A. Resource pools

    B. Private clouds

    C. Fabric extender

    D. Community clouds

14. Which of the following two statements are true about Intercloud? (Choose two.)

    A. Centralized management portal

    B. Operates with specific hypervisors

    C. Service provider and business application components

    D. Interconnects community clouds to the Internet

15. The primary function of the ICX VM includes which of the following? (Choose two.)

    A. Local cloud or premise switch interaction

    B. VM management

    C. Initiates secure tunnel to remote ICS

    D. VM-to-VM firewall services

16. What Intercloud offering encapsulates Ethernet frames into IP packets and uses Datagram Transport Layer Security to ensure confidentiality?

    A. ICX

    B. VSG

    C. ICX

    D. ICFD

17. What is the public cloud VM application that is an overlay in the cloud that tunnels to the ICS for VM-to-VM communications and also collects overlay statistics for monitoring?

    A. ICS

    B. ICA

    C. ICFD

    D. CSR

18. The grouping of all Intercloud products working together is called what?

    A. Secure Intercloud Fabric Shell

    B. ICA

    C. ICFD

    D. SaaS

19. What Intercloud offering uses APIs to communicate with specific public clouds?

    A. Intercloud Exchange

    B. Intercloud Fabric Director

    C. Intercloud Fabric for Providers

    D. Intercloud Routing Services

20. What Intercloud product provides routing between VLANs, direct network access to VMs, NAT functionality, and edge firewall services?

    A. Cloud services router

    B. Intercloud Fabric Director

    C. Intercloud Fabric for Providers

    D. Intercloud Fabric Shell

Chapter

5

The Cisco Unified Computing System

THE FOLLOWING UNDERSTANDING CISCO CLOUD FUNDAMENTALS CLDFND (210-451) EXAM OBJECTIVES ARE COVERED IN THIS CHAPTER:

✓ **3.1 Identify key features of Cisco UCS**

- 3.1.a Cisco UCS Manager
- 3.1.b Cisco UCS Central
- 3.1.c B-Series
- 3.1.d C-Series
- 3.1.e Server identity (profiles, templates, pools)

An Introduction to the Cisco Unified Computing System

In this chapter, we move away from the general overview of the cloud and the investigation into the different service and deployment models. You will now learn about the enabling technologies deployed in data centers. The CCNA Understanding Cisco Cloud Fundamentals exam covers a broad array of topics, and one of the most interesting is the Cisco *Unified Computing System (UCS)*. Figure 5.1 shows a 12-rack UCS configuration connected to a pair of fabric interconnect systems.

FIGURE 5.1   Cisco UCS configuration

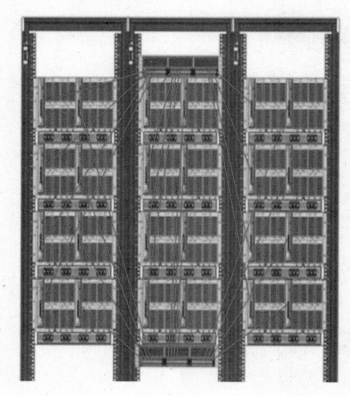

Cisco has traditionally had its roots as a routing and switching company with almost an exclusive networking focus. However, over the years as Cisco searched for new sources of revenue, it has been actively expanding into new markets in an effort to diversify its product and services portfolio. This expansion has been accomplished either with internally developed products or with acquisitions. Sometimes, as is the case with the UCS product family, it is a combination of the two approaches that has led to new and interesting product offerings from the company.

In 2009 Cisco publically announced its internally developed line of servers, converged fabric networking products, network adapters, storage, and management software under the UCS label. Internally, the engineering undertaking came to be known by the codename Project California, with many of the subsystems named after cities in California. Project California turned out to be a much larger undertaking than the server product lines that were currently being offered by the major server manufacturers. This was a huge undertaking even for a company the size of Cisco, and it took a long time for most of the industry to really understand the scope of the release. The UCS product line has been hugely successful for Cisco, and in a short amount of time it has taken a significant amount for market share away from the established server vendors. With constant innovation and improvements, the UCS family of products is continually expanding and evolving the cloud technology landscape.

As you could imagine, this was a big shift in focus for Cisco as it had traditionally partnered with the big server manufacturers. Cisco would supply the networking equipment, while companies such as Dell, IBM, HP, and others provided the computing components. Cisco is now competing with these companies, instead of acting in its traditional role as a business partner, and gaining market share from them in the server marketplace.

The one big advantage that was apparent from the announcement was that Cisco did not have any legacy server install base to worry about and could design its UCS product line from the ground up with no migration, integration, or upgrade concerns. This is what is called a *greenfield* approach and allowed Project California to use the most current architectures, technologies, and convergence design principles available. What a great opportunity this gave the company to completely develop a new product line from a blank sheet of paper! The UCS product family was much more than just *bare-metal servers*, however; it was designed for virtualization, convergence, and automation technologies from the ground up that are, as you have learned, central to enabling a cloud data center. By utilizing the UCS architecture, cloud service providers could collapse many legacy servers into a smaller number of Cisco UCS servers and realize cost savings in rack space, cabling, power, and cooling requirements in their data centers. Also, with the UCS design and management software, automation and deployment techniques were introduced to greatly enhance the rapid deployment of cloud services.

The UCS family allows cloud providers to have efficient, scalable, and manageable data centers based on converged, *open system* products. By designing the UCS product line with virtualization in mind, resources can be virtualized and pooled together, which is a primary enabling technology for cloud deployments. The UCS family virtualizes not only the compute operations but also networking and storage all in one integrated system. The lines between servers, networking, and storage began to go away with the UCS family of products. To provide flexible options when designing and implementing a *converged network* in the cloud data center, Cisco released a wide variety of I/O options for network and server interconnectivity.

The UCS product family is highly integrated and combines computing, networking, and storage into a *unified fabric* that has centralized management applications for the complete system. The UCS hardware is configured, as you will learn, by policies defined in the management applications that have effectively virtualized the hardware as well as the applications. UCS was designed for automation from the beginning and offers open APIs and high-level tools to configure, monitor, and manage a complete UCS deployment.

Many of the required underlying components were designed to accommodate the virtualization advances made in the cloud data centers. Hypervisors were running on the servers that had the ability to migrate virtual servers from server to server in real time. Failover and deployment of new servers were automated and deployed widely in large public and private cloud data centers. Advanced cloud data center management and automation software systems were developed to enable this advanced capability.

On the server side, the hypervisors allowed the underlying hardware to be hidden from the guest operating systems, but there was still the issue of some very fundamental and limiting server hardware characteristics that were present on the legacy servers. Each server had unique identifiers such as Ethernet *MAC addresses*, Fibre Channel *World Wide Names*, the system *UUID*, very specific *BIOS* settings, and other configuration parameters that prevented an easy replacement of failed hardware. You could not simply remove the drives from one server and install them into another without expecting a number of addressing and driver issues. This became especially painful if the server replacement was between different models of the same vendor or, much worse, servers between different manufacturers. Server management often meant logging into each server individually to manually make changes or to monitor its operation. With the massive scale of cloud data centers, this was no longer feasible. Legacy servers would traditionally contain at least two Ethernet cables for traditional LAN connections, another LAN cable for management, and two pairs of fiber-optic cables for storage connections. If a data center had 1,000 servers, for example, that would mean more than 5,000 cables just for the server connectivity! These issues were all addressed and mitigated in the UCS products, as you will investigate in this chapter.

The UCS family of products were designed from the beginning for programmability and automation. UCS integrates x86-based server technology with data networking, storage networking, automation, virtualization, and management creating what can best be described as a large pool of racks of servers into virtualized systems that allow for elastic on-demand provisioning for the cloud.

Exploring the Key Features of the UCS Product Family

Before getting into the details of all the products and technologies that make up the UCS product family, we will cover the key features that make up the UCS product line. This is truly a system and not just a collection of products marketed under a common brand name.

These systems are designed to all work together as a complete, converged, and unified data center offering. All of the UCS products are configured and managed by centralized UCS management applications that control a large number of physical servers. The servers come in a complete range of form factors and performance levels. The underlying networking fabric is converged with both LAN data and SAN data sharing the same switching fabric that greatly reduces cabling and simplifies the cloud infrastructure design. You will also learn about the management software that ties all of the hardware components into a unified system. These include the Unified Computing System Manager (UCSM) and the UCS Central applications.

To best understand the benefits of the UCS server systems, let's take a moment to review what was required to implement a new server in the past and, in most cases, still in the present. First, the server needs to be designed around the needs of the operating system and applications running on it. When the server's processing, memory, storage, networking, and scalability configuration are determined, the purchasing department usually puts the requirements out for bid. Once all of the bids are received, a purchase order is generated, and the order is placed for the hardware. After some time passes, the equipment is delivered at the data center. You then uncrate the systems, complete any additional hardware installations, and mount the server into the rack in the data center. The next steps are connecting power, network, and storage cabling, which, as we discussed, is usually quite a few cables for each server. At this point, weeks may go by, and you still have a long way to go before the server goes live in production. Next up is the configuration of the Ethernet access switches, in other words, the needed VLANs with their associated layer 3 *switched virtual interfaces*. You may need to add new routing entries and configure the firewall and load balancing policies to complete the networking setup. Also, additional VSAN interfaces for the storage network from the storage engineering group need to be configured. You need to create LUNs and masking and configure SAN zones for *Fibre Channel*. For Internet Small Computing System Interface (*iSCSI*), the storage administration group needs to define mappings and storage permissions. When the server is connected to the network, then you can configure all of the BIOS settings needed to allow the server to run most efficiently in a virtualized environment. If local drives are attached, the HDD configurations will need RAID group settings. The boot order, NIC redundancy, and host bus adapter (*HBA*) configurations all need to be configured.

Now you are to the point where you can install the operating system on the server. This would usually take a fair amount of time to load the image and create the base configuration to get it talking on the network. Then all required patches, required management, and automation software would be installed on top of the operating system. Once all of that is done, it comes time to install and configure the application. Now, imagine having hundreds or maybe even thousands of servers to manage under this approach.

The previous example highlights the configuration and setup issues that the UCS products were designed to reduce or alleviate. Also, it underscores the importance of virtualization and automation to provide rapid server deployments in today's hyper-scale cloud networks.

UCS Blade Server B-Series

In modern cloud data centers, servers are designed to provide high-density compute resources in the smallest form factor possible and to be as power efficient as possible. Other design considerations include reduced cabling, ease of maintenance, and management. A primary way to achieve these objectives is to mount the servers in a common chassis that shares either a midplane or backplane, power, and cooling. The blade chassis are complete systems that allow power and management of the blade servers inserted in the chassis.

The Cisco UCS blade server family is appropriately called the B-series, and while the central focus will be on the blade servers themselves, we will discuss the complete system and components that make up the B-series, explain why this family is much more than another line of blade server products, and explore what makes them unique in the marketplace. Figure 5.2 and Figure 5.3 show the UCS blade system chassis with server B-series servers installed.

FIGURE 5.2   Cisco UCS B-series chassis front view

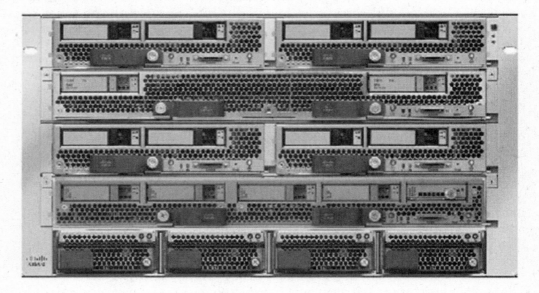

FIGURE 5.3   Cisco UCS B-series chassis rear view

Blade Server Overview

The UCS B-series combines many different data center technologies into a common unified platform that can be centrally managed and is specifically designed for today's cloud-based computing operations. Compute, storage, and networking are integrated into a common switching fabric with the UCS B-series platform. The platform is based on a 10 and 40Gb Ethernet converged switching fabric, industry-standard x86 servers that are delivered in a multichassis, highly scalable platform that is managed under a unified management domain.

Each blade server uses the latest Intel Xeon processors and features enhanced highly scalable memory options; they are also designed to be energy efficient. The B-series servers come in a variety of models designed to meet all levels of compute and scalability requirements. The servers implement converged networking adapters for a unified switching fabric that combine both LAN and SAN traffic on the same forwarding plane.

B-Series Architecture

The 5108 blade series chassis is the primary enclosure for the UCS B-series family of products. The *5108 chassis* consists of a six-RU enclosure that fits into a standard 19-inch rack. Up to seven 5108 chassis can fit into a standard data center rack for up to 56 servers per rack. The chassis consists of eight half-width or four full-width server slots to accommodate the B-series blade servers.

The chassis contains four front-loaded power supply slots that support a variety of data center power connections including 48 VDC, 200–380 VDC, and both 100–120 or 200–240 VAC power supply options. All four power supplies and eight fan trays are hot-swappable and allow the chassis to continue to operate with either the power supplies or fans removed during maintenance windows.

Each chassis is managed by and connects directly to the *6300 series fabric interconnects* that contain the UCS Manager application. The chassis has autodiscovery capabilities and is completely managed by the UCSM application running on the model 6300 fabric interconnects. There is no local management of the chassis. Each slot in the 5108 enclosure supports two 40Gb Ethernet fabric connections to the chassis midplane for a total of 1.2Tb of throughput per enclosure.

All blade servers can be either inserted or removed when the chassis is in operation for noninterrupted service in the cloud data center. The chassis performs constant management and environmental monitoring, and alarm thresholds can be configured to alert operations if a trap metric has been met.

Each 5108 enclosure has two switch fabric extension modules installed that are used to connect to the 6300 fabric interconnects; each fabric module is integrated with the complete system and does not require local configurations. The blade chassis to the fabric interconnects are interconnected, as shown in Figure 5.4, to provide complete redundancy.

FIGURE 5.4   Fabric interconnects

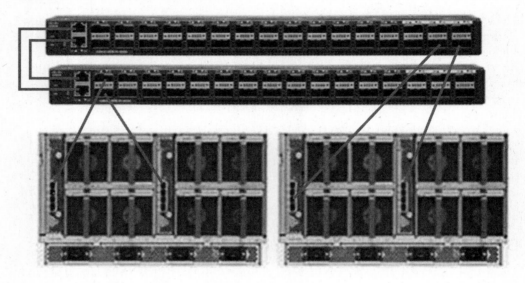

USC B-Series Models

The B-series of UCS blade servers is a constantly evolving and changing product line that follows advances in technologies with both increments (gen levels) or model releases being offered by Cisco on a regular schedule. For the most current offerings, it is best to check the Cisco website under the Unified Computing topic in the Products and Services section. As new generations of servers are released, the older generations are depreciated to maintenance mode and eventually end-of-life status. You can find up-to-date information on Cisco.com.

The most current and available B-series servers and their key features follow so you can be familiar with what is available in the marketplace:

UCS B22 M3

Half-width blade (See Figure 5.5.)

2 Intel Xeon CPU sockets

12 memory slots supporting 322GB of memory

2 mezzanine slots for 80Gbps total Ethernet/FCOE throughput

2 hard-drive bays

2 SAS, SATA, SSD hard-drive bays

FIGURE 5.5 Cisco UCS B22 M3

UCS B200 M4

General-purpose cloud computing (See Figure 5.6.)

Half-width blade

2 Intel Xeon CPU sockets

24 memory slots supporting 1.5TB of memory

1 mezzanine slot for 80Gbps total Ethernet FCOE throughput

2 SAS, SATA, SSD hard-drive bays

FIGURE 5.6 UCS B200 M4

UCS B420 M4

Full-width blade (See Figure 5.7.)

4 Intel Xeon CPU sockets

48 memory slots supporting 3TB of memory

2 mezzanine slots for 160Gbps total Ethernet/FCOE throughput

4 SAS, SATA, SSD hard-drive bays

FIGURE 5.7 UCS B420 M4

UCS B460 M4

Large enterprise and cloud applications, designed for memory-intensive workloads used by databases, analytics, bid data, and business intelligence (See Figure 5.8.)

Full-width double-height blade

4 Intel Xeon CPU sockets

96 memory slots supporting 6TB of memory

4 mezzanine slots for 320Gbps total Ethernet/FCOE throughput

4 SAS, SATA, SSD hard-drive bays

FIGURE 5.8   UCS B420

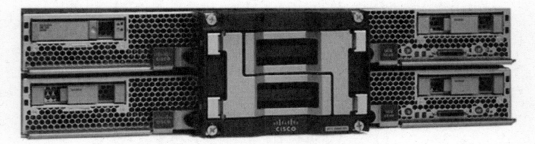

UCS Rack Server C-Series

In this section, we introduce you to the second part of the Cisco UCS server family, the C-series (or *Chassis series*). We will start with a basic overview of the family of servers, and then you will learn about the architecture of the server series platforms. Finally, we will end the section with a look at eight different models in the C-series of chassis servers.

The Chassis Server Overview

In addition to the blade servers that Cisco released with Project California, Cisco introduced a complete line of chassis, or rack-mountable servers, called the *C-series*. These servers feature a range of models that are designed for both general and specific uses. They are all based on industry-standard components such as the Intel Xeon family of CPUs. All servers are designed to be operated as a virtualized server with a hypervisor installed and supporting a large number of virtual machines or with the operating system installed directly on the server.

The C-series product family is constantly evolving, with new versions and models being released regularly from Cisco and older models going through the end-of-life process. It is advised to check the Cisco.com website for the latest and most up-to-date information on the server family.

C-Series Architecture

The UCS C-series design is based on the industry-standard server architecture found in all Intel-based servers found in the marketplace today. There will be a variety of options between each server model for CPU slots, memory slots, capacity, the types of interface cards supported, and hard drive slots available. Cisco also supports the Cisco Extended Memory Technology for increased RAM capacity that allows for large pools of memory often required in a virtualized cloud data center.

The servers offer out-of-band management with both Ethernet and serial ports used to remotely manage the servers. Also, with the use of fabric extenders, the C-series servers can be managed as a domain using UCSM, the same manager application that is used to control the B-series blade server. However, using UCSM is not a requirement, and the C-series servers can operate in a stand-alone environment.

USC C-Series Models

The C-series of the UCS server product line is also constantly evolving as new models are released and existing servers are upgraded to keep pace with new technology introductions and advances. Just like you learned with the B-series, the C-series will release new versions of existing models with new generations such as Generation 1, Generations 2, and so forth. The nomenclature will be in the format of Cxx-M1, M2, M3, and so forth. The Cisco.com website will have the latest information on server models and releases.

We will introduce the current models in the C-series and then give a list of the key features so you can be familiar with what is currently available.

UCS C22 M3

Designed for a wide range of scale-out applications (See Figure 5.9.)

1 rack unit high

2 Intel Xeon 8-core CPU sockets

12 memory slots supporting 384GB of memory

2 PCIe slots

8 SAS, SATA, SSD hard-drive bays

Redundant hot-swappable power supplies

FIGURE 5.9   UCS C22 M3

UCS C24 M3

Entry-level virtualizations, expandability, web applications (See Figure 5.10.)

2 rack units high

2 Intel Xeon 8-core CPU sockets

12 memory slots supporting 384GB of memory

5 PCIe slots

8 SAS, SATA, SSD hard-drive bays

Redundant hot-swappable power supplies

FIGURE 5.10   UCS C24 M3

UCS C220 M3

High-density general compute platform (See Figure 5.11.)

1 rack unit high

2 Intel Xeon 8-core CPU sockets

16 memory slots supporting 512GB of memory

2 PCIe slots

8 SAS, SATA, SSD hard-drive bays

Redundant hot-swappable power supplies

FIGURE 5.11   UCS C220 M3

UCS C220 M4

High-density general compute platform (See Figure 5.12.)

Entry-level virtualizations, expandability, web applications

1 rack unit high

2 Intel Xeon 8-core CPU sockets

24 memory slots supporting 512GB of memory

2 PCIe slots

8 SAS, SATA, SSD hard-drive bays

Redundant hot-swappable power supplies

FIGURE 5.12   UCS C220 M4

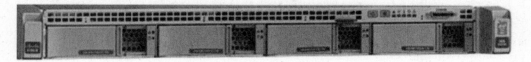

UCS C240 M3

High-density general compute platform (See Figure 5.13.)

2 rack units high

2 Intel Xeon CPU sockets

24 memory slots supporting 768 GB of memory

5 PCIe slots

12 SAS, SATA, SSD hard-drive bays

Redundant hot-swappable power supplies

FIGURE 5.13   UCS C240 M3

UCS C240 M4

High-performance and scalable compute platform used for big data, collaboration, virtualization, storage, and high-performance computing applicators (See Figure 5.14.)

2 rack units high

2 Intel Xeon CPU sockets

24 memory slots supporting up to 1TB of memory

6 PCIe slots

24 SAS, SATA, SSD hard-drive bays

Redundant hot-swappable power supplies

FIGURE 5.14 UCS C240 M4

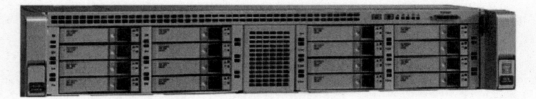

UCS C420 M3

High-performance and scalable compute platform used for big data, high storage density applications for compute, I/O, storage, and memory-intensive stand-alone and virtualized applications (See Figure 5.15.)

2 rack units high

4 Intel Xeon CPU sockets

48 memory slots supporting up to 1.5TB of memory

4 PCIe slots

16 SAS, SATA, SSD hard-drive bays

Redundant hot-swappable power supplies

FIGURE 5.15 UCS C420 M3

UCS C460 M4

Very high-performance server for compute and memory-intensive mission-critical and virtualized applications (See Figure 5.16.)

4 rack units high

2 to 4 Intel Xeon CPU sockets

96 memory slots supporting up to 6TB of memory

10 PCIe slots

12 SAS, SATA, SSD hard-drive bays

Redundant hot-swappable power supplies

FIGURE 5.16   UCS C460 M4

UCS Interconnect and Unified Fabric Products

The 6300 fabric interconnects act as the central control and interconnection point for the USC products. Operating in a pair, the 6300 is directly connected to each 5108 blade chassis and also the outside network in the cloud data center. As you will learn, the fabric interconnects play a critical role in the operation of a UCS deployment.

They offer up to 320Gbps of bandwidth per connected blade server chassis, with a total of 2.56Tbps of switching capacity. The fabric interconnects reduce network cabling and serve as the compute platform for the UCS Manager application. Redundant cooling fans, power supplies, front-to-back airflow, and rear cabling are standard features along with out-of-band management interfaces.

The fabric interconnects serve as the central management point for a cluster of blade server chassis. They also act as the interconnection point between the UCS domains to the rest of the cloud data network. The fabric interconnects are operated in active pairs for redundancy and come in either 24- or 32-port models offering both 10G and 40G LAN interfaces. The interfaces support Ethernet for data and either Fibre Channel over Ethernet or iSCSI for storage traffic. The converged fabric architecture enables both LAN and SAN data to simultaneously share the same forwarding plane. The unified fabric reduces the NICs, HBA switches, and cabling required by eliminating the need for separate LAN and SAN interfaces. Fibre Channel traffic is encapsulated into Ethernet frames, and the servers utilize converged network adapter technology to further reduce the number of interfaces required per blade server.

The embedded UCS Manager can manage from one to twenty 5100 series blade chassis as well as the C-series servers that we will introduce later in this chapter.

The fabric interconnects operate in a redundant configuration that allows for two converged network paths from each individual blade server chassis to the cloud data center network, as shown in Figure 5.17. It is important to understand that while the fabric interconnects switching fabric is active on both switches, the UCS Manager application that also resides in each fabric interconnect operates in an active standby mode. During operation, the cluster is designed for resiliency and continuous operation. The UCS cluster can continue to operate with a failed 6300 interconnect. In fact, B-series server cards can be removed and inserted (as well as the power supplies and fan trays in the 5108 chassis). Changing the fabric interconnect switching mode from Ethernet to Fibre Channel will cause service disruption and should be performed only during initial setup.

FIGURE 5.17   Redundant fabric interconnect modules

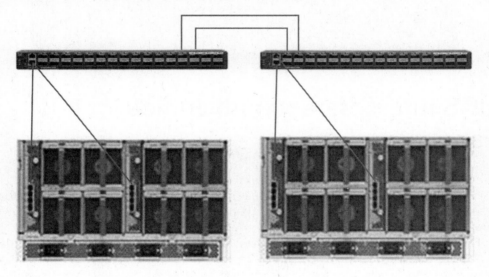

Cisco Data Center Unified Fabric Interconnects

The current shipping model on the UCS fabric interconnects is the 6300. There remains a large installed base of 6100 and 6200 interconnects, but both models have been discontinued by Cisco. The exam will focus on the model 6300 fabric interconnect family.

Currently there are three products in the 6300 family, and each is designed to support a specific use case and features different form factors and interface speeds. They are similar in that each model hosts the same UCS Manager application needed to control and manage the complete UCS domain. We will outline the different models to get you up to speed on this critical UCS component.

UCS 6332 Fabric Interconnect

The 6332 rack mount fabric interconnects operate in a pair, and the UCS Manager application resides in the 6332. They serve the function of being the central management point of the UCS domain (See Figure 5.18.)

32 40Gbps interfaces that can be configured for 4×10 breakout requirements

High-density, line-rate Ethernet and Fibre Channel over Ethernet support

Supports up to 160 UCS C-series rack and UCS B-series blade servers

Supports up to 20 5108 B-series chassis

2.56Tbps throughput

Redundant power

FIGURE 5.18   Cisco UCS fabric interconnect model 6332

UCS 6332-16UP Fabric Interconnect

The 6332-16UP fabric interconnects extend the functionality of the 6332 model with the addition of 16 unified ports that can be configured for either Ethernet or Fibre Channel interfaces. The unified ports allow for converged LAN and storage traffic in the UCS domain. External to the domain, the 6332-16UP offers Fibre Channel interfaces to interconnect to the cloud SAN network. These 16 ports have the flexibility to be configured either as Ethernet or as Fibre Channel. Since changing the modes of the unified ports requires a reload of the fabric interconnect, the mode of the interfaces is usually only set at the time of the initial installation (see Figure 5.19).

Twenty-four 40Gbps interfaces that can be configured for 4×10 breakout requirements

Sixteen 1Gbps or 10Gbps and Fibre Channel over Ethernet or 4Gbps, 8Gbps, and 16Gbps Fibre Channel unified ports

High-density, line-rate Ethernet and Fibre Channel over Ethernet support

Supports up to 160 UCS C-series rack and UCS B-series blade servers

Supports up to 20 5108 B-series chassis

2.43Tbps throughput

Redundant power

FIGURE 5.19   Cisco UCS fabric interconnect model 6332-16UP

UCS 6324 Fabric Interconnect

The 6324 is also known as UCS mini. It is designed to insert directly into the 5108 blade chassis for smaller installations that do not require external rack-mounted fabric interconnects such as the 6332 and the 6332-16UP models (see Figure 5.20).

Inserts as a line card into the 5108 enclosure

The UCS Manager application resides in the 6324.

Four 1Gb to 10Gb Ethernet and Fibre Channel over Ethernet external interfaces

One 40G (4×10G) external interface

2Gbps, 4Gbps, and 8Gbps Fibre Channel interfaces

Supports up to 20 UCS C-series rack and UCS B-series blade servers

Sixteen 10Gbps interfaces to servers in the 5108 chassis

500Gbps throughput

FIGURE 5.20   Cisco UCS fabric interconnect model 6324

Combining Data and Storage on the Same Switching Fabric

One of the key features of the UCS switching fabric is that of convergence of dissimilar network traffic. *Convergence* refers to the ability of the switching fabric to support both LAN data traffic and SAN storage traffic on the same forwarding plane. With a converged network fabric, there is a reduction in the amount of hardware required as multiple networks are collapsed into one unified switching architecture. Also, cabling to the servers is greatly reduced as a single high-speed Ethernet connection to the server supports both LAN and storage traffic.

This design approach eliminates the need for a separate Ethernet network for LAN data and another network for SAN or storage traffic in and out of the UCS clusters. The B-series and C-series servers support converged network adapter cards that allow for convergence into the servers themselves, eliminating the need for separate LAN and SAN cards to be installed in the servers. The Converged Network Adapter (CNA) connects to the unified fabric on the 5108 backplane or by using 10Gbps or 40Gbps Ethernet to the chassis servers. However, and this is where the magic takes place, the operating system running on the servers is fooled into thinking there are two individual interface cards, one for LAN traffic and a second for SAN traffic. This approach reduces cabling and interface ports and the need to manage separate networks in the UCS products. This is the primary objective and feature of using a converged network switching fabric.

UCS Manager

The Unified Computing System Manager (UCSM) is the central configuration and management point for UCS products. UCSM is an application that runs on the 6300 series fabric interconnects in a hot-standby or active/standby mode. The UCSM combines the management functions of networking, storage, and compute into a central application that can be configured with a Java-based graphical interface, a CLI, or XML APIs that allow machine-to-machine automation, configuration, and management from third-party vendors. Up to 20 5108 B-series chassis can be managed as well as the C-series UCS servers. UCSM provides a common management platform that consolidates individual applications and utilities that were commonly needed in the past to manage individual blade racks, storage, networking, and compute. All UCS products are designed to be managed under the UCSM umbrella for a consolidated point of configuration. This allows you to quickly scale, integrate UCS into the cloud data center's automation systems, pool resources, allow enhanced virtualization technologies, and commission or decommission servers automatically for rapid deployment.

The UCS Manager allows for the virtualization of all compute hardware, networking, and storage in the system, and by treating these as virtualized pools, you can create on-demand, highly scalable service offerings in the cloud. Compute services can be preconfigured or provisioned on demand.

At the beginning of this chapter, we discussed the traditional model of bringing servers online and discussed the limitations you encounter when replacing server hardware. The MAC, WWN, and UUIDs were all hard-coded on each server, and there were also BIOS and storage configurations that needed to be contended with. This was all taken into account when UCS was developed, and the addressing issues of the past have all been virtualized and are now managed with UCSM. BIOS settings, MAC addresses, WWNs, and BIOS settings are all stored in UCSM as configuration objects instead of on the server itself. With the UCS, replacing server hardware is as simple as connecting the replacement server and having UCSM automatically download the configuration with all of the required parameters to the new server. Zero-touch provisioning has become a reality. Service profiles allow you to virtualize what used to be hard-configured on a server, and those profiles can be dynamically applied to the UCS hardware.

Every configurable item in the UCS product family is an object; there is an autodiscovery system that scans for changes in the environment and updates the configuration object database.

Profiles and templates allow for ease of use and replication in the data center by creating templates for use cases of service offerings and then replicating the template across many devices in the UCS servers.

Role-based administration allows for the allocation of resources and security by defining roles and applying users to those roles. For instance, you can define server administration, networking, and storage roles for the cloud operations staff. New roles can be created, and existing roles can be modified to meet the requirements of your cloud operations center.

The UCSM is designed to be an open management system. The architecture uses XML APIs, and Cisco publishes the APIs to allow third-party companies to write automation and orchestration code as well as for integration into their internal products. Cisco offers scripting tools and software development kits to assist companies in creating application interconnects to the UCS system.

UCSM supports ongoing maintenance and operations with the support of alarm and usage reporting. Thresholds can be defined that allow for automation systems to make changes when scaling up or out for on-demand cloud service offerings. Internal maintenance can be scheduled for automated firmware updates that are periodically offered by Cisco in pretested bundles that mitigate the risk of firmware interoperability issues.

The UCSM is a software application that runs on the 6300 fabric interconnect platforms. The UCS Manager is the glue that ties all of the UCS components together under a single management application, as shown in Figure 5.21. All blade and rack-mount servers are managed from the UCSM domain using a graphical user interface, command line, XML, or APIs. The server, storage, and networking configuration functions are included with the applications and with the integration of these disparate technologies. The UCSM offers rapid deployment in near real time, which is critical for on-demand rapid provisioning found in cloud operations. No longer do you need to have the server group make their needed configuration additions and then the follow up with the networking department connecting the servers to the network and configuring all VLANs, routing, switched layer 3 interfaces, quality of service, and so on. Traditionally, the storage group would also need to configure and connect the SAN to the servers. This was usually a manual process prone to errors and long delay. With the UCSM, you can now complete all of these tasks with preconfigured policies or with the help of higher-level cloud orchestration and provisioning tool interconnects using XML API calls to the UCS domain via UCSM.

FIGURE 5.21   Cisco UCS Manager

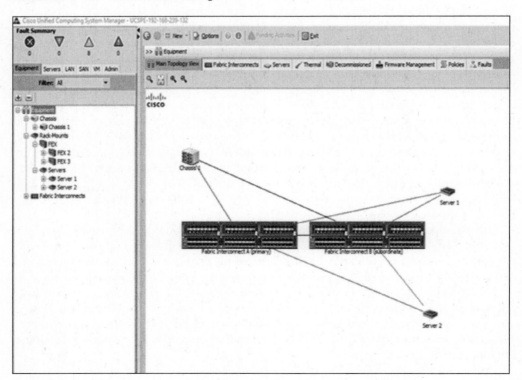

The management software can be partitioned for use by multiple discrete and separate entities.

UCSM GUI

When accessing the GUI, a standard web browser can be used for HTTP/HTTPS web access to the UCS Manager application. Then the web screen loads, and you will be able to select the UCSM Java application to download and run on your local system. The UCS Manager client is a Java based application that runs on the remote client to access UCSM. A standard username and password are required to access the user accounts defined in the application. Figure 5.22 illustrates the UCSM graphical interface.

FIGURE 5.22   UCS Manager interface

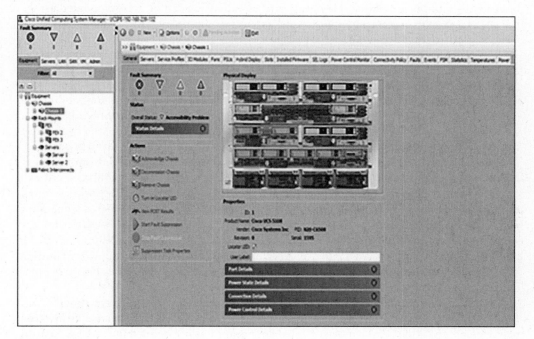

UCSM Use Cases

The UCSM controls, monitors, and configures the complete Cisco Unified Computing System environment. The application is the most critical component in the UCS. Without its operations, the complete UCS domain would not be able to be controlled. The use cases for the system are to provision, monitor, and manage the UCS deployment. You are familiar with the Java-based graphical interface for human interactions. However, there are also the XML APIs that Cisco has made public that allows for machine-to-machine communications. The use of the APIs enables third-party developers and even Cisco to write applications that communicate directly with the UCSM. This allows for rapid provisioning, monitoring, and applications such as billing and on-demand provisioning. Statistics can be collected for a dashboard type of operational screens. Trouble ticketing, security, and different service model deployment applications all use the UCSM as the interconnect to each UCS domain.

UCS Central

For large cloud installations, the UCSM management limit of 20 chassis or 160 servers can be reached, limiting scalability. However, further expansion can be accommodated using the UCS Central management application that controls multiple UCSM domains. UCS Central offers multi-UCS node management.

The UCS Central application is a global management platform that allows administrators to define polices that will then be applied to a number of UCS Manager systems that are each managing an individual UCS domain.

UCS Central is a configuration tool, serves as the central repository for configuration objects, is a workload management tool, and provides an information dashboard.

The configuration tools provide functions such as monitoring, changing the configuration of each individual server or complete systems, updating the servers' firmware and drivers, and providing backup and restore operations and user-based roles. Information displayed as a dashboard function provides information such as statistic counters, critical event logging, fault monitoring, and device inventory. The object storage repository stores all information on ID pooling and offers a centralized database of IDs selected from global pools with usage statistics and ID conflict resolution. Pools can be used for UUIDs for server identification, PWWNs for Fibre Channel adapters, Ethernet MAC addresses and IP addressing profiles, policies, VLANs, VSANs, and a large number of system configuration objects. The workload manager concerns topics such as changes and moves occurring in the domain as well as system definitions.

Global policies are defined on the UCS Central system and pushed out systemwide for a centralized enforcement and consistency point that includes maintenance, firmware management, backups, and exports. Global configurations are defined in the UCS Central system using the policy manager and then applied to each UCS domain. Domains can be grouped together to match a public cloud region or availability zone but still maintain a centralized management system.

UCS Central runs as a virtual machine application that is external to the fabric interconnects where, as you recall, the UCS Manager applications reside. UCS Central is installed on a hypervisor and accessed by either the APIs or a GUI interface.

The architecture of UCS Central allows for a programmable platform that can accept configuration parameters from systems above it (northbound) and push the polices to the UCS products below it (southbound).

The northbound interface uses the eXtensible Markup Language or XML as its API. This allows for an open system that any vendor can write interfaces to from their own applications as well as internally developed systems such as portals, management systems, and compliance adherence. Scripting languages can be written for machine to UCS Central interfaces, and there is a Java-based user interface similar to that of the UCS Manager. Companies that integrate their applications with UCS Central include VMware, IBM, EMC, Computer Associates, HP, and Microsoft, to name just a few.

UCS Central GUI

The UCS Central graphical interface is similar to the UCSM and is illustrated in Figures 5.23 and 5.24. The GUI is accessed from a web browser to allow for remote access. Configuring and managing a complete UCS domain using UCS Central is beyond the scope of the Understanding Cisco Cloud Fundamentals exam, and all examples are for information only. The Cisco data center certification covers UCSM and UCS Central in more extensive detail.

FIGURE 5.23   UCS Central main screen

FIGURE 5.24   UCS Central graphical interface

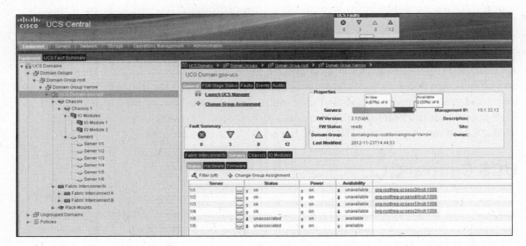

UCS Central Use Cases

UCS Central is required when you exceed the operational limits of the UCS Manager application. Each UCSM can manage up to 160 UCS servers and 20 5108 blade chassis. UCS Central allows for many UCSM systems to be controlled by one UCS Central controller.

Other common use cases include using the application as a central repository of information in a multidomain UCS environment. Statistics, firmware updates, object pools, statistics, and configuration policies are all stored in the UCS Central application for the global installation and pushed down to each domain's UCSM application. This consolidates many domain configuration points into one central control point.

Server Identity (Profiles, Pools, and Templates)

In this section, we provide an introduction to the basic UCS configuration concepts as they relate to server configurations. This section is intended to make you familiar with the basic concepts for server identity, including profiles, templates, and pools.

UCSM Configuration Concepts

The exam blueprint for the Understanding Cisco Cloud Fundamentals exam expects you to be familiar with the UCSM application and to be aware of the general UCS configuration concepts that you will learn about in this section. It is important for us to be clear that this is a large topic that whole books and training courses cover exclusively. The UCS configurations are large and sometimes complex. For the CCNA Cloud certification, it is not expected that you know all of the thousands of configuration options available.

The UCSM application can be extensive and detailed; many resources can be found online for specific UCSM operational issues that are beyond the scope of the Understanding Cisco Cloud Fundamentals exam.

Understanding UCS Profiles

The configuration of UCS components can be a large undertaking given that there are so many configuration points, servers, interconnects, network adapters, LANs, SANs, and many other objects to be configured. It can at first seem overwhelming. However, Cisco has designed the application to allow configurations to be placed into groups, or *profiles*, and makes those profiles reusable by all systems in the UCS domain. A large number of configuration objects are combined into a profile and stored in the UCS Manager, which greatly simplifies the configuration process. Each UCS server in a domain has to be associated with a profile to operate as it needs a basic configuration like all servers and network equipment. Only one profile can be assigned to a server at a time, which makes sense when you consider that it can have only one configuration applied to it at any given time.

When administering a UCS server, all configuration changes are applied to the profile. As shown in Figure 5.25, all servers associated with that profile will automatically inherit the configuration changes. Figure 5.26 shows a more detailed policy configuration where the server's boot order is defined. As you can see, there are a large number of configurations to define in a policy. This applies not just for the server itself but for all attached controllers, interface cards, and converged fabric connections.

FIGURE 5.25   UCS service profiles

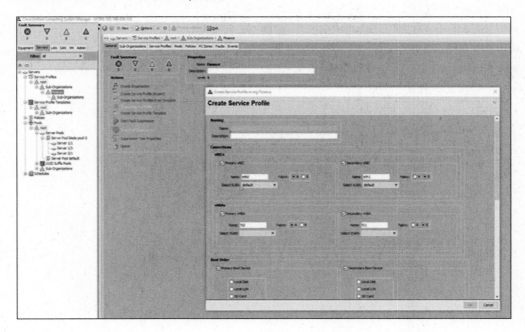

FIGURE 5.26   UCS service boot profile

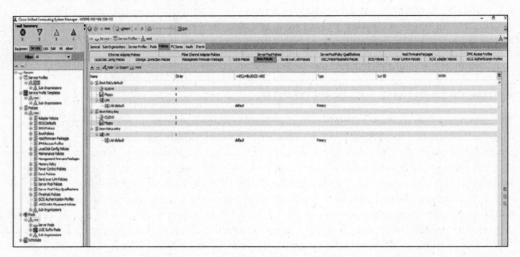

With the rapid growth of cloud data centers, rapid hardware provisioning becomes an important feature to facilitate the timely installation of UCS hardware. The UCSM allows you to define profiles for servers that are yet to be installed. The system can be preconfigured, and when the server arrives and is inserted into the system, it will automatically download its profile and configure itself for use in the cloud data center.

Service profiles are created using any of the standard user interfaces including the GUI, CLI, or XML API.

Examples of profile objects to be configured for the fabric interconnects include the following:

- Virtual interfaces
- Uplink selection
- VLAN tagging
- VSAN selection
- QoS settings (for LAN-based SAN)

UCS blade chassis service profile objects include the following:

- Server identifier
- MAC address
- WWN addresses
- Firmware packages
- BIOS settings
- Boot order
- Management IP address

Understanding UCS Pools

Pools are used in UCS configuration setups when a range of identifiers is required but when it is desirable to abstract them from the underlying hardware. For example, each domain will require a pool of Ethernet MAC addresses to allocate to Ethernet LAN NIC cards on each server. Pools are defined in UCSM and are assigned to devices in the domain as needed. These pools can then be assigned to a service profile to allow the server to pull addressing as required. Figure 5.27 shows the GUI of the UUID pool configuration screen.

FIGURE 5.27   UUID pool configuration screen

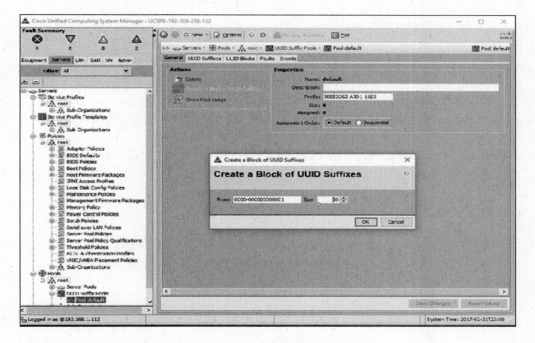

Pools can be created for many objects, including the following:

- **UUID:** A server universally unique identifier assigned to servers
- **MAC:** Media Access Control addressing used to identify LAN NIC adapters
- **nWWN:** Node World Wide Name for Fibre Channel node identification on a host bus adapter
- **pWWN:** Port World Wide Name for Fibre Channel host bus adapter port identification
- **Management IP:** A pool of IP addresses available to be assigned per server for management access

Pools can also be created for servers, where a number of servers share common characteristics such as memory, CPUs, or network bandwidth that are grouped into a pool and all assigned the same policies.

Understanding UCS Templates

Templates group configuration objects together that form a base configuration for a server in the UCS product family. Templates allow you to define a group of policies, pools, and other objects into a template. The UCSM provides a configuration wizard that is used to build a template.

The wizard allows you to include the following in a template:

- Identity service profile UUID pool assignment
- Networking options such as virtual NICs, MAC address pools, and many other options
- Storage polices for disk host bus adapter configurations and SAN configurations
- Fibre Channel SAN zoning information
- vNIC and vHBA configurations to create on the servers
- vMedia information to define storage shares such as NFS, CIFS file systems, and HTTP/HTTPS access, and any virtual media mounts such as hard drives and CDs
- Server boot order to define the preferred order of devices to search to locate the boot loader

Figure 5.28 and Figure 5.29 illustrate the server configuration screens in UCSM. As you can see, this is an extensive and detailed application that, over time, becomes intuitive to operate.

FIGURE 5.28 Server pool configuration screen

FIGURE 5.29   General server configuration screen

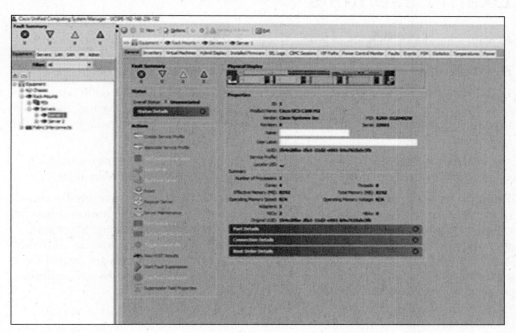

Summary

This chapter moved away from cloud theory and models and covered the Unified Computing System. UCS is Cisco's line of server products that introduced a completely new server platform than was currently offered in the marketplace.

We started out with an introduction to the complete UCS setup, the components that are used, and how they interconnect with each other. The fabric interconnects are the heart of the system and are the interconnection point to all blade chassis, the external data, and storage networks, and you learned that the fabric interconnect is the host-processing platform for the UCS Manager configuration and management application.

Then you learned about the B-series architecture of blade compute systems, you learned about the 5108 blade chassis, and you became familiar with the current models of blade server hardware.

The chassis servers in the UCS product lineup are the C-series, and you saw many of the current models and what their primary use cases are. You learned that the system is managed by the UCS Manager application for each domain, and for large cloud deployments the UCS Central application is used to manage multiple UCS domains.

The chapter ended by taking a deeper look at the UCSM and UCS Central applications, and you were introduced to the basic configuration concepts of pools, policies, templates, and profiles.

Exam Essentials

Explain what the UCS family of products are.   Know all the primary components in the UCS family such as the fabric interconnects, the 5108 chassis, B and C-series servers, and the UCS Manager and UCS central applications.

Define the fabric interconnect converged networking capabilities.   The 6300 fabric interconnects support native Ethernet frames and iSCSI storage data over Ethernet, and the UP or unified ports can be configured for either Ethernet or Fibre Channel but not both at the same time.

Understand the UCS configuration protocols supported.   The UCS Manager and UCS Central applications support XML APIs, a command line, and graphical interface.

Know the basics of the UCSM configuration concepts.   Understand what profiles are and where they are used. Know that server profiles are a collection of configuration objects that get applied to the UCS server instead of directly configuring the server. Many common addressing requirements are now virtualized in the UCS products, and the addresses are no longer physically applied to the server. With the UCS setup, pools are created for such objects as UUID, MAC, WWN, IP addresses, and others that are then dynamically assigned to systems in the UCS domain.

Written Lab

Fill in the blanks for the questions provided in the written lab. You can find the answers to the written labs in Appendix B.

1. The UCS converged switching fabric combines which two technologies into one shared forwarding plane?

    _____ and _____

2. In large cloud installations with multiple regions and availability zones throughout the world, the _____ _____ application is used to manage multiple domains.

3. UCSM management access methods include _____ _____ or _____ interfaces.

4. The _____ UCS chassis provides redundant power and cooling with eight half-width server slots.

5. Logical groups of device addressing that are allocated to servers from UCSM are called what?

Review Questions

The following questions are designed to test your understanding of this chapter's material. You can find the answers to the questions in Appendix A. For more information on how to obtain additional questions, please see this book's Introduction.

1. Where are specific UCSM boot settings used by a server stored?

    A. Pools

    B. Profiles

    C. BIOS

    D. UUID

2. World Wide Names are primarily used for what function?

    A. LUN masking

    B. Zoning

    C. HBA addressing

    D. iSCSI target mapping

3. UCS Manager API communications are based on what structure?

    A. Perl

    B. JSON

    C. XML

    D. Python

4. Which UCS application manages a cluster of domains?

    A. UCSM

    B. Java

    C. XML

    D. UCS Central

5. 6332 fabric interconnect downlinks can operate at which speeds? (Choose two.)

    A. 1Gbps

    B. 10Gbps

    C. 40Gbps

    D. 100Gbps

6. Fabric interconnects do which of the following? (Choose three.)

    A. Connect 5108 chassis into a domain.

    B. Virtualize server systems.

    C. Host the UCS Manager.

    D. Provide a converged switching fabric.

    E. Host the UCS central management application.

7. Multiple UCS domains are managed by which application?

   A. JSON

   B. UCS Manager

   C. XML

   D. UCS Central

8. UCSM operates in which mode?

   A. Primary/primary

   B. Active/standby

   C. Cluster

   D. Network function virtualized

9. What is the maximum number of full-width servers that can be installed in a 5108 chassis?

   A. 2

   B. 4

   C. 6

   D. 8

10. The UCS family of products includes which technology areas? (Choose three.)

   A. Networking

   B. Storage

   C. Firewall security

   D. Intrusion detection

   E. Servers

   F. Load balancing

   G. Cloud orchestration

11. The 6300 converged fabric operates in which mode?

   A. Active/passive

   B. Active/standby

   C. Active/active

   D. On-demand provisioning

12. What are the main features of the UCS product line?

   A. 10Gb converged fabric, decentralized management, optimized for virtualization, individual device configuration, isolated LAN and SAN networking

   B. 10Gb converged fabric, centralized management, optimized for virtualization, centralized configuration profiles and templates, variety of I/O options

   C. 1Gb Ethernet switching, centralized management, optimized for virtualization, variety of I/O options

   D. 10Gb converged fabric, centralized management, proprietary APIs

13. What is a layer 3 network interface called?

   A. SVI

   B. UUID

   C. FC

   D. HBA

14. UCS C-series servers support which types of local storage? (Choose three.)

   A. Flash

   B. SSD

   C. SAS

   D. SATA

   E. DAT

15. A 6332-16UP unified port supports which two protocols?

   A. JSON

   B. Fibre Channel

   C. Fabric path

   D. Ethernet

16. Which UCSM feature assigns configurations to a B22M3 server?

   A. pWWN

   B. Global policy

   C. BIOS boot order

   D. Server profile

17. What can pools be created for? (Choose four.)

   A. UUID

   B. MAC addresses

   C. XML addresses

   D. Management IP addresses

   E. IaaS server groups

   F. Hybrid cloud availability zones

   G. Fibre Channel worldwide names

18. The UCS Central application configures what southbound service?

   A. SaaS

   B. Python

   C. SNMP

   D. UCSM

19. What objects can be configured in a fabric interconnect with the UCS Manager? (Choose four.)

A. VSAN

B. Uplinks

C. Boot order

D. WWN address

E. VLAN tagging

F. UUID

G. QoS settings

20. What are the primary differences between the B-series and C-series products? (Choose three.)

A. Internal storage

B. Rack density

C. Processing capacity

D. Number of interface slots

Chapter 6

Cisco Data Center Products and Technologies

THE FOLLOWING UNDERSTANDING CISCO CLOUD FUNDAMENTALS CLDFND (210-451) EXAM OBJECTIVES ARE COVERED IN THIS CHAPTER:

✓ **4.0   Basic Knowledge of Cloud Networking**

- 4.1 Describe network architectures for the data center
  - 4.1.a Cisco Unified Fabric
    - 4.1.a.1 Describe the Cisco Nexus product family
    - 4.1.a.2 Describe device virtualization
  - 4.1.b SDN
    - 4.1.b.1 Separation of control and data
    - 4.1.b.2 Programmability
    - 4.1.b.3 Basic understanding Open Daylight
  - 4.1.c ACI
    - 4.1.c.1 Describe how ACI solves the problem not addressed by SDN
    - 4.1.c.2 Describe benefits of leaf/spine architecture
    - 4.1.c.3 Describe the role of APIC Controller

Data Center Network Architectures

The data center is the place where the servers and storage environments live. The primary use case of the data center is for the many devices and systems to efficiently communicate within the confines of the data center and to the outside world. Data centers are usually measured by their efficiency and speed, and those metrics closely revolve around network architecture.

Data centers are often measured by several key attributes. You'll find this in the Cisco documentation or other network and data center vendor sites.

The following are the most common attributes you find ascribed to the data center:

Resiliency and Availability   A data center design needs to achieve high availability for the compute nodes that are installed. This is often done by having multiple tiers and layers of design, which we'll discuss in this chapter.

Flexibility   This is the ability to accept designs and equipment that were not originally thought of. The network design needs to be flexible enough to take on unforeseen obstacles. This could be as simple as extra networking ports or as complex as managing cooling, power systems, and rack layouts.

Scalability   The data center must be able to scale logically and physically. The design should offer the ability to accommodate future growth, to receive sudden surges of traffic, and to offer mobility for hosts within the data center.

Monitoring and Management   Data center operations need to be able to monitor all the devices and components and effectively alert immediately on issues. Being able to monitor and offer good management systems is critical to maintaining cloud availability.

Data Center LAN Fabric Design

Data center network fabric design has evolved over time. One of the main layouts has been the same for decades, the *three-tier* design. This design revolves around the *core*, *aggregation*, and *access* layers. Take a look at Figure 6.1 to see this at a high level.

FIGURE 6.1   Three-tier design

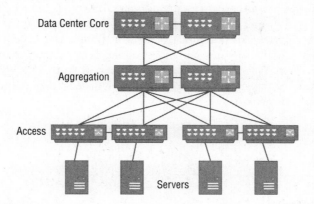

Before the three-tier approach, there were several other design models that were used in data center and enterprise installations. It was common in the past to have a single core device with many servers connected and just expand the number of connections from a modular perspective by adding line cards into a chassis-based switch or router. While this might work, it leads to catastrophic failures if the core device fails. The three-tier design was developed to split up the failure domains and offer more flexibility and resiliency with the ability to scale. With the network design split into functional silos, failures can be absorbed and not impact the entire network. Figure 6.2 shows the evolution of the data center network.

FIGURE 6.2   Evolving to the three-tier design

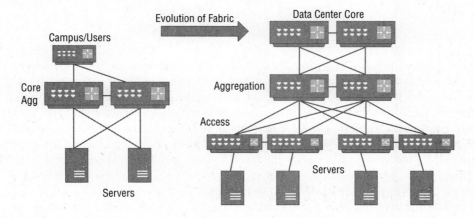

In Figure 6.2 the integrated core and aggregation network has been transformed into the three-tier model using the access, aggregation, and core layers that are commonly found in cloud data centers today. The core tier is primarily a layer 3 router or switch that interconnects the aggregation areas. This is where the north-south traffic from the data center flows between areas. Usually there are no services here, as the core tier is kept to one job and one job only: forwarding traffic reliably at a very high rate. In some cases, data centers might design a supercore around mini-cores for flexibility and scale. Figure 6.3 shows this design. You'll notice that the supercore layer connects to many other core layers, which feed into their aggregation layer and finally on to the access layer. This allows for a larger scale-out architecture. Choosing one or the other is solely dependent upon the size and functional needs of your network.

FIGURE 6.3 Core design

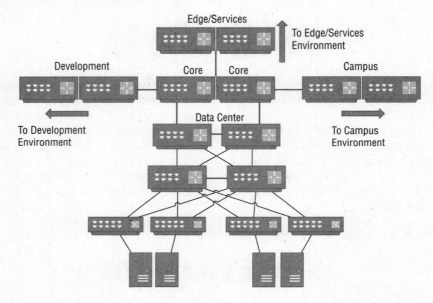

The aggregation tier is traditionally the east-west traffic flow between access tiers that connect servers. East-west refers to traffic inside the cloud data center as opposed to north-south, which is traffic entering and leaving the data center. Depending on the design, the aggregation tier can implement VLANs with layer 3 routing here for server default gateways. This design enables mobility in the access tiers as the server would have access to the same VLAN regardless of where it is in the access layer. Other designs might call for the access layer to run the layer 3 gateways with local routing, making the aggregation tier for routing only. This design works but doesn't lead to flexibility and mobility in modern data center design. The aggregation tier is also a common place to find firewalls, load balancers, and shared services. Take a look at Figure 6.4 to see an aggregation design.

FIGURE 6.4   Aggregation design

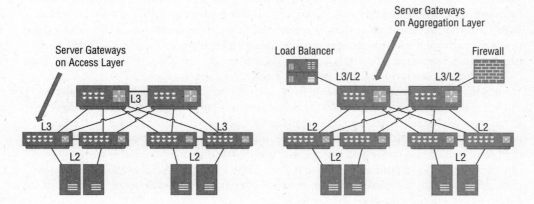

Cisco Unified Fabric

Servers traditionally have multiple types of network connections that are used for separate functions. There are no hard or fixed requirements for server connections to the cloud network fabric.

The following are some of the more common server connection types:

Public Interface   The public interface is the one most thought of when considering how a server connects to the external network. This is generally where the server's public-facing IP address occurs and is the main in-out interface on the server. In some cases, there is no need for public connectivity, and this interface can be omitted.

Management Interface   This is usually a dedicated management interface for out-of-band connectivity or just plain management connectivity. Server vendors have different methods to use this, but most revolve around using Ethernet for connectivity.

Private Interface   This is an interface usually found in cloud networks or ISP networks for the customer server. This allows two servers to communicate with each other through a private interface. On the data center side, it can simply interconnect servers in the same cluster needing a separate path for communications. The private interface is usually an interface that is not billed for bandwidth transfer.

Backup/Storage Interface   This interface is dedicated to providing a path to the backup services. This could be iSCSI, NFS, Fibre Channel, or any other common storage interconnect technology.

It was common in the past to have servers connected to the external network as outlined earlier, but it leads to several problems. Each of these connections requires a separate cable, a separate adapter/NIC on the server, and in some cases a separate switch upstream. This design is hard to scale up in the data center, especially when it requires deploying unique switches. One of the main issues on the server side is bandwidth sharing. Some of the interfaces may not need a line rate connection or may not transfer enough data to warrant it. Even with that being the case, these interfaces can't share with each other. If one interface needs more throughput, the design would require configuring multiple LAN interfaces together into port channels or migrating to higher-speed interfaces.

The previous scenario is solved by using a converged network and I/O architecture. Network convergence includes placing both storage and data traffic on the same shared unified switching fabric; this allows for several separate physical networks to be consolidated into one single switching fabric. This design is a key point for the Cisco Unified Fabric. I/O consolidation is about taking the large number of interfaces and combining them into one or two converged interfaces. Usually you'd find them combined with two interfaces as a port channel, either in a 1Gb or 10Gb configuration. Network virtualization technologies are deployed to keep the traffic separate from each other. Take a look at Figure 6.5 to see the high-level differences.

FIGURE 6.5   I/O consolidation

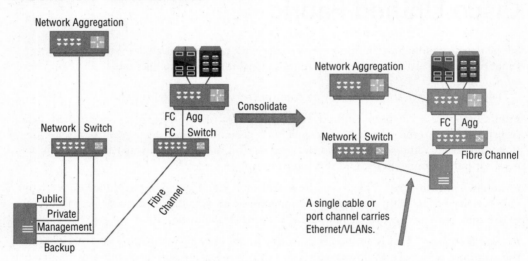

When the converged network design approach is employed, a data center gains multiple benefits for the server infrastructure including but not limited to the following:

Cable Count   The amount of cables to each server decreases significantly.

Bandwidth Sharing   Multiple applications are consolidated into a larger pipe and are able to share the available load.

Network Device Count   The number of network switches and separate infrastructure to support data and storage networks are reduced.

Creating this type of design leads to challenges on the network side with traffic priority and who gets queued first when there is network congestion. This is especially true for storage-related services in the unified infrastructure. IP-based storage such as NFS, iSCSI, and others can get quality-of-service profiles configured on the network. Since they're built around TCP/UDP, these protocols fit into the QoS paradigm. However, there is one that does not, Fibre Channel, which is a lossless protocol and has nothing to do with TCP or UDP and, as such, must be treated differently.

Fibre Channel employs a buffer-to-buffer credit system for transmission. Essentially this means the Fibre Channel fabric does not transmit unless it knows for sure there is buffer space available at the remote end allowing for transmission to the remote receiver. This ensures the lossless connectivity for Fibre Channel. Everything transmitted is guaranteed to make it to the other side without any loss of data. Fibre Channel over Ethernet (FCoE) arose to run Fibre Channel over Ethernet and is a critical component of the converged unified fabric.

Before we can talk more about FCoE, we need to cover how a lossless protocol like Fibre Channel exists over Ethernet. *Data Center Bridging* deals with the lossless connectivity over Ethernet, and it is a collection of standards. DCB is essentially multiple extensions to Ethernet that allows dynamic resource allocation and congestion notification. In the next sections, we'll briefly discuss these extensions and how they operate.

Priority-Based Flow Control (IEEE 802.1 Qbb) is one of these extensions. The standard Ethernet pause mechanism pauses all traffic on the link and does not take into consideration the requirements of the many traffic flows over that link. In lossless applications, you can't have this. Priority-based Flow Control (PFC) addresses this issue by allowing pauses on a specific queue of traffic, or class of service. Imagine a physical link divided into eight virtual links or service classes. The PFC mechanism provides the capability to pause one of these lanes while the others proceed unaffected. This allows for no drop queues and allows the enablement of FCoE, which requires no traffic loss. All other queues can maintain normal congestion management and drop without affecting the virtual lane of FCoE or any other no-drop application. Take a look at Figure 6.6 to see the PFC queues.

FIGURE 6.6 Priority-based flow control

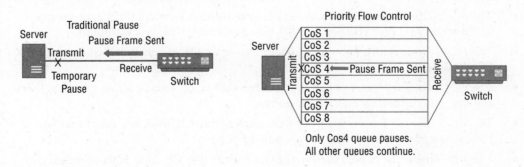

Enhanced Transmission Selection (IEEE 802.1Qaz) is another extension belonging to the data center bridging family of congestion management standards. ETS, like PFC, enables bandwidth management of virtual links or lanes. As previously mentioned, PFC can create eight virtual links on a physical link, each with a different class. ETS extends this concept by providing priority processing on bandwidth allocation, reservation, and best-effort classes. This creates a flexible per-group traffic class allocation. When a traffic class is not using all of its bandwidth, it can be shared among the other classes to optimize link utilization. The network administrator is then able to carve out guaranteed classes with minimum bandwidth assignments per class. As long as there isn't congestion, anyone can transmit and share bandwidth. When congestion occurs, ETS will ensure a fair distribution of available bandwidth as defined by the administrator.

Data Center Bridging Exchange (DCBX) is the final extension belonging to the DCB family of protocols. DCBX is a discovery and exchange protocol to find peers and exchange capability and configuration information with DCB-capable bridges.

These include the following:

- DCB peer discovery
- Any mismatched configuration detection
- DCB link configuration of peers

DCB uses Logical Link Discovery Protocol (LLDP) to exchange these attributes. DCBX is meant to make the administrator's life easier by identifying mismatched configurations and identifying what the current configuration is by communicating with directly connected devices that also support DCBX.

Fibre Channel over Ethernet (FCoE) is the main application for DCB and one of the primary protocols operating on a unified fabric. The main concern with running Fibre Channel on standard Ethernet networks is the lossless nature of storage. The Fibre Channel standard does not allow any dropped data between the sender and the receiver; it requires a lossless switching fabric. DCB solves this and allows you to encapsulate Fibre Channel frames into Ethernet frames. To Fibre Channel, Ethernet is just a transport to get the Fibre Channel frames between *Virtual Fibre Channel (VCF)* ports.

Here are some key terms that you should be familiar with when dealing with an FCoE fabric:

- The *FCoE Controller* performs the FCoE Initialization Protocol (FIP) and is responsible for the VFC port creation and deletion as well as FCoE link endpoints.
- The *FCoE Node* is also known as Enode. This is simply an endpoint that can transmit FCoE frames.
- The *FCoE Forwarder* is a switch that can forward FCoE frames across a lossless fabric and may or may not have native FC ports.
- The *VF_Port* is an F port carryover from native Fibre Channel. It's a port that is a Fibre Channel switchport that connects to an N port.
- The *VN_Port* is the N port carryover from native Fibre Channel. It's a port that connects to an F port, typically the HBA or CNA of the host.
- The *VE_Port* is the E port carryover from Fibre Channel; it's an interswitch link that connects Fibre Channel switches together.

The previously discussed subjects all make up the unified fabric from a Cisco perspective. A big part of this is the convergence of storage and LAN traffic on the same network switch. FCoE isn't a requirement, as you can simply use another IP-based storage protocol in its absence. The primary benefit of the converged fabric is cost savings and simplified management. Figure 6.7 shows what the fabric looks like. Now Cisco Nexus and MDS edge access switches can provide the SAN and LAN entrances. Traditionally these are two entirely different fabrics. Converged fabrics allow this merging and offer a large variety of products to converge the LAN and the SAN onto the same unified switching fabric.

FIGURE 6.7   The converged fabric

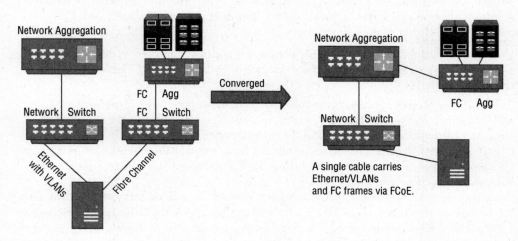

Cisco Nexus Data Center Products

Cisco launched the Nexus product line of data center networking products in 2008, and it has been one of its most successful and widely deployed lines in the history of the company. Here's a quick summary of some of the shared features:

- They are capable of DCB and Cisco Unified Fabric with FCoE.

- *Virtual Device Contexts* (*VDC*) offers the ability to create separate logical instances of switches and routers that run their own OS on the same physical hardware platform.

- *Virtual Port Channels* (*vPC*) offers a technology to virtualize two switches to appear as one to a connected device for resiliency.

- *Fabric Extender* (*FEX*) is an extension of the control plane to manage remote line cards as part of the same switch.

- *FabricPath* is a specialized routing protocol for layer 2 allowing all interconnect links to be active and forwarding.

- *Application Centric Infrastructure* (*ACI*) is an SDN network/fabric developed by Cisco that runs on the Nexus line of switches.

Nexus 1000v Switches

The Nexus 1000v is a software-only switch that operates as a virtual machine or in the hypervisor. We will introduce the Nexus 1000v in this chapter and then go into more detail in Chapter 8 on this product family. The 1000v controls the switching between VMs and is multihypervisor capable. The 1000v brings the familiar Cisco CLI and toolset to network administrators dealing with virtual networks. These features include but are not limited to SPAN, SNMP, CLI, LACP, CDP, QOS, ACLs, and more. The following are the primary components that make up the 1000v:

Virtual Ethernet Module (VEM)   This runs in the hypervisor and is the actual data (forwarding) plane of this software-based switch. Think of this as a line card with ports that connect the VMs but that exists only as software.

Virtual Supervisor Module (VSM)   If you have line cards, you need a controller, right? The VSM is the supervisor that controls multiple VEMs (line cards). The VSM is the control plane of the 1000v.

The 1000v is multihypervisor capable and currently supports the Hyper-V, KVM, and VMware hypervisors. The 1000v comes in two separate editions, the essential and advanced editions. You can download the essential edition for free, but it will cost money to gain support and help. The advanced edition is the same as the essential but is a chargeable product that adds extra features such as DHCP snooping, TrustSec security, Cisco Virtual Security Gateway, and more.

Cisco also offers a Nexus 1100 series that it refers to as a cloud services platform. Don't let the branding fool you. The 1100 is a hardware UCS appliance dedicated to running the 1000v. The similarities end there. The 1100 allows *virtual service blades (VSBs)* to extend the offering of the 1100. The three main offerings of the VSB category are as follows:

Citrix Netscaler 1000v   This is a standard application delivery controller (ADC) appliance in software form running on the 1100.

Virtual Security Gateway (VSG)   VSG is a multitenant firewall that offers zone-based and context-aware policies. In the VM world, this is basically an east-west firewall to control policy between VMs.

Cisco Prime Network Analysis Module (NAM)   This allows data analysis and packet capture from the VMs. The NAM also provides comprehensive statistics of virtual ports and other entities on the switch.

Nexus 2000 Switches

The Nexus 2000 Fabric Extender line is a series of 1U *top-of-rack (TOR)* remote line cards. These operate through a parent switch. It's tempting to call the 2000 series "switches," but in reality they are not. None of the 2000 series switches provides any local switching capability or has a local control function; there is no CLI or configuration interface of any type on a Nexus 2000! They are solely reliant upon their parent switch to provide this functionality. To understand this, look at Figure 6.8. While the 2000 series do indeed provide data plane functionality, they cannot switch flows east-west belonging to the same fabric extender. These flows will go through the parent switch for switching operations, and traffic may return to the same Nexus 2000 FEX for local forwarding if required. In Figure 6.8, you see this with Server C and Server D. Even though they are connected to the same FEX, the flow of traffic will traverse the parent switch. Because of this, the 2000 series is thought of more as remote line cards that make up a distributed modular chassis with a Nexus parent switch. If you've used catalyst chassis in the past, this is essentially removing the line cards, racking them in a remote cabinet, and connecting them to the parent switch with fiber-optic cables. Figure 6.9 shows the Nexus 2000 product family.

FIGURE 6.8   Nexus 2000 switching

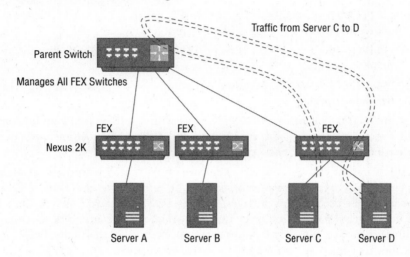

FIGURE 6.9   Nexus 2000 product line

Even with that being the case, the 2000 series is a popular data center access layer product. Nexus 2000 products are compact with a 1U footprint and a small power draw. Scaling with them is easy, and if you use them as TOR switches, they can almost operate as patch panels. Since every 2000 connects to a parent switch, a patch panel may not even be needed.

Some of the common models are listed here:

- **Nexus 2224TP:** This has 24 ports of 1000BaseT with dual 10G uplinks, making it an oversubscription ratio of 1:2 to 1.

- **Nexus 2248:** Several models make up the 2248, and all offer 48-port 1000BaseT connectivity and four 10G uplinks, also making it a 1:2 to 1 oversubscription device. The 2248 includes the E model, which has enhanced buffering. You would use this for bursty traffic such as storage.

- **Nexus 2232PP/TM/TM-E:** All of these models include 32 ports of 10G connectivity. The PP model is SFP+, and the TM model is 10GBaseT. All of these models have eight 10G uplinks, making them a 4:1 oversubscription ratio. The *E* stands for enhanced buffers.

- **Nexus 2232TQ:** This has 32 ports of 10GBaseT, but this time with QFSP+ uplinks and four 40G uplinks, making it a 2:1 oversubscription.

- **Nexus 2348PQ:** This has 48 10G SFP+ ports with four 40G QFSP+ uplinks, making it a 3:1 oversubscription.

- **Nexus 2348TQ:** This has 48 10GBaseT ports but with six 40G QFSP+ uplinks, making it a 2:1 oversubscription.

- **Nexus 2348UPQ:** This has 48 10G SFP+ ports with six 40G QFSP+ uplinks, making it a 2:1 oversubscription. The *U* stands for unified. This extender has ports that can be Ethernet, FC, or FCoE depending on the SFP inserted.

The 2000 series line can also use less expensive optics than are normally available in the marketplace to connect to parent switches known as *Fabric Extender Transceivers (FETs)*. These optics can't be used for anything else besides a 2000-to-parent switch connection. This is an important consideration given that optical interconnects can be a substantial financial investment in a cloud data center network. Because of their inexpensive nature, they are a popular choice to use for FEX-to-parent connections. Only the Nexus 5000, 5500, 5600, 6000, 7000, and 9000 can be used to drive fabric extenders. Cisco has gone through some Nexus number rebranding, and there may be different Nexus models or older lines that allow FEX control, but the previous are the core models.

Nexus 5000 Switches

The Nexus 5000 line shown in Figure 6.10 is perhaps one of the more well-known lines of Nexus switches. The 5000 series is often used as the parent switch for fabric extenders and converged fabrics. The numbering scheme jumps around, with 5000 being the older first-generation models and 5600 being the newest. The 5500 platform was the first to offer unified ports and fabric path. The 5500 was able to configure its unified ports as Fibre Channel, FCoE, or Ethernet simply based on the SFP you used. This drove adoption for converged networking. The 5600 continued this trend and added more features such as integrated layer 3 capabilities, VxLAN, and the NX-API. Let's take a brief look at some of the models you'll see as of this writing. All models are SFP+ unless noted.

- **Nexus 5548UP:** This has 32 unified ports of fixed 10G connectivity with the ability to add an expansion module, bringing the total count up to 48 ports.

- **Nexus 5596UP:** This has 48 unified ports of fixed 10G connectivity with the ability to add three expansion modules, bringing the total count to 96 10G ports.

- **Nexus 5596T:** This is the same as the 5596 except a Base-T version, which makes 32 of the ports 10G-BaseT and 16 of them support SFP+ unified ports.

- **Nexus 5672UP:** The next generation after 55xx is the 56xx series. The 5672UP includes 32 10G ports fixed with an additional 16 unified fixed-speed 10G ports. The 5596T has no expansion modules. It includes six QFSP+ 40G ports that can be broken out into four 10G ports each.

- **Nexus 56128P:** This includes 48 fixed 10G ports with four 40G QFSP+ ports that can be broken out into 10G interfaces. The fixed ports aren't fully unified, as they support only FCoE and Ethernet. However, you can also use two expansion modules, which are unified.

- **Nexus 5624Q:** This includes 12 ports of 40G QFSP+. It supports FCoE or Ethernet, and one expansion module slot is available.

- **Nexus 5648Q:** This includes 24 ports of 40G QFSP+, with support for two expansion modules. It is also an FCoE or Ethernet switch like the 5624Q.

- **Nexus 5696Q:** The 5696 is the big one, coming in at a 4U form factor with zero fixed ports. It has eight expansion slots and can support 10, 40, and 100G ports. At line rate, the 5696 can handle 384 10G ports, 96 40G ports, or 32 100G ports. It supports up to 60 unified ports as well. The 5596 also boasts the highest fabric extender (Nexus 2000) count, coming in at 48 FEXs. This means you could run 48 remote Nexus 2000 series fabric extenders from one 5696 or, in other terms, 2,304 10G/1G Ethernet ports.

FIGURE 6.10 Nexus 5000 switches

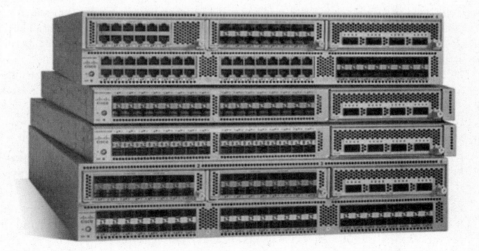

The expansion modules on the 55/56xx series are not all the same nor are the routing features. Figure 6.11 shows some of the Generic Expansion Module (GEM) cards, but there are more that fit into each series. Some are installed internally.

FIGURE 6.11   Nexus 5000 GEM cards

The models support the following:

- **16 port 10G:** This has a 16-port expansion (not unified).
- **8 port 10G 8 port FC:** Half of the ports are 10G, and half are FC.
- **16 port 10G:** This is a later version and supports unified FCoE, FC, and Ethernet.
- **16 Port 10GBaseT:** Only the 5596T supports this 10GBaseT module.
- **L3 Daughter Card:** Only the 5548 supports this. It adds layer 3 services and is internally installed so it does not use up the external expansion slot.
- **L3 160Gbps:** Only for the 5596, it takes up one external expansion slot and adds layer 3 services to the switch.
- **12 port 40G:** 40G interfaces are supported only on the 5624Q and 5648Q platforms; the 5648Q adds 12 more 40G ports.
- **5696:** Each slot can take cards that support either twelve 40G, twenty 10G unified ports, or four 100G ports.

The 5600 series has native layer 3 services, something the 55xx series does not have, which required a layer 3 daughter card or expansion module depending on the 5500 model. It's worth noting that the performance jumps up significantly between the generations. The 55xx series supports 32,000 MAC addresses and up to 24 FEX modules in layer 2 mode. If you install a layer 3 daughter card and run L3 services, that drops down to 16 FEXs.

The 5600 series supports 256,000 MAC addresses and 24 FEXs regardless of whether it is configured for layer 2 or layer 3 operation. As noted earlier, the 5696 can support 48 FEX/N2K modules.

Cisco sells the 55x/56xx series products with licenses, and there are a few you need to be aware of when purchasing said gear:

- **Layer 3 Base:** This is the base license with static routing, HSRP/VRRP, and limited OSPF/EIGRP/RIP routing support. It also has PIM multicast support (sparse only), IGMP, and VRF Lite.
- **Layer 3 Enterprise:** It contains everything the base does, but with no limitations on the features. This license adds BGP and IS-IS; includes all PIM multicast modes; and supports policy-based routing, VxLAN, and other layer 3 features.
- **Enhanced Layer 2:** This has a FabricPath license only.
- **DCNM:** This enables management via the Data Center Network Manager (DCNM) management application.
- **FCoE NPV:** This enables Node Port Virtualization (NPV) mode.

- **8 port storage protocols:** This allows FCoE and FC to be enabled on eight unified ports.
- **Storage Protocols:** This allows FCoE and FC on any supported port.
- **VM-FEX:** This is a *v*irtual FEX extension (blade series chassis, and so on).

Nexus 7000 Switches

The 7000 series was the first series released along the original 5000 products to fill the core and aggregation capacity scenarios. They are a modular chassis, and some refer to them as Catalyst 6500 replacements, an often-chosen choice for data center aggregation. The 7000 series has a capacity of just under 18Tbps forwarding rates with more than 11 billion packets per second throughput. The 7000 series is a completely modular chassis that supports upgradeable line cards, supervisor modules, power supplies, and switch fabric cards.

At the time of this writing, there are several options for the 7000 series, as shown in Figure 6.12.

- **Nexus 7004:** This is the 7U version and has four slots that correspond to the model number. Two of the slots are for supervisors, and two of the slots are for I/O line cards.
- **Nexus 7009:** This version is 14U and is a smaller footprint than its 7010 big brother. The reason is the orientation of the line cards. In this 7009, the line cards are horizontal. It has two slots for supervisors, five slots for switch fabric modules, and seven slots for I/O line cards.
- **Nexus 7010:** This 21U 7000 chassis predates the 7009 chassis. The line cards run vertical in this chassis, making the chassis taller than the 7009. However, you get more line cards. The same slot counts for supervisors and switch fabrics as the 7009.
- **Nexus 7018:** This 25U monster retains the same switch fabric and supervisor card count as other models but lets you install 16 I/O line cards. The 7018 achieves this by running the line cards horizontal like the 7009 and being almost double the height.

FIGURE 6.12   Nexus 7000 switches

Nexus 7700 Switches

The Nexus 7700 is the next generation of the 7000 series. The 7700 series quadruples the forwarding capacity achieving 83Tb of forwarding capacity. One additional switch fabric module is added, and there is a smaller model for edge connectivity and other uses cases.

At the time of this writing, these are the current models:

- **Nexus 7702:** This 3U version has a slot for a supervisor and a slot for an I/O line card. It supports almost all of the Nexus line cards and can fulfill some unique scenarios because of its small footprint.

- **Nexus 7706:** The 7706 is 9U high and supports six switch fabric modules, two supervisor modules, and four slots for I/O line cards.

- **Nexus 7710:** The 14U version runs the cards vertically instead of horizontally. The same switch fabric and supervisor card support as the 7706 but accepts eight slots for I/O line cards.

- **Nexus 7718:** At 26U, this is the largest 7000/7700 series switch with two supervisor modules, six switch fabric modules, and sixteen I/O line cards. At the time of this writing, the 7718 can support up to 768 10G ports, 384 40G ports, or 192 100G ports.

Both the Nexus 7000 and 7700 series share the same supervisor modules. Currently, only supervisor 2 is shipping, and supervisor 1 is at end-of-life status and discontinued. There are two versions of supervisor 2 that are sold. The only difference is enhanced vs. standard. The largest differences between the two are the number of virtual device contexts supported (four vs. eight) and the number of FEX devices supported (32 vs. 48). Based on how you deploy these switches, you should be careful which supervisor you purchase. The Understanding Cisco Cloud Fundamentals exam does not cover this material, so we will not expand on it further here. Complete Nexus details are available in the Cisco data center certification.

There are stark differences in the switch fabric modules, and they are specific to each chassis model. For example, you cannot use a 7000 switch fabric in a 7700, and vice versa.

The switch fabric 1 is at end-of-life, so only switch fabric 2 is currently available as of this writing.

- **Nexus 7000 Switch Fabric 2:** This has 110Gbps total forwarding capacity per switch fabric with five switch fabrics per chassis (except the 7004) for a total of 550Gbps forwarding to each I/O card.

- **Nexus 7700 Switch Fabric 2:** This doubles the forwarding at 220Gbps per switch fabric, with six total switch fabrics per chassis (except the 7702). This enables 1.32Tbps per I/O card.

There are many different line card models available for both chassis systems, with 7000 and 7700 requiring different, specific line cards between models. All cards focus on 1/10G, 40G, or 100G connectivity. The difference is merely the density, L2/L3 support, and forwarding throughput. The 7000, for example, has a six-port 100G card, while the 7700 answers with a 12-port 100G card. There are differences in the versions that you should know, mainly the F and M series cards.

- **Nexus 7700/7000 M series cards:** Both the 7700 and 7000 have M series cards. Currently shipping as of this writing are the M2 and M3. M series cards are primarily routing cards with a large table space for routes. The M3 on the 7700 can support two million routes, for example. They usually do not support LISP, FCoE, FC, FabricPath, and other layer 2 types of services.

- **Nexus 7700/7000 F series cards:** These cards are thought of as more layer 2 service cards because of their support for FabricPath. They, however, have smaller routing tables and are lower cost than the M series cards, so each use case is different.

Like the 5000 series, the 7000 series has specific licenses you need to be aware of. They are as follows:

- **Transport Services:** This enables OTV and LISP, provided you have a line card that can actually use these features (M vs. F cards).

- **Advanced Services:** This enables virtual device context (VDC) support.

- **VDC:** This adds an extra four virtual device contexts to the base four VDCs supported, making eight the total number of VDCs supported. This license requires the supervisor 2 module to operate.

- **Enterprise Services:** This enables layer 3 services such as VxLAN, EVPN, BGP, OSPF, ISIS, RIP, EIGRP, PIM, PBR, GRE and MSDP, and ACI-WAN interconnect.

- **Scalable Services:** This enables higher route tables on M series cards that support the XL option.

- **Enhanced Layer 2:** This enables FabricPath support, RISE, and ITD.

- **MPLS:** This enables MPLS services.

- **Storage Enterprise:** This enables FCoE and VSAN services.

- **DCNM LAN:** This enables Data Center Network Management application support.

Nexus 9000 Switches

The Nexus 9000 series is the most recent Nexus line aimed at the data center, as shown in Figure 6.13. The 9000 series represents the next generation of Nexus switching and is a large leap forward in how data center switches operate. The Cisco IOS NX-API is fully baked into the 9000 series along with Linux shell access. The 9000 series is the first product family to support the Cisco SDN architecture referred to as ACI, which we'll discuss later in this chapter. In addition, the 9000 series offers superior power, performance, and lower latency than the previously discussed models.

The Nexus 9000 series has three families of switches. An important distinction to understand is ACI mode vs. NX-OS mode. Nearly all models are capable of NX-OS, but not all are capable of operating in ACI mode, mainly the 9200 series.

FIGURE 6.13   Nexus 9000

Nexus 9200 Switches

The 9200 switches are the one line in the 9000 series that operate only in NX-OS stand-alone mode; they do not support the ACI operational mode. The 9200 series is the first Cisco product line to support multirate, 10/25/40/50/100G ports in the same switch.

Here are SFP+ native switches only as of this writing.

- **Nexus 92160YC-X:** This is a 1U top-of-rack switch with 3.2Tbps throughput. It has 48 SFP+ total downlink ports capable of 10/25Gbps. Four out of the six uplink ports are 100Gbps capable; the others are 40Gbps.

- **Nexus 9272Q:** This is a 2U top-of-rack or aggregation switch with 5.76Tbps of throughput. The 9272Q has 72 fixed 40G QFSP+ ports. Using breakout cables, it can support 1G and 10G ports.

- **Nexus 92304QC:** This is a 2U top-of-rack or aggregation with 6.08Tbps of throughput. It has 56 fixed ports of 40Gbps with eight uplink ports of 100Gbps each. Using breakout cables, the ports can support 1/10G speeds.

- **Nexus 9236C:** This is a 1U aggregation switch with 7.2Tbps of throughput and 36 fixed 100Gbps ports that can be broken out into 4×10GBps, 4×25Gbps, 1×40Gbps, or 1×50Gbps. This flexibility makes the 9236C a good choice for any deployment where a wide range of speeds are needed.

- **Nexus 92300YC:** This has slightly more than 1U, at 6.0Tbps of throughput. The 92300YC offers 48-wire rate 10/25Gbps ports. It does this by also having 18 100Gbps ports for uplinks. It is designed for high-density 1:1 subscription 25Gbps racks.

Nexus 9300 Switches

The 9300 switches were the first top-of-rack switch introduced in the 9000 series of switches. All 9300 switches support ACI mode, and nearly all support NX-OS operations. They also have Base-T models for copper, something the 9200 series does not have yet as of this writing.

The main models are shown here, but this list is not comprehensive, as there are many variations of the models:

- **Nexus 9332PQ:** This is a 1U top-of-rack switch with 2.56Tbps of throughput and 32 fixed QFSP+ 40G ports, which makes it ideal for use as an aggregation switch.

- **Nexus 9336PQ:** This is a 2U aggregation switch with 2.88Tbps of throughput. It runs only in ACI mode and is a mini-spine switch with 36 QFSP+ 40G ports.

- **Nexus 93180LC-EX:** This is a 1U top-of-rack switch with 3.6Tbps of throughput. This model operates in ACI mode as a leaf with 24 QFSP+ 40G ports and six 100G uplink ports. NX-OS support for this product has been announced.

- **Nexus 9372PX/TX:** This is a 1U top-of-rack switch with 1.44Tbps of throughput. It has 48 1/10G ports and six QFSP+ 40G uplink ports. The TX version is for Base-T ports.

- **Nexus 9396PX/TX:** This is a 2U top-of-rack or aggregation switch with 1.92Tbps of throughput. It has 48 fixed 1/10G ports with an expansion module that enables either six or twelve QFSP+ 40G uplink ports or four 100G ports. TX model is for Base-T support.

- **Nexus 93180 YC|TC-EX:** This is a 1U top-of-rack switch with 3.6Tbps of throughput. It has 48 fixed 1/10/25G ports with six uplink ports that support 10/25/40/50/100G speeds. The TC model offers Base-T support.

- **Nexus 93120TX:** This is a 2U top-of-rack switch with 2.4Tbps of throughput. It has 96 fixed 1/10G Base-T ports with six fixed QFSP+ 40G uplinks.

- **Nexus 93128TX:** This is a 3U switch with 2.56Tbps of throughput. It is identical to 93120 but adds an expansion slot to get twelve 40G uplinks or six 100G uplinks.

Nexus 9500 Switches

The Nexus 9500 series is the modular version of the 9000 series, the answer to the 7000-series generation. There are currently three different versions to choose from:

- **Nexus 9504:** This is a 7U chassis that supports four I/O line cards, two supervisors, and six switch fabrics supporting 15Tbps of system capacity.

- **Nexus 9508:** This is a 13U chassis that doubles the line card support to eight, including 30Tb of system capacity. The switch fabric and supervisor counts are the same as all 9500s.

- **Nexus 9516:** This is a 21U chassis that again doubles the line cards to 16 total modules, as well as 60Tbps of system capacity. The switch fabric and supervisor counts are the same.

The 9500 series has two variations of the supervisor and fabric modules:

- **Supervisor A:** This is a four-core 1.8GHz CPU with a built-in 64GB SSD drive along with 16GB of RAM.

- **Supervisor B:** This is a six-core 2.2GHz CPU with a larger 256GB SSD drive and 24GB of RAM.

- **FM Generation 1:** There is a specific fabric module version for each 9500 chassis, all sharing 320Gbps per slot per FM for up to a maximum of 1.92Tbps a slot if you installed all six fabric modules.

- **FM-S Second Generation:** This greatly increases the fabric module performance by offering 1.5Tbps per slot, per fabric module. Also, 9Tbps per slot is possible if you install all six FMs into a 9500 series chassis.

Nexus 9500 Modules

We won't cover every module here, but you need to know that they skew heavily in the 40G/100G offerings. A large difference between cards is whether they support ACI.

Currently, three models support ACI operation:

- **N9K-X9536PQ:** This is a 36-port 40G module that supports ACI leaf as well as stand-alone NX-OS.

- **N9K-X9732-EC:** This is a 32-port 100G module that supports ACI spine as well as stand-alone NX-OS.

- **N9K-X9736PQ:** This is a 36-port 40G module that operates only as an ACI spine, with no NX-OS support.

Here are the Nexus 9500 licenses:

- **Layer 3 License:** This is the layer 3 feature set license that enables full OSPF, EIGRP, and BGP.

- **Data Broker License:** This enables the TAP aggregation feature for the 9500 series.

- **DCNM:** This enables management via the data center network manager application.

- **ACI:** This is a separate ACI license, which we'll cover later in this chapter.

The 9500 series out of the box supports 160,000 MAC entries and 128,000 IPv4 routes. These metrics can change heavily based on line card, switch fabric, and software. The 9500 series also supports ACI mode, which we've lightly discussed and will cover in more detail later in this chapter.

Software Defined Networking

Traditional networking revolves around making manual changes to the network and has been the normally accepted method since the beginning of networking. Most network engineers are familiar with their CLI or, in some cases, GUI interfaces. Provisioning things as simple as adding a new VLAN to the network may require a network engineer to log into many devices in the cloud or enterprise data center to build the topology. Over the years, protocols and software have been introduced to speed up this process. Things such as the VLAN trunking protocol (VTP) or new commands in the CLI to configure groups of interfaces at one time have been introduced. There are other approaches as well, but none of these solved the basic configuration overhead problem and some even created other issues!

In fact, the previously mentioned examples give credence to the recent industry complaints that network departments often slow down IT deployments by taking so long to implement changes in the network. When a networking engineer must manually define a gateway, VLAN, ACL, and many other items by hand, there is an operational slowness that is incurred. Throw in IT change governance processes, and network configuration changes often slow down to a crawl. The inverse of adding changes to the network is removing or deleting old configurations in the network. Since these processes are all manual, usually the removal processes are as well. VLANs, ACLs, subnets, firewall rules, routing configurations, and many other things are left untouched for long periods of time after the original use case has been decommissioned. This was done over concern that what they were added for has completed and is long gone but nobody knows for sure. This problem compounds when engineers discover these older configurations during troubleshooting. This makes it even worse, as no one remembers or knows when these configurations were last in use and no one wanted to delete them for the risk of causing an outage! The manual operational processes led to these types of issues and created a huge demand for network automation.

Enter in cloud computing. Amazon Web Services launched in 2006 and has risen to become one of the leaders in the public cloud marketplace. Cloud computing in this model changed the conversation for the data center model as cloud computing rose in popularity. Cloud providers must have automatic processes for turn-up and turn-down cloud services because of the highly dynamic and constantly changing dynamics of the cloud. Not all tenants stay, and tenants want the ability to rapidly change their footprint. These delivery models were discussed in earlier chapters.

This began the conversion into a software defined network (SDN) centric model that could behave like cloud computing does. Enterprises have loved the agility and ability to consume cloud services at will and wanted their own internal network to respond in the same way.

Depending on what you read online or who you talk to, you might get a different answer on what SDN is. SDN is an ever-expanding definition, but we'll list some of the more common ideas that surround SDN:

Dynamic   This means it's fluid and easy to change. The SDN topology should work like cloud computing does.

Manageable   It is easy to manage from a centralized perspective. Users should not have to manage individual elements beyond certain circumstances such as initial configuration. The management plane should be separate; we will discuss this in the next section.

Programmable   It is directly programmable. SDN should let users manage and deploy via SDN applications that they can write themselves or that are supplied by SDN application vendors.

Software Services   Where available, software services should be favored over tied-down hardware services. You'll find software-based overlays in this definition as well as other services.

Independent Data Plane   When possible, the data plane should be independent from other network components. This leads to the creation of programmable, dynamic, and manageable cloud networks.

You might find different examples and definitions, and that's OK. SDN is a hotly contested term and definition since its inception, and now that the marketing departments have gotten excited, confusion is at its peak right now. One thing that is agreed upon is the programmability aspect and how the data plane and control plane should be separate.

Separating the Control and Data Plane

Control plane and data plane separation are the cornerstone of most if not all SDN definitions and key attributes. Traditional networking is usually unified in its control and forwarding. This simply means that every network device is self-contained from a forwarding and management perspective. Routing and many other protocols exist to help this matter by exchanging state information between network devices. This doesn't change the fact that each network device is running its own control and forwarding processes.

Let's break down the control and data plane definitions:

Control Plane   The controller of the network device. In the Nexus line of 9500 or 7000, this would be the supervisor module. The control plane is responsible for programming line cards, running dynamic routing protocols, responding to certain types of requests, and overall management of the network device.

Data Plane   This is where the hardware ASIC magic happens and where data forwarding is performed in the device. These are the interfaces on the network device that transport packets.

It's easy to understand the difference when looking at the large modular chassis switches. The Catalyst 6500 can still be found throughout data centers around the globe. It represents the legacy issue of a joined control and data plane. The 6500 had supervisors as the control plane, but they also included the switch fabric hardware for the line cards. Without the supervisor, the chassis can't actually function. Take a look at Figure 6.14 to see this setup.

FIGURE 6.14   Modular control and data planes

Modular 6509e Chassis

Supervisor (Control)	Fabric
Supervisor (Control)	Fabric
Line Card (Data Plane)	**Supervisor has the switch fabric.**
Line Card (Data Plane)	
Line Card (Data Plane)	
Line Card (Data Plane)	
Line Card (Data Plane)	
Line Card (Data Plane)	
Line Card (Data Plane)	

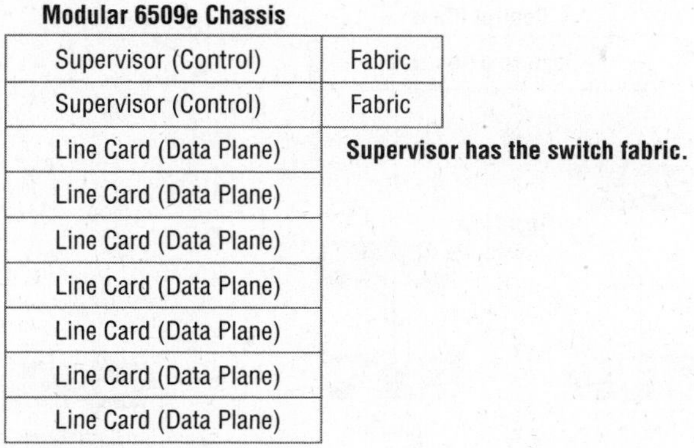

Each line card in the 6500 is in the data plane, providing the forwarding interfaces for moving packets in and out of the chassis. But as mentioned previously, the supervisor also has the switch fabric on it and is tightly coupled with the data plane. This is shown on the drawing, but it's not something you see physically on the chassis. It's built into the supervisor and connects to the other line cards.

Contrast that with the Nexus 7500 or Nexus 9500. Both lines have separate switch fabric modules installed into the chassis. This choice was easy; separate the control and data planes as much as possible to gain new features like in service upgrades and SDN capabilities. In this design, the control plane programs the line cards with the forwarding information they need. This includes adjacency tables and other next hop-related information. If the control plane goes down, the line cards still have this information programmed. Any preexisting flow can still function. There are of course limits to this concept. Eventually tables and adjacencies would expire or become stale. They would need a refresh like gratuitous ARP or other control-related information to retain accurate and up-to-date state tables. This would again require the use of the control plane. The concept, however, is sound, and one that leads to larger scenarios than just the chassis design. If the forwarding plane takes instructions only from a central control plane, you are able to construct larger SDN designs.

One of the first SDN protocols was *OpenFlow*. The project originally began at Stanford University in 2008, with version 1.0 being released in 2009. This is often thought of as the standard of what the industry wanted SDN to be, at least at the time. OpenFlow uses a centralized controller to program the downstream switches to implement routing and traffic steering. See Figure 6.15 for an example. In this example, the SDN controller is the control plane. It sends instructions to the individual switches to control the data plane. The switches are merely a data plane waiting to be programmed from the controller.

FIGURE 6.15   OpenFlow

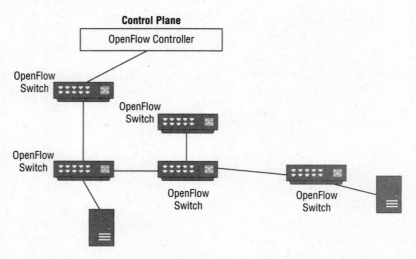

An important point to understand here is that there is no routing protocol used! OpenFlow *is* the protocol. The controller has a central view of the network and program rules into each switch. The controller acts on a collection of rules and statistics. This could be as simple as "This MAC address source to this MAC address destination egress port 5." There are many rules and several actions to choose from, including drop.

The benefits to OpenFlow can be summarized as follows:

Programmability   One of the key concepts of SDN is programmable access to the OpenFlow network through the controller. You can even add your own extensions and features by using publically available APIs.

Centralized Management   Again, one of the key concepts of SDN is that the controller is the brains of the operation here. With a granular policy and simplistic provisioning, this problem is easily solved.

Abstraction   OpenFlow has real decoupling of the control and data plane. Use your own switches or different vendors' switches that support OpenFlow. The control and data planes are truly separated.

Exploring Device Programmability

As explained earlier in the chapter, most traditional networks are configured on an individual device basis. That means the administrator must log in to each device to push policy. This is one of the features of SDN. Even before SDN, the network industry trended toward this with *Network Management Systems (NMS)*.

Administrators would use an NMS to deploy configuration on a large scale. Instead of logging in individually, the NMS would send commands to routers, switches, and firewalls and configure the network. Usually this revolved around using either SSH or SNMP-based applications. The NMS tool will usually send a single command or batches of commands to fulfill a request.

Imagine an operator wants to install a new VLAN, with a layer 3 gateway at the aggregation layer and VLAN trunks all over the access layer. The operator for an NMS would likely set up several configurations to be sent:

- Send VLAN configuration to the aggregation layer (add VLAN).
- Set up SVI in the aggregation layer (add a layer 3 interface).
- Set up trunks on the access layer and the aggregation layer.

One of the main issues with an NMS tool is the way each vendor implements their network and software. Because each NMS is usually custom to that vendor, the operator needs to have a deeper understanding of exactly how that network vendor functions. This also limits or prevents cross-vendor NMS tools, as most NMS tools may not work with other vendors.

The vendor-specific NMS gave rise to the larger tool called an *orchestrator*. The orchestrator doesn't necessarily have to be vendor specific and usually is not. There are many tools on the market that specialize in network orchestration that revolve around the concept of treating a network with separate instructions that work together to perform an end goal or action. It is not limited to switching or routing but could also work with load balancing gear, firewalls, and other services. The difference here is how the changes are perceived and interact with the network. The orchestrator would consider the previous example of VLAN addition via NMS a workflow management application. These instructions would be grouped together and could be even run on different vendors' gear. Not only that, they would be run via a preset action or click. It may be something as simple as "Create New VLAN."

For example, the operator clicks Create New VLAN in the Orchestration GUI and then does the following:

1. Fill in the field for VLAN number.
2. Fill in the field for IP address.
3. Decide where server ports are (via drop-down menu).
4. Click Deploy.

The large difference here is the way the actions are deployed. The NMS has no understanding of the larger use case and sends separate instructions. The orchestration tool is most likely multivendor and knows what is required for each workflow. Usually via the GUI, the operator would fill in details and with one-click deploy workflows.

How do you get beyond this to even more fully automated networks? This all works with the subjects previously discussed.

You know you need the following:

- Orchestration capabilities that go beyond the GUI
- A common framework to speak to network elements
- Custom automation and applications

This is where SDN has evolved to provide a *network controller.* Think of a network controller as the gateway to the network. It's the centralized control plane we previously discussed in the section on SDN. It does not have to replace high-level orchestration; rather, it can complement them. The network controllers use a few common terms to describe their functions. *Northbound* and *southbound* communications are the most common when referring to the network controller.

The northbound side of the controller is the traditional GUI/interface a user or application might use. Its job is to abstract the network complexity and present it as a programmable interface to the user. The southbound side is the protocol used by the controller to go and do the hardware-level functions on the network. In the OpenFlow style, the southbound protocol is OpenFlow. The controller uses this protocol to go and configure the actions the operator dictates. See Figure 6.16 to illustrate this concept with OpenFlow.

FIGURE 6.16   OpenFlow controller north and south

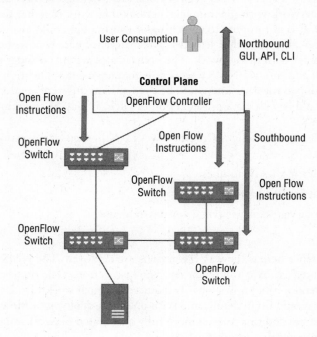

Introduction to OpenDaylight

One of the issues with OpenFlow is that it primarily is a southbound protocol without a standard definition for northbound communications, including to the controller. Vendors have offered solutions, but there wasn't a standard unified way to approach network control. A multivendor effort began in 2013 called OpenDaylight to address this issue. Many vendors are members of the project, including Cisco, HP, Juniper, Arista, and Red Hat, as well as many other vendors, end users, cloud providers, universities, and government agencies.

The goals of the OpenDaylight project are as follows:

- Provide an industry-standard controller and framework to be used for SDN and Network Function Virtualization use cases.

- An interoperable multivendor platform that works with many protocols, with Open-Flow being the largest

- A common SDN foundation for the industry to use and expand on that is entirely based open standards and software

As you can see in Figure 6.17, OpenDaylight has a well-defined framework that includes north and southbound communications. Everything above the API is considered the northbound side. Through the GUI or API, requests are processed and received. The API is RESTful and supports REST, RESTCONF, and NETCONF.

FIGURE 6.17   OpenDaylight operational view

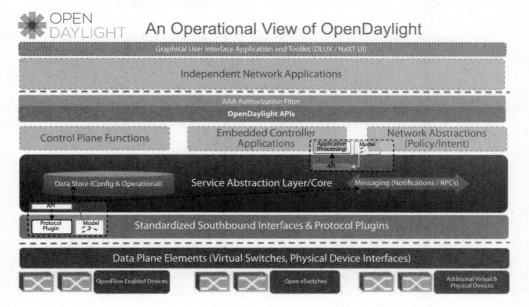

Below the API/northbound layers, the control plane functions include things like AAA, Host Tracker, OpenFlow Forwarding/Switch/Stats managers, and more. Embedded applications include an open source router, open stack plug-ins, NAT applications, virtual tenant network manager, and more. Their job is to process requests made through the API or from the northbound side.

The services abstraction layer exposes these services to the actual network devices below, at the bottom of Figure 6.17. The Service Abstraction Layer (SAL) works with standards protocols like OpenFlow, SNMP, BGP, and others. It also allows for vendor-specific southbound protocols, allowing for some great flexibility. There are many moving parts here and several use cases for deployment. OpenDaylight defines several use cases for ODL in the enterprise and service provider realm.

These are the major uses as identified by OpenDaylight:

Automated Service Delivery   It provides a services platform on demand that can be controlled by the service provider or even the end user. Examples might be dynamic bandwidth adjustments, automated firewall services, and L2/L3 VPN services.

Network Resource Optimization   This is a service provider feature and one that several are using. It's an optimization of the network based on the load and state and uses protocols like BGP-LS and OpenFlow.

Cloud and NFV   It provides service delivery in a cloud-like environment, frequently using OpenStack and the OpenDaylight plug-ins to facilitate cloud automation and service delivery.

Visibility and Control   It provides centralized management and administration of the network.

Cisco contributed heavily to the development of the OpenDaylight controller and is still a platinum member. The work that went into the ODL controller Cisco spun off as a commercial project called the Cisco Open SDN Controller.

Cisco offers the following benefits in the Open SDN Controller:

Commercial Distribution   Using the Open SDN controller gets end users a validated and supported OpenDaylight software distribution. Essentially, it's commercial support for the open source software.

Clustering   It offers increased availability and scale.

Northbound REST APIs   It offers easy development and integration of custom applications.

Network Service Java APIs   It allows the creation of new embedded network services to deliver customer controller capabilities.

Southbound Device Plug-ins   It connects compatible Cisco and third-party virtual and physical networks allowing multivendor networks. It supports multiple protocols such as BGP-LS, NETCONF, and PCEP.

ACI Solutions to Enhance SDN

Cisco *Application Centric Infrastructure (ACI)* was developed by Cisco to address issues seen in other SDN offerings. Offerings like OpenFlow were a good start, but they still suffered from some limitations. It's important to note that since that time, some of these problems have been addressed. However, understanding this history is important to the beginnings of ACI.

Running the network on OpenFlow and other flow architectures can be cumbersome. Managing flow tables for each switch leads to operational challenges and specialized rules on a per-hop basis. It works well for some applications but doesn't scale out to a large enterprise. The reliability of the network can also be an issue. The controller and the switches are tightly coupled and integrated. Without the controller, the switches can fall out of state. Some of this has been addressed in headless mode and third-party controllers not relevant to this book, but they're the reason, among others, for Cisco developing the ACI framework and family of product offerings.

The ONF whitepaper "Software Defined Networking: The New Norm for Networks" describes several imitations to current networking. Cisco looked at these and built ACI with these in mind.

The traditional network approach suffers from the following limitations, which ACI attempts to solve:

Complexity   Traditional networks have protocols and features defined for single purposes, leading to complexity. VLANs are a perfect example of this and something that was defined merely as a broadcast domain separation technology. Now they are used as security domain separation as well, creating further complexity for administrators. Changes to a VLAN not only might affect broadcast domains but could now affect security rules.

Policies That Are Inconsistent   This is related to large-scale enterprises that might have hundreds if not thousands of policies and rules. Traditionally these are configured via scripts or manual intervention. This approach is prone to human error and drives the result of inconsistencies in network configurations. These can cause dramatic security holes or applications simply not working.

Scalability Issues   Traditional networks aren't designed with scaling in mind, especially when related to mobility in single-subnet broadcast domains. Usually increasing the number of endpoints on a traditional network requires a complete redesign and more hardware deployed.

Cisco ACI can address all the limitations just discussed. The goal of ACI is to use an approach that combines hardware and software to work in a unified fashion. The management is centralized, and the policy can be consistent.

Cisco ACI removes complexity from the networking architecture by decoupling policy from the forwarding logic. This policy is then distributed throughout the fabric. This is accomplished through a combination of merchant silicon while also using custom Cisco silicon for added features and capabilities at the same time. Standards-based VxLAN is used throughout the fabric to bridge and route traffic. Cisco refers to the fabric as *penalty free*. This means there is no performance impact on the application latency because of the overlay of VxLAN and lookup of unknown host locations. The spine is the mapping database of where hosts are, so a leaf switch must traverse a spine switch regardless to locate another host elsewhere. Hence, this term is called *penalty free*.

Cisco ACI uses a 16-bit ID in the VxLAN header to uniquely identify a source group in the ACI fabric. This approach allows policy to be defined without being held down to the usual network semantics. Most traditional policies are defined on the IP address and port level. ACI is not limited to this methodology because of its use of the 16-bit ID in the VxLAN header.

Inconsistent policies are solved using the *Application Policy Infrastructure Controller (APIC)*. A user of ACI needs only to use APIC to offload the task of policy deployment. The APIC will program the fabric based on the desired intent of the policy. Since policy configuration is centralized in one place and programmed across the fabric, the policy remains consistent.

It's important to know that ACI works only with certain hardware, mainly the Nexus 9000 series. The 9000 series has the ability in some models to run in ACI mode vs. NX-OS mode, as we discussed earlier in this chapter. In addition to the 9000 series, the ACI fabric requires an APIC controller. The APIC is a centralized controller responsible for provisioning the policy to the fabric. The APIC can interact with other controllers and solutions besides the Cisco 9000, such as VMware vCenter, Microsoft Virtual Machine Manager, Cisco products like ASA, and other third-party products. See Figure 6.18 to get a brief look at the ACI fabric.

FIGURE 6.18   Cisco ACI fabric

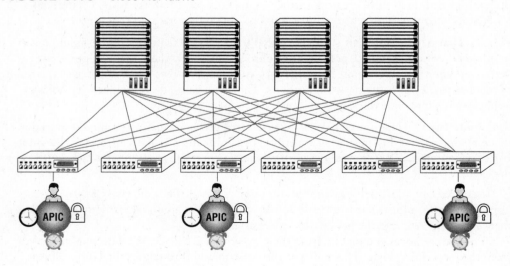

The ACI policy model differs greatly from the traditional networking paradigm. Traditionally almost all firewalls and access control lists (ACLs) use rules based on IP address, a layer 4 port, or the IP subnet. The issue with this, as any network administrator knows, is how intertwined these items become. You can't make changes to a subnet, VLAN, or IP address without causing a waterfall effect downstream. The IP address *is* the identifier of an endpoint in traditional networking. The ACI policy model is a key benefit to the ACI fabric.

Let's define what exactly makes up the policy model and objects.

Tenant   In the service provider world, this would likely be other customers. This is an administrative and traffic segregation domain. In the enterprise world, this could be different domains such as quality assurance and production or organizations and business units. Tenants can be isolated from other tenants or share resources.

Context   This in the traditional networking sense is a VRF. It is a separate layer 3 domain. Multiple contexts can exist within tenants.

Bridge Domain   This represents a layer 2 forwarding construct within the ACI fabric. This is required to be linked to a VRF context and at least one subnet. A context may have multiple bridge domains.

Subnet   This is the classic layer 3 subnet that traditional networking uses. It is linked to a bridge domain. Multiple subnets may exist on the bridge domain.

Endpoint   This is a physical or virtual device connected to the ACI fabric.

Endpoint Group (EPG)   This is perhaps the most important part of the ACI fabric. The policy applies to endpoint groups, not endpoints. EPGs represent a collection of endpoints that share a common policy requirement. This could be a group of VMs and physical servers or even a single host in its own EPG.

Contract   This is the rule that gets applied between EPGs in the traditional networking sense. By default, an EPG cannot contact another EPG. A contract must be specified that allows that behavior. Intra-EPG (in the same EPG) communication is allowed by default.

Application Profile   This is the container for an application that contains all the EPGs and contracts between them.

External Networks   This controls connectivity to networks that are outside of the ACI fabric. It could be a layer 2 extension or a routed layer 3.

Figure 6.19 shows a single tenant with context. For a small customer, this may be enough. Remember that the tenant could be something that refers to a customer or business unit or environment. The context is next, which is the VRF in traditional networking. Notice the two bridge domains and two subnets. A bridge domain can have more than one subnet if needed. These link to downstream endpoint groups (EPGs), which are a collection of hosts that belong to the subnet above. The contract specifies the rules between the EPGs. The external EPG specifies connectivity to an outside network. Finally, the application profile is the box around the EPGs and external EPG. The APIC takes these logical constructs and pushes the policy to the hardware throughout the fabric.

FIGURE 6.19   Cisco ACI policy hierarchy

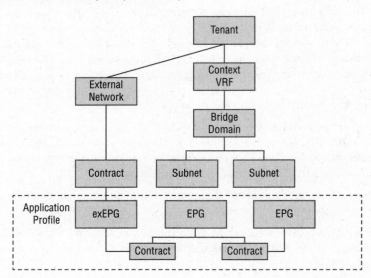

You should begin to see the possibilities of a fabric designed with logical groupings in mind. An ACI fabric can identify physical and virtual entities, regardless of where they are, through several different methods via the EPG construct. An organization might be tempted to stick with a policy defined by IP addresses, but the EPG construct offers so much more flexibility. EPGs are not bound to hosts within the same subnet. They can be mixed. This enables a per-IP policy even within the same subnet. Two different hosts in the same subnet might belong to two different EPGs, allowing a contract/policy to be defined. As of this writing, the endpoint can be defined by the following:

- VLAN identifier
- VxLAN identifier
- Specific IP/subnet
- A DNS hostname

The contract in the fabric is the main construct that defines rules between EPGs. ACI defines the following roles from a contract perspective:

Provider   This is the EPG that offers the service, or the destination endpoints that are defined in the contract.

Consumer   This is the opposite of the provider, in other words, the source endpoints for the traffic defined in the contract.

Both   A provider can provide and consume at the same time, but it must be set that way. This consists of just two EPGs talking to each other; it includes defined rules through the contract. This is an important point. Only consumer-originated traffic can initiate to providers. Provider-initiated traffic to a consumer is dropped. By defining both ways, bidirectional initiation is allowed.

A contract is composed of the following:

Subjects   Subjects are a group of filters for a specific application or service.

Filters   Filters are the classification of traffic based on traditional layer 2 to 4 attributes such as TCP ports and IP addresses.

Actions   These are the actions to be taken on filtered traffic:

- Permit the traffic.
- Mark DSCP/CoS.
- Redirect the traffic (service graph).
- Copy the traffic (service graph or SPAN).
- Block the traffic (taboo contracts only).
- Log the traffic (taboo contracts only).

The service graph concept allows a redirect to an appliance like a load balancer or firewall. Think of this as traditional policy-based routing but dynamically scalable. You could define a contract from web servers in an EPG that states return traffic with source port 80 must redirect back to the load balancer.

In Figure 6.20 you can see how this is defined with a standard three-tier web application. The web EPG defines a contract that is consumed by the L3 EPG. Again, the consumer initiates here. The traffic flow is the outside world flowing into the web EPG. Moving further along, the web EPG consumes the contract provided by the application EPG. This allows the web EPG to initiate communication to the application EPG. Finally, the application EPG consumes the database-provided contract. Don't let the provider and consumption fool you. In the traditional ACL world, the consumer is simply the source. The provider is the destination. This is simply the provider saying, "I'll let you connect to me" and the source consumer agreeing. In the end, it's an ACL rule with source to destination on ports.

FIGURE 6.20   Cisco ACI contract consumption

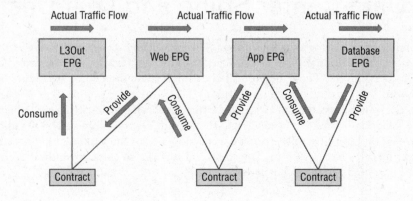

The Cisco ACI APIC

The APIC system is the true brains and single point of control for the ACI fabric. Its job is to maintain the fabric as a whole. It is not, however, a single point of failure. The APIC does not participate in the control plane or the data plane of the fabric. This means you can completely power off the APIC and the fabric will still function. There are obvious limitations with attempting this, such as new policies cannot be deployed. But the previous defined network state can continue to run.

The APIC is deployed in a cluster from three to thirty-one appliances. This is done for redundancy and fault tolerance. There is a special method called *sharding* to distribute the data across the clusters. The APIC architecture can support up to one million endpoints with 200,000 ports and 64,000 tenants.

The APIC also acts as a fabric manager and handles all aspects of the switch configuration. This includes the boot image management, IP address management, and overall configuration. LLDP is used through the fabric for autodiscovery of the Nexus switches and APIC appliances. The APIC offers more than just a GUI, including a full RESTful API and even a CLI. Accessing these features is delegated to traditional role based access control (RBAC) methods that can work with TACACS+, RADIUS, or LDAP servers.

APIC uses *OpFlex* to communicate to the devices in the fabric. These can be physical and virtual switches as well as networking services. OpFlex is an open and extensible protocol developed by Cisco. Its purpose is to transfer object-based policies between a controller, in this case the APIC, and the aforementioned devices.

APIC can also integrate with VM managers from VMware, Microsoft, and OpenStack. This allows APIC to gather information about the VMs, especially live migrations that happen. When the APIC senses this, a policy push can follow to ensure the fabric is programmed appropriately after VM moves.

The Data Center Spine and Leaf Design

The ACI fabric uses a spine and leaf design. New data center design trends are evolving to this direction. In traditional three-tier designs, multiple aggregations were used to connect to multiple access layers. These all connected through a common core. See Figure 6.21 for this depiction.

One of the issues illustrated in Figure 6.21 that has been previously discussed is mobility. You could keep scaling out the core/aggregation design, but mobility suffers. Traditionally these aggregation layers are in their own layer 2 domain for fault tolerance. This eliminates newer features like VMotion. The spine and leaf design came from these scenarios. Reference Figure 6.22 to see the difference.

FIGURE 6.21 Core aggregation design

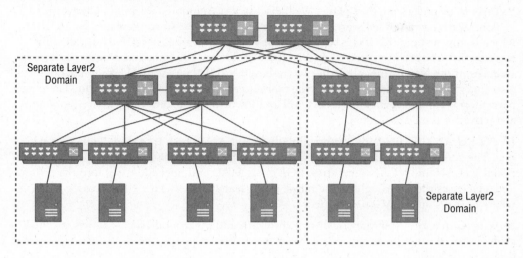

Separate Layer2 Domain

Separate Layer2 Domain

FIGURE 6.22 Spine and leaf design

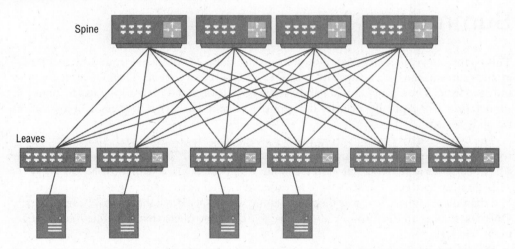

Spine

Leaves

One large benefit to such a design is the predetermined hop count between devices. Each leaf is only one hop away through the spine to another. This design leads to fast and efficient east-west traffic patterns.

If you're looking at the design and thinking it's one big gigantic layer 2 fault domain, you'd be correct. This, however, applies only if it were deployed in the traditional method, using classic trunks and the Spanning Tree Protocol. These types of designs are usually deployed with some type of layer 2 routing technology, such as FabricPath or VxLAN. ACI uses VxLAN as its underlying data plane. We'll discuss VxLAN more in depth in Chapter 8.

FabricPath has provided a great deal of use, but it is being slowly replaced by VxLAN, which is now a standard. VxLAN encapsulates Ethernet frames in UDP datagrams that traverse the network as routed packets. All the 9000 series switches (and other various switches in the Nexus line) allow hardware-based VxLAN gateways. Virtual machines can also run VxLAN gateways, allowing the fabric to extend into the virtual world. There have been several enhancements to the VxLAN architecture that makes these fabric topologies attractive for the Data Center.

EVPN VxLAN   EVPN adds a control plane to VxLAN, which traditionally did not have one. The control plane is MP-BGP. Using BGP avoids the flood and learns aspects of traditional VxLAN and VLAN semantics. BGP takes MAC and host addresses into the protocol and advertises them throughout the fabric to the leaf switches. This allows leaves to learn where host IPs and MACs are located.

Anycast Gateway   Seen previously in FabricPath and other models, this allows for the leaf switches to all function as a gateway. No matter where a host is, the closest gateway in this design is the leaf.

Summary

This chapter covered a large set of topics for the exam. We discussed traditional network architectures in the data center and how they've evolved over time. Then we discussed the unified fabric. The Cisco Unified Fabric converges storage and networking traffic onto the same fabric. Concepts like priority flow control were induced that help create a lossless fabric on Ethernet.

The line of Nexus products from Cisco was introduced. The 5000 and 7000 series are some of the older lines of Nexus products. The more recent 7700 and 9000 series are current. The 2000 series is a remote line card technology that can be used with most Nexus lines.

Beginning concepts for SDN were introduced as well as the separation of the control and data plane. OpenFlow was discussed along with OpenDaylight for SDN controllers. OpenDaylight is an open source alternative to SDN controllers that has contributions from many vendors.

Finally, we discussed the ACI solution and spine and leaf fabrics. These solutions round up the current and next-generation fabric technologies you'll find in the data center.

Exam Essentials

Know the differences in network architectures.   Understand the classic three tier and older core only model and why it evolved to later fabrics. Understand the three network layers of access, aggregation, and core and what function each performs. Know that the end devices connect to the access, and the aggregation interconnects the access to the core and provides services and routing. The core is the high-speed and highly reliable central routing for the network.

Understand the unified fabric and its role in I/O consolidation.   Know converged adapters and FCoE play into the converged network. Understand data center bridging and why it was created to deal with storage on a converged fabric. Know the concepts of priority flow control.

Know the difference between the Nexus product lines and where they're used. Understand the FEX architecture of the Nexus 2000 and know the limitations and capabilities. Know the differences in each product family, for example, the 2000 compared to the 5000 or 7000. Know that the Nexus 9000 line was developed for network automation and supports commands from the Cisco ACI APIC controller. Also, be able to identify the differences between the 9200, 9300, and 9500 models and what their intended use is.

You should be able to explain where SDN originated and the difference between OpenFlow and traditional architectures.   Know the control plane role and the data plane role in networking. Know the concept of their separation and what that achieves. Understand the OpenDaylight initiative and how Cisco's contributions affected it.

Understand the ACI fabric and the benefits it brings.   Know the policy model and how it vastly differs from other solutions on the market. Understand the gear required to run ACI and what the APIC controller is used for. You should be able to explain its basic setup and redundancy. Make sure you understand the spine and leaf architecture and what the benefit of one is.

Written Lab

Fill in the blanks for the questions provided in the written lab. You can find the answers to the written labs in Appendix B.

1. Cisco has a three-tier design model for network deployments; list the three layers Cisco defines in this model.

    1. _____

    2. _____

    3. _____

2. The protocols that enable lossless connectivity over Ethernet by enabling dynamic resource allocation and congestion notification are collectively referred to as _____ _____ _____.

3. The _____ _____ _____ design is used to shorten cable runs and offer deployment flexibility, reliability, and high-density access requirements.

4. The _____ tier operates at layer _____ and provides high-speed aggregation interconnections.

5. The Nexus _____ product line acts as the primary aggregation switch model.

6. The ability of data center network architectures to accept new equipment and designs that allow for growth is referred to as a(n) _____ design.

7. A data center network design must allow for _____ to accept surges of traffic and to allow for expansion of hosts.

8. A(n) _____ _____ accommodates both LAN and SAN traffic on the same forwarding plane.

9. The Nexus _____ series access switches allow a distributed topology that supports a top-of-rack architecture with a central control plane and distributed remote line cards.

10. The Nexus technology that extends VLANs between data centers is known as _____ _____ _____.

Review Questions

The following questions are designed to test your understanding of this chapter's material. You can find the answers to the questions in Appendix A. For more information on how to obtain additional questions, please see this book's Introduction.

1. What are key components of Cisco data center network architecture? (Choose four.)
   A. Resiliency and availability
   B. Flexibility
   C. RBAC
   D. ACI
   E. Overlay Transport
   F. Scalability
   G. Centralized control plane
   H. Monitoring

2. Which Nexus product is software only?
   A. 1000
   B. 2248
   C. 5600
   D. 7700

3. Which networking technology requires a lossless switching fabric?
   A. DCB
   B. OTV
   C. FC
   D. VDC

4. Which of the following products acts as a Nexus remote line card?
   A. ASA
   B. 2248TP
   C. 56963UP
   D. 7004

5. Which model of Cisco switch supports FEX and unified ports for a converged network fabric?
   A. 1000V
   B. MDS9624
   C. 569623UP
   D. 7010

6. What is the discovery protocol used with data center bridging to discover neighbor capabilities?

  A. 802.1az

  B. DCBX

  C. Priority-based bridging interconnect

  D. 802.1bb

7. The ability of a Nexus 7000 series switch to create separate virtual instances and appear as many separate logical switches is referred to as?

  A. VDC

  B. FEX

  C. ACI

  D. VPC

8. What Nexus series can support the ACI mode of operation?

  A. 2200

  B. 5600

  C. 7700

  D. 9000

9. What Nexus product family is designed for a spine/leaf data center deployment?

  A. 1000

  B. 6000

  C. 7700

  D. 9000

10. What technology replaces the manual configurations of VLANs, ACLs, subnets, SVIs, and firewall rules?

  A. SaaS

  B. NFV

  C. VTP

  D. SDN

11. The Cisco three-tier design consists of which components? (Choose three.)

  A. Access

  B. Unified fabric

  C. ACL

  D. Core

  E. Aggregation

  F. Switch block

12. What is a Cisco remote line card interconnect technology?

    A. VDC

    B. FEX

    C. ACI

    D. VPC

13. What is a specialized routing protocol used to provide a loop-free layer 2 topology in a data center?

    A. Data center bridging

    B. Unified fabric

    C. ACI

    D. FabricPath

14. What Nexus technology allows remote data centers to be interconnected at layer 2 across a routed WAN?

    A. PVSTP

    B. OTV

    C. FEX

    D. FabricPath

15. Which of the following is a technology used to virtualize two Nexus switches to appear as a single device?

    A. VDC

    B. FEX

    C. ACI

    D. VPC

16. What Nexus series supports 10, 25, 40, 50, and 100G Ethernet ports?

    A. 2200

    B. 5600

    C. 7700

    D. 9000

17. What technology automates the provision of network topologies?

    A. SDN

    B. VTP

    C. OTV

    D. SNMP

18. SDN centralizes and virtualizes what network component?

   A. Forwarding plane

   B. Converged fabric

   C. Control plane

   D. Core layer

19. What is a Cisco-developed SDN controller that interoperates with the Nexus 9000 series of switches?

   A. VPC

   B. ACI

   C. DCB

   D. VDC

20. What are examples of an SDN controller's northbound user interfaces? (Choose two.)

   A. GUI

   B. JSON

   C. API

   D. OpenFlow

21. Which of the following is a Cisco virtualized control plane processor designed to control a Nexus leaf/spine data center deployment?

   A. SDN

   B. VDC

   C. APIC

   D. FabricPath

Chapter 7

Server Virtualization in the Cloud

THE FOLLOWING UNDERSTANDING
CISCO CLOUD FUNDAMENTALS
CLDFND (210-451) EXAM OBJECTIVES
ARE COVERED IN THIS CHAPTER:

✓ 3.2   Describe Server Virtualization

- 3.2.a Basic knowledge of different OS and hypervisors

Introducing Virtualization

In this chapter, you will take a deep dive into the virtualization technologies used in cloud computing. You will get a thorough overview of this critical technology and then learn about all of the many different components of virtualization. This will give you a detailed understanding of the many different areas that make up a virtualized cloud offering.

We cannot stress enough that virtualization is the primary enabling technology for all of the cloud models and services. If it were not for advances in virtualization, it is clear that the move to the cloud would not be as prevalent or cost effective as it is today. While it may be tempting to think of virtualization in terms of servers and applications, it is important to know that along the way the industry has virtualized all aspects of the cloud data center. This includes not only the server operating systems but also applications, storage subsystems, networking switches, routers, load balancers, firewalls, Ethernet NICs, storage host bus adapters, and many other functions.

It is not an understatement to say that the widespread deployment of virtualization technologies, not only in the technology industry but in society as a whole, has fundamentally changed the technology field. At the center of all of these cloud innovations is the concept of virtualization, or the idea of abstracting the physical world of data center operations into that of a virtualized world.

While today's virtualization technology has been disruptive to the industry, it has actually been around for a long time. The large mainframe computers dating back to the 1960s utilized virtualization software to take one large mainframe computer and logically create many virtual computers from the one central machine. Over time this technology has been improved and expanded upon, as you will learn in this chapter.

In computing, *virtualization* describes the process of abstracting a physical object into a logical object. The logical object is a digital replica of the real system. This replication is created in software in an attempt to make a copy of the hardware. With virtualization technology, resources can be used more effectively and efficiently to introduce new capabilities and to reduce operational costs.

When the physical is converted to the logical, greater flexibility and expanded options are realized. For example, with networking in the days before VLANs came into use, completely separate LANs, each with their own groupings of hardware switches, were deployed. This created a sprawling mess of Ethernet switches since the only way to separate the traffic was to keep each user or server group on their own set of switches. When VLANs became popular, all of the separate LANs could share and reside in the same physical switched network. The need for hardware was greatly reduced, and higher efficiencies were achieved. Now each switch could be fully utilized and support many networks instead of a lower utilization supporting only a single network. Along with the greater hardware utilization came the added benefit of less rack space and less power. With less power came fewer cooling requirements in the data center.

Once a physical device is virtualized, it can be manipulated in software. This greatly expands the capabilities of the modern cloud data center that could never have been realized in the physical-only world of computing. Since the virtualized server is no longer a physical server bolted into a cabinet in a cloud data center, it can now be copied, replicated, cloned, moved from location to location, and redeployed. Furthermore, additional servers can be created in seconds instead of months. As you will learn, memory, CPUs, storage, networks, and many more physical assets can now be virtualized and interconnected with management software in the cloud data center.

When applications are deployed in a production environment, it is common and often required that the single application run on the operating system and not have many different applications installed on the same server hardware. This is done to increase reliability and resiliency. With multiple applications installed and running on a single server system, there is an increased risk of interference, resource contention, and conflict between the running applications. Also, if the server or one of the applications running on the server should fail, the outage would be more widespread than if the compute workloads were distributed. This one-application-per-server architecture, while adding stability to a company's operations, has many downsides; in addition to the space, power, and cooling issues, it is common that the servers have very low utilization rates and run day-in and day-out at CPU rates often as low as 10 to 15 percent! With server virtualization, multiple operating systems and applications can safely run on the same server platform, which allows for a much more efficient use of resources. Today, with the use of virtualization, server utilization rates as high as 90 to 95 percent are common.

With Intel, AMD, and others designing faster and more powerful CPUs at an amazingly fast pace, the computing power in a standard server has dramatically increased over the years. Today it is common to deploy multiple CPUs on a server motherboard with each CPU housing many logical cores each. Also, these CPUs now have features designed specifically to enhance virtualization. Each server in a modern cloud data center today has the computing power of literally hundreds or even thousands of single-core servers that were common in the past!

With the dramatic increase in the need for ever-higher server performance driven by the growth of the Internet, the architecture of the past (one server running one application) became highly inefficient as data centers were overflowing with hardware consuming massive amounts of power and cooling resources. This was the driver that allowed for the explosion of virtualized data centers. It became feasible to consolidate hundreds of traditional servers into a single, powerful server! The economics of consolidation in the data center were too great to ignore, and the race was on to virtualize. Multiple file, print, e-mail, database, web, and application servers filling up data center racks could all be installed onto one virtualized server. With the ability to consolidate dozens or even hundreds of individual servers into a single virtualized server, the industry was able to save substantial amounts of money and operate more efficiently. By moving to virtualization, companies can save money in power and cooling, downsize support agreements, and lower costs for upgrading, repairing, and supporting equipment.

Virtualization allows applications to be more manageable, available, and scalable than they could have been before when they were on individual servers, as you will learn as you progress through this chapter.

Understanding the Benefits of Virtualization

In this section, you will learn about the many benefits that virtualization technologies bring to cloud deployments. Benefits include the following:

- Efficient use of hardware resources
- Almost instantaneous provisioning of servers
- Increased system uptime and resiliency
- The ability to rapidly scale computing resources
- Enabling cloud elasticity
- Providing the technology that enables the move to the utility model
- Cost savings attributable to operational efficiencies and reduced hardware costs
- Lower power and cooling requirements
- A smaller data center footprint

Let's look in more detail at the advantages gained when implementing virtualization in the cloud.

Shared Resources

Virtualization allows for the physical hardware on a server to be converted into a software representation and then shared among many virtual machines (VMs) running on the server platform. This sharing of resources allows for full utilization of the server's CPU, memory, and storage systems that are often underutilized when a single server operating system is running on the hardware. Also, the CPU, memory, and storage capacity can be dynamically allocated and migrated between VMs based on real-time or scheduled demands.

For example, a traditional e-mail server would be designed to meet its peak workloads during the day. When these peaks were not being realized, the server platform would have a very low utilization rate. In a shared resource environment, these unused cycles could be used by other applications.

Rapid Deployment

When a resource becomes a software representation of the real or physical hardware, it can be allocated by the virtualization management and orchestration software such as Cisco Intercloud. Since it is no longer a physical entity, it can be allocated in near real time for a rapid deployment for new VMs, disaster recovery, scaling, or other purposes. As we discussed earlier, there are no longer extended procurement cycles to bring a new server or application online. With the widespread deployment on virtualization technologies, rapid deployment becomes a reality in the cloud.

Portability

Portability is the ability of a virtual machine to move to different hosts inside and between data centers on the fly with minimal or zero downtime.

As you know, a virtual machine is a software representation of a real server. Since a VM is a virtual representation of the physical asset, it can be moved from server platform to server platform. This portability has created a wide range of new capabilities. For example, a VM can be moved in real time from one data center to another, as shown in Figure 7.1, or to a server that has a lower utilization rate. As shown in Figure 7.2, if the VM is running on a server that experiences a failure, portability provides rapid migration to a backup server, preserving the uptime requirements of cloud customers. The Cisco Intercloud suite of applications is a key enabler of this capability.

FIGURE 7.1   VM portability between clouds

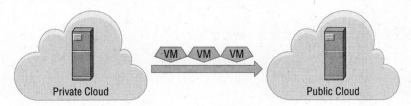

FIGURE 7.2   VM portability due to server failure

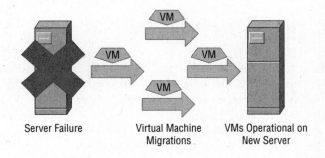

Isolation

The process of a cloud provider isolating customers in a data center is important for security and privacy. The network can be segmented with VLANs, firewalls, and even virtual private clouds (VPCs) to enable isolation security so that only a single customer can access their computing resources in a cloud.

Virtual machines, appliances, and applications in the cloud are isolated from other processes running on the same physical hardware. This *isolation* prevents a failure on one virtual operation from taking down all others running on the same platform.

Consolidating the Network

The cloud data centers are moving toward unified computing that often includes a shared or common switching fabric. *Infrastructure consolidation* is used for both Ethernet LAN and storage area networking (SAN) data over the common switching platform and is also referred to as a *converged fabric*. Converged networking was covered in detail in Chapter 5 when we discussed the Cisco UCS product family.

Consolidation of Servers

With server hypervisors, the underlying hardware has been virtualized, enabling many servers to simultaneously operate on one platform where in the past only the operating system and application were installed on one physical server. You will learn about the many pieces of technology that are used to consolidate servers throughout this chapter.

Consolidating the Infrastructure

Just as servers can be consolidated by converting the physical into the virtual and then running many virtual instances on a single hardware platform, the same can be done for the infrastructure such as LANs, SANs, adapters, networking appliances, storage arrays, and anything else that can be converted into a software representation of the underlying hardware. This topic will be explored in later chapters on network function virtualization and storage systems.

Introducing the Hypervisor

The primary enabling technology behind virtualization is the hypervisor. The hypervisor is a layer of software installed on the server hardware that allows server operating systems to be installed on top of it. The real magic is that the operating systems and other virtual devices all think they are installed directly on the bare-metal server's hardware and have no idea that there is a hypervisor running between the OS and the hardware.

Traditionally a server operating system would be installed directly on a bare-metal server, and the operating system would manage all of the underlying hardware of the server, as shown in Figure 7.3.

FIGURE 7.3   OS running directly on a bare-metal server

Server Operating System

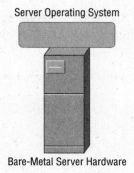

Bare-Metal Server Hardware

The job of the hypervisor is to virtualize the underlying server's hardware components, such as CPU, memory, storage, and networking into resource pools, and then allocate these resources to the virtual machines it supports. The hypervisor masks physical server resources from server users. In this section, you will explore the critical role the hypervisor provides in enabling today's massively scalable clouds.

Taking a Closer Look at the Hypervisor

Hypervisors can provision hardware resources into virtualized pools and then assign them to virtual machines running on top of it. This allows for the segmentation of resources and the ability to isolate failures or keep events in one VM from impacting others running on the same server platform. The VMs run in their own protected containers on the hypervisor, and this fault isolation contains failures to a single container and not the whole server. All other VMs will continue to operate as normal, and the hypervisor is not affected by a single VM issue, as is illustrated in Figure 7.4.

FIGURE 7.4   One VM failure will not affect other VMs.

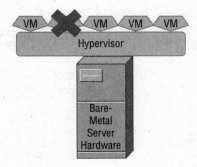

The primary responsibility of a hypervisor is to create a virtual environment that emulates the physical hardware of a server with as little overhead to the performance of the server as possible. The hypervisor will also provide complete control over the underlying hardware resources.

For the *guest operating system* to function properly, it must have access to hardware resources, such as storage, memory, compute, video, and networking, as if it were directly installed on the server. The role of the hypervisor is to provide for and manage the operations of these resources for multiple guest operating systems, with each guest believing it has exclusive use of the server, as shown in Figure 7.5.

FIGURE 7.5   Guest OS access virtualized hardware resources

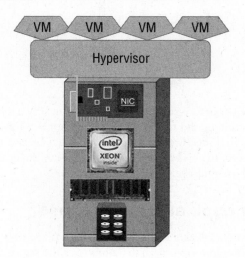

The hypervisors basically fool the operating system into believing that it is running directly on a server with no other guest operating systems installed. However, the guest is presented with only a small section of the installed hardware. For example, a server may have 256GB of memory installed but only 4GB allocated per virtual machine.

The hypervisor is also the traffic cop for all guest VMs. Each guest will request server resources, and it is the job of the hypervisor to manage and balance these requests in a timely and efficient manner.

We like to think of the hypervisor as its own operating system with the difference being that instead of supporting applications, it supports other operating systems. It is also a bit of a magician in that it fools the guest OSs into thinking it is running on a real server when in fact it is all an illusion!

The hypervisor itself will take a minimal amount of resources from the bare-metal server to operate. Also, some of the resources in the pools will be reserved for rapid deployments of new VMs.

Type 1 Hypervisors

The primary type of hypervisor deployed in the cloud today is called a Type 1 hypervisor. A Type 1 runs directly on top of the server's hardware and does not require any external code to support it; there is no underlying operating system with a Type 1 hypervisor. It is illustrated in Figure 7.6. With the hypervisor running directly on the server, it is referred to as a *bare-metal* server. Sometimes the term *native supervisor* is used when referring to a Type 1 hypervisor. Type 1 hypervisors are the more advanced and most prevalent type used in the cloud today.

FIGURE 7.6 Type 1 hypervisor

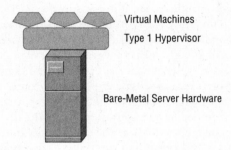

Since a Type 1 runs directly on top of the server hardware, it is more efficient and offers higher performance, higher stability, less overhead, and more security than other hypervisor designs. These advantages are obtained when the hypervisor is installed directly on top of the server hardware and does not rely on any operating system underneath it. Also, a Type 1 can interact directly with the server hardware, allowing greater control, faster response, lower processing requirements, and increased stability.

Type 2 Hypervisors

When the hypervisor is installed on top of an existing operating system as an application, it is referred to as a Type 2 hypervisor, as shown in Figure 7.7. The operating system manages all underlying hardware resources, and the Type 2 hypervisor runs as any other application and utilizes the hardware resources that are managed by the operating system. When a Type 2 is installed, there are no configuration requirements for networking, storage, memory, and processing that is required by a Type 1 since the operating system that the Type 2 is running on has that responsibility. Remember, a Type 2 hypervisor is actually an application running on a Windows or Linux device.

FIGURE 7.7 Type 2 hypervisor

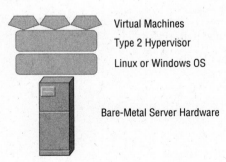

For example, if a VM running on a Type 2 hypervisor needs to make an I/O request to the server hardware, the VM would pass the request to the hypervisor running as an application on the server, and then the hypervisor would in turn pass the I/O request to the operating systems to access the hardware.

Since the Type 2 hypervisor does not have to interact with the underlying hardware, it can be installed on a wide variety of platforms with an easy installation process. All of the hardware configuration responsibilities are addressed by the operating system.

Type 2 hypervisors are commonly used for testing and validations on a laptop or personal computer and not found in a cloud data center. However, because of the requirement for a master operating system and given that a Type 2 hypervisor is essentially just another application running on the server, it is much less efficient, and there are far fewer capabilities than a Type 1 hypervisor. Therefore, Type 2 will not be found in the cloud data center; as mentioned, Type 1 is the primary hypervisor in cloud computing.

A Type 2 hypervisor is installed as an application on an already existing operating system and allows you to then install the VMs as the application. For example, a PC running Windows can install a Type 2 hypervisor and run it just as it would any other application such as a web browser or word processor. The amazing part is that inside the hypervisor application, multiple operating systems can reside as VMs.

Several Type 2 hypervisors are available on the market today including VMware Workstation from VMware and VirtualBox from Oracle. Many are open source and free for use, while others are offered at no charge for bare-bones versions with licensing available for the full-featured versions.

Type 2 hypervisors are good for locally testing operating systems, applications, or situations where dedicating a server to be virtualized is not desirable. This type of hypervisor does not offer the higher performance of a Type 1 hypervisor since the Type 2 hypervisor is running on top of another operating system but is easy to install and use.

Commercial and Open Source Hypervisors

Hypervisor product suites are offered in both the commercial and open source marketplaces, with each approach having its good and not-so-good points. Also, both Type 1 and Type 2 versions are available in the commercial and open source marketplaces.

Commercial offerings are often sold with many added features and benefits, with the hypervisor itself being only a subsystem of a larger integrated suite of virtualization products. Examples of proprietary hypervisors are *Hyper-V* developed by Microsoft and *ESXi* from VMware, as shown in Figure 7.8.

FIGURE 7.8   Commercial hypervisors

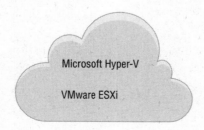

Microsoft Hyper-V

VMware ESXi

Open source hypervisors are free and readily available for download and by the public. Open source software is in the public domain, and there are no licensing fees. A good place to find open source code is at www.sourceforge.net.

Examples of open source hypervisors are *Kernel-based Virtual Machine* (*KVM*), VirtualBox from Oracle, and *XenServer* by Citrix, as shown in Figure 7.9. They are all complete virtualization systems that allow for one or more VMs to run on the same server hardware platforms as the proprietary hypervisors.

FIGURE 7.9 Open source hypervisors

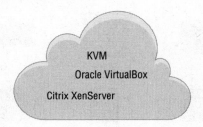

There are advantages and disadvantages to each approach. Commercially available hypervisors are fully supported by the vendor's support agreements and have regular updates for bug fixes and feature enhancements. Open source offerings rely on a community of development and support teams that offer a large feature list and are also reliable. Most public clouds are running on open source software, and as such, open source has extensively proven itself in large cloud production environments. Open source support is generally offered in community forums, with managed service companies offering support agreements.

Most cloud data centers operate on ESXi, Hyper-V, or KVM as the primary hypervisor as they are all Type 1 and offer a complete set of management utilities.

Understanding Server Virtualization

In this section, you will learn more about the virtual machines that are central to the cloud service models. *Server virtualization* refers to making a software representation of the physical hardware-based server to allow multiple operating systems, or VMs, to operate on a single server. It appears to the VMs that they are each running exclusively on their own server.

Virtual Machines

Virtual machines are basically the emulation of a real server in software; the VM will run a guest operating system such as Windows or a version of Linux with applications running on it just as in the real world. A *virtual machine* is an operating system or application environment that imitates dedicated hardware.

The VM does not run directly on the hardware platform but, rather, in the virtualized environment on the hypervisor. So, as you have learned, the VM cannot directly access the resources it needs to operate such as memory, CPU, network, storage, and so on. The hypervisor will virtualize all of these resources into pools and share them with multiple VMs operating in the environment. These include virtual CPUs, virtual RAM, a virtual hard drive or storage, a virtual storage controller, virtual network interface card, virtual video cards, and other peripherals such as the CD/DVD, USB, or even floppy drives, as shown in Figure 7.10.

FIGURE 7.10   VM resources

Snapshots

A *snapshot* is a file-based image of the current state of a VM. The snapshot will record the data on the disk, its current state, and the VM's configuration at that instant in time, as illustrated in Figure 7.11. Snapshots can be created while the VM is in operation and are used as a record of that VM's state at the time the snapshot is taken. Snapshots can be saved and used to roll back or restore the VM at a later time.

FIGURE 7.11   Virtual machine snapshot

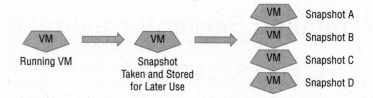

The process of taking a snapshot is usually performed in the management tools that are used to control the virtual environment.

Cloning

In addition to snapshots, there is a second type of VM replication called *cloning*, as shown in Figure 7.12. Cloning is similar to snapshots but has a different use in managing cloud deployments. With a snapshot, an exact copy is made of the running VM. Cloning, on the other hand, takes the master image and clones it to be used as another separate and independent

VM. A clone is a master reference image that is used as a template for further VM deployments. Important components of a server are changed to prevent address conflicts; these include the UUID and MAC address of the cloned server. A standardized clone image should include the operating system with all current patches and security configurations applied.

FIGURE 7.12   Virtual machine cloning

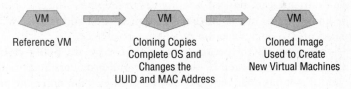

Reference VM   Cloning Copies   Cloned Image
                  Complete OS and   Used to Create
                  Changes the   New Virtual Machines
                  UUID and MAC Address

Keep in mind that snapshots are used to restore an existing machine server, and cloning is when you take a VM and duplicate it to create a new and separate VM.

Virtual Machine Migrations

When migrating your servers to the cloud, there are several options to consider.

Online migrations are "over the wire" and are preferable to offline migrations because they can be completed in a much shorter period of time. One restriction of an online migration is the amount of networking bandwidth that is available between the data center, where the existing server resides, and the cloud data center, where the new virtual machine will be migrated to. If there is insufficient bandwidth to perform the migration in a reasonable amount of time, then performing an offline migration should be your second choice.

In an *offline migration*, the virtual server is stored on storage media and shipped to the cloud provider to be installed. This requires a delay in the migration because of the transport times of the files to the remote data center. In addition, experienced staff may be required at the remote location to complete the process at the cloud provider's data center. Offline migrations are usually required if there is insufficient network capacity to upload the large amount of data sometimes required during a migration.

Once the virtual machines are operational in the cloud, additional migrations can be, and often are, performed. The Cisco Intercloud management system allows migrations of VMs between systems inside a cloud and even between clouds. Automation and control software can be configured to perform migrations based on predefined thresholds such as utilization rates, errors, and response times.

Virtual Machines and Server Virtualization Offerings

This section discusses the different types of virtualization product offerings in the marketplace. There are a large variety of both commercial and private products on the market, and the offerings seem to be expanding exponentially!

Open Source

For open source hypervisors, many vendors offer scaled-down versions of their commercial products to the community at no charge. Also, there are offerings of very complete and stable open source hypervisors and VMs that are widely used in commercial public, private, and community cloud deployments.

Many companies offer preconfigured VM images to the open source community that save a lot of time and effort to install since they are preloaded and tested. In addition, many online marketplaces offer a huge selection of VMs at no charge.

Open source hypervisors are the predominate types used in the public cloud; they have been extensively developed and tested by the largest cloud providers and private corporations in the world. Each has contributed code and utilities to enhance the products. Examples of open source hypervisors include Linux KVM, Citrix XenServer, and Oracle VirtualBox, to name just a few that are available.

Commercial Offerings

Commercial hypervisors are provided from companies such as VMware with the ESXi product line and Microsoft with its Hyper-V offering. Commercial hypervisors are available at a charge or included in a larger offering. Commercial systems are fully supported by the vendors and are undergoing constant development and improvement. These offerings are extensive, with many additional applications available to enhance the management and operations of the cloud. For example, VMware offers enhanced management, storage, networking, and cloud orchestration products in addition to its core hypervisor offerings. The advantages of commercial offerings are vendor support agreements and integration testing.

Orchestration

Orchestration systems offer management platforms to control all aspects of the cloud management and deployment operations. The Cisco Intercloud suite of products is an orchestration system that manages a hybrid cloud deployment model and is a key focus point of the Understanding Cisco Cloud Fundamentals exam and is covered throughout this exam guide. Also, many other commercial systems are offered or developed internally at cloud service providers. Orchestration systems are usually web-based for graphical user interaction and offer extensive APIs that are used for automating machine-to-machine communications between cloud server applications. These APIs include a huge array of interactions from hypervisors, switches, routers, load balancers, firewalls, storage systems, billing, reporting, monitoring, and so on.

Bare-Metal Servers

A hardware computer server platform is often referred to as a *bare-metal server*. That is, it is a piece of hardware! This is in comparison to the term *server* now being used to refer to virtualized, or software-only, servers.

Also, bare-metal servers are used to describe servers that are used, or belong to, a single tenant as compared to a multitenant server that is shared in the cloud by multiple entities. Most cloud computing service providers offer the option to reserve, or lease, a single server for a period of time such as one to three years at a fixed rate.

Server Resource Virtualization

Resource pooling is the concept of creating a group of storage, memory, processing, I/O, or other types of resources and sharing them in a virtualized cloud data center environment. The hypervisor will use what is available in these resource pools to provide infrastructure to be shared as the VMs need to consume them.

The physical or hardware resources are installed inside the bare-metal server and utilized by the hypervisor to provide resources to the installed VMs. For example, if a server has 256GB of RAM installed on its memory slots, the Type 1 hypervisor will create a memory pool from the physical memory and then allocate the memory to each VM running on the hypervisor. The VMs will assume they are accessing the memory directly and not have any idea that they are being fooled by the hypervisor!

This example also applies to other hardware resources on the bare-metal server such as CPU cores, network interfaces, storage host bus adapters, and storage arrays. There are also logical or nonhardware virtual devices running on the hypervisor such as virtual network interface cards, storage adapters, and network switches that we will discuss in this section.

Virtual Memory

Memory that is physically installed in the server will be shared by the VMs installed on it. These VMs will all need memory to operate. The hypervisor will create a pool of *virtual memory* from memory physically installed inside. This pool will then be allocated to the VMs where each VM sees the memory as if it were running directly on the bare-metal server.

The pool of RAM will be created and shared through the hypervisor to the VMs. This allows for memory to be dynamically allocated as needed and reclaimed later when the additional memory is no longer required. Virtual memory can be provisioned for growth and ordered by the cloud consumer from the cloud provider on the fly as needs dictate.

Virtual Network Interfaces

It would stand to reason that a VM running on a hypervisor in the cloud would need a method to connect to the outside world. Since there is no physical interface slot in a VM, you would use a virtual network interface card. Big surprise on that one!

Actually, the VM will use the vNIC to connect to the virtual switch that is also running in the hypervisor. This allows many VMs to connect to a single vSwitch that will in turn have only a few physical connections to the cloud data center network infrastructure.

Virtual network interface cards (vNICs) are the virtualized equivalent of a standard Ethernet LAN NIC installed in a server. The vNIC is installed on the virtual machine, and the operating system sees that as a connection to a real LAN. The vNIC in turn connects to a virtual switch running on the hypervisor.

Virtual Storage

Virtual storage is the pooling of one or more physical storage devices into what appears to be a single, logical storage device. These logical storage systems can then be allocated to virtual machines as locally attached storage, as you will learn in a later chapter.

By virtualizing the cloud storage function, storage can be dynamically allocated and relocated inside the cloud to allow for growth, elasticity, and recovery.

Virtual Switches

In a hypervisor, a *virtual switch* is a software representation of an Ethernet switch that provides the Ethernet interconnection from the VMs to the external and physical cloud data center network. The idea is that all vNICs connected to each virtual machine image are in turn connected to this virtual switch also running on the hypervisor.

The hypervisor will have one (or more) actual hardware NIC installed that is the external connection to the real world. These are usually high-speed Ethernet interfaces running 1, 10, 25, 40Gbps, or higher speeds.

In the next chapter, you will learn about virtual switches in much greater detail.

Virtual CPUs

Virtual CPUs operate under the same principles as the other server components that are virtualized and allocated to VM instances running on the hypervisor. The CPU or processing component will be virtualized by the hypervisor and will then be allocated as needed by the cloud computing consumers. CPU processing power can be elastic in that it can be created and used when additional processing power is needed and returned after the period of higher demand subsides.

Migrating Servers to the Cloud

Server migration to the cloud consists of moving servers from your private cloud to another cloud such as a community or public provider's data center. The servers will most likely need to be converted into the format used by the cloud provider, and as such, a migration will need to be performed. If you are already operating in a virtualized environment, then a virtual-to-virtual conversion will be in order. Or if the server is running directly on bare metal, then a physical-to-virtual migration is needed. Changing the format of one virtual server to that of another will be discussed.

You will also learn the processes for migrating to the cloud and what is involved in a migration project.

Understanding the Move to the Cloud

While beyond the scope of the Understanding Cisco Cloud Fundamentals exam, a successful migration to the cloud requires much research, planning, and testing. You need to make a complete inventory of all operating systems, servers, and applications that are running in the private data center. Then you need to record baselines of operations. Once you have created a complete and accurate representation of your current operations, the process of selecting and matching cloud requirements can begin. You must select virtual server instances to match the compute, graphics, memory, networking, and storage requirements of the resources being migrated to the cloud.

Depending on the cloud service model, many preconfigured virtual instances are offered by the public cloud providers or are available on the marketplaces. The public cloud providers offer storage as a separate service offering, and there are many options available to meet any requirement for the migration. The SaaS option, of course, offers a wide selection of applications available that can make for a smooth transition to the cloud.

Undertaking the Migration Project

Migrating to the cloud is not usually a trivial undertaking. As you have learned, there is much planning and research required for a successful project. The details of migration are vast, diverse, and often highly technical. As such, a migration is not in the CCNA Cloud blueprint, but we bring it to your attention here for completeness.

Most companies will require that a cloud migration be made an official project with an assigned project manager. Many of the different groups in a company, such as applications, server OS, networking, storage, finance, and others, will all need to participate in the planning and actual migration process.

Fortunately, many companies have done this, and you will find many case studies, white papers, and research available to reference to help make your project a smooth one. In fact, many of the cloud providers and consulting companies have staff available to assist in the migration.

Virtualizing the Operating System

In this section, you will learn about the process of preparing and converting the servers into virtualized resources that can be migrated to the cloud. There are many different aspects to this, and we will cover the background information needed to build a solid foundation on server virtualization and then go into detail on the different virtualization processes you will encounter as a cloud engineer.

Migration Models

There are three migration methods that can be performed when preparing an operating system to run on a hypervisor in the cloud.

- The most common is probably a server operating system that is running in a nonvirtualized environment and requires a conversion to the format needed to run in the cloud. This is known as the physical-to-virtual technique.

- If you need to migrate a virtual machine that is running on a specific vendor's hypervisor that is not compatible with the hypervisor you are planning on migrating to, you can perform a virtual-to-virtual migration.

- If everything goes wrong and there is a need to return to a server running on a bare-metal server, there is the less common but not unheard of virtual-to-physical migration.

The following sections will introduce you to these migration options. However, be aware that all of the major public cloud providers offer preconfigured and tested VMs to run on their environment that may eliminate the need to even perform a migration. Also, there are marketplaces on the Internet where companies and individuals sell or sometimes offer for free packaged VM solutions, often with the applications pre-installed and tested.

Physical-to-Virtual (P2V)

If you need to perform a migration, you have several options. P2V defines the *physical-to-virtual* migration, which includes taking a server that is running an operating system and applications directly on it in a nonvirtualized environment and then migrating it to a VM running on top of a hypervisor (see Figure 7.13). A P2V migration may require reinstalling the operating system, application, and data files onto a new VM from scratch. Many companies offer software utilities, such as VMware vCenter Converter and Microsoft Virtual Machine Manager to perform the conversion. Several third-party software companies offer fully automated P2V utilities.

FIGURE 7.13   Physical-to-virtual migration

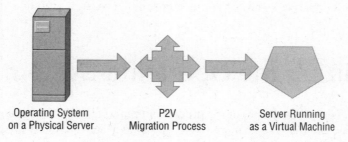

Operating System   P2V   Server Running
on a Physical Server   Migration Process   as a Virtual Machine

Virtual-to-Virtual (V2V)

Virtual-to-virtual migrations are much more straightforward than P2V migrations. Generally, a V2V migration involves cloning the existing VM and installing that image at the cloud provider's hosting center, as shown in Figure 7.14.

FIGURE 7.14 Virtual-to-virtual migration

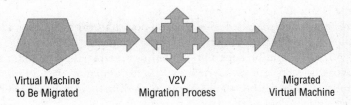

Virtual Machine to Be Migrated   V2V Migration Process   Migrated Virtual Machine

Virtual-to-Physical (V2P)

While not as common, there is an option of converting from a virtual server to a physical server, called a *virtual-to-physical* option, as shown in Figure 7.15. A use case for this type of migration is if more processing power is needed and can be provided if the server is hosted on its own server hardware or if there is a compatibility issue that requires the use of a dedicated server. Virtual-to-physical conversions have a lot of details that must be sorted through based on the hardware and virtualization software being used. It may be that a fresh installation of the operating system and application will be required. This type of migration would need to be researched and the options explored based on each migration's unique requirements.

FIGURE 7.15 Virtual-to-physical migration

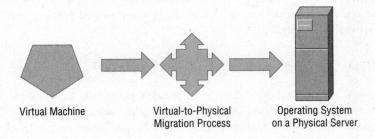

Virtual Machine   Virtual-to-Physical Migration Process   Operating System on a Physical Server

VM Resiliency in the Cloud

Modern cloud data centers are designed to be highly redundant regardless of the deployment model used. In this section, you will learn about redundancy from the cloud provider, the migrations of virtual machines, and the important concept of availability zones.

Cloud Provider Redundancy

Competition in the cloud marketplace is fierce, and given the visibility of hyperscale cloud service providers, any failure tends to be rather catastrophic and highly noticeable. Faced with widespread outages of large customers and the potential for large monetary losses for each hour of downtime, cloud provider redundancy is a critical metric for any cloud offering. Often with large e-commerce sites or large corporations that have migrated to the cloud, downtime is simply not an option.

Modern data centers are designed to withstand both natural and manmade events and remain in operation. Power systems that are directly connected to the public power grid also have local power generation capabilities; cooling systems are redundant as well as the server and network infrastructure. Carriers and cloud companies will interconnect data centers using multiple Internet peering locations with directly connected fiber optics that have diverse routes in and out of the data center.

All efforts are made to ensure that there is no single point of failure. Should there be a critical event, VMs can be quickly moved from one server platform to another or even to other cloud data centers with very little disruption of services.

Migrating Virtual Machines

Automation applications such as the Cisco Intercloud offer the ability to migrate VMs not only inside of a cloud data center but between them. This function can be automated for disaster recovery in case of an event in your primary cloud data center that causes you to have degraded or a loss of services. Cloud automation applications can quickly move the affected VMs to restore operations. Cloud dashboard applications can offer the ability for your company's cloud administration staff to invoke a migration at their own discretion. Cluster management software has features that will move VMs to underutilized servers automatically and also to shut down a VM if it is lightly used and bring it back online when an activity threshold is reached.

Availability Zones

As we covered in the chapter on cloud deployment models, many large public cloud providers segment their extensive clouds into regions around the world. Each region is isolated from the others to provide security and isolated failure domains. If one region should experience catastrophic problems, the intent is that it does not spread to other areas. Each region will have its own dedicated infrastructure for storage, networking, and compute, for example.

To further segment the failure domains, each region is often divided into smaller areas called *availability zones*. Each region will have two, or usually many more, availability zones. If one availability zone should have a failure, the VMs in the cloud can automatically resume operations in another availability zone, and often the failover is never seen outside of the cloud operations staff. When migrating to the cloud, you will often be given an option as to which region, and which availability zone inside the region, you want to install your VMs and operations in. Then, as a second option, you can define a backup availability zone to use in case the zone you are operating in should have a failure.

Summary

This chapter on virtualization is central to enabling the cloud and all the benefits offered that you have learned about. Virtualization allows multiple server operating systems to run on a single bare-metal server platform where in the past only a single operating system could run a server.

After the Introduction, you learned that virtualization enabled many benefits to cloud computing. Then the different types of hypervisors were introduced, with Type 1 being the most common cloud-based hypervisor because it runs directly on the server hardware. A Type 2 hypervisor is less efficient and capable since it relies on the underlying operating system such as Windows or Linux and runs as an application.

Commercial hypervisors include ESXi from VMware and Hyper-V from Microsoft. Examples of open source hypervisors are KVM, VirtualBox, and XenServer.

The topics of cloning, snapshots, and migrations were introduced and examined.

There are several server migration options including physical-to-virtual, virtual-to-virtual, and virtual-to-physical. Each migration type was detailed in this chapter.

A primary benefit of moving to virtual computing includes the sharing of hardware resources such as memory, CPU, network, and storage. New VMs can be created rapidly and moved from one server to another with little or no downtime. The consolidation offered by virtualization reduces the hardware requirements in the data center and saves on power and cooling expenses. You also became familiar with sharing hardware resources, network, and application isolation and the ability to consolidate hardware for use by multiple systems instead of having a hardware platform for each system running in a data center.

As you learned, virtualization is a key component in the cloud computing world, and the various aspects need to be well understood for the exam and for success in the field of cloud computing.

Exam Essentials

Know virtualization terminology and concepts.   The basic terms and concepts are important to know for the exam and are covered in this chapter. Study the benefits of virtualization and how virtualization enables cloud services.

Understand the differences between the two types of hypervisors.   Know what a hypervisor is and that a Type 1 runs directly on top of the hardware and that a Type 2 hypervisor is run as an application on another operating system.

Understand the various components that can be virtualized.   Systems, such as disks, network interface cards, CPUs, memory, Ethernet switches, and storage area networks, can all be represented as virtualized components.

Be able to answer questions regarding the process of migrating servers to the cloud.   Know that the most common is migration of a physical server to a virtual server, referred to as P2V. There is also a virtual-to-virtual (V2V) migration, and the less common process of migrating from a virtual server back to a physical server (called a V2P migration).

Understand the benefits of virtualization.   You may be tested on your understanding of the benefits of virtualization, so be able to answer questions about consolidation and the sharing of resources.

Written Lab

The following questions are designed to test your understanding of this chapter's material. You can find the answers to the questions in Appendix B. For more information on how to obtain additional questions, please see this book's introduction.

1. Name two commercial hypervisors.

   1. _____

   2. _____

2. A _____ to _____ migration allows a private cloud virtual machine to run in the public cloud.

3. Name four physical resources that become pooled virtual resources in the public cloud.

   1. _____

   2. _____

   3. _____

   4. _____

4. Cloning will change the ____ and ____ addresses on the cloned VM image.

5. The ability of a VM to move from one cloud to another is referred to as _____.

6. A ____ ____ hypervisor runs directly on top of a bare-metal server.

7. Name three open source hypervisors.

   1. _____

   2. _____

   3. _____

8. An instant-in-time image of a running virtual machine is referred to as a _____.

9. A ____ ____ hypervisor runs as an application on an existing operating system.

10. When migrating servers from your local data center to a public cloud, sometimes it is necessary to copy an image of the server and physically send it to the cloud provider for installation. This is known as a _____ migration.

Review Questions

The following questions are designed to test your understanding of this chapter's material. You can find the answers to the questions in Appendix A. For more information on how to obtain additional questions, please see this book's Introduction.

1. What best describes software that enables a server to be logically abstracted and appear to the operating system running on it as if it is running directly on the server hardware itself?

   A. Virtualization

   B. Abstraction

   C. Hypervisor

   D. SaaS

2. What kind of hypervisor runs directly on the bare-metal server?

   A. Virtualized

   B. Type 1

   C. Type 2

   D. Cloud

3. What kind of hypervisor runs as an application on top of an already installed operating system?

   A. Type 1

   B. Type 2

   C. Virtualized

   D. Cloud

4. Which two of the following are open source hypervisors?

   A. ESXi

   B. KVM

   C. Hyper-V

   D. VirtualBox

5. Cloning a server creates a reference install image for new virtual machines. Which two of the following objects need to be changed between the cloned image and the running VM? (Choose two.)

   A. BIOS

   B. UUID

   C. SAN name

   D. MAC address

6. When creating a cloned VM, name three components that should be included in the master image. (Choose three.)

    A. Operating system

    B. Service packs

    C. Security configurations

    D. Hypervisor settings

7. A virtual server image created at a specific moment in time is called what?

    A. Clone

    B. Hyper-V

    C. Snapshot

    D. Virtual replica

8. What software running in a hypervisor acts as a network interconnection between the virtual machines and the outside network?

    A. vNIC

    B. VSAN

    C. vSwitch

    D. Fibre Channel

    E. VLAN

9. What are the benefits of virtualization? (Choose the best answer.)

    A. Shared resources

    B. Rapid deployment

    C. Portability

    D. All of the above

10. What is used in place of a hardware Ethernet card in a virtual machine?

    A. VLAN

    B. Virtual switch

    C. vNIC

    D. Host bus adapter

11. Where does the hypervisor get installed?

    A. Virtual pool

    B. VM

    C. Guest operating system

    D. Computer node

12. The self-serve automated cloud is enabled by what technology?

    A. Dashboard

    B. JSON

    C. BIOS

    D. Orchestration

13. What is an example of a hypervisor control system?

    A. Orchestration

    B. SDN central

    C. vCenter

    D. Splunk

14. What migration type is used when cloning an existing virtual machine and installing it on a cloud provider's hypervisor?

    A. Type 1

    B. P2V

    C. Type 2

    D. V2V

15. When undertaking an online storage migration to the cloud, what must be taken into consideration?

    A. Application restore point

    B. WAN bandwidth

    C. Migration type

    D. Hypervisor capabilities

16. The use of a real-time migration from the private cloud to a public cloud of a VM is referred to as what?

    A. V2V

    B. Online migration

    C. Transposing

    D. vMotion

17. What hypervisor models are commonly found in the public cloud data centers? (Choose three.)

    A. ESXi

    B. VirtualBox

    C. Hyper-V

    D. KVM

    E. VMware

18. A bare-metal server contains which devices? (Choose four.)

    A. Host bus adapter

    B. RAM

    C. CPU

    D. IOS

    E. Hypervisor

    F. NIC

    G. IaaS

19. What technology enables Linux and Windows virtual machines? (Choose two.)

    A. Pooling

    B. KVM

    C. Orchestration

    D. ESXi

20. The ability to dynamically commit and reclaim resources, such as storage, memory, and CPU, is referred to as what?

    A. Elasticity

    B. Autoscaling

    C. Virtualization

    D. Dynamic allocation

    E. Resource pooling

Chapter

8

Infrastructure Virtualization

THE FOLLOWING UNDERSTANDING CISCO CLOUD FUNDAMENTALS CLDFND (210-451) EXAM OBJECTIVES ARE COVERED IN THIS CHAPTER:

This chapter covers the details of infrastructure virtualization that you'll be expected to know for the exam. We'll discuss infrastructure virtualization as it relates to both network switching and routing services. Once you understand the virtualization of networking functions, you will then learn how to integrate them with hypervisors and virtual servers. We'll also cover the details of VxLAN and some of the ways it is different from a traditional VLAN. Finally, we'll discuss some fabric options and how to join them together, a continuation of where we left off in spine leaf design from Chapter 6.

Network Switch Virtualization

In Chapter 7, we discussed virtualization and its impact on the data center. One aspect of server virtualization that deserves a lot more detail is network switch virtualization. Virtual servers running on a hypervisor have their physical components extracted for them at a higher level. Don't forget about the networking aspects between VMs and the virtual and physical worlds. Who deals with the networking functions between the VMs, adapters, and the physical world? The hypervisor, as explained in Chapter 7, is responsible for this. The hypervisor is the best choice for traffic management as it can offer centralized control, management, and security.

Virtualized switching was an obvious choice for vendors to connect multiple VMs. This would carry over the classic paradigm of layer 2 switched networks in the data center server farms that all network engineers are familiar with. The hypervisor extracts this functionality and presents a basic layer 2 software virtual switch to the hosts running on top of it. Take a look at Figure 8.1 to see this concept compared with a normal switch.

FIGURE 8.1 Virtual switch versus physical switch

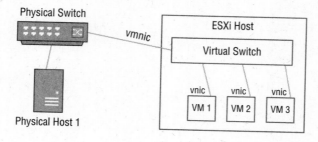

You can see that there isn't really that much of a difference in Figure 8.1. The physical hosts connect to a real switch, with its VLANs and other configurations that implement uplinks to the rest of the data center via the aggregation layer. The virtual hosts are essentially the same. It just so happens that this is all virtualized, and upstream is where you'll find the real physical switches and routers. Understand that Figure 8.1 is showing the inside virtual networking of a physical host, such as ESXi.

VMware Virtual Switching

Multiple vendors have their own version of the virtual switch, and they usually refer to it as a *vSwitch*. We'll discuss the aspects of one of the most common ones, the VMware vSwitch, but first let's discuss some of the basics that most vendors offer with virtual switching.

As previously mentioned, a vSwitch still operates as a normal layer 2 switch but in virtual form. The VLAN concept is still used for standard configuration, segmenting or sharing broadcast domains with virtual hosts. This is an important point that might get lost to those unfamiliar with virtualized switching. As with traditional switches and hosts, virtual hosts in the same VLAN can communicate freely with each other on the same IP subnet without the requirement to use a router. Extending this concept to the virtual world, you end up with traffic that never leaves the hypervisor if the VMs running on the same hypervisor share the same VLAN. Take a look at Figure 8.2 to see this concept. The VM hosts 2 and 3 for whatever reason have a private network on VLAN 50. Notice this doesn't trunk outside of the virtual switch. The physical world never sees this. These VMs can communicate freely on VLAN 50, and traffic stays in the ESXi hypervisor.

FIGURE 8.2   vSwitch traffic flow

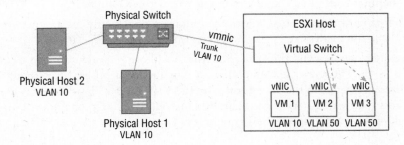

Not only can the traffic flow stay inside the hypervisor, but it can also be extended to the outside world. Nothing special is happening here; you're just using the traditional VLAN semantics of data center design and intermixing where devices are. A mixture of physical and virtual hosts on the same VLAN could aggregate through the same firewall providing a common policy for physical and virtual hosts, as shown in Figure 8.3.

FIGURE 8.3   Virtual hosts and physical

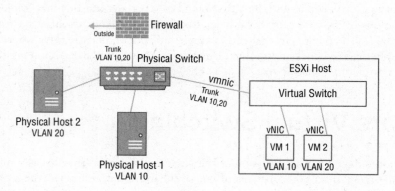

In a basic configuration of VMware ESXi, the standard switch offering is included in the application and is simply referred to as the vSwitch. The vSwitch is managed for each ESXi host on an individual basis. One large difference from the standard configuration of switches is how the ports are configured. In the virtual switch, ports aren't used in the same way the physical world would use them. VMware uses a concept called *port groups*. A port group is a set of configurations applied to ports sharing a common requirement. This is usually the VLAN identifier. VM hosts therefore connect to port groups on the virtual switch. Any VM connected to the same port group is part of the same network.

A port group defines the following for a VM:

- **VLAN ID:** The standard 802.1q tag that is used internally on the vSwitch and the connection to the outside physical world

- **Security:** Allowing MAC address changes, settings for promiscuous mode, and forged MAC addresses

- **Traffic shaping:** Outbound shaping of traffic to a defined data rate

- **NIC teaming parameters:** Load balancing options, failback options, and network failover detection methods

See Figure 8.4 to understand this concept better. VM host 1 uses port group A, and VM hosts 2 and 3 use B. The names are simplified for illustrative purposes. More than likely, the major difference between the port groups are the VLAN IDs. This concept is used to group hosts together with a similar configuration instead of trying to maintain a logical virtual switch port configuration for every single VM port.

FIGURE 8.4   vSwitch port groups

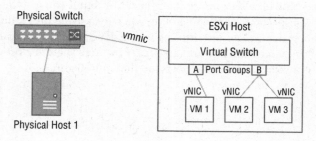

As mentioned, the standard vSwitch is managed on a host-by-host basis, and configuration consistency can be difficult to maintain. If the network requires only a few hosts, this may not be an issue. However, for larger-scale and expanding operations, operational challenges may arise. Live migration of hosts is a common use case, but to do this, the VLAN must be properly configured on both hosts. Since port groups are configured on a host-by-host basis with separate vSwitch management applications per hypervisor, this needs to be reconciled somehow. Usually scripts are used to make sure the vSwitch and port group configurations remain consistent among the various hypervisors. Figure 8.5 illustrates this concept. Each hypervisor runs its own set of VMs and a vSwitch that connects them with separate management for each. For proper operation in Figure 8.5, the network administrator and VM administrator would not only need to make sure the trunks are set up properly for every physical connection but also that each port group meant the same thing to each hypervisor. Looking at Figure 8.5, you could assume VM hosts in the same group are the same VLAN ID. This may be the case, but it needs to be configured as such across all equipment, physical and virtual.

FIGURE 8.5   vSwitch on multiple hosts

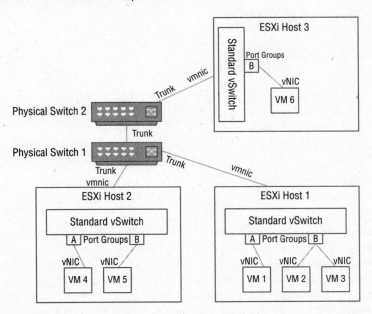

The management limitations and scalability issues of the standard vSwitch when dealing with large deployments led VMware to introduce the *distributed vSwitch (DVS)*. DVS introduced the concept of *distributed port groups*. This greatly simplified the consistency and management challenges of the single vSwitch configuration. Distributed vSwitches are managed from VMware's centralized configuration application called vCenter and not at the individual host level like standard vSwitches require. Distributed port groups are configured and replicated across the enterprise wherever a host attaches to the same DVS. This means that a change such as VLAN ID will get replicated to all distributed vSwitches. One

then no longer needs to keep manual consistency by having to configure each vSwitch individually if they deploy their port groups correctly.

The DVS also offers some advanced features that the standard vSwitch does not. One of
the main features missing in the standard vSwitch is the Link Aggregation Control Protocol
(LACP) for Etherchannel. Other DVS-specific features are Link Layer Discovery Protocol
(LLDP), private VLANs, port mirroring, NetFlow, and inbound traffic shaping. Also, new
features are added with each ESXi release, so this is not a complete list.

You are not limited to using one type of switch over the other. There can be a mixture of
both types of switches in an environment. See Figure 8.6 for more detail.

FIGURE 8.6   vSwitch and dvSwitch deployment

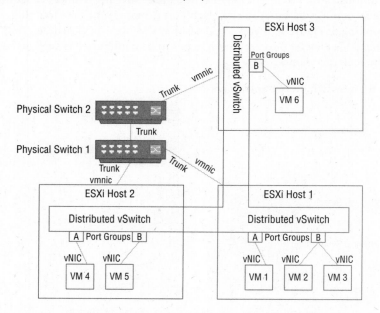

It's important to understand that the distributed vSwitch is a configuration construct and
that the switches are still confined to the hypervisor. Drawings online may make it seem like
the DVS is logically stretched between all hosts. Even Figure 8.6 looks like this. This is true
from a configuration standpoint, but if the hosts are separate, they still need to connect to a
common physical layer 2 backbone to exchange frames in the same VLAN. In Figure 8.6, all
the physical hosts would have to trunk the appropriate VLAN for port group B to function.

Now that you have learned about local and distributed virtual switches, you'll take a
closer look at the internal port names that are shared between them. The following is a list
of the internal ports of vSwitch and DVS:

- *vmnic*: This is the uplink port of the vSwitch or DVS that connects to the physical
  world. It stands for *virtual machine network interface controller*. In short, it is the
  physical adapter of the host running virtualization as it connects to a real switch or
  router upstream.

- *vnic*: This is the representation of the NIC to the virtual host running on the hypervisor. This is the NIC associated with a port group in vSwitch or distributed port group in DVS. It stands for *virtual network interface controller.*

- *vmknic*: A virtual adapter to the ESXi host kernel used for management purposes, live migrations, and IP storage access. It stands for *virtual machine kernel network interface controller.*

Figure 8.7 illustrates everything we've discussed.

FIGURE 8.7   vSwitch and dvSwitch interfaces

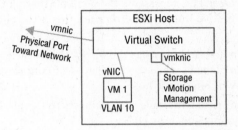

In the next section, we'll discuss the 1000v and the features it provides, but first let's address some of the issues traditional networking faced with the vSwitch architecture.

Visibility in virtual networking is one of the largest hurdles for the network support staff to overcome. Traditionally network engineers would trace locations of servers on physical switches and be able to draw and troubleshoot an entire path between all of the network devices in the data center. This concept is completely changed in the virtual world, with many of the networking functions virtualized and moved inside of the hypervisor. This creates a network visibility problem that compounds itself when the virtual hosts are entirely internal to a hypervisor. In situations such as these, no network management visibility at all is usually the result. Often, the most troubleshooting that a network administrator can do is tell whether the virtual host is up with a ping test and what physical host it's running on.

Another aspect is the actual configuration on the port, including the VLAN or QoS policies. If a virtual host doesn't ping, the next steps available could be limited based on the network administrator's access to the vSwitch infrastructure. Correct configurations of VLAN and network settings would be assumed or trusted to be right. This is similar to the visibility problem.

Depending on how the infrastructure is deployed, control and security could become a concern as well. VM admins have the ability to deploy virtual hosts into any VLAN the physical layer gives them access to. In certain circumstances, this VLAN may be a DMZ or a security-related VLAN that has special requirements for the VMs it attaches to. As long as an organization has governance around these processes, things will turn out fine. However, that still doesn't address visibility and cross-team collaboration.

Cisco Nexus 1000v

Cisco addressed the shortcomings of virtual network visibility by releasing the 1000v. The Nexus 1000v is a software-only replacement for the distributed virtual switch, as shown in Figure 8.8. Just like the DVS, the 1000v runs in the hypervisor of the VMware kernel. It uses the familiar NX-OS CLI syntax and management so network engineers acquainted with traditional Cisco Nexus products will have a small learning curve.

The items that make up the 1000v deployment are as follows:

- *Virtual Ethernet interface*: This represents the virtual Ethernet port to the host from the 1000v's perspective. Also known as *vEthernet*, this is the equivalent to the vNIC in the vSwitch or DVS.

- *Virtual Ethernet module*: Also known as the *VEM*, this is the extrapolation of the module that is the data plane for the switch. The *VEM* contains the uplinks to the physical world and downlinks to the hosts.

- *Ethernet interface*: This is the interface that connects to the physical world, which is equivalent to the vmnic in vSwitch or DVS.

- *Virtual supervisor module*: Also known as *VSM*, this is the supervisor for the 1000v and is deployed as a VM in hot/standby state. The VSM is the control plane for the 1000v, providing synchronization to vCenter and managing the Ethernet ports and modules.

FIGURE 8.8   Cisco Nexus 1000v

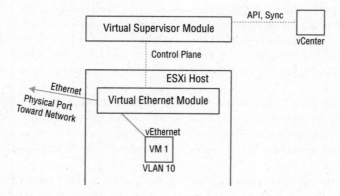

The Nexus 1000v can be thought of more like a modular chassis, much like the Nexus 7000/9000 or other Cisco chassis-based switches. The VSM serves as the supervisor, with two VSMs able to provide redundant operations. The VEM can be thought of as a modular line card. The VSM is essentially the control plane and is responsible for VEM configuration. This includes the VLANs, policies, and other functionality offered via the 1000v. The active VSM synchronizes with the standby VSM and is ready to take over in case of failure of the primary or master VSM.

It's important to note that the VSM operates as a VM and is the Nexus 1000v control plane only. The VSM should be installed redundantly by using different ESXi hosts with different upstream switches to eliminate any single point of failure. As of this writing, the VSM can support up to 64 VEMs, which make the similarities to a modular switch even more obvious.

Note that there wasn't a switch fabric module for what was discussed in this section. This is because like vSwitch and DVS, the VEM is local to each ESXi host. The VSM does indeed manage multiple VEMs on multiple hosts, but the switching fabric itself resides only on the physical network. A VM connected to a particular VLAN on one host can't talk to a VLAN on a different host in the same VLAN if the physical network doesn't support it. Look at Figure 8.9 to see this concept now that we've discussed these points.

FIGURE 8.9   Cisco Nexus 1000v fabric

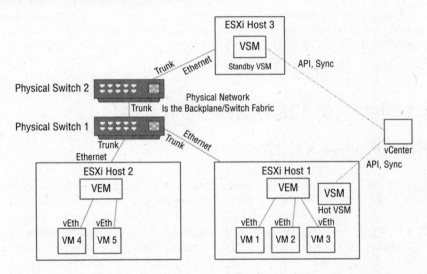

There are advanced features gained when deploying the 1000v over the DVS or vSwitch offerings from VMware. These features are listed here:

- **Cisco Discovery Protocol:** CDP is useful in the mapping of your network and seeing your neighbors, especially Cisco switches and routers. ESXi hosts support this as well, making troubleshooting easier and knowing where you're connected.

- **TrustSec:** It allows the 1000v to use security group tags from the Cisco offering to manage devices as security groups with tags. This lessens the burden on access control lists and security configurations.

- **SPAN:** It supports SPAN and ERSPAN, providing port mirroring of the vEth interfaces to an analyzer tool elsewhere in the network. SPAN helps with troubleshooting and monitoring the VMs and traffic from them.

- **QoS:** It applies quality-of-service policies to the physical NICs connecting to the external network.

- **Private VLAN:** Using the private VLAN feature, you can isolate VMs or groups of VMs in the same broadcast domain from speaking to each other. When deployed properly, it assists in east-to-west segmentation even in the same VLAN.

- **DHCP snooping/IP source guard/dynamic ARP inspection:** These security features allow DHCP server enforcement and snooping protection on the VM network.

- **VM Tracker:** It offers the ability to see the VMs running on the ESXi host. You can see not only their names but powered-on state, memory allocated, uptime, migration, vMotion logs, and much more. This feature has also been added to some of the Nexus physical switches as well.

In addition to those features, the 1000v also offers a Cisco *Virtual Switch Update Manager (VSUM)* to the server team. This lessens the burden on the server team from installing and managing the 1000v and its updates. From the vSphere web client, it enables automatic updates and installation of the 1000v with simple clicks. It also enables automatic port profile creation. The VSUM operates as a virtual appliance installed on the ESXi hypervisor.

Cisco Nexus 1100 and Virtual Network Services

We've discussed the Nexus 1000v VSM that operates as a VM in the previous sections, but it's important to know that it's also offered as a dedicated physical appliance. As of this writing, the most recent version is the Cisco 1100, with the 2100 series replacing it soon. This was briefly discussed in Chapter 6. The 1100 series manages *virtual service blades (VSBs)* using the Cisco traditional NX-OS as its operating system. There are several VSBs available for the 1100 series, including the 1000v VSM that you became familiar with in the previous section. The VEMs are still installed on the ESXi hosts; however, the VSM is simply relocated to the Nexus 1100 physical appliance that the network team controls. This sits better with some teams because the supervisor that controls and manages the 1000v switches is now under the management of the networking team. Traditional physical redundancy can be deployed, and the network support group can own the appliances that manage the virtual 1000v switches. We've mainly discussed the 1000v from a VMware perspective, but it is a multihypervisor and supports Microsoft Hyper-V, OpenStack, and KVM.

We'll now move into virtual networking services and learn about the other Cisco 1000v and virtual appliances that are offered in the cloud and the data center. *Networking services* can be defined as devices offering specialized network functions or multiple services. Generally, network services include routers, firewalls, load balancers, and WAN accelerators.

In the past, these services were all delivered as physical appliances or modules installed in appliance option slots. As virtualization in the server space grew, the network space was an easy virtualization target. The 1000v portfolio grew to release several other virtual versions beyond the switch as well as stand-alone virtual products. Before we discuss the virtual versions, let's look at how the physical versions were deployed. Some of the virtual versions borrow the same technology. Look at Figure 8.10 to see the physical deployment models.

FIGURE 8.10   Network service deployment

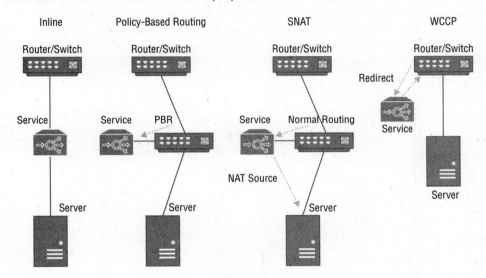

The following list isn't a comprehensive list of all options, but it is the most common physical deployments of network services. As shown in Figure 8.10, the following are often found in physical deployments:

- **Inline:** There are several ways to accomplish inline mode, the most common being *VLAN manipulation* and layer 2 bridged inline. VLAN manipulation uses different inside and outside VLANs to steer traffic appropriately.

- **Policy-based routing (PBR):** One of the most classic examples, PBR uses filtering to direct traffic via the IP source address to a different next hop, and then the routing table will normally direct the traffic. This allows traffic in either direction to be sent or returned to the appliance appropriately. PBR is often used in load balancing.

- **Source NAT (SNAT):** Instead of using PBR to direct return traffic, the appliance NATs the source address to something owned by the appliance. The routing tables then return traffic to the appliance. Source NAT is also often used in load balancer scenarios.

- **WCCP reverse proxy:** The Web Cache Control Protocol uses a protocol on the router or switch to direct traffic to an accelerator. Via defined ACLs, the switch or router can encapsulate and redirect web-based traffic to a proxy. This requires little configuration and effort on the network side and allows for a load-balanced proxy deployment without the client having to adjust their browser configuration.

To combat some of these complexities, when dealing with virtual networking, Cisco introduced *Virtual Services Data Path (vPath)*. This was briefly discussed in Chapter 4, as it is a component of the Cisco Intercloud product family. vPath deploys special port profile configurations to instantiate network service insertion.

vPath steers traffic to or from a VM to a services node via *forwarding policies*. The virtual service node can process this traffic or offload it back to vPath, which increases the performance of service delivery. vPath uses an encapsulation method to tunnel frames between VEMs. The forwarding policies are used to program the VEMs on how to do this and what particular VMs need special services beyond traditional networking. The underlying detail of how this works is beyond the scope of the test and this book, but look at Figure 8.11 to see an illustrative example. In this example, VM 4 gets redirected via vPath to a service provided elsewhere before normal routing happens. The VEM handles this redirection.

FIGURE 8.11   vPath service insertion

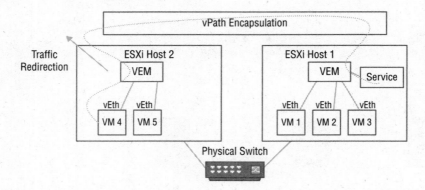

Let's look at some of the popular virtual networking appliances that Cisco offers and list their use cases and benefits. Remember that these can run as a VM in the cloud and are also available for physical deployments. Some of products also have the option to use Nexus 1100/2100 physical appliances.

The Cisco *Virtual Security Gateway (VSG)* is one of the virtual security services offered to protect virtual hosts and applications. Intercloud uses the VSG, and this topic was also briefly covered in Chapter 4. The VSG is made up of several primary components:

- **Cisco Prime Services Controller:** This is the controller responsible for programming the VSG and policies configured for servers and applications. The controller is deployed as a VM.

- **VSG:** This is the actual virtual appliance that executes the rules and enforces policy based on what is configured from the controller.

- **VSM:** This is the supervisor of the 1000v that can insert security profiles into the vEth port profiles of the VEMs running on the ESXi host. This was explained earlier with how the VEMs can be programmed with policy.

- **VM Manager:** This keeps track of the policies from VSM and pins them to the appropriate VMware NIC port.

With these parts working together, you end up with a virtual firewall that can intercept cloud traffic even if that traffic is an east-to-west traffic flow that never leaves the virtual switch in a hypervisor. The VSG receives this traffic via vPath and inspects the first packet of the flow. The security policy is acted upon and then, if able, offloaded to the VEM for the rest of the session. What this means is that traffic need not always tunnel to the VSG for policy inspection. Normal traffic may only need the first SYN and last RST to terminate the flow. The VEM maintains state and *flow tables* on what is and isn't allowed. This allows for a flexible deployment in the cloud data center.

VSG profiles also allow policies to be defined beyond just the traditional IP addresses. Policies can be defined that reference the guest OS, VM hostname, cluster name, port profile, and DNS names. *Virtual zones (vZones)* take this a step further and can aggregate the common devices into groups such as all web servers running Linux.

This was a high-level overview of the VSG, and there are obviously more intricate details involved; however, they are beyond the scope of the test and this book. Look at Figure 8.12 to see an example of east-to-west traffic policies and the flow between the components.

FIGURE 8.12   VSG and traffic flow

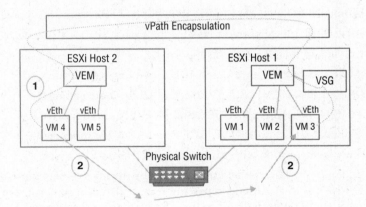

① First packet and setup through vPath to VSG

② Subsequent packets might take a normal path without vPath encapsulation.

The Cisco *Adaptive Security Virtual Appliance (ASAv)* is the classic Cisco ASA ported to a virtual machine. The VSG is more for the intracloud filtering of tenants and VM-to-VM communications. The ASAv fulfills the edge firewall role. It can, however, be used as intraclient filtering but was more designed for the edge role. It's important to note that the ASAv doesn't currently support vPath, so other technologies need to be used to get traffic there. Usually this is accomplished by setting the default gateway of the VM to the ASAv.

Briefly, these are some of the important features the ASAv offers:

- **VPN:** IPsec VPN support as well as remote-access VPN support like Cisco Anyconnect or clientless VPN users.

- **Inspection:** Deep packet inspection on certain protocols such as FTP, HTTP, DNS, and more.

- **Single-policy domain:** Since the physical ASA and virtual ASAv support the same policy constructs, the physical and virtual world can reuse these policies as hosts are provisioned or moved. This enables a single policy construct that can be applied in both scenarios, enabling rapid cloud and on-site deployment of security.

The ASAv can be managed via the standard command-line interface (CLI). Management can also be done via the Adaptive Security Device Manager (ASDM) and the Cisco Security Manager (CSM), both GUI tools. ASAv also offers a RESTful API for integration with cloud automation and monitoring systems.

The Cisco *Cloud Services Router 1000v (CSR)* is a virtual routing appliance running the IOS-XE software, the same software powering the physical ASR 1000 series. Whether in the cloud or in the enterprise data center, the CSR can be the gateway for your VM hosts. In the Cisco 1000v series products, the 1000v CSR is the product that supports the most extensive list of features. The large ones that stand out are the following:

- **IP:** Both IPv4 and IPv6 are supported.

- **OTV/VxLAN:** The CSR can run as a layer 2 extension for VxLAN and OTV. Both of these features we'll discuss shortly.

- **Routing protocols:** BGP, OSPF, EIGRP, RIP, ISIS, and PBR are all supported.

- **HSRP/VRRP:** Both are supported to enable multiple CSRs for first-hop redundancy.

- **Multicast:** PIM and IGMP are both supported.

- **VRF:** VRF lite and full VRF are supported, depending on licensing.

- **MPLS:** EoMPLS, MPLS, VPLS, L3VPNs, and L2TPv3 are supported.

- **VPN:** IPsec VPN, EasyVPN, DMVPN, and FlexVPN are supported.

- **Security:** Zone-based firewall, NAT, ACLs, and AAA are supported.

- **WCCP:** There is integration with caches and accelerators.

As you've undoubtedly guessed by now, the CSR is the Swiss Army knife of virtual routers. This list isn't even an all-encompassing feature list. Not only can the CSR be your router, but it could potentially fill in for a firewall as well. Utilizing the zone-based firewall, many requirements could be met by those who do not need the more extensive features that the ASAv or VSG provides. The CSR provides a RESTful API like the ASAv and can also be managed by the CLI and Cisco Prime Network Services Controller (PNSC).

From a cloud perspective, one of the bigger integrations is between MPLS, VxLAN, and OTV. These protocols allow extensions of the data center and bridge the gap between on-premise and cloud.

As shown in Figure 8.13, the CSR excels in cloud deployments. With the built-in tools for separation and multitenancy, choosing to implement the 1000v CSR is easy. This is not the only use case, of course, but it makes for a compelling example to highlight the capabilities of the 1000v CSR. Using the CSR for an enterprise deployment has similar benefits as well. One of them is the VxLAN or OTV extension. Using these features, the enterprise can bridge layer 2 traffic from the local on-site network to the remote cloud network across a layer 3 routed network. This may be required for scenarios where layer 2 mobility is needed between clouds for application reasons. The CSR can also be your VPN gateway in absence of the ASAv or other VPN software. See Figure 8.14 for these use cases.

FIGURE 8.13   CSR and the multitenant cloud

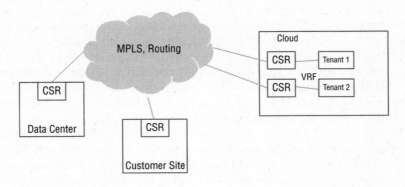

FIGURE 8.14   CSR and enterprise cloud

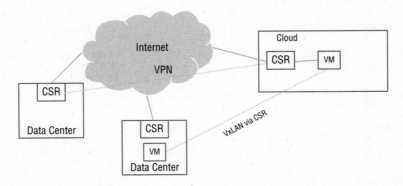

The Citrix *Netscaler 1000v* is a virtual version of the popular Citrix Netscaler line of load balancers. Using the Netscaler 1000v allows for virtual load balancers to live close to the hosts they load balance for, the VMs. The NetScaler 1000v supports the following major features and more:

- SSL offloading
- Layer 4 load balancing and layer 7 content switching
- Global server load balancing

- Application acceleration and optimization
- Application firewall and security
- URL rewrite
- TCP and SQL multiplexing

The Netscaler 1000v also supports vPath, as described earlier in this chapter. This ends up being a large bonus for the virtual version of the Netscaler, as traffic steering is an issue when return traffic is required. As shown earlier in Figure 8.10, PBR or SNAT is the traditional model to fix this problem. A load balancer in almost all use cases requires traffic in both directions to pass through it.

The problem generally occurs on the return traffic from the server. The load balancer owns the virtual IP (VIP) address that a client will connect to. The client requesting services connects here, and the load balancer, on behalf of the client, connects to the real servers in the load-balanced pool. If the load balancer changes the IP address to something the load balancer owns (SNAT), then the server replies to the load balancer. The end server never sees the original client IP address. When the load balancer receives the reply, the original client source IP is restored and sent back to the client. In some cases, this is actually a proxy request via the LB, but it is beyond the scope of this book. The underlying mechanics might be different between load balancing vendors, but the concept is the same.

If SNAT isn't used, then PBR is the next logical choice. In this case, the LB doesn't change the source address of requests to real servers. Because of this, the real server sees the real client's IP address. Replying to the real client IP will require intervention if the load balancer isn't deployed inline. This is where PBR would be deployed to intercept traffic on the way out to the client and redirect it back to the load balancer. Figure 8.15 illustrates both concepts.

FIGURE 8.15 Traditional load balancing return

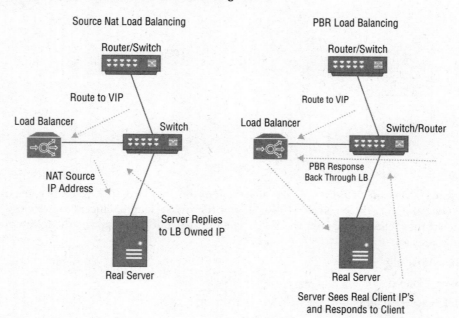

The Netscaler 1000v can use vPath to bypass the previous scenarios and simply steer traffic from the VEMs to the Netscaler 1000v. This completely eliminates the need for PBR or SNAT. The bonus to server owners is that they are seeing the real client's IP address and not the IP address of the load balancer. The VEMs keep a table of this information and know when to switch traffic back to the Netscaler 1000v for return traffic from the servers to the client. See Figure 8.16 for this example. In this illustration, traffic arrives destined to a load balancer VIP owned by the NetScaler 1000v. The VEM sees this and knows it should encapsulate this traffic in vPath and redirect it to the NetScaler 1000v. The NetScaler 1000v can then route normally to the real server or, in this case, VM 3. Return traffic is subjected to the same policy, and it returns through the Netscaler 1000v via vPath.

FIGURE 8.16 Netscaler 1000v and vPath

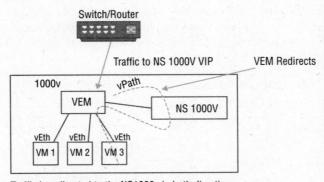

Traffic is redirected to the NS1000v in both directions.
Return traffic from the VM follows vPath back to NS1000v.

The Cisco *Virtual Wide Area Application Services (vWAAS)* is a virtual version of the Cisco WAN acceleration platform, WAAS. WAN accelerators largely function the same and offer the following features:

- **Compression:** This works in conjunction with deduplication and implements standards-based compression to compress the amount of data in a TCP flow.

- **Deduplication:** You identify and remove redundant data patterns with a marker or signature. Instead of sending large patterns, signatures can be used to represent them that are smaller in data size.

- **Application optimization:** There are specific application optimization features for things such as NFS, CIFS, SMB, HTTP, and more.

- **TCP proxy and optimization:** Perhaps the largest feature, the appliance or virtual appliance proxies connections on the client's behalf. This ends up fooling the client nearest to the proxy because the response time is much greater on the LAN than the WAN. The client then sends data faster, as it believes the end server is closer. The acceleration appliance uses a combination of the previous features to keep data moving fast.

The deployment of vWAAS is supported via traditional methods such as on the network edge inline and WCCP from a router. One of the bigger benefits, though, is the vPath integration. Like the Netscaler 1000v, the vWAAS can use vPath to steer traffic accordingly. When traffic can't be accelerated or there isn't an acceleration device on both ends of the connection, vWAAS can tell the VEM to bypass for that flow or host. This allows for more efficient deployments without having to deal with inline, PBR, or WCCP.

Now that we've discussed the virtual appliances Cisco can provide along with vPath, you will take a quick look at *vPath Service Chains* in the 1000v. Let's look at an easy example that puts all of this together. As you read, vPath can program the VEM to intercept and redirect traffic to the virtual appliance. The service chain can actually take that a step further, and traffic can loop through each virtual appliance on the way to the host. Again, the encapsulation and low-level details are beyond the scope of the test, but you need an understanding of how it works. Look at Figure 8.17 to see an example.

FIGURE 8.17   vPath service chains

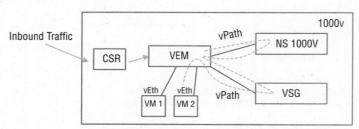

Traffic is redirected to the NS1000v, then to the VSG for policy.
If the VSG allows the traffic, then traffic continues to the real VM.

Looking at the diagram, you can see the path involved. Traffic is routed to the CSR 1000v, which then routes traffic to the Netscaler 1000v VIP, which then sends traffic to the VSG and finally to the host. This is the service chain and how the VEM programs traffic in and out of the appliances. Remember that in vPath, some of these decisions can be offloaded as well. For example, the VSG may only need to see the initial traffic flow at first packet, depending on protocol. This helps accelerate traffic when not all packets need to flow through the virtual appliance. Return traffic is redirected to the appropriate appliances. If a VM migrates via VMotion or moves to another physical server, the service chain moves with it. This enables a programmable insertion policy that scales.

What happens if a virtual appliance fails? The Nexus 1000v VSM can detect this with keepalives and take appropriate actions. There are two actions that can be taken when an appliance is deemed failed. vPath can decide to fail open, which behaves as if the virtual appliance is removed from the chain. This means that all subsequent packets will flow through the chain but avoid the failed appliance. This could be a massive security issue depending on your scenario but could also be exactly what you want. A good example of this is acceleration. You may not want the service chain to stop entirely just because the accelerator has dropped out, so a failed open scenario is desirable. However, that case might be entirely different should a VSG security appliance fail. In that case, you'd likely want a fail closed approach, which is the next supported option. In the VSG failure, the vPath chain will stop working until it's repaired.

Cisco Virtual Application Containers

Cisco *Virtual Application Container Services (VACS)* is a technology by Cisco for the rapid provisioning of custom containers. A container in this case is a group of virtual appliances like the CSR, VSG, and other services discussed in this chapter. The Cisco solution uses a few main components to spin up containers.

- **UCS Director:** This is the orchestration for the container solution as a whole, providing the frontend GUI to deploy and monitor the solution.

- **CSR 1000v:** This is the router of the container, providing the routing services in and out of it.

- **Nexus 1000v:** This is the switch of the container. A single 1000v instance can manage multiple containers implementing VEM switching.

- **VSG:** The virtual service gateway provides the security and segmentation policies within the container.

- **Prime Controller (PNSC):** This defines and monitors the policies within the containers. A single PNSC instance can span multiple containers and manage the policies.

VACS uses *virtual application container templates* for rapid provisioning of similar containers. These containers are isolated with their own components using VLAN or VxLAN and the virtual components attached to them. A VM manager is used to spin up the VMs. See an example of this in Figure 8.18. Ultimately, UCS Director gets information via an administrator or API call from another orchestration tool to turn up a new container. The next steps could be based on templates, which we'll discuss shortly. VMs can be spun up in response as well as the 1000v stitching together vPath-enabled services within the container itself.

FIGURE 8.18   VACS and containers

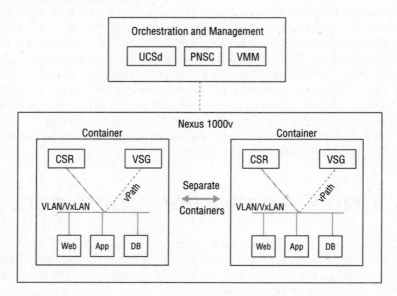

VACS provides three distinct container templates revolving around the tiered setup. Based on template, certain rules and policies are already applied and ready to go. The templates are as follows:

- *Three-tier internal template*: This is where external networks can only access the first web tier of the container network.

- *Three-tier external template*: This is where external networks can only access any of the internal container networks.

- *Three-tier custom template*: This enables you to design your own container without restriction on tier, zones, networks, or application types. You can choose the services and policies attached and then reuse it again and again for automated provisioning.

The templates require configurable pools for VLAN and IP assignment to make sure each container has unique assignments. Briefly, these are as follows:

- *Static IP pool*: This is anything in the container that would be used for uplink, management, and VM networks.

- *IP subnet pool*: This is a large supernet with the number of subnets specified that can be created from it.

- *VLAN/VxLAN pool*: These pools contain the VLAN or VxLAN ranges that can be used for instantiating new networks.

EIGRP is used as the default routing protocol for the container templates, but you have the option to use static IP addressing as well. As you can see, VACS offers multiple options including your own for orchestrating rapid deployment of virtual services in containers.

VLANs and VxLAN

We've discussed VLANs and VxLAN but have yet to contrast the two and explain VxLAN in detail. *Virtual eXtensible LAN (VxLAN)* received its start around 2010 with an Internet Engineering Task Force (IETF) draft proposal. Cisco, VMware, Arista, Brocade, and many others contributed to the initial drafts and ideas behind VxLAN. There are several short-comings with VLANs that led to the creation of VxLAN. We'll briefly discuss these and then move on to VxLAN and the problems it solves.

One of the shortcomings of VLAN-based networks is the difficulty in scaling them beyond local areas. Before virtualization kicked in, a lot of networks defined layer 3 (routing) boundaries as close to the access layer as possible. This made VLAN scalability easy, as the VLAN significance remained local. A network administrator could reuse VLAN 100 in two different places with two entirely different subnets. This worked well until VLANs needed to scale and move beyond the access layer to achieve mobility. Then, virtualization came along and demanded machine mobility while keeping the network subnet information the same. Figure 8.19 shows a good example of this. In this example, the aggregation layer trunks VLAN 10 through to both sides of the access layer. These access layer switches might be on different floors or different parts of the data center. VLAN 20 is not trunked through, and the ID is even reused elsewhere. This leads to problems later in network planning.

FIGURE 8.19 VLANs and local vs. stretched

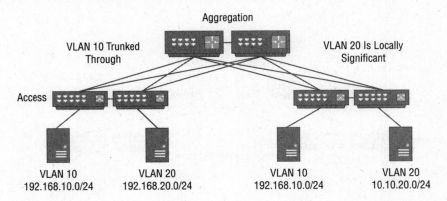

This stretching of the VLAN domain led to another problem, mainly configuration of trunks and equipment throughout the data center. Figure 8.19 shows only a few aggregation switches in the stretch design, but imagine that the network had 20 more switches. Stretching VLAN 10 in the illustration means that every switch requires a layer 2 switch trunk with that VLAN allowed. If there's one break in the chain, nothing works. This is cumbersome and annoying to network administrators as well as the server administrators. There are ways to combat this, but none of them is foolproof. You could predefine your configurations on all switches in the hope that nothing new ever gets added. Or, you could also simply allow all VLANs to transit your network aggregation trunks. This seems like an easy fix, but any network engineer would deem that unwise. Blindly allowing any VLAN to transit the network is asking for security issues, unwanted broadcast traffic, and more issues.

MAC address exhaustion is also a cause for concern in large stretched VLAN domains. Every switch that must carry the VLAN will learn the MAC addresses that pertain to that VLAN. Not all switches have large content addressable memory tables to store a large number of MAC addresses that are common in large cloud data centers. This means that all your switches must have roughly the same limits for memory and table size to address that need. Carry this over to cloud providers, and the problem multiplies far faster. See Figure 8.20 for an illustrated example. Notice that every switch learns all MAC addresses in VLAN 10. In one case, the upper-right switches don't even have a host in VLAN 10. But because the VLAN is stretched and trunked, the switch hears broadcast frames and learns MAC addresses.

FIGURE 8.20   VLANs stretched and MAC exhaustion

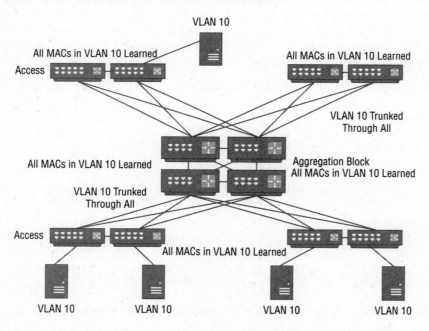

We're not done beating up on traditional VLANs yet! We mentioned the scaling issue and that it becomes apparent with cloud providers. You also need to contend with the issue that the VLAN identifier allows only 4,094 total VLANs. In addition, some vendors reserve VLANs for specific internal purposes. You may not be able to use all 4,094. Even if the number were 4,000, imagine the cloud provider scale. If a provider of cloud services used traditional VLANs, how would their network be scoped? They obviously have more than 4,000 customers. You could build their model with local significance like we discussed earlier, but this also creates growth problems. VLANs that are scoped locally have no mobility outside of their area. This would simply mean that subnets stay attached to certain physical hardware in certain physical areas that can never move. This obviously wouldn't work for most cloud customers.

While the test doesn't specifically cover it in detail, it's worth calling out that the Spanning Tree Protocol (STP) is one of the most well-known shortcomings and aggravations of large layer 2 networks. STP prevents layer 2 loops in bridged networks by blocking redundant path ports, making load balancing impractical if not very hard in large layer 2 domains.

VxLAN radically changes the way VLANs transit a network. VxLAN is an encapsulation method. It takes an Ethernet frame and encapsulates it in an IP packet using UDP as its transport. Another name for this is MAC in IP encapsulation (some call it MAC in UDP) because the layer 2 frame is untouched and wrapped in a normal IP/UDP packet.

Let's start addressing some of those shortcomings with traditional VLANs. Figure 8.21 shows a sample format of what VxLAN looks like from a header level. An original Ethernet frame is wrapped in a UDP packet that is wrapped in IP. This is where the MAC in UDP we just discussed comes from. You'll also notice the VxLAN header is 8 bytes or 64 bits. The *VxLAN Network Identifier (VNI)* uses 24 bits of that header. The VNI is synonymous with the traditional VLAN identifier discussed. In the VxLAN case, however, the VNI scales to more than 16 million segments. These are private segments too. Show us a cloud provider that doesn't want 16 million segments belonging to millions of customers! The traditional VLAN ID maps to the VxLAN ID. For ease of use, some networks map similar numbers to a higher numerical number in VxLAN. You'll see it in Figure 8.22. In this case, VLAN 200 maps to VxLAN 2000 for ease of identification.

FIGURE 8.21   VxLAN header

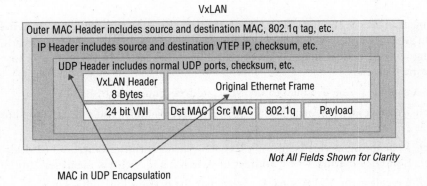

So, how do you scale and move these subnets around? VxLAN introduces a concept of a *VxLAN Tunnel Endpoint (VTEP)*. A VTEP is any device that can process VxLAN packets. This includes encapsulating them for routing or bridging or removing the encapsulation to natively route or bridge. When a VTEP receives a packet that is destined to a local host, it removes all the fancy encapsulation and the original frame is left. The VTEP then switches this normally. From a host or network perspective, the original frame is simply standard Ethernet again. Figure 8.22 shows an example with physical switches and physical hosts so you can see VTEPs and VxLAN in action.

FIGURE 8.22 VxLAN forwarding

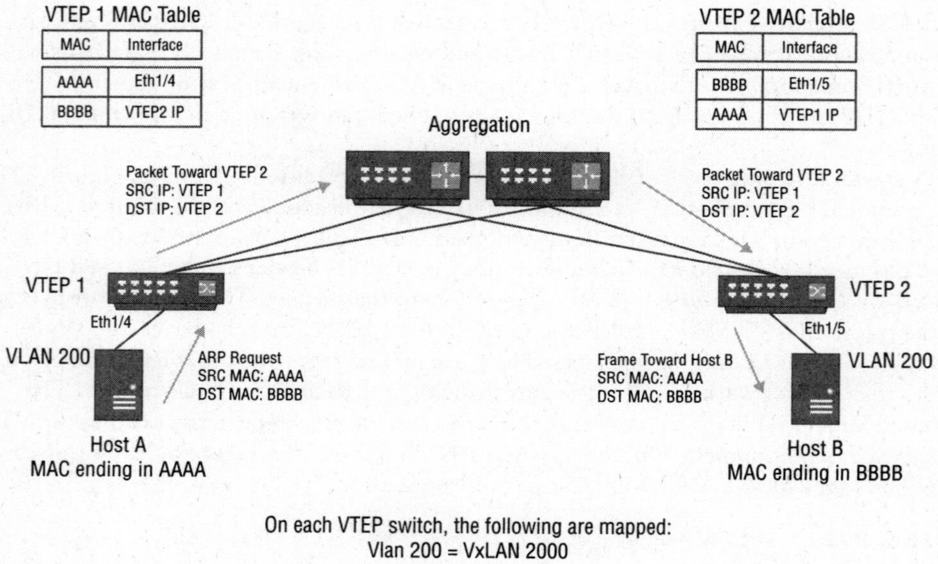

Looking at Figure 8.22, you can see a few things. There are two aggregation switches separating switch 1 and switch 2. Let's assume for this example that ARP has already taken place along with MAC learning. We'll cover that next. If host A sends a frame to host B, the following happens:

- Host A sends a frame destined to the MAC address ending in BBBB.

- Switch 1 receives this frame, checks the MAC address table, and sees the next hop is switch 2.

- Switch 1 encapsulates this frame in a VxLAN packet with the source VTEP address of switch 1 and destination VTEP address of switch 2 and VxLAN identifier 2000.

- Switch 2 receives the VxLAN packet, sees that the destination address is itself, and begins to process the packet.

- The VxLAN identifier is checked along with the destination MAC address, encapsulation is removed, and it is forwarded out the proper port where host B is connected.

Did you notice that the MAC address table had a next hop of an IP address? This is different from traditional bridging. The MAC address table usually points to a physical port. In the VxLAN case, the MAC address table may point to a remote VTEP address where traffic needs to be tunneled. Also, another interesting item here is the separation between switch 1 and switch 2. The aggregation switches need only know how to reach the VTEP IP addresses of switch 1 and switch 2. Remember, VxLAN is still IP. Any switch not running VxLAN can still forward traffic between VTEP source and destinations. All the aggregation switches see is a normal IP packet with a source and destination IP address. This helps solve the MAC address exhaustion discussed earlier. The aggregation switches will not learn any of the MAC addresses in this case, as they are just routing packets between VTEP IP addresses. The aggregation switches only know how to route to those IP addresses.

Let's shift and discuss learning and traditional VxLAN with multicast. Traditional VLAN forwarding using broadcast domains with spanning tree blocking loops along redundant paths. A broadcast frame is flooded everywhere in a traditional layer 2 domain, and the mechanics of that need to carry over to VxLAN. Since VxLAN is routed and not traditionally bridged, how do we get a broadcast frame like an ARP packet everywhere? VTEPs do this with multicast. Each VTEP maps a VxLAN to a multicast address to deal with Broadcast, Unknown Unicast, and Multicast (BUM) traffic. Let's focus on the underlying mechanics of broadcast. This time we'll start from the beginning. In this case, nothing has happened, no host knows about the other, and all VTEP MAC address tables are clear. For this example, see Figure 8.23. The following information is known:

FIGURE 8.23   VxLAN learning, ARP request

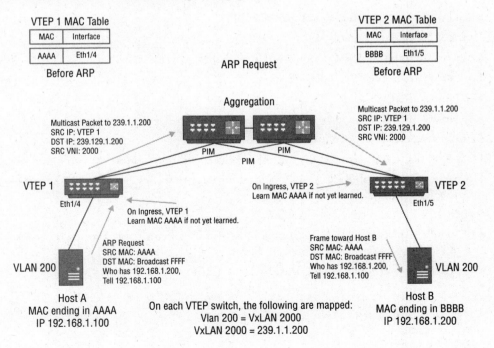

FIGURE 8.24 VxLAN learning, ARP response

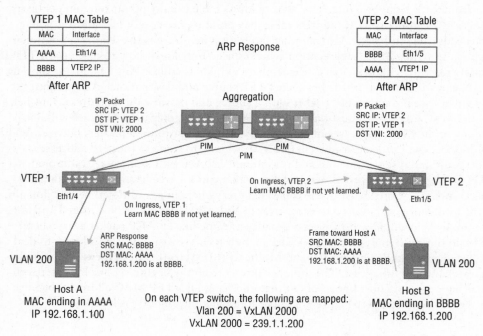

- Each host is in VLAN 200 and VxLAN 2000.
- VxLAN 2000 maps to multicast address 239.1.1.200.
  - This is configured and mapped on the switches.
- Both hosts are in the 192.168.1.x/24 range.
  - Host A is .100.
  - Host B is .200.

The following events happen in Figures 8.23 and 8.24:

- Host A wants to locate the MAC address for the IP address of Host B to communicate.
- Host A sends out a standard ARP broadcast message that says "Who has IP address 192.168.1.200? Tell 192.168.1.100."
- Switch 1 (VTEP 1) receives this frame.
  - Switch 1 learns the MAC address of Host A if it hadn't already learned it because of Host A generating the broadcast frame.
  - Switch 1 floods out the broadcast to 239.1.1.200.

- Switch 2 (VTEP 2), having joined the multicast group 239.1.1.200, receives this packet.
  - Switch 2 (VTEP 2) learns that Host A can be reached via switch 1 (VTEP 1) by inspecting the source VTEP address of the packet and removing the encapsulation to see the inner IP information.
  - Switch 2 forwards the broadcast frame to any member of VxLAN 2000 locally, in this case VLAN 200.
- Host B receives this frame and replies with a unicast response to the MAC address of Host A with the ARP reply information.
- Switch 2 (VTEP 2) receives this reply and learns the MAC address of host B if it had not done so already via other means.
- Switch 2 (VTEP 2) already knows the MAC address of host A, so it will now encapsulate the reply in a VxLAN packet destined for the VTEP address of switch 1 where host A's MAC address resides.
- Switch 1 (VTEP 1) receives this reply and learns the MAC address of Host B can be reached via Switch 2 (VTEP 2).
- Switch 1 removes the encapsulation and forwards the response to Host 1.

While we didn't dive into the underlying mechanics of multicast domains, the concept of forwarding should be easy to see here. This is all routed traffic between the VTEPs, leaving spanning tree behind. One concept that we didn't cover is the concept of local significance in VLANs. This is highly effective for cloud providers. Referring to the previous example, let's assume switch 1 and switch 2 are in different data centers for a cloud provider. Now knowing that, let's also assume that VLAN 200 is taken up on switch 1 but not on switch 2. For the cloud provider, VLAN 200 might be a different customer on each switch. This is where VxLAN can save the day. The mapping is the most important key here. We'll still map each VLAN to the correct VxLAN and multicast group, and we'll be fine. The following could happen:

- Switch 1 (VTEP 1) has VLAN 200 available, and it maps VLAN 200 to VxLAN 2000 and multicast group 239.129.1.200.
- Switch 2 (VTEP 2) has VLAN 500 available, and it maps VLAN 500 to VxLAN 2000 and multicast group 239.129.1.200.

Nothing changes from the previous examples save the local VLAN number. The significance in VxLAN is the unique VxLAN ID. Each switch respects the mapping when encapsulating or removing the encapsulation. This helps cloud providers significantly, as there are more than 16 million VxLAN IDs. This solves the VLAN ID starvation aspect we discussed earlier.

The previous examples all work for the virtual environment as well. The 1000v was one of the first devices to support functioning as a VTEP. The underlying mechanics are identical. The previous examples also only discussed layer 2 forwarding. Indeed, layer 3 forwarding exists, but its details are beyond the scope of the initial test and this book.

A *VxLAN gateway* is a device that can connect traditional VLANs to VxLAN. This device can be physical or virtual. All our previous examples were physical. The gateway can also function as a layer 2 or layer 3 gateway. In the layer 3 model, the destination frame might be a different VxLAN identifier than the source that generated the request. This is the same concept as inter-VLAN routing on Cisco routers and switches. There is a lot more behind the scenes; look at Cisco's site or search out the forwarding models of layer 3 VxLAN, which are beyond this book. The Nexus 1000v, 5600, 7000, 9000, CSR 1000v, and ASAv are just some of the products that support VxLAN forwarding. More are added and updated each day; this list may not be all of them as of this book's writing.

There are other control models besides multicast VxLAN, mainly *Unicast VxLAN* and *VxLAN EVPN*. There are proprietary vendor models as well, but they are not covered in this book. As of this writing, EVPN is gaining traction as the more popular way to deploy VxLAN with a standards-based control plane. Unicast VxLAN replaces multicast with head-end replication. What happens here is each VTEP keeps a list of all other VTEPs belonging to the same VxLAN identifier. When a broadcast frame needs to go out, the VTEP makes a duplicate copy and forwards to each VTEP on the list. This is less efficient than multicast, but it works. The replication is the job of the first VTEP that receives the packet to be broadcasted and, hence, the name head end replication.

The Cisco 1000v takes this a step further and gives the option of deploying VxLAN as *Enhanced VxLAN*. This is very like the head end replication, but it only does that as a last resort. The VSM of the 1000v learns when hosts come online and distributes the MAC addresses to all active VTEPs. This drastically cuts down on the unknown unicast floods as the VSM learns where MAC addresses are via the 1000v VEMs as virtual hosts come online.

A pitfall of the 1000v method is that the learning only occurs for the 1000v hosts and the VEMs that it controls. Combine it with any standard vSwitch or physical host, and the mappings aren't there for those segments. Vendors have been headed toward the EVPN method. Most major switch vendors support it. It is an open standard and not proprietary.

EVPN uses Multiprotocol BGP as its controller, or control plane. While the technical details in full are not covered by the exam, we'll briefly discuss how this works. EVPN uses a data plane learning method when hosts come online to generate an MP-BGP update to other hosts in the BGP domain. What this means is that BGP in this case carries the IP to MAC mappings of all hosts in the domain. BGP distributes these mappings as host routes with a MAC address and a next-hop VTEP address. This almost eliminates flooding and unknown MAC addresses as the domain knows about every single host attached to the network. Hosts come online, and BGP immediately floods out a host route for the VM or physical host. A lot of these networks are deployed in the spine and leaf method where the spine switches are route reflectors to all leaf switches. In this deployment, the leaf switches can run VxLAN locally and MP-BGP with the spine switches. The loopback reachability can be any other IGP protocol. See Figure 8.25 for a better look.

FIGURE 8.25 VxLAN and EVPN

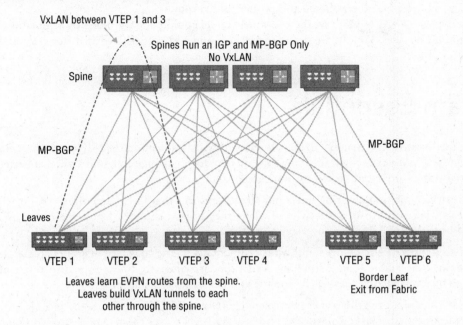

VxLAN between VTEP 1 and 3

Spines Run an IGP and MP-BGP Only
No VxLAN

Spine

MP-BGP

MP-BGP

Leaves

VTEP 1   VTEP 2   VTEP 3   VTEP 4   VTEP 5   VTEP 6

Leaves learn EVPN routes from the spine.
Leaves build VxLAN tunnels to each
other through the spine.

Border Leaf
Exit from Fabric

What's happening here is the leaf switches are access switches connected to servers. They could be virtual or physical. These switches run VxLAN like in previous examples. The aggregation layer is the spine, and its sole job is to reflect EVPN routes throughout the domain and route traffic from VTEP to VTEP. The spine is learning these EVPN routes from the leaf switches. The spine is in place to aggregate all the VTEPs together and rapidly move traffic between them.

In this case, VTEP 1 can communicate with VTEP 3 just like in previous examples, but its tables were likely populated via EVPN. Once a VTEP learns of a local host, a BGP host route is triggered and sent upstream so the network can learn where hosts are. This model scales well and as of this writing is getting a lot of attention as a scalable VxLAN fabric.

Summary

This chapter covered a large range of topics. We initially discussed the difference between virtual switching and physical switching. We then went over the different types of virtual switches offered by VMware. We discussed the Nexus1000v and its use in the multihypervisor VM world. The inner workings of the 1000v were discussed, and we covered some of the extra features it provides.

We then covered some of the virtual networking services provided by Cisco in the cloud and on-premise at the data center. The 1000v line was discussed along with the security products Netscaler 1000v and vWAAS. We covered how vPATH works with the virtual services to program service chains and proper return routes.

We discussed VACS and how the container model could be used to deploy segmentation and spin up services. Finally, we discussed VLAN and VxLAN with their differences and problems alike.

Exam Essentials

Know the features and benefits of the Nexus 1000v.   Understand the differences between the standard VMware switch offerings. Know why the distributed virtual switch is better than the standard virtual switch in some scenarios.

Be able to explain and describe the cloud virtual services that Cisco can offer.   Know the differences between ASAv and VSG and where they fit in the model. Know the feature sets of 1000v, CSR, vWAAS, and the Netscaler 1000v.

Understand how vPATH works and what problem it's trying to solve.   vPATH creates service chains that enable service stitching across the virtual environment by redirecting traffic through multiple virtual services before the end device is reached.

Be ready to explain the differences between VLAN and VxLAN.   Know the pitfalls of VLAN in traditional layer 2 networks and how VxLAN solves them. Make sure you understand the replication model of VxLAN in multicast or unicast mode.

Written Lab

Fill in the blanks for the questions provided in the written lab. You can find the answers to the written labs in Appendix B.

1.   Which term is used to describe devices offering specialized network functions or multiple services?

2.   _____ _____ _____ uses filtering to direct traffic via the IP source address to a different next hop, and then the routing table will normally direct the traffic.

3.   Virtual networking containers that use Cisco VSG and other virtual appliances can be rapidly deployed using the Cisco _____ _____ _____ _____.

4.   _____ _____ _____ is the control plane of the Cisco 1000v providing management and control to the virtual Ethernet modules.

5.   The identifier used in VxLAN that serves to identify the segment is called _____ _____ _____, or ____ for short.

6. The _____ is the name used to describe the virtual device that connects VMs with port groups in VMware.

7. _____ _____ _____ _____ _____ is used by the server team to lessen the burden on installing and managing multiple 1000v instances.

8. Virtual devices offered on the physical Cisco 1100 cloud series platform are also referred to as _____ _____ _____.

9. Multiprotocol BGP combined with the _____ address family is gaining popularity for building VxLAN fabrics.

10. The term _____ _____ is used for any device that can bridge and route traditional VLANs and VxLAN. This device can be physical or virtual.

Review Questions

The following questions are designed to test your understanding of this chapter's material. You can find the answers to the questions in Appendix A. For more information on how to obtain additional questions, please see this book's Introduction.

1. How many VxLAN identifiers can be used in one network?

   A. 16,000

   B. 1,024

   C. 4,096

   D. More than 16,000,000

2. What Cisco-developed protocol steers traffic to or from a VM to a services node via forwarding policies?

   A. WCCP

   B. vPath

   C. LACP

   D. VSG

3. Enhanced VxLAN refers to:

   A. An extension of the VxLAN standard

   B. A specialized configuration for EVPN

   C. A 1000v option for using VxLAN

   D. A CSR tunnel from the cloud to data center

4. EVPN is an extension to:

   A. VxLAN

   B. BGP

   C. OSPF

   D. ISIS

5. Which virtual switch offerings consolidate the configuration into a central site? (Choose two.)

   A. ESXi

   B. VMware DVS

   C. VCenter

   D. Nexus 1000v

6. Virtual switching is implemented where?

   A. Distribution

   B. Hypervisor

   C. Virtual machine

   D. Aggregation

   E. SaaS

7. What virtual switch components connect multiple VMs together?

   A. VSM

   B. CSR

   C. VEM

   D. LACP

8. Virtual switching supports which of the following features? (Choose three.)

   A. Layer 2 VM connectivity

   B. 802.1q

   C. LACP

   D. OSPF

   E. DNS server

9. Which of the following is not a Nexus 1000v feature?

   A. TrustSec

   B. CDP

   C. QOS

   D. BGP

   E. VM Tracker

   F. Private VLANs

10. Intercloud uses which virtual networking service to protect virtual hosts and applications?

   A. vWAAS

   B. CSR

   C. VSG

   D. MDS

11. Which virtual networking server supports IPv4 and IPv6 routing, VRRP, MPLS, and OTV/VxLAN operations?

   A. Netscaler 1000v

   B. CSR

   C. VSG

   D. ASAv

12. Which virtual networking server supports SSL offloading and content switching?

    A. Netscaler 1000v

    B. CSS 1000v

    C. VMware distributed vSwitch

    D. ASAv

13. vPath Service chains enable what feature?

    A. Custom VSG rules

    B. Service stitching

    C. Special CSR NAT services

    D. vWAAS deduplication

14. SNAT is used to solve what problem?

    A. Incorrect firewall rules

    B. VxLAN forwarding policies

    C. Properly return traffic to an appliance

    D. Correctly forward traffic to the right destination

15. Which protocol does the CSR support? (Choose all that apply.)

    A. OTV

    B. VxLAN

    C. IPsec

    D. DMVPN

16. VM Tracker enables what capability?

    A. LLDP between ESXi and network gear

    B. ARP snooping to monitor VM movements

    C. Connection to vCenter to monitor VM information

    D. VM allocation limits and tracking

17. A benefit of the 1000v over vSwitch could be:

    A. LLDP

    B. BGP

    C. OSPF

    D. SPAN

18. On the Nexus 1000v, the Ethernet interface connects to the what?

  A. VM

  B. Physical switch port

  C. VEM

  D. Hypervisor

19. The vmknic in the VMware switch does what? (Choose the best answer.)

  A. Ensures the VM is in the right policy group

  B. Is the virtual adapter for management purposes

  C. Is the uplink port to the physical switch

  D. Is the virtual adapter that takes care of IP groupings

20. What purpose does a port group serve in VMware?

  A. Allows VM to boot their proper OS

  B. Configures the VM security policies for separation

  C. Groups configurations together to apply to a group of VMs

  D. Applies individual interface configurations to a group of VMs

Chapter

9

Cloud Storage

THE FOLLOWING UNDERSTANDING CISCO CLOUD FUNDAMENTALS CLDFND (210-451) EXAM OBJECTIVES ARE COVERED IN THIS CHAPTER:

✓ **5.1 Describe storage provisioning concepts**

- 5.1.a Thick

- 5.1.b Thin

- 5.1.c RAID

- 5.1.d Disk pools

Introduction to Cloud Storage

It would be an understatement to say that data storage in the cloud is an extremely important topic not only for the Understanding Cisco Cloud Fundamentals exam but also when working with cloud deployments. While it seems like there are an unlimited number of storage options available from cloud service providers, if you have clarity on the basic storage terms and concepts, it will make the storage offerings much easier to understand.

We have discussed storage throughout this book. In this chapter, you will learn about the types of drives, storage hardware, interfaces, redundancy options, the concept of tiers, and what storage provisioning options exist in the cloud. You will also learn about many of the most common file systems found in the cloud today. This chapter is all about understanding and provisioning basic storage systems. In the following chapter, we will cover the topic of storage area networking in great detail.

You will learn about the differences between the direct-attached and networked storage options. Once you have that down, we will introduce the differences between file- and block-level access. All storage systems require a file system to operate, so we will explain what a file system is and then present the most common file systems found in the public cloud.

Since there are varied requirements and use cases for storage, we will cover the concept of tiering to allow you to understand the different ways that storage is deployed in both cloud and enterprise data centers. Next up, you will see how storage is deployed in the public cloud by exploring the concepts of thick and thin provisioning. The main types of storage systems are solid state, magnetic, and, to a lesser case, tape; these will be important to know as a CCNA Cloud professional.

We will wrap up this chapter by presenting the storage redundancy options found in the RAID specification and then take a closer look at disk pools, which were introduced in Chapter 7.

Cloud Storage Models

The two cloud storage models are direct-attached storage and network storage. In the public cloud, the most prevalent is network-attached storage. We will discuss both of these implementation models.

Direct-Attached Storage

In *direct-attached storage (DAS)*, the storage systems, usually either a spinning disk drive or a solid-state drive, are installed and connected directly in the server chassis for high-speed local access, as illustrated in Figure 9.1. While this has traditionally been a common server design, it has several drawbacks that can cancel out its desirable traits.

FIGURE 9.1   Direct-attached storage

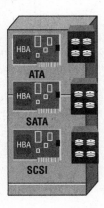

Direct-attached storage is common in desktops, laptops, and consumer devices. A drive is cabled directly to the motherboard and is dedicated to the operating system running on the system. Modern interfaces, bus designs, and disk architecture allow for high-performance read and write access in a DAS implementation.

The storage devices can be spinning magnetic hard drives, solid-state drives, flash drives, or any other type of storage that is directly connected to the computer and not over a network. The connection from the motherboard to the storage system is commonly ATA, SATA, or SCSI, which will be introduced later in this chapter.

Network-Attached Storage

Network-attached storage (NAS) is file-level access to data across a network. For example, a file server sitting on an Ethernet-based LAN and hosting shared directories would be a type of NAS. In a NAS configuration, data files are sent over the network rather than as blocks of data like in storage area networks (SANs). The data is not stored on a local computer, as with direct-attached storage; instead, it is accessed over a LAN as network-attached storage, as shown in Figure 9.2.

FIGURE 9.2   Network-attached storage

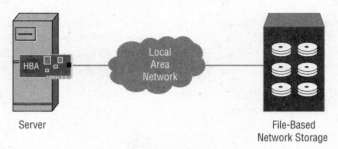

Server   File-Based Network Storage

Network-attached storage can be shared between many servers and serve as a central-ized, highly redundant storage pool in the cloud. Using network-attached storage enables many VMs to share a single data store and eliminates the need to store a local copy of files physically on each server. Also, by separating the physical storage from the server, the VMs running on a server can be migrated from that physical hardware to another platform or even anther data center without the need to migrate the storage since the storage resides on the network and can be accessed from servers at multiple local or remote locations.

Network-attached storage is easy to implement and maintain and is highly reliable.

File-Level Access

In a NAS deployment, the data files are sent over the LAN using a protocol such as TCP/IP as the common transport. However, data structures are dependent on the operating system used. For example, with Microsoft Windows, the Common Internet File System (CIFS) and Server Message Block (SMB) are the most commonly deployed data structures. Linux has a multitude of file systems, with the Network File System (NFS) commonly implemented. *File-level access* is a common solution for sharing files between servers and users on the network.

With file-level storage, data is stored in the familiar files/folders format, and access-ing the stored data looks the same to the VMs running on the hypervisor as if the drive was locally attached. Also, file-level access supports access control, integration with directory services, encryption, redundancy, and the features that are found in DAS implementations.

File-level storage is inexpensive and requires less maintenance than block-level storage, which we will cover next.

Block-Level Access

In *block-level access*, the VM sends reads and writes directly to a hard disk rather than relying on a file-level protocol like Common Internet File System (CIFS) or Network File System (NFS). Block-level access allows the reading and writing to a hard disk drive (HDD) at the physical hardware level. A disk controller on a server reads and writes the disks at the block level.

Compared to a file-based system, block level is both a faster and more efficient storage access method for an operating system. Block-level storage will be deployed over a storage area network in the cloud rather than a LAN as is most common for file-level access.

Block storage supports booting of server operating systems and is commonly deployed in a remote boot model. Virtual machines, hypervisors, databases, and operating systems running directly on a server platform all can access block storage remotely over the SAN.

Storage Controllers

The physical storage devices will need specialized interfaces to attach to the motherboard of the SAN. In this chapter, you will learn about the options available for direct-attached storage, and then in the next chapter we will introduce you to the connectivity options available for network-attached storage.

Serial Advanced Technology Attachment (SATA) is the serial implementation of the parallel ATA or IDE interface. SATA uses a point-to-point cable for data and a separate cable to supply power to the storage device. SATA I/O speeds extend up to a 6Gbps data transfer rate. SATA interface technology is common in modern cloud data centers.

Serial Attached SCSI (SAS) uses the standard SCSI command set over a serial interface instead of the standard parallel cable found in traditional SCSI connections. SATA SCSI supports 3Gbps, 6Gbps, or 12Gbps transfer rates over a point-to-point full-duplex serial interface. Also, there is a separate power cable that is required. However, when combined with SATA, the power can also be supplied with a single interface connection.

Advanced Technology Attachment/Integrated Drive Electronics (ATA/IDE) has been around since the early days of computing and has gone through many revisions and versions over the years. ATA/IDE uses either a 40 or 80-pin cable and is considered slow and obsolete by today's standards. Transfer speeds vary from 16Mbps to 133Mbps. The ATA/IDE interface is not common in modern cloud data centers and is largely obsolete.

Peripheral Component Interconnect Express (PCIe) is a serial version of the standard PCI bus. PCIe is implemented as a hub installed on the server's motherboard and has I/O data rates up to 4Gbps per lane. This is an internal server interface, so the drive is in the server chassis and plugged into a PCIe slot on the motherboard.

Universal Serial Bus (USB) is a simple serial bus with integrated power in a single interface cable. The USB system's base data transfer rate is 12Mbps. Newer versions support a data transfer rate up to 5Gbps. USB has several versions that all use a 4-pin bidirectional serial bus based on a hub-and-spoke topology. USB interfaces are able to connect up to 128 devices per master controller.

File System Types

Storage terminology and concepts can often be one of the more challenging aspects of becoming a CCNA Cloud professional. Next you will look at the storage file systems used by various operating systems on the market today. A file system defines the format in which files are stored on media and generally uses the concept of a *sector*. A sector is a group of data that is the minimum amount of data stored in physical storage. The file system is a structured representation of a set of data that is being written to a disk partition.

UFS

The *UNIX File System (UFS)* is available in most Linux and UNIX operating system file systems. UFS is one of the most common file systems for these operating systems and uses the familiar structure of a slash (/) being the root of the file system's multilevel tree structure.

The root is at the top of the tree structure. Three levels follow: /bin, /usr, and /tmp. The file hierarchy flows down from these directories to complete UFS.

EXT

The *Extended File System (EXT)* is a Linux-based file system that is common across all distributions. EXT comes in many variants with EXT 2, 3, and 4 being the most commonly deployed.

The differences between the versions of the EXT file system are in the number of files that can be stored, the size of the files and volumes, and the number of tables in the directory. EXT includes the ability to attach metadata to the files and is based on UFS.

While there are many different file system offerings in Linux, EXT is the most common.

NTFS

Microsoft developed the *New Technology File System (NTFS)* for its Windows operating system and, over the 20 years since it was introduced, it is still the main file system for Windows-based systems.

NTFS features include access control and encryption. The master file table contains all the information about the file stored on the disk, including the size, allocation, and name. Also, the first and last sectors of NTFS include the boot record and file system settings.

FAT

The *File Allocation Table (FAT)* file system was the basic storage file system found on Microsoft operating systems. FAT has its roots going back all the way to the days of the MS-DOS operating system. FAT is now considered to be a legacy and has been replaced by the NTFS file system.

However, many systems still support the FAT file system for backward compatibility, and FAT is still common on USB thumb drives, floppy drives, and other removable storage systems. FAT files are stored in directories, with each directory being either a 16 or 32-bit value. The directories and associated subdirectories and files are linked together in a block allocation table that contains the block descriptors detailing the filenames, extensions, file attributes, creation date, and file size.

VMFS

VMware is a leader in the server virtualization market, as you learned in Chapter 7. To optimize file systems for the VMware product line, the *Virtual Machine File System (VMFS)* was developed.

VMFS is used in the vSphere system as the primary file system format for virtual machine images. VMFS was designed exclusively for the virtualized environment and supports features such as virtual machine migrations and the ability to dynamically add and remove disk space allocations. VMFS also incorporates file recovery features. This file system eases the provisioning of virtual machines and includes features as point-in-time snapshots and disk imaging that are used as backups and for cloning and testing.

Storage Tiering

Data stored in the cloud will have different storage requirements based on its current or intended use. In this section, you will learn about *storage tiering,* and while we will not do a deep dive into this topic, after reading it, you will be able to answer any questions on what the different storage tiers are in the cloud and what their intended uses are.

Cloud service providers offer a wide selection of storage options that can be bewildering at first. However, each storage option serves the many different storage requirements of customers' cloud operations. For example, certain applications may require high read or write speeds for better performance as is common in many database or big data environments. These will require high-speed, low-latency access with optimized I/O and low-latency read-write performance.

If the data is seldom accessed and is archived in the cloud, there might only be a requirement for very infrequent access that fits a near-offline storage model that can be implemented as a cost-savings measure.

Storage Tier Levels

As you can see, some data may need to be accessed frequently, whereas other data can be stored and seldom accessed by an application. Different storage tiers have been defined to address the levels of storage a cloud customer may require.

- *Tier 1 storage* is used for the most critical or frequently accessed data and is generally stored on the fastest, most redundant, and highest-quality media available. With a standard Tier 1 implementation, it is important to use a storage configuration that will allow one or more disks to fail with no data being lost and access still available. Tier 1 storage arrays have the greatest manageability and monitoring capabilities and the highest performance, and they are designed to be the most reliable.

- *Tier 2 storage* is a notch below Tier 1 and is generally used when the data does not require as fast a read or write performance as Tier 1 or does not require as frequent access. Tier 2 data can use a less expensive storage option that still meets the storage needs of the cloud consumer. For example, e-mails, file sharing, and web hosting files are generally well-suited for a Tier 2 storage environment. With these applications, storage read-write speeds are important but do not require the high capacity and low latency that, for example, a highly utilized database may require. Why pay a premium for a storage solution that is overkill for your use case?

- For data that is at rest and rarely accessed or for general storage and backup uses, data can be stored at the Tier 3 level. Examples of *Tier 3 storage* media are DVD, tape, or other less expensive media types.

There can be many different tiers in a cloud storage design depending on each cloud provider's individual offerings. Multiple tiers can be implemented by customers based on the complexity and requirements of their storage needs.

Performance Levels of Each Tier

As you learned while examining storage tiers, the higher the tier, the more critical the data is considered to be and the more the design focuses on faster performance, redundancy, and availability. For example, a Tier 1 data set would generally offer better performance than a Tier 2, which in turn would have higher performance than Tier 3. This is by design; for example, a Tier 3 storage system may need to be accessed infrequently and has no need to offer the performance of a Tier 1 or 2 data set. By properly classifying the data needs in a multitiered cloud storage system, you can realize extensive cost savings by not paying for more than what you require in your cloud design.

Storage Provisioning Concepts

In this section, you will be introduced to the provisioning or deployment process that is used by cloud providers when provisioning virtual storage for a Virtual Machine (VM).

Thick Storage Provisioning

Thick provisioning is a virtual storage provisioning technique where the amount of storage on a disk is pre-allocated, or preconfigured, when the physical storage is created. For example, if you deploy a new virtual machine in the cloud and allocate a 30GB volume for storage, the orchestration software that spins up the new VM will also allocate the full 30GB of disk space to be available even if it is not initially going to be used. The full storage allocation is reserved specifically for that specific VM.

Thick provisioning has a lower latency as compared to other provisioning techniques because it allocates all storage capacity up front, and as such, there are no delays incurred with having to dynamically expand the storage volume. However, it is less efficient because it sets aside the full volume capacity for each specific use and precludes efficiencies gained by allocating the storage in a dynamic, as-needed deployment model.

Thin Storage Provisioning

Thin provisioning allocates only a portion of the requested storage capacity at the time it is created. This is done to optimize the storage systems in the cloud data center. When there are many hundreds, thousands, or even tens of thousands of virtual servers accessing the storage systems, it is more efficient to allocate storage on the basis of what is required at any given moment and then to expand up to the maximum allocated storage requirements as needed.

Thin provisioning allows for a more efficient allocation of the storage pool than the thick provisioning model. A smaller storage volume size is initially allocated for each VM and then is dynamically expanded as the storage needs require. This prevents storage capacity in a pool to be allocated that is never used. With the thin model, the storage capacity is consumed and added, up to the maximum contracted volume size.

Exploring Cloud Storage Technologies

The hardware options for storage systems in the cloud are almost exclusively either solid-state drives or the traditional spinning disk that has been the tried-and-true method of storage for many years. In this section, you will be introduced to solid-state drives, magnetic drives, and, for completeness, tape media.

Solid-State Drives

The most recent storage technology quickly gaining momentum for cloud storage is the *solid-state drive (SSD)*. SSDs do away with the mechanical spinning platter of traditional HDDs and instead use flash silicon for storage. This approach makes for a highly reliable storage medium since there are no moving parts as was required with the spinning platter hard disk drives that were most common in storage arrays until recently. Also, SSDs can have very fast read and write times, dramatically increasing server performance in cloud computing centers.

Solid-state drives offer the same external attachment interfaces as traditional HDDs and can be used as a direct replacement. Figure 9.3 shows a common SSD drive.

FIGURE 9.3 Solid-state drive

Magnetic Drives

The traditional and still most widely deployed storage media is the spinning platter design of traditional *magnetic hard drives*, as illustrated in Figure 9.4. The magnetic drive consists of multiple spinning magnetic platters with read/write heads floating just above the surface. Magnetic drives are on the market in a wide variety of densities, number of heads, platters, and external interfaces. The basic HDD design has been around for decades and has evolved into an extremely high storage density option with small form factors and high-speed interfaces.

FIGURE 9.4   Magnetic spinning hard drive

Tape Drive

For the sake of completeness, we will mention *tape storage*. This medium was common in enterprise data centers as a long-term, Tier 3 storage media type. However, because of its slow performance and heavy reliance on mechanical systems, it was considered to be too slow and not as reliable as other storage types for today's requirements. Tape drives are rarely seen in cloud data centers and are being depreciated from corporate data centers. Figure 9.5 shows a typical tape cartridge.

FIGURE 9.5   Tape drive

Understanding the RAID Technologies

A universal method of deploying drives in a data center is the concept of a Redundant Array of Independent Disks (RAID), which is a method of grouping drives together into storage arrays that offer fault tolerance and enhanced performance. There are many RAID designs. In this chapter, you will learn about the most commonly deployed models.

What Is RAID?

It is rare to see a single drive attached to a server in modern cloud data centers. What is commonly done is to group a set of drives together to achieve performance gains, redundancy, and high storage densities above what a single drive installed in a server is able to achieve. In this section, you will learn about the storage technologies used to group many disks together into one logical drive. Many advantages are gained with this storage technique, and you will become familiar with the many RAID methods that are used to group these drives together and the advantages each approach offers you.

The term *RAID* has several definitions, however; the most common is a Redundant Array of Independent Disks. By combining multiple physical disks together, you can achieve redundancy without having to sacrifice performance, and in some cases, you can achieve increased performance when using certain RAID architectures. The groupings of many disks can also be used to create large volume sizes that are required in today's cloud deployments. Individual drive densities cannot scale to these sizes. However, by grouping many drives together, you can create petabyte-scale storage systems. When a storage logical unit spans multiple hard drives, you get increases in performance, speed, and volume size.

Disks can be configured in various ways using RAID arrays. These are referred to as RAID levels, and you will explore them in the following sections to see where they are best used, the benefits and drawbacks of the different RAID types, and the differences between the various levels.

The configuration and operation of RAID arrays can take place either in software running on the operating system or on hardware cards called *RAID controllers*. In the cloud and in data centers, hardware RAID is almost exclusively used because of the performance gains over the software approach. The hardware RAID controller relieves the CPU of cycles that are required when RAID is implemented in software.

RAID 0

RAID 0 (pronounced as "raid zero") is a striped disk array without fault tolerance. What does this mean? Well, a stripe is when you split up the data and write it across two or more disks. RAID 0 uses *striping* across disks but does not use any parity information, which makes it nonredundant with no fault tolerance.

Although RAID 0 is a simple design and is easy to implement, it provides no redundancy or error detection, so if one of the drives in a RAID 0 array fails, all the data for the affected files is lost. Why would anyone want to use RAID 0 then? Well, since RAID 0 allows for parallel read and write operations, it offers high-performance I/O operations and works well in storage-intense environments such as many database applications where storage speed can often be the main performance bottleneck. Also, as you will learn, RAID 0 can be combined with other RAID options to obtain fault tolerance without sacrificing the high read-write performance that is its main benefit.

Figure 9.6 shows striping across multiple disks with RAID 0.

FIGURE 9.6 RAID level 0

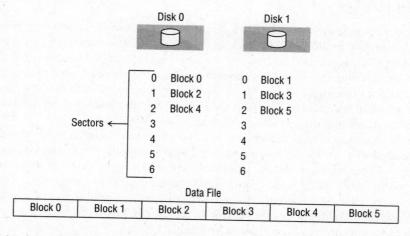

RAID 0 uses a striped disk array, where data to be stored is divided into separate blocks and each block is written to a separate disk drive. The advantage is that I/O performance is dramatically increased by spreading read and write I/O operations between more than one channel and drive. Also, since there is no fault tolerance, there is no overhead to create and write a parity bit during I/O operations.

The best RAID 0 I/O performance is achieved when data is striped across multiple controllers with only one drive per controller.

The RAID 0 architecture has some disadvantages that usually preclude it from being widely deployed in production environments. First, it is not redundant; if just one drive in the array fails, all of the data is lost. RAID 0 is not fault tolerant and does not fit well for mission-critical deployments.

However, there is a place for RAID 0 in any environment that requires or benefits from high-bandwidth I/O disk operations such as video editing, video production, streaming applications, and many other storage-intensive requirements.

RAID 1

RAID 1 is the first version of RAID that actually is fault tolerant, and if one drive were to fail, there would be no data loss.

RAID 1 is a simple implementation of RAID given that all it does is mirror, or write the same data file onto two or more disks. So, if one disk fails, the same copy of the file is also stored on the other disk and can be retrieved. As you can see, by storing the same file on two or more separate disks, fault tolerance or data redundancy is obtained. RAID 1 requires a minimum of two drives to implement.

Another feature of RAID 1 is that the data can be read off two or more disks at the same time, which improves read times when compared to reading off a single disk because the data can be read in parallel. However, write performance suffers since the file needs to be written out twice, once to each drive in the mirror set.

RAID 1 is the most inefficient RAID implementation since half of the disk capacity is lost, or used up, for redundancy. This is because of the requirement of a backup drive to store the same file as the primary, as explained earlier and illustrated in Figure 9.7.

FIGURE 9.7   RAID level 1

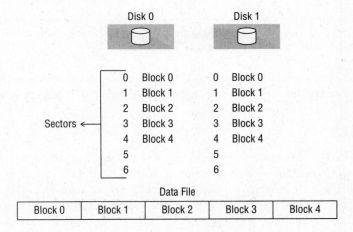

Advantages of RAID 1 include two times the storage read throughput rate of single disks with the same write throughput as a single-disk implementation. It is a good redundancy solution for environments that require high availability.

With mirroring, 100 percent redundancy is achieved by storing the same block of data twice, once to each drive. This means that a data rebuild is a requirement if there is a disk failure. Block storage transfer rates are equal to that of a single disk.

However, there are, of course, disadvantages to a RAID 1 deployment that must be considered. First, RAID 1 has the highest disk overhead of all RAID types at a whopping 100 percent inefficiency because of the same file being written twice, once on each drive. Also, it is common for the RAID function to be implemented in the operating system. A software RAID 1 deployment adds to the CPU load with the risk of degrading other applications that require CPU cycles. Also, a software approach may not allow for the hot swap of failed drives. For this reason, it is suggested that RAID 1 be implemented in hardware instead of software.

RAID 1+0

RAID levels can be combined in different configurations to achieve different objectives. One popular implementation found in cloud-based storage systems is to create two separate RAID 1 arrays and then combine or mirror them by using a RAID 0 design. This is referenced as a RAID 1+0 array, as shown in Figure 9.8. With *RAID 1+0*, the data is mirrored, and then the mirrors are striped. This configuration offers higher performance than RAID 1; the trade-off is a higher cost, and it takes a minimum of four drives to deploy.

FIGURE 9.8   RAID level 1+0

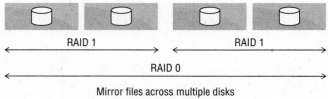

Mirror files across multiple disks
and stripe each mirror.

RAID 1+0 is closely related to RAID 0+1, which you will learn about next, and then you will explore the advantages and disadvantages of these two RAID implantations.

RAID 0+1

So, when you thought this could not get any more confusing, hold on, because along comes the *RAID 0+1* implementation! Actually, this is close to RAD 1+0; in fact, they are pretty much identical. The only difference is the order of operations, with the 0+1implementation creating the stripe first and then writing to the disk mirror, as shown in Figure 9.9. With 0+1, an individual drive failure will cause the 0+1 array to become what is essentially a RAID 0 array.

FIGURE 9.9   RAID level 0+1

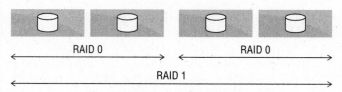

Stripe files across multiple disks
and mirror each stripe.

RAID level 0+1 does require a minimum of four drives to implement and is a mirrored array of RAID 0 arrays. RAID 0+1 offers the same fault tolerance level as RAID level 5, which you will learn about shortly. This design also has the same overhead for fault tolerance as mirroring alone, and very high disk I/O rates are possible by using the multiple striped segments.

Having gone over what is great about this approach, you also need to be aware of the disadvantages of using RAID 0+1, which includes a relatively higher expense than other RAID implementations. There is a high overhead with I/O operations that requires limited scalability. Also, all drives must move in parallel to properly track operations, which has the side effect of lower sustained performance than other RAID types.

Please understand that there is also a RAID level 10 (yes, there are a lot of them!). Do not confuse RAID 10 with 1+0 or 0+1 as they are not the same in any way.

RAID 5

In *RAID 5*, stripes of the file data and check parity data are written over all disks in the array. There is no longer a single parity check disk or write bottleneck. RAID 5 is illustrated in Figure 9.10. This design dramatically improves multiple I/O write performance since writes are now performed in parallel across multiple disk systems. Disk reads offer a slight improvement over other implementations since more disks are used for parallel read operations. If any disk in the array fails, the parity information stored across the remaining drive can be used to re-create the data and rebuild the drive array. While there is a delay to rebuild the array, RAID 5 offers efficient disk utilization and the ability to replace drives when the array is in production with no downtime requirement.

FIGURE 9.10   RAID level 5

Disk 0	Disk 1	Disk 2	Disk 3
0 Block 0a	0 Block 0b	0 Block 0c	0 Block 0p
1 Block 1a	1 Block 1b	1 Block 1p	1 Block 1c
2 Block 2a	2 Block 2p	2 Block 2b	2 Block 2c
3 Block 3p	3 Block 3a	3 Block 3b	3 Block 3c
4 Block 4a	4 Block 4b	4 Block 4c	4 Block 4p
5	5	5	5
6	6	6	6

Sectors ←

Data File

Block 0	Block 1	Block 2	Block 3	Block 4

There is a minimum of three disks that are required when constructing a RAID 5 array. However, it is more common to see five or more drives implemented in cloud production environments.

RAID 5 features read and write performance close to that of RAID level 1 where individual block data transfer rates are comparable to those of a single disk. However, RAID 5 requires much less disk space compared to other RAID levels and is widely deployed in production storage arrays found in cloud data centers.

One of the drawbacks when implementing RAID 5 is it may be a poor choice for applications that can benefit from write-intensive storage systems. This is because of the performance hit received when calculating and writing parity information. Also, when a single disk in a RAID 5 array fails, it can take a long time to rebuild the array during a disk rebuild, and the performance of the array is degraded.

The advantages when deploying RAID 5 in the cloud is that it offers the highest I/O read transaction rates of the many RAID different types. Medium I/O write transaction rates are common. Since there are multiple disks, there is a low ratio of error correction parity data written onto each disk. This means there is a high efficiency rate of the amount of data stored on the disk compared to overhead.

As you have learned, there will always be disadvantages with any technology option chosen. In the case of RAID 5, there is the issue that when there is a disk failure, you can expect that there will be a negative impact on disk I/O performance. RAID 5 also has a complex controller design with advanced driver requirements and sometimes complex configurations. Operational management of a RAID 5 array includes the issue that it can sometimes be difficult and time-consuming to rebuild the array should there be a disk failure as compared to other implementations.

RAID 5 is a versatile option and is widely deployed in the cloud data center. Common use cases are for file and application servers; database servers; web, e-mail, and news servers; intranet servers; and many more applications that can benefit from high performance and fault tolerance.

RAID 6

RAID 6 is an extension of the capabilities of RAID 5. The added capability offered in the RAID 6 configuration is that a second parity setting is distributed across all the drives in the array, as shown in Figure 9.11. The advantage gained by adding the second parity arrangement is that RAID 6 can suffer two simultaneous hard drive failures and not lose any data. However, there is a performance penalty with this configuration as disk write performance is slower than with RAID 5 because of the need to calculate and then write the second parity stripe.

FIGURE 9.11   RAID level 6

Disk 0		Disk 1		Disk 2		Disk 3		Disk 4	
0	Block 0a	0	Block 0b	0	Block 0c	0	Block 0p1	0	Block 0p2
1	Block 1a	1	Block 1b	1	Block 1p1	1	Block 1p2	1	Block 1c
2	Block 2a	2	Block 2p1	2	Block 2p2	2	Block 2b	2	Block 2c
3	Block 3p1	3	Block 3p2	3	Block 3a	3	Block 3b	3	Block 3c
4	Block 4p2	4	Block 4a	4	Block 4b	4	Block 4pc5	4	Block 4p1
5		5		5		5		5	
6		6		6		6		6	

Data File

Block 0	Block 1	Block 2	Block 3	Block 4

Two independent parity computations must be used in order to provide protection against two or more disks failing in the array. Two different algorithms are employed to achieve this purpose. RAID level 6 requires a minimum of four drives to implement.

RAID 6 is an extension of RAID level 5 but adds additional fault tolerance by using a second independent distributed parity scheme (dual parity).

Data is striped at the block level across a set of drives, as is done in RAID 5; however, with RAID 6, a second set of parity is calculated and written across all the drives. RAID 6 provides for extremely high data fault tolerance, can sustain multiple simultaneous drive failures, and protects against multiple bad block failures. It is a good RAID solution for mission-critical applications.

Some of the drawbacks of a RAID 6 solution are that the controllers are more complex than other RAID implementations, and they require additional overhead to compute the parity values for the striping. Also, N+2 drives are needed because of the dual parity scheme.

Disk Pools

In Chapter 7 you learned that disk pooling is the grouping of one or more physical storage devices into what appears to be a single, logical storage device. By creating a pool from a group of physical drives, you can then assign the storage to virtual resources in the cloud by allocating storage space to virtual machines that appear as locally attached storage. The physical storage installed inside the server (or more commonly, in a remote storage array) is grouped into pools and utilized by the hypervisor to provide storage resources to the installed VMs.

By virtualizing the cloud storage function, storage can be dynamically allocated and relocated inside the cloud to allow for growth, elasticity, and recovery. When you create virtual storage pools using one or more storage devices, the virtualized storage appears as one large storage volume. The VMs consume the resources of the storage pool, which appears to the VM as a locally attached drive.

The cloud management and orchestration tools as well as the proprietary utilities supplied by operating system and storage system vendors allow for the dynamic creation and management of storage pools.

Summary

This chapter on cloud storage may be a challenge for many as it deals with technologies commonly not seen by Cisco routing and switching professionals.

The chapter explained the different types of storage access with a focus using the direct-attached storage model by directly connecting the storage devices or using the network-attached storage model where the files are accessed over a LAN.

This chapter explored the drives themselves and compared hard disk drives to the newer solid-state drives. The different types of hardware interfaces were examined such as ATA, SATA, and the always present SCSI. It is important that the hardware interfaces and internal drive architecture be well understood for a CCNA Cloud certification.

Any discussion of storage deployments would not be complete unless you have a full understanding of RAID. In this chapter, we went into detail on how more than one drive can be combined to achieve higher performance and redundancy by using RAID. After learning about basic RAID technologies, you were introduced to the many different RAID levels. You can be sure in your career as a cloud professional that when the topic of storage hardware design arises, RAID will be included.

You also learned that each operating system has several file system types to choose from and what they are.

Storage tiers are standard offerings that allow cloud customers to select the appropriate types of storage to meet the needs of their operations. Tier 1 is high-speed and redundant storage that is commonly used for production deployments. If some of the features and benefits of Tier 1 storage are not required, significant cost savings can be realized by deploying a less robust and slower Tier 2 offering or by deploying the near-offline storage options available with Tier 3 options.

Thick provisioning allows for the full volume size of a VM to be made available at launch time. This means that there will be no associated delays like with the thin provisioning model, which implements a small percentage of the full volume size and dynamically provisions additional storage as the need requires.

We ended the chapter with a review of logically grouping storage volumes into pools to be accessed by servers.

Exam Essentials

Understand what direct-attached storage and network-attached storage are. Know that direct-attached storage is cabled directly to the server using ATA/IDE, SATA, PCIe, or USB interfaces. Network-attached storage is accessed over a network that is usually a LAN.

Understand the various types of physical hard drives and their characteristics. Traditional hard drives use mechanical components and spinning platters, and performance limitations are inherent because of this fact. However, hard drives are still the most common drive deployed in the data center. Know that solid-state drives offer much higher performance and do not have any moving parts.

Be able to define the various types of drive interfaces. ATA and IDE have integrated controllers and are parallel bus types. SATA uses a serial link to the drives and is higher speed and more commonly used in data centers than ATA interfaces. SCSI interfaces are also common physical interfaces.

Know the basics of storage tiering. Understand that the different types of storage have different needs. Tier 1 storage is mostly used in production networks by critical data that requires high-performance read and write operations. Tier 2 is used for data that does not need the higher performance of Tier 1, such as mail and file storage or for web servers. Tier 3 is for data at rest that is infrequently accessed, such as backup data. It is less expensive but has lower performance compared to the Tier 1 and Tier 2 storage types.

Know the difference between thin and thick provisioning.   Thick provisioning allocates the full storage volume size at the time of deployment and allows for better performance with the trade-off being that it may be an inefficient use of storage space. Thin provisioning deploys a smaller amount of storage than the maximum volume size to allow for efficient use of disk utilization. As additional storage space is required, thin provisioning allows for dynamic expansion of the volume size up to the maximum size of the storage volume purchased from the cloud provider.

Understand what RAID is and know the various RAID types.   Knowing the various methods used to connect drives to storage arrays and what each RAID type offers is the most important area of this chapter for the exam. RAID is connecting drives together in different configurations that offer redundancy and fault tolerance. Review RAID 0, 1, 1+0, 0+1, 5, and 6 and know how each is configured and what the advantages and disadvantages are of each RAID type.

Know the basic storage file systems.   UFS and EXT are common Linux/UNIX file systems. VMware uses the VMFS file system that is tailored to the unique requirements of hypervisors and VMs. Microsoft operating systems support NTFS and the older FAT file system for backward compatibility.

Understand disk pools.   Disk pools are simply the logical aggregation of storage space into a grouping, called a *pool*, that is then allocated to virtual resources.

Written Lab

The following questions are designed to test your understanding of this chapter's material. You can find the answers to the questions in Appendix B. For more information on how to obtain additional questions, please see this book's Introduction.

1. _____ arrays write a block of data to be stored on two or more disks, and then it mirrors the striped arrays with a second array.

2. _____ _____ reserves all storage volume capacity at the time of deployment.

3. The most common physical storage media found in the public cloud are _____ and _____ drives.

4. VMware storage volumes that are designed specifically for VM usages are known as _____.

5. The concept of creating groups of storage requirements in a hierarchy to match optimum storage offerings from the cloud service provider is known as _____.

6.   Two common Linux/UNIX file systems are _____ and _____.

7.   _____ _____ allocates a subset of the contracted storage capacity at the time of deployment and dynamically expands as required.

8.   The storage resiliency deployment that supports the ability to have several simultaneous drive failures while the array remains available is known as _____.

9.   _____ creates an array of hard drives that allows for any single hard drive to fail while still being able to recover all data.

10.   File systems are implemented in operating systems to standardize the data structures on the HDD; Microsoft offers _____ and _____ in its operating systems.

Review Questions

The following questions are designed to test your understanding of this chapter's material. You can find the answers to the questions in Appendix A. For more information on how to obtain additional questions, please see this book's Introduction.

1. What type of storage is available on a network?
   A. Shared
   B. SCSI
   C. NAS
   D. RAID

2. What type of storage interconnections is commonly found installed on standalone servers, laptops, and desktops?
   A. RAID
   B. NAS
   C. FC
   D. DAS

3. Logically grouping storage devices together for VM access is referred to as what?
   A. Tiering
   B. VMFS
   C. Pooling
   D. Thick

4. What storage model is low cost and used for near-offline requirements such as backups?
   A. Tier 1
   B. Tier 2
   C. Tier 3
   D. NAS

5. This file system was specifically designed for virtualized systems.
   A. NTFS
   B. EXT
   C. VMFS
   D. UFS

6. A cloud user wants a storage implementation from his public cloud provider that can support the loss of two disks simultaneously while still operating. As a CCNA cloud professional, what would you recommend?

    A. DAS

    B. RAID 5

    C. NAS

    D. RAID 6

7. What are Windows-native file-based protocols? (Choose two.)

    A. UFS

    B. NFS

    C. NTFS

    D. FAT

8. What provisioning model is used by cloud-based orchestration systems to allocate the maximum purchased storage capacity at deployment?

    A. Tier 1

    B. Tier 2

    C. Thick

    D. Thin

9. What are two common Linux file systems deployed in a hybrid cloud? (Choose two.)

    A. EXT

    B. FAT

    C. UFS

    D. NTFS

10. This model allows for data that can use a less expensive storage option that still meets the storage needs of the cloud consumer. E-mails, file sharing, and web hosting files are generally well-suited for this storage environment.

    A. Tier 1

    B. Tier 2

    C. Thick

    D. Thin

11. Which of the following are HDD architectures? (Choose two.)

    A. NTFS

    B. Spinning

    C. SSD

    D. EXT

12. Which of the following are standardized hardware storage interconnects? (Choose three.)

   A. ATA

   B. SATA

   C. SCSI

   D. Block

   E. File

13. What storage model was developed to address the different types of storage needs in the cloud for availability, response times, and economics?

   A. RAID

   B. Multipathing

   C. Tiering

   D. Policies

14. What is the grouping of hard drives in a storage array that offers redundancy and performance called?

   A. Multipathing

   B. RAID

   C. Masking

   D. Tiering

15. You are asked to recommend a storage array that stripes file data and performs a parity check over multiple disks that can recover from a single hard disk failure. What do you recommend?

   A. RAID 0

   B. RAID 1

   C. RAID 1+0

   D. RAID 5

16. Which file system was developed for the UNIX operating systems and is now commonly found in many Linux distributions?

   A. ZTS

   B. VMFS

   C. UFS

   D. FAT

17. Which provisioning model is used by cloud-based orchestration systems to preserve storage capacity at deployment but allows for dynamic expansion as required?

   A. Tier 1

   B. Tier 2

   C. Thick

   D. Thin

18. What storage array deployment does not offer data recovery?

   A. RAID 0

   B. RAID 0+1

   C. RAID 1+0

   D. RAID 1

19. What storage array deployment features fast read-write times using two disks and allows data to be recovered if a disk fails?

   A. RAID 0

   B. RAID 0+1

   C. RAID 1+0

   D. RAID 1

20. What storage array model uses mirroring and striping across four or more disks? (Choose two.)

   A. RAID 0

   B. RAID 0+1

   C. RAID 1+0

   D. RAID 1

Chapter 10

Storage Area Networking

THE FOLLOWING UNDERSTANDING CISCO CLOUD FUNDAMENTALS CLDFND (210-451) EXAM OBJECTIVES ARE COVERED IN THIS CHAPTER:

Introducing Storage Area Networking

Five critical areas of cloud computing are compute, networking, storage, virtualization, and automation. The Understanding Cisco Cloud Fundamentals exam requires knowledge of storage in order to be able to obtain the certification, but more importantly a knowledge of storage networking is critical to be effective in your role as a CCNA Cloud professional.

Learning about storage can be challenging to Cisco professionals since most primarily have routing and switching backgrounds. Usually there is just a vague familiarity of what is going on over on the storage side of the house. Traditionally, storage networking has been completely separate from data networking with similar but different technologies and a dedicated staff of storage administrators to maintain operations.

However, with a background in data networking, you have a strong base of knowledge to build on to master storage networking. In fact, you will find that much of storage networking is the same as data networking but uses different terminology.

In Chapter 9, you learned about storage media, direct and network-attached storage, file systems, storage tiers, and RAID. In this chapter, you will build upon that knowledge and learn what storage networks are, their unique requirements, and many of the architectures and protocols that are used on a storage area network (SAN). With that knowledge, in Chapter 11, you will then learn about the storage hardware in the Cisco MDS and Nexus product lines.

In modern cloud data centers, the primary storage access technology is the SAN. While SANs can be complex and are often a separate area of specialization in the cloud, it is critical that, as a CCNA Cloud professional, you have a solid understanding of SANs just as you would with compute, virtualization, automation, and networking.

SANs traditionally have been deployed as separate networks from the traditional Ethernet LANs in the data center, as shown in Figure 10.1. This was because of the unique requirements of storage traffic. Storage systems are intolerant to loss and require a lossless underlying network. The conflict with this is that Ethernet was never intended or designed to be lossless and has always relied on upper-layer protocols for recovery and retransmission of any data lost across the network.

FIGURE 10.1 Traditional storage area network

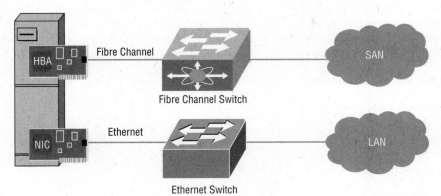

As shown in Figure 10.1, there is a specialized storage networking protocol known as Fibre Channel that was designed specifically to handle storage traffic across a SAN. You will learn about Fibre Channel in this chapter. After you learn about the basics of Fibre Channel, you will then dig a bit deeper into the details of its operation.

In cloud and enterprise data centers, the advantages of convergence of the local area network (LAN) and SAN networks into a unified fabric are readily evident, as we discussed in Chapter 5 on the Cisco UCS line of unified computing products. The cabling and the administrative overhead of managing multiple networks are reduced with a converged network switching fabric, as illustrated in Figure 10.2. There are special protocols such as iSCSI and Fibre Channel over Ethernet that were developed to support storage traffic over LANs, which you will also learn about in this chapter.

FIGURE 10.2 Unified network

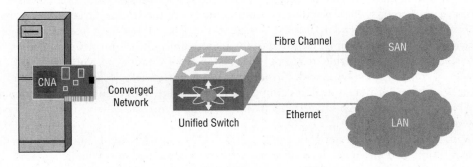

The SAN is defined as a high-performance network dedicated to storage traffic that is independent of all other traffic in the cloud. The SAN allows for shared storage resources to be remotely accessed by servers in the cloud data center.

Since storage is such a critical component of any cloud operation, SANs are designed to be highly fault tolerant to avoid any disruptions or errors in the communications path from the server to the storage devices. It is a typical architecture to deploy two completely separate storage area networks for redundancy and fault tolerance, as shown in Figure 10.3.

FIGURE 10.3   Redundant SAN networks

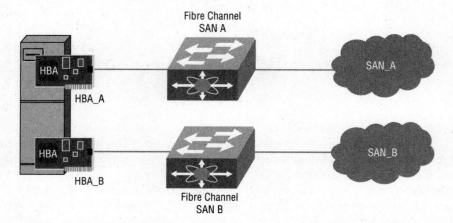

Servers may utilize redundant host bus adapters for resilient storage connectivity. One HBA will be connected to SAN_A, and the second will be connected to SAN_B as a backup. Should one of the SAN fabrics fail, the backup is designed to take over with no loss of service.

The SAN uses a specifically designed storage protocol called *Fibre Channel* and extends the SCSI command set across the network to remote storage arrays. Fibre Channel uses the concept of credits where the initiator communicates to the storage target when there are buffers available to send additional storage traffic. This allows for a lossless network since storage traffic is never transmitted to the remote unless it is informed that there are sufficient buffers available to accept the transfer. Fibre Channel networks are high speed and constantly evolving with introductions of new technologies and higher data rates. While there is a great deal of complexity in setting up, maintaining, and managing a SAN, Fibre Channel SANs have a reputation of being stable and reliable in production networks.

With the advantages of network convergence, SANs and LANs will continue the trend of being combined into a single, unified network to be combined into a single network. Special protocols were developed to assist in the collapsed network topology. iSCSI and FCoE are the two primary storage overlay protocols found in the cloud today; these protocols encapsulate the SCSI command set and Fibre Channel operations respectably over an Ethernet-based LAN. This approach of merging the LAN and SAN traffic together is referred to as a *converged network*.

As mentioned earlier, the storage array is essentially a collection of hard disks, as pictured in Figure 10.4. Storage is allocated to hosts based on logical unit numbers (LUNs), not on physical disks. When the storage systems administrator requests the creation of 100GB of disk space on the storage array, a 100GB LUN portion is allotted, which can comprise quite a few kinds of physical storage devices underneath such as spinning disks or solid-state drives (SSDs). The storage administrator can increase or decrease the LUN size, with some LUNs being used by a single host for things such as booting or other normal OS operations. Shared LUNs are accessible by multiple hosts.

FIGURE 10.4   Typical storage array

The entire storage array connects to the Fibre Channel SAN via *storage processors (SPs)*. There are typically two storage processors such that one is available for connecting to each SAN fabric. Individual SPs have their own unique addresses, which host devices use to connect to the storage system.

Back when fiber-optic speeds were reaching gigabit levels, the ability to send SCSI requests over fiber media using the Fibre Channel protocol was developed. Fibre Channel used the SCSI commands to read and write from the remote storage and replaced the physical layer with higher-speed fiber-optic technologies and extensive networking capabilities. Like SCSI, Fibre Channel is a lossless block-based protocol that encapsulates SCSI commands, as shown in Figure 10.5.

FIGURE 10.5   Fibre Channel frame

During the time of development of storage networking technologies, the traditional networking industry standardized on TCP/IP as its primary network layer protocol. Development was done to encapsulate the SCSI into the TCP/IP protocol using TCP for reliable transport. The outcome of this development was the *Internet Small Computer System Interface (iSCSI)* protocol.

The iSCSI protocol allows for converged networking in the cloud data center by collapsing the storage network into the data network by combining LAN and SAN into the same switching fabric. The iSCSI protocol is popular, with its basic operation to encapsulate SCSI commands into a TCP packet for transmission over a TCP/IP Ethernet network, as shown in Figure 10.6.

FIGURE 10.6   iSCSI frame

Block Storage Technologies

Before going deeper into storage networks, let's pause and review two main storage concepts you will be working with when implementing storage solutions in the cloud. First we will review what block storage is and where it is most commonly used, and then we'll review file-based storage in the next section. In Chapter 9, you were introduced to block storage; in this chapter, we will do a quick review since a deep understanding of block storage is critical to SAN support and operations.

With locally attached storage and drive architectures, a *block* is a unit of storage allocated in the drive. With block storage specific to storage networks, the definition is different; a *storage block* is a raw volume of storage you create and is managed and accessed as if it were an individual hard drive. Each block can be formatted by the server's operating system using file systems such as NTFS, NFS, or VMFS and mounted as a volume. Yes, it can be confusing that *block* has two separate meanings depending on the context. Just remember that we will be talking about block storage in the networking context as compared to the individual drive geometry, so you will have the correct perspective.

Storage arrays are connected to a SAN and allow the server's operating system to access these blocks of storage data remotely instead of being locally attached to a server. When the storage is located across a network, many additional features and capabilities are introduced that allow much more flexibility over the directly attached storage model of operation. For example, by disaggregating the compute component from storage, the VMs can be moved from one physical server to another physical server in a cloud data center or even across data centers in a hybrid, multi-availability zone, or multicloud design. The storage remains at a fixed address on the network that the virtual machines access regardless of their locations.

Block-level storage is commonly found in a SAN deployment residing in a data center and offers server boot capabilities that allow the server operating system to boot over the SAN and not have to rely on locally attached drives in the hosting server. Block storage over a network is reliable and can store file systems, databases, virtual machine file systems, and many other storage requirements. Each storage volume is independent from the other volumes and can be accessed by either a single or multiple operating systems over the network.

File-Based Storage Technologies

File-based storage technologies contrast with block storage in that they are at the file level and configured with a file system such as NFS for Linux or SMB/CIF for Windows-based systems. File storage can be accessed over an existing Ethernet-based network and does not have the loss restrictions found in block storage architectures.

File storage systems are much easier and cost effective to implement and operate because of the reduced restrictions as compared to block storage. Files are stored in the familiar folder format that you are used to seeing. Network-attached storage systems are usually file-based systems. Since they are based on standard file systems, features such as user access control, rights, access control lists, and directory systems integration are available. You will learn about file-based permissions later in this chapter.

Network-Attached Storage

Network-attached storage (NAS) is network-based file-level access. For example, a cloud server connected to an Ethernet-based LAN hosting shared data directories would be a type of NAS. In a NAS configuration, data is transmitted over an Ethernet network as files rather than blocks of data, as we discussed earlier in this chapter. NAS systems do not require a SAN but instead operate over a traditional Ethernet-based LAN.

Network-attached file storage systems are highly scalable and support a distributed architecture that can scale from a small single volume to massive systems with many nodes spread across multiple availability zones in the cloud supporting hundreds of thousands of clients. NAS systems scale into the multiple petabyte range with both vertical and horizontal scaling. A NAS system supports user and system authentication for security and also can define permissions. Figure 10.7 illustrates a NAS architecture.

FIGURE 10.7 NAS architecture

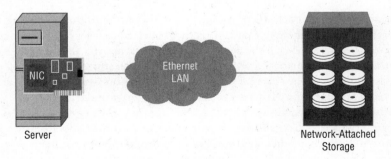

Direct-Attached Storage

Direct-attached storage (DAS) is just as it sounds; it consists of storage devices that are directly cabled to the server and do not require any type of networking technologies to access. A server will either have a storage adapter on the motherboard or a card installed that is used to connect the drives. As we discussed in Chapter 9, there are many different types of DAS interconnect standards including IDE, ATA, SATA, and SCSI, as shown in Figure 10.8.

FIGURE 10.8   DAS architecture

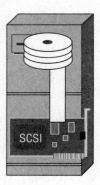

NAS Storage Concepts

In this section, you will learn about the administrative options of shares and mount points as they relate to network-attached storage.

Shares

Network-attached storage consists of storage arrays connected to the cloud data network; this is different from DAS storage that is directly connected to a server. The volumes on the NAS are shared by the devices in the cloud, each of which has the ability to access the data on the drive arrays inside a storage system. By using various storage networking protocols and access arrangements, the stored data can be security protected and still be shared in the cloud even when multiple clients are accessing the same storage hardware.

Shares allow servers to access data on the volumes; they are a system of rights and permissions that allow a user or operating system to perform storage operations on a volume, directory, or file. Such rights include the ability to write to the volume, read from it, and erase or delete a file. For example, files may be set to read-only to prevent a system from changing a critical file, while other operations may require that a file be modified; in that scenario, read-write access can be granted.

Network shares are created and managed using many different utilities and applications that are beyond the scope of the Understanding Cisco Cloud Fundamentals exam. Most cloud management dashboards allow the cloud consumer to create and modify shares to meet their individual requirements. When creating a share, it is customary to create groups of users or servers that share common requirements and then to assign the share permissions to the groups as compared to individual users or servers. This approach makes administration easier to manage as your operations scale.

Mount Points

When storage is remote from the Linux operating system, there must be a means to logically connect the volume to the local server's NFS-based file systems. The *mount point* is an NFS directory where the remote file system is mounted (logically attached or connected). The mount point contains the directory tree and file system of remote storage that can be accessed from a Linux-based server as if it were locally attached. Mount points can be created over both NAS and SAN systems. The mount process is based on the Linux mount application and is a component of the NFS stack.

Before data can be accessed by an NFS Linux client, it must first be mounted as a file system in the local operating system. Often in the cloud, on a virtual machine that is booting, there is a script that is run on bootup to automatically perform an NFS mount operation to the volume. Once the volume is mounted, the shares take effect, and data can be accessed by the operating system as if it were a locally attached storage system.

SAN Protocols and Hardware

With a solid understanding of block and file storage systems and network- and direct-attached storage, you can now explore the storage technologies used in a modern cloud data center.

We will explain the communication protocols that are commonly found when connecting large cloud-based storage systems to servers using a SAN network that interconnects the storage systems and the servers that access the data. These protocols include Fibre Channel, Fibre Channel over Ethernet, and iSCSI.

In this section, you will be introduced to the details of the hardware and protocols that make up a SAN. The most widely deployed protocol that was developed specifically for storage networking is Fibre Channel. In this section, we will introduce Fibre Channel and then explain the many different hardware and software components that come together for a complete SAN solution. In Chapter 11, we will complete our storage discussion by detailing the Cisco MDS and Nexus product lines that support SAN switching.

A *storage area network* is a high-speed network composed of computers and storage devices. A SAN removes the requirement of servers having locally attached storage with hard drives installed. Instead, the SAN allows the storage arrays to be remote from the servers and to be accessed over the SAN.

In cloud data centers, this allows dedicated storage arrays that can hold massive amounts of data and that are highly redundant to be shared by a large number of VMs and servers in the cloud. The servers and their host operating systems can now be replaced or relocated via host virtualization techniques since the hard drives remain stationary and do not need to be moved with the servers.

Servers may use multiple storage protocols, such as Fibre Channel, iSCSI, and FCoE, over standard Ethernet or Fibre Channel switching fabrics to access storage shares. A server platform will communicate with the Fibre Channel network using cards installed in the bus called *host bus adapters (HBAs)*. HBAs are similar to the Ethernet NIC cards used to connect to the LAN. The server's OS sees the storage as attached locally when it talks to the HBA. However, behind the scenes, the HBA takes the SCSI storage commands and encapsulates them into the Fibre Channel networking protocol. Fibre Channel is a high-speed, optical SAN, with speeds ranging from 2Gbps to 32Gbps. There are usually two SAN networks, SAN A and SAN B, for redundancy, and they have traditionally been separate from the LAN. With that background, let's jump in and take a look at the details of a modern SAN.

Fibre Channel

Fibre Channel (FC) is the predominant storage protocol in storage area networking. The protocol was developed specifically for the transport of storage data from storage systems to servers and other devices that require I/O access to storage systems. Fibre Channel is a high-speed protocol that was developed as data speeds reached 1Gbps and higher. It is a lossless protocol that takes into consideration the requirements of storage systems to not tolerate lost frames when transmitting across the network.

Fibre Channel is its own protocol that is separate from Ethernet. This is an important point to keep in mind. While a Fibre Channel switch or cable may look similar to an Ethernet switch, a Fibre Channel SAN and the traditional Ethernet-based LAN are completely different and incompatible. The frame formats, optical coding "on the wire," and upper-level protocols of Fibre Channel are not compatible in any way with a TCP/IP-based LAN.

Fibre Channel encapsulates inside its headers the SCSI command set to allow the server and storage controllers to exchange information on disk read, write, and other types of disk operations between the host operating systems and the remote storage arrays. Just as Ethernet networks have hardware LAN switches that interconnect all devices, SAN switches serve the same function with the additional intelligence required by the Fibre Channel protocol.

The SCSI protocol uses a standards-based command set between the storage initiator and the storage provider or target. This is an important concept to understand; remember that SCSI encompasses the communications commands and also the hardware interfaces used between a server and a storage system. One of the limitations of SCSI is that it is a relatively short distance from the host to the storage drives because of cable restrictions. To resolve this issue, the Fibre Channel protocol was developed. Instead of using the Ethernet protocol to carry SCSI commands and disk read-write data over a network, the Fibre Channel protocol is used. The reason for this is that Ethernet was never intended to be a lossless protocol, and storage systems are intolerant of data loss in transmission. Because of this limitation of Ethernet, Fibre Channel was developed to provide standards-based protocols for end-to-end, high-speed, low-latency storage network communications.

The frame formats and encapsulation are similar to Ethernet but differ in purpose and operation; the Fibre Channel and Ethernet frame formats are not compatible and will not communicate with each other. Figure 10.9 shows a basic Fibre Channel–based frame.

FIGURE 10.9   Fibre Channel

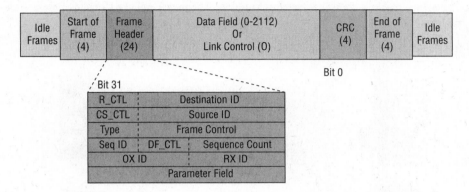

The Fibre Channel–based network uses a switched fabric topology, enabled by Fibre Channel–compatible SAN switches to connect the nodes of a network together. Figure 10.10 provides a simple example where Fibre Channel–based devices connect to a single network or fabric. While this implementation is functional, it does not offer any fault tolerance; it's used only in a nonproduction environment.

FIGURE 10.10   Simple single fabric

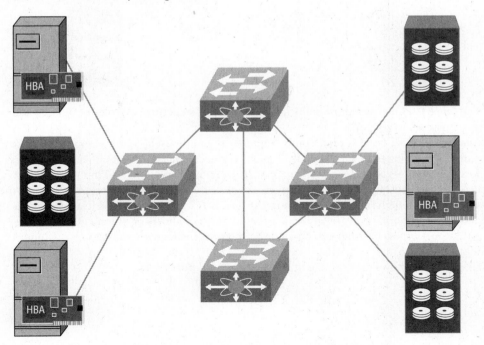

The more common SAN implementation for cloud and enterprise production networks utilizes two separate SAN switching fabrics, as shown in Figure 10.11. Note that unlike with Ethernet switches, there is no interconnection between the two fabrics. Keep that in mind! The end nodes have two separate ports, and each of them connects to one fabric, adding vitally important fault tolerance. If one fabric fails, the end node can use the other fabric to communicate. Again, these are completely separate networks that operate independently of each other.

FIGURE 10.11 Dual SAN fabric

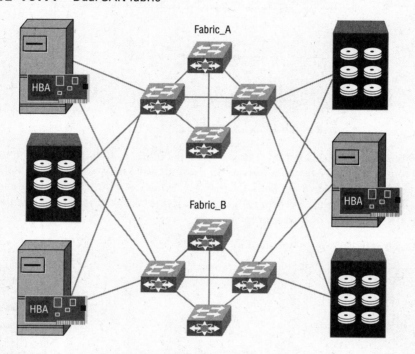

The Fibre Channel standard defines port types that structure the roles of devices and ports connected to the SAN.

A *node port (N_port)* is predictably found on the node itself, and it operates just like a port in a storage array or on a server. N_ports connect point-to-point either to a storage enclosure or to a SAN switch. A *fabric port (F_port)* is located on the Fibre Channel switch and connects to an N_port. An *E_port*, or *expansion port*, connects one switch to another switch for interswitch link (ISL) communications. In a loop, whether arbitrated or via a hub, the *node loop ports (NL_ports)* are the ports on the hosts or storage nodes. There are other port types, but they are beyond the scope of the Understanding Cisco Cloud Fundamentals exam.

Figure 10.12 shows an example of the various SAN port types.

FIGURE 10.12   Port types

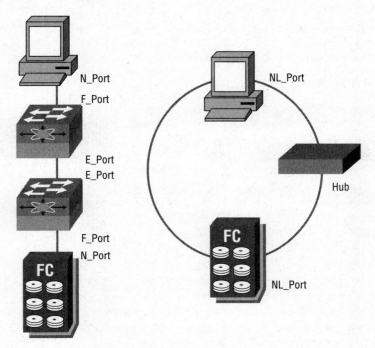

It is helpful to view Fibre Channel as the lower-level communications NL_Port protocol used to create communications paths through a switched SAN network that allows for the SCSI storage commands to be passed from the operating system to remote storage devices that are also connected to the same SAN switching fabric. The server, also known as the *initiator*, logs into the switch and requests remote storage from the network. A path then gets set up that allows the initiator to talk to the target over the Fibre Channel network. After the Fibre Channel connection is created, it acts as a tunnel through the switching fabric that the SCSI protocol uses between the initiator and the target to store and retrieve information off the hard drives.

World Wide Names

Each Fibre Channel device is assigned a unique identifier called a *World Wide Name (WWN)* that allows the port to be uniquely identified on a Fibre Channel network. The best way to understand this is to think of a WWN as being the same concept as a MAC address found in Ethernet-based LANs.

A WWN is a globally unique identifier that is hard-coded into a Fibre Channel device usually at the time of manufacture, whether it be an HBA, storage array controller, or part of a SAN switching system. The WWN is assigned to a hardware Fibre Channel SAN device when it is manufactured and is a 128-bit value. The first 64 bytes identify the manufacturer, and the remaining bits uniquely identify the individual device; Figure 10.13 illustrates a WWN frame format. This is known as hard-coding the WWN. Any device with multiple Fibre Channel ports will require a WWN for each port to identify each individual port on the SAN. The WWN is also used as a device identifier to log in and register the device on the SAN switching fabric during the Fibre Channel login process.

FIGURE 10.13 WWN

WWNs from a Single-Ported Device	
WWNN	20:00:00:00:00:01:EF:25
WWPN	21:00:00:00:00:01:11:01

WWNs from a Dual-Ported Device	
WWNN	20:00:00:00:00:01:EF:25
WWPN A	21:00:00:00:00:01:11:01
WWPN B	21:00:00:00:00:01:11:02

There are several different types of WWNs, and they are based on their location in the network. The WWN that identifies an endpoint in a SAN is referred to as the *World Wide Node Name (WWNN)*. An endpoint can be any termination point in the Fibre Channel network; for example, HBA's SAN switch ports and storage array controllers that terminate a Fibre Channel connection are all endpoints that each use a unique WWNN.

When a WWN is used to identify a port on a SAN switch, it is referred to as a *World Wide Port Name (WWPN)*. WWPNs are used, for example, on a dual-FC port HBA card where the card itself will have a hard-coded WWNN, and then each of its two Fibre Channel ports will be distinguished with separate WWPNs.

When a storage controller first connects to the Fibre Channel SAN switch, it registers its WWNs to the SAN switch fabric; this is known as a *fabric login* or *FLOGI*, which is probably the coolest acronym in all of networking. The FLOGI process identifies the WWN on the network and assigns defined rights to the connection and is part of the Fibre Channel standard.

Host Bus Adapters

The *host bus adapter* is a hardware device that resides in a server and provides connectivity from the server to the SAN switch. The HBA provides storage I/O processing and the physical interconnection to the SAN switch. HBAs support different storage interfaces such as Fibre Channel, SATA, and serial-attached SCSI. Different form factors include connecting to a server PCIe slot or as a mezzanine card in a blade server. HBAs are critical to the storage I/O performance of a server and provide offload SAN processing that frees up CPU cores from processing Fibre Channel storage and retrieval operations. The result is better server performance.

It is helpful for a network engineer to think of an HBA as being similar to the Ethernet NIC card; however, instead of connecting to a LAN, the HBA is used to connect to storage networks or devices. The HBA provides the interconnection from the server to the remote storage systems across a SAN. They require drivers unique to the operating system and support SFP interfaces to match the optics and speeds of the Fibre Channel SAN.

Each HBA will use the WWN addressing scheme as its endpoint identifier on the SAN; there will be a worldwide node name for the HBA and a world wide port name for each of its FC ports. The HBA will log into the SAN fabric and register itself on the fabric that it is connected to. The storage controller will also be registered on the SAN, and if configured to allow the target and initiator to communicate, the server can access the remote storage LUN across the SAN through the HBA. Figure 10.14 illustrates a common HBA card on the market today.

FIGURE 10.14   HBA image

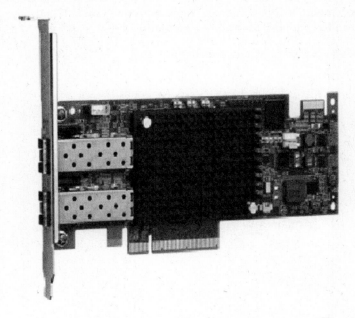

Converged Network Adapters

Cisco UCS servers and fabric interconnect products support the convergence of storage and traditional LAN traffic on the same switching fabric. With a converged network, the number of connections and cable requirements are greatly reduced, saving on complexity, cabling, and the number of switch ports required, and only one server bus slot is required to support both data and storage connections to the network. The *converged network adapter (CNA)* combines the functions of an Ethernet NIC and a storage HBA in a server and provides a single converged network interface for both functions.

However, since Fibre Channel and Ethernet are completely different protocols with different frame formats and physical layer connections, the CNA must perform a conversion of Fibre Channel into an Ethernet LAN–based frame and protocol such as iSCSI or Fibre Channel over Ethernet (FCoE). The switching fabric must also support converged networking to accommodate both LAN and SAN traffic on the same switch forwarding plane. The converged switch may also support the conversion from Ethernet-based storage to Fibre Channel to interconnect to the Fibre Channel SAN or devices that only support FC interfaces but need to communicate to each other. As you can assume, there will be a heavy traffic load on the interface since it is supporting both LAN and SAN traffic, and given the need that SAN traffic has for lossless connections, the interface speeds will need to operate as fast as possible. CNAs commonly support 10Gbps Ethernet with 25 and 40Gbps interface speeds now appearing on the market.

The CNA server drivers support both the Ethernet network and the Fibre Channel drivers. The operating system sees these as two completely separate interfaces and does not have any knowledge that both LAN and storage connections share the external converged network using a single interface for both traffic types. Figure 10.15 shows an image of a common HBA.

FIGURE 10.15   Converged network adapter

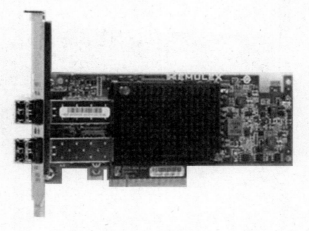

Fibre Channel over Ethernet

With the introduction of the converged fabric in the data center, a new spin on the Fibre Channel protocol is called *Fibre Channel over Ethernet*. The Fibre Channel frames are encapsulated into an Ethernet frame, and the switching hardware is shared with the LAN. This approach saves on switching hardware, cabling, power, and rack space by collapsing the LAN and SAN into one converged network, also called *unified switching fabric*.

Storage requires a lossless connection between the server and the storage array. By design, Ethernet is not lossless and will drop Ethernet frames if there is congestion. This could cause an operating system to fail. To make the storage traffic lossless, there are several mechanisms that use quality of service (QoS) and the various networking layers to identify which traffic is storage and to make it a higher priority than the normal LAN data on the same link.

To support the transport of storage traffic, new networking protocols were developed that encapsulated the Fibre Channel protocol into TCP/IP packets for transport over an Ethernet network. Keep in mind that the standard Fibre Channel–based SAN is its own standard, all the way from framing to how the initiator and target interact; it is not Ethernet, and it is not TCP/IP.

When FCoE is implemented, storage data traverses the same network as the Ethernet LAN traffic. When the SAN and LAN traffic are collapsed into a single switching fabric, it is called a *converged fabric*, as shown in Figure 10.16.

FIGURE 10.16   Converged network FCoE

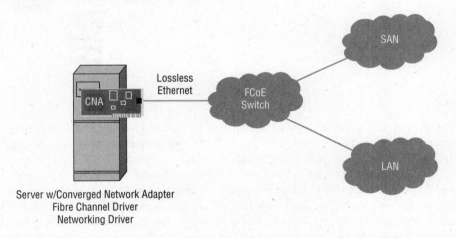

With FCoE, the Fibre Channel traffic is encapsulated once again, this time with an Ethernet header. The storage traffic is sent over the LAN along with all other traffic types in the cloud data center. However, special quality-of-service considerations to make sure that no storage traffic is dropped and that sufficient bandwidth is reserved for storage are implemented.

Block-level storage has historically not worked very well with the Ethernet protocol. Ethernet was never designed to be lossless and will drop a frame if there is a collision, buffer starvation, or any type of congestion on the LAN; it will rely on its upper-level protocols to provide recovery and retransmission services. These recovery services were never included in the Fibre Channel protocol; Fibre Channel relies on a different scheme that uses buffer credits and assumes that the underlying network was lossless. To reconcile these differences, there has been extensive quality-of-service enhancements created to allow storage traffic priority over traditional LAN frames to ensure that the underlying network requirements of the SAN are met when connected through a converged network. Figure 10.17 shows a storage network based on Ethernet LANs.

FIGURE 10.17   Storage networking using Ethernet

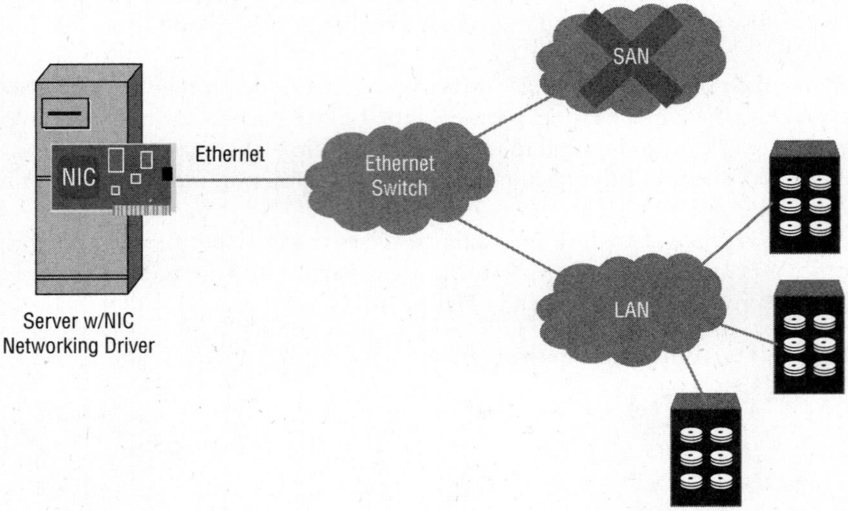

iSCSI

Another method used to connect storage traffic over a standard Ethernet-based LAN is to encapsulate the standard SCSI commands into a TCP frame for transmission over the cloud TCP/IP-based LAN. The iSCSI *Internet Small Computer Systems Interface (iSCSI)* protocol enables storage traffic to traverse an Ethernet LAN but is different from FCoE in that it does not encapsulate the FC frame into Ethernet but rather encapsulates the SCSI command set directly into Ethernet frames, and by using TCP with its connection-orientated operation and ability to retransmit missing packets, the storage traffic is not lost across the network. This is shown in Figure 10.18. One of the big advantages of implementing iSCSI for storage traffic is that there is no requirement for an HBA to be installed in the server, and a standard Ethernet switching backbone fabric can be used since iSCSI is seen on the network as standard TCP/IP traffic.

The SAN Initiator

The SCSI protocol has standardized how block read and write requests are communicated between the device requesting storage data and the drive providing that information. For example, if a server needs to read or write to the storage device, it will do this using the SCSI protocol. To the server, it appears that the storage device is directly connected as DAS; however, this may not be the case, and the storage resources may be across a SAN, as is usually the case with cloud-based storage. When data is requested, the OS will send a disk read request to its storage subsystems. The SCSI controller with act as the initiator and request from the target the specified data. The initiator acts as the consumer of stored data. This is straightforward to understand as the initiator is the end that initiates the connection over the SAN to the target and requests the data, as shown in Figure 10.19.

FIGURE 10.18   An iSCSI-based network

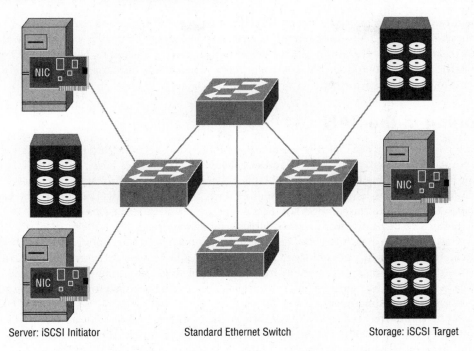

Server: iSCSI Initiator   Standard Ethernet Switch   Storage: iSCSI Target

FIGURE 10.19   SAN initiator and target

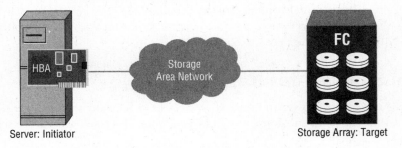

Server: Initiator   Storage Array: Target

The initiator is the endpoint device that will request a read or write operation for a block of data. When the initiator transmits that request to the target, it is then up to the storage controller on the target to carry out the storage request operations. As you learned earlier, the storage array contains blocks of storage space called *logical unit numbers (LUNs)*. A LUN can be considered to be a remote volume or hard drive. After the LUN is made visible on the SAN, then the initiators will request the data stored on the LUN as if it was a storage device directly attached to the operating system.

The SAN Target

The target receives the storage operation request from the initiator and carries out the requested operation. When the request is received, the storage controller will perform the operation that may be a read, write, or delete request to its attached storage arrays. Then, using the SCSI command set, the controller replies back to the initiator that the requested operation has been performed.

Zoning in the SAN

Zoning is the process of logically segmenting a Fibre Channel SAN into multiple logical SANs. Zoning provides security and segmentation on the SAN fabric. Zoning is used to provide isolation and protection of LUNs in the storage arrays by restricting access between specifically defined storage initiators and targets. All devices placed into the same zone and logged into the same SAN fabric are permitted to talk to each other.

Zoning also helps protect storage volumes from data corruption. For example, if a Linux server attempted to attach to a storage device that is formatted to support a Microsoft file system, there is a strong possibility that the volume could become corrupted. Zones can be created to separate operating systems from each other, to group storage by application and use case, and to isolate sensitive data. Multiple zones can be grouped together into a zone set on a SAN switching fabric.

Zoning is implemented in the SAN fabric switches and is a fabric-wide service that allows the hosts you define to connect only to the LUNs or targets they are intended to connect to and to be isolated from the LUNs they are not configured to attach to.

Security is achieved by mapping hosts to LUNs. Members that belong to a zone can communicate with each other but not to endpoints in another zone. However, you can define a device to be in more than one zone at a time. When creating and implementing zoning on a SAN, a common use case is to configure a zone for each initiator port and the target LUN that the initiators need to connect to.

Virtual Storage Area Network

In much the same manner that an Ethernet switch can be logically segmented into individual and separate switching domains by implementing VLANs, SANs can be segmented with the use of VSANs.

The *virtual storage area network* (VSAN) operates in a SAN much the same way that a VLAN is used in an Ethernet-based switching network found in the cloud. Storage devices in each individual VSAN are allowed to communicate with each other without special provisions but not outside of their assigned VSANs.

A VSAN creates a separate SAN that is configured in the SAN switch, and all fabric processes such as SAN login services and the zone server are duplicated in each VSAN. VSANs are used in multitenant implementations such as in cloud computing to consolidate multiple SAN fabrics into a smaller number and to provide isolation. VSANs are normally defined by the physical ports as is also common when configuring a VLAN on an Ethernet switch. A VSAN is a logical SAN created on a physical SAN network. Each VSAN is separated from the other VSANs on the same fabric so that the same Fibre Channel IDs can be used in each VSAN.

Understanding Storage Logical Unit Numbers

The *logical unit number (LUN)* provides a unique identifier that designates both physical and virtual storage devices that execute storage operations on a SAN. The LUN is created using a block storage array on a storage controller connected to the SAN.

The SCSI command set uses LUNs and the SCSI commands, as you have learned, encapsulated into FC, FCoE, or iSCSI to allow remote networking from the server. LUNs allow for an administrative control point for the management of storage systems and is where access control and other configuration options can be assigned.

A LUN can be a block of storage, can be the complete drive, or, usually, can be made up of multiple storage drives in a RAID array for redundancy. With RAID, a LUN can be the entire array, or the array can be partitioned into multiple LUNs. The LUN is identified and managed as a single device regardless of its underlying configuration.

When using *LUN masking* in a SAN, a logical unit number is a unique value used to specify remote storage systems such as a hard disk or an array of storage devices. The remote storage devices are block-level arrays of disks. A LUN mask is used to divide a SAN port so that the same SAN port on the storage controller can restrict a server's access to a storage area by limiting it to specific LUNs. LUN masking is the process of making storage LUNs available for access by some host computers and restricted to others in the SAN. LUN masking is normally configured on the server's HBA or on the SAN switch and defines the LUN of the remote storage system. LUN masking can be thought of as a filter to permit or restrict storage visibility between the servers and the storage controllers.

SAN Permissions

SAN permissions are security mechanisms that are used to control access to data stored on a volume in a SAN storage array; this can be accessed as defined by the initiator or at the user or server level. Permissions can be defined on the storage array head end controller, in the SAN switching fabric, or, most likely, as a combination of the two solutions.

Access controls, user-based roles, and filters can be used when implementing SAN permissions. The permissions define the ability of an initiator to perform file operations. Common permissions are read-write, read-only, and delete.

Many cloud service providers allow the cloud consumer to create and modify these permissions via a web-based or API interface.

Summary

In this chapter, you explored the critical cloud infrastructure components of storage area networking. This chapter built upon the previous chapter on storage technologies by introducing the concepts of placing a storage network between the servers accessing the volumes that are connected to the storage arrays. You learned about how storage resources can be placed at different points in the cloud data center and can be directly attached or network-attached over a dedicated SAN. Traditional SANs were introduced, and then you learned about combining both the LAN and SAN traffic into a single converged network. Both redundant and nonredundant SAN topologies were compared and contrasted.

The chapter then explored the two main techniques used to store data on a storage device, file-based and block-based storage, and you learned the differences between the two and how each is used by the compute resources.

You learned about the various SAN protocols and associated hardware used in storage networks, specifically the Fibre Channel, FCoE, and iSCSI storage protocols. We explained in the level of detail needed to be a CCNA Cloud professional. The storage hardware covered host bus adapters, converged network adapters, and SAN switches. In the next chapter, we will go into greater detail on the Cisco storage product offerings in both the MDS and Nexus products.

The chapter ended with additional details about SANs, such as world wide names, the concept of a VSAN, logical units, initiators, and targets, and finally you learned about SAN permissions.

The topic of storage networking is a critical component of any cloud data center, and your understanding of SAN offerings is critical to your success as a CCNA Cloud professional. It is important that you study and feel comfortable with all of the technologies presented in this chapter.

Exam Essentials

Understand the difference between a NAS and a SAN. Network-attached storage is file system based and connected to an Ethernet-based LAN. A storage area network is Fibre Channel-based and a completely different protocol than Ethernet. Also, know that a Fibre Channel SAN uses block storage.

Understand block and file storage. Block storage is used with the SCSI, iSCSI, and Fibre Channel protocols. Block storage, whether local or across the network, requests individual sections of stored data residing on a storage device. File storage communicates across the network by requesting files, and it is used by all file systems including VMFS, CIFS, and NFS.

Understand what Fibre Channel is and the basics of its operation. For the Understanding Cisco Cloud Fundamentals exam, know the Fibre Channel topologies. Point-to-point topologies directly connect a storage array to a workstation. The Fibre Channel Arbitrated Loop is used within storage arrays. Fabric-switched networks allow for complex networks to be created using Fibre Channel switches that are similar to Ethernet switches but are designed specifically for storage applications. Recognize the different Fibre Channel port types. Ports on end nodes are N_ports. Ports on switches are F_ports to connect to end nodes and E_ports to connect to other switches. NL_ports connect to a Fibre Channel hub or in an arbitrated loop.

Know what World Wide Names are and what they are used for. A world wide name is a hardware address assigned to a device at the time of manufacture that is used to uniquely identify a Fibre Channel endpoint on a SAN; it is similar in concept to a MAC address in the Ethernet world.

World Wide Node Names (WWNNs) represent a device, and World Wide Port Names (WWPN) represent each individual port on an HBA or storage array. If an HBA has multiple ports assigned to it, then it will have both a WWNN and multiple WWPNs assigned to it.

Know what a VSAN is. A VSAN is a Fibre Channel term for virtual storage area network. It creates a separate logical SAN that is assigned on the SAN switching fabric; all fabric processes such as the SAN login services and the zone server are duplicated in each VSAN. VSANs are used in multitenant implementations such as in cloud computing.

Understand Logical Unit Numbers. The logical unit number provides a unique identifier that designates both physical and virtual storage devices that execute storage operations on a SAN. The LUN is created using a block storage array on a storage controller connected to the SAN. The SCSI command set uses LUNs, and the SCSI commands are encapsulated into FC, FCoE, or iSCSI to allow remote networking from the server. LUNs allow an administrative control point for the management of storage systems, and that is where access control and other management options can be assigned.

Be able to explain the SAN concept of zoning. Zoning is the process of logically segmenting a Fibre Channel SAN into multiple logical SANs. Zoning provides security and segmentation on the SAN fabric. Zoning is used to provide isolation and protection of LUNs in the storage arrays by restricting access between specifically defined storage initiators and targets. All devices placed into the same zone log into the same SAN fabric and are permitted to talk to each other.

Be able to explain the differences between a SAN initiator and a SAN target. The server acts as the storage initiator and logs into the SAN switch, and a path is established for the initiator to talk to the target across the Fibre Channel network. The initiator requests storage operations, and the target receives the request from the initiator to store and retrieve information off the hard drives.

Know what storage shares and mount points are. Shares create the ability of servers to access data on the volumes; it is the system of rights and permissions that allow a user or operating system to perform storage operations on a volume, directory, or file. Such rights include the ability to write to the volume, to read from it, and to erase or delete a file.

The mount point is an NFS directory where the remote file system is mounted (logically attached or connected). The mount point contains the directory and file system of remote storage that can be accessed from a server as if it were locally attached. Mount points can be related over both NAS and SAN systems.

Know what SAN access controls are.   Access controls, user-based roles, and filters can be used when implementing SAN permissions. The permissions define the ability of an initiator to perform file operations. Common permissions are read-write, read-only, and delete.

Written Lab

Fill in the blanks for the questions provided in the written lab. You can find the answers to the written labs in Appendix B.

1. _____ networks are the result of Ethernet and Fibre Channel networks sharing the same switching fabric.

2. _____ _____ provides file-based storage on a LAN.

3. A _____ _____ _____ provides a communications path from the CPU to a storage area network.

4. A SAN utilizes _____-based storage systems.

5. _____ _____ _____ _____ are used to identify unique Fibre Channel interfaces on an HBA.

6. The _____ _____ _____ combines both HBA and NIC functions on a card that allows for LAN and SAN traffic to share a common fabric.

7. _____ _____ does not require any networking technologies to access storage resources.

8. NAS storage is based on an _____-based storage system.

9. A SAN _____ requests storage operations from the _____.

10. The SAN _____ provides a unique identifier that designates both physical and virtual storage devices that execute storage operations on a SAN.

Review Questions

The following questions are designed to test your understanding of this chapter's material. You can find the answers to the questions in Appendix A. For more information on how to obtain additional questions, please see this book's Introduction.

1. What device is used to connect a server to a Fibre Channel SAN?

    A. IaaS

    B. VSAN

    C. HBA

    D. SCSI

2. A converged fabric consists of what two protocols? (Choose two.)

    A. SCSI

    B. Ethernet

    C. Fibre Channel

    D. VSAN

3. Which storage design is file-based?

    A. iSCSI

    B. NAS

    C. SAN

    D. FCoE

    E. DAS

4. Which protocols encapsulate storage requests and data that can be transported over a LAN? (Choose two.)

    A. Fibre Channel

    B. iSCSI

    C. Ethernet

    D. FCoE

    E. SCSI

5. After the FLOGI process is complete and the HBA in a server requests a file read operation, what role is the server in the SAN?

    A. FCSPF

    B. Target

    C. Initiator

    D. N_node

    E. LUN

6. Which two are common NAS file systems? (Choose two.)

    A. HBA

    B. VSAN

    C. Fibre Channel

    D. NFS

    E. iSCSI

    F. CIFS

7. What is the port type for a Fibre Channel HBA connected to a Fibre Channel hub?

    A. N_port

    B. E_port

    C. NL_port

    D. F_port

8. What are the port types defined in a connection between a Fibre Channel HBA and cloud SAN switch?

    A. N_port to F_port

    B. E_port to N_port

    C. N_port to E_port

    D. F_port to E_port

9. The storage initiator and target perform which function when first connecting to a SAN?

    A. VSAN

    B. FLOGI

    C. FCNS

    D. User authentication

    E. Permission assignment

10. A SAN fabric service that restricts initiators' connectivity to specific targets is known as what?

    A. LUN masking

    B. VSAN

    C. Zoning

    D. Access control lists

11. Which technology encapsulates a storage access standard directly to a LAN?

    A. FCoE

    B. Fibre Channel Ethernet

    C. iSCSI

    D. CNA over LAN

12. What segments a SAN switching fabric where ports are assigned into separate groupings on the SAN switches with each running a separate FLOGI process and only communicating with themselves?

   A. Zoning

   B. VSAN

   C. LUN masking

   D. ACL

13. What devices connect to a SAN switch? (Choose all that apply.)

   A. Storage array

   B. ACE

   C. HBA

   D. LAN

14. Which of the following are block-based storage protocols? (Choose three.)

   A. CIFS

   B. NFS

   C. NTFS

   D. Fibre Channel

   E. iSCSI

   F. HBA

   G. LUN

   H. FCoE

   I. FAT

15. SAN permissions define which of the following? (Choose three.)

   A. Write

   B. CNA

   C. Read

   D. Access

   E. VSAN

   F. WWPN

16. A LUN is made up of which of the following? (Choose two.)

   A. A block and a single SSD

   B. A unique identification number

   C. LUNs support spanning multiple disks.

   D. LUNs create their own file systems.

17. What are two characteristics of NAS? (Choose two.)

    A. Authentication

    B. File-based

    C. Block access

    D. iSCSI support

18. Which technology encapsulates Fibre Channel frames into a format that can be sent over a converged fabric?

    A. FCoE

    B. Fibre Channel Ethernet

    C. iSCSI

    D. CNA over LAN

19. A converged switching fabric supports which two storage options? (Choose two.)

    A. HBA

    B. VSAN

    C. FCoE

    D. NFS

    E. iSCSI

    F. FC

20. When FLOGI registration completes, the storage array assumes what role in the SAN?

    A. N_node

    B. Target

    C. LUN

    D. FCSPF

    E. Initiator

Chapter

11

Cisco Storage Product Families and Offerings

THE FOLLOWING UNDERSTANDING CISCO CLOUD FUNDAMENTALS CLDFND (210-451) EXAM OBJECTIVES ARE COVERED IN THIS CHAPTER:

✓ **5.5   Describe the various Cisco storage network devices**

- 5.5.a Cisco MDS family

- 5.5.b Cisco Nexus family

- 5.5.c UCS Invicta (Whiptail)

Introducing the Cisco Storage Network Product Lines

This chapter will conclude the Understanding Cisco Cloud Fundamentals exam objectives covering storage technologies by introducing you to the Cisco family of storage networking products. In Chapter 9, you learned all about basic storage such as hard drives, file systems, drive and HBA interface types, and storage redundancy with RAID. Then, in Chapter 10, we focused on SANs and converged networks with a discussion of NAS, DAS, and SAN file and block storage; you also learned about the Fibre Channel, iSCSI, and FCoE storage protocols.

There are two primary product lines for storage area and converged networks offered by Cisco. The first series of products you will learn about is the Multilayer Director Switch (MDS) family that is dedicated specifically to storage networking. We will then go into deeper detail than we did in Chapters 5 and 6 on the storage networking integration in the Cisco Nexus and UCS products. The chapter will conclude with an introduction of the Invicta SSD storage arrays.

This chapter will prepare you for any exam questions relating to the physical networking hardware for storage systems in the Cisco product line. It will also give you a look at the products used in the cloud and prepare you to be an effective Cisco Cloud professional.

This chapter is intended to introduce you to the many different storage products that Cisco offers. In each product family there are often many different models that make up each subgroup. Our intention is not to overwhelm you with the details of each family or to do a deep dive into the configuration complexities. It is good to know that the configuration steps are mostly the same across all the product offerings, and once you learn them for one platform, your knowledge is easily transferred across all the Cisco storage networking products. With that perspective on the storage products, you will find that it is not at all complex; it's storage networking is just different than standard Ethernet routing and switching.

The Cisco MDS Family

The Cisco Multilayer Director Series (MDS) family is purpose-built for the storage networking group of SAN switching hardware platforms. The MDS line has been available for many years and is still evolving by adding support for new technologies, faster interface speeds, and application software capabilities. In addition to the hardware offerings, many different types of management applications can be deployed to provision the MDS products, including the NX-API application programmable interface for cloud automation and orchestration.

When working with the MDS command line, if you have a data center background, you may notice that the CLI structure appears to be similar to the Nexus line. This is no coincidence since the *SAN-OS* operating system that was developed for the MDS line was used as the code base for the Nexus line of data center switching products and was labeled as *NX-OS*! So, you can see that the MDS products are not all that different after all; they just are focused on storage whereas the Cisco Nexus and Catalyst lines were designed primarily for Ethernet LAN operations.

Overview of the MDS Product Family

In this section, you will learn about the current models available in the MDS line of storage networking products from Cisco.

MDS products are used in the cloud and enterprise data centers for storage connectivity from servers to storage arrays. Cisco's primary storage offerings are the 9100, 9200, 9500, and 9700 series switches in the MDS family. While each series includes several products and a wide variety of line cards, interfaces, and software, you will find that they are more alike than different. The primary differences are the scalability and use cases. For example, you will learn that the MDS 9100 series is designed for the small installations or at the edge of the network, whereas the 9500 series is for large core cloud installations.

The MDS 9100 Series

The *MDS 9100* family is designed for implementation at smaller sites and businesses, while still offering the manageability, features, and high availability and virtualization capabilities of the larger members of the MDS family. The 9100 models, as shown in Figure 11.1, are the most cost effective of the MDS line and are still feature rich; installations that do not require the high port densities of the larger MDS products can still get the features they require in an MDS FC SAN switch.

FIGURE 11.1   MDS 9100 series switches

The 9100 features include the following:

- Top-of-rack SAN switch
- For small cloud and enterprise SAN connectivity requirements

- Edge switch to core SANs
- Stand-alone SAN switch with fixed interfaces
- Power-on autoprovisioning, allowing multiple switches to be configured together
- Intelligent diagnostic features
- High availability with hot-swappable redundant power supplies and in-service OS upgrades
- SAN extensions
- Virtual fabric support
- Switch-to-switch connections and SAN extensions
- Switch fabric management and monitoring application software

The MDS 9148 features include the following:

- 16, 32, and 48 ports
- 1Gbps, 2Gbps, and 8Gbps Fibre Channel interfaces
- Fixed configuration
- Advanced traffic management
- Virtual SAN support
- Inter-VSAN routing
- Port-channel support up to 16 links

The MDS 9148s model has the same feature set as the 9148 but offers Fibre Channel interface speeds of 16GB in addition to the 2GB, 4GB, and 8GB interfaces of the standard 9148 model. It is important to note that neither the 9148 nor the 9148S supports Fibre Channel over Ethernet or iSCSI; all interfaces are Fibre Channel only.

The MDS 9200 Series

Medium to large enterprise and cloud SAN support is the primary use case for the *MDS 9200* series. The 9200 series supports the full feature set of the MDS line in a small form factor modular design. High-performance SAN extensions and a distributed architecture are a natural fit for the 9200 series. The 9200 offers multiprotocol support for both cloud and enterprise installations.

The MDS9222i has just recently been flagged for retirement from the MDS 9200 lineup. For the sake of completeness and to show you the common features found in SAN switches, we have decided to include a description of the 9222i for learning purposes and because it may still show up on the CCNA exam. The 9222i is a modular switch that supports from 18 to 66 4Gbps Fibre Channel ports. iSCSI and FCIP are supported with Gigabit Ethernet interfaces and software support. There is a modular expansion slot that allows for the addition of ports as required. Trunking support between SAN switches and end devices is included. Figure 11.2 shows the 9222i.

FIGURE 11.2   MDS 9222i SAN switch

Courtesy of Cisco Systems, Inc. Unauthorized use not permitted.

The MDS 9222i features include the following:

- SAN extensions for distributed networks
- Up to 66 4Gbps Fibre Channel interfaces
- Four 1Gbps Fibre Channel over IP and iSCSI interfaces
- *IBM Fiber Connection (FICON)*, iSCSI, and Fibre Channel over IP support
- One expansion slot module
- Power-on autoprovisioning, allowing multiple switches to be configured together
- Intelligent diagnostic features
- High availability with hot-swappable redundant power supplies and in-service OS upgrades
- VSAN extensions and inter-VSAN routing support
- Virtual fabric support
- Switch-to-switch connections and SAN extensions
- Switch fabric management and monitoring application software

The fixed-configuration MDS 9250i is the second product in the family. The 9250i offers integrated multiprotocol support for Fibre Channel, Fibre Channel over Ethernet, and Fibre Channel over IP interfaces in a small fixed-configuration enclosure. Figure 11.3 shows the 9250i.

FIGURE 11.3   MDS 9250i SAN switch

Courtesy of Cisco Systems, Inc. Unauthorized use not permitted.

The MDS 9250i features include the following:

- SAN extensions for distributed networks
- IP and FCoE for multiprotocol storage networks
- Up to 66 Fibre Channel interfaces

- Eight Fibre Channel over Ethernet (FCoE) interfaces
- Two 1/10Gbps Fibre Channel over IP (FCIP) interfaces
- IBM Fiber Connection, iSCSI, and Fibre Channel over IP support
- Data encryption
- Power-on autoprovisioning, allowing multiple switches to be configured together
- Intelligent diagnostic features
- High availability with hot-swappable redundant power supplies and in-service OS upgrades
- VSAN extensions and inter-VSAN routing support
- Virtual fabric support
- Switch-to-switch connections and SAN extensions
- Switch fabric management and monitoring application software

The MDS 9300 Series

Let's move higher up the technology ladder and introduce you to the *MDS 9300* series and the 9396s multilayer fabric switch, as shown in Figure 11.4. This product is a fixed-configuration 2RU and supports from 48 to 96 line-rate 16Gbps Fibre Channel connections. You can deploy this in medium-size cloud SAN deployments and large-scale installations where it is a good fit for a top-of-rack or end-of-row SAN switch.

FIGURE 11.4   MDS 9396s

Courtesy of Cisco Systems, Inc. Unauthorized use not permitted.

The MDS 9396s features include the following:

- Up to 96 2Gbps, 4Gbps, 8Gbps, 10Gbps, and 16Gbps line-rate Fibre Channel connections
- SAN extensions for distributed networks
- Expanded buffer to buffer credits
- VSAN support
- Inter-VSAN routing support
- Virtual output queuing to eliminate head of line blocking
- In-service software upgrade offering reduced downtime for maintenance and software updates

- High-performance interswitch links with up to 16 ISLs in a bundle with load sharing
- SPAN and RSPAN switch port analyzer support
- Data Center Network Manager (DCNM) support
- Redundant power supplies

The MDS 9700 Series

The *MDS 9700* series, as illustrated in Figure 11.5, features chassis-based Fibre Channel SAN switches that support Fibre Channel speeds from 2Gbps all the way up to 32Gbps 1/10Gbps and 40Gbps Ethernet FCoE and FCIP interfaces for large-scale converged networks. The MDS 9700 family is for large-scale virtualized cloud and enterprise installations. By implementing the 9700 series, SAN networks can be consolidated into a small number of large 9700 systems that offer a centralized highly available architecture. Features include multiprotocol support, a nonstop operational design, and scalability. An analytics module is available that offers extensive insight into the data traversing the fabric. The family is designed for high availability to achieve zero downtime that is critical for storage networks in cloud data centers.

FIGURE 11.5   MDS 9700 series

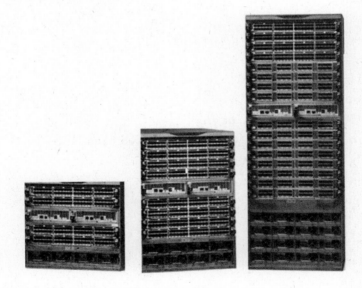

The 9700 comes in the following models:

MDS 9706

- Small to medium enterprise and cloud
- 12Tbps Fibre Channel switching bandwidth

- 10.5Tbps of FCoE bandwidth
- 192 32Gbps FC connections
- 192 10Gbps FCoE interfaces
- 96 40Gbps FCoE interfaces
- 32 1/10Gbps Ethernet FCIP interfaces
- Eight 40Gbps Ethernet FCIP interfaces
- Four line-card slots
- Two supervisor slots
- Six crossbar switching fabric slots
- Three fan trays at the back of the chassis
- Four power supply bays
- Name server per VSAN
- Registered State Change Notification (RSCN)
- Fabric login services
- Fabric configuration server (FCS)
- VSAN support
- Inter-VSAN routing IVR
- Port channel with multipath load balancing
- Flow-based and zone-based QoS
- N-port ID virtualization (NPIV)
- Internal port loopbacks
- SPAN and RSPAN switch port analyzer
- Fibre Channel traceroute, Fibre Channel ping, Fibre Channel debug
- Cisco Fabric Analyzer and syslog support
- Online system health reporting
- Extensive port-level statistics
- VSANs
- SAN access control list support
- Per-VSAN role-based access control (RBAC)
- Fibre Channel zoning support
- N-port world wide name (WWN)
- N-port FC-ID
- Port security and fabric binding support
- Out-of-band management access
- SSHv2 with Advanced Encryption Standard (AES) support

- SNMPv3 network management with AES encryption
- Cisco TrustSec Fibre Channel link encryption
- Software upgrades can be performed online and will not disrupt the flow of traffic.
- Supervisor module failover retains state information and does not disrupt traffic flows.
- Redundant supervisor, fabric, SFP, fan trays, and power supplies are hot-swappable.
- Individual software process restart capabilities
- Fabric services per VSAN
- Online diagnostic support

See Figure 11.6 for an illustration of the MDS 9706.

FIGURE 11.6   MDS 9706 series

Courtesy of Cisco Systems, Inc. Unauthorized use not permitted.

MDS 9710

- Medium to large-scale cloud and enterprise storage
- Edge and core deployments
- 24Tbps FC bandwidth
- 1.5Tbps of FCoE bandwidth per chassis slot
- 384 32Gbps FC connections
- 384 10Gbps FCoE interfaces
- 192 40Gbps FCoE interfaces
- 64 1/10Gbps Ethernet FCIP interfaces
- 16 40Gbps Ethernet FCIP interfaces
- Nine line-card slots
- Two supervisor slots

See Figure 11.7 for an illustration of the MDS 9710.

FIGURE 11.7 MDS 9710 series

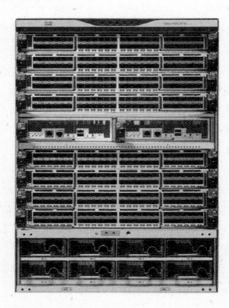

Courtesy of Cisco Systems, Inc. Unauthorized use not permitted.

MDS 9718

- Large-scale cloud and enterprise storage
- SAN consolidation
- 24Tbps FC bandwidth
- 1.5Tbps of FCoE bandwidth per chassis slot
- 768 32Gbps FC connections
- 768 10Gbps FCoE interfaces
- 384 40Gbps FCoE interfaces
- 128 1/10Gbps Ethernet FCIP interfaces
- 32 40Gbps Ethernet FCIP interfaces
- 16 line-card slots
- Two supervisor slots

See Figure 11.8 for an illustration of the MDS 9718.

FIGURE 11.8   MDS 9718 series

Courtesy of Cisco Systems, Inc. Unauthorized use not permitted.

The Nexus Product Family

The Cisco Nexus family of data center and cloud networking products were introduced and covered in Chapter 6. In this chapter, you will learn about the SAN features in the Nexus products in greater detail to better prepare you for the exam.

The Cisco Nexus Family Storage Networking Features

As we discussed earlier in this chapter, the Nexus product line adopted its operating system (NX-OS) from the MDS product family. However, the Nexus products are not intended to be a replacement for the MDS offerings and actually have only a limited storage networking feature set. The design intent of the Nexus products is for converged LAN/SAN networks and using the Nexus as a Fibre Channel gateway to the cloud SAN.

The design intent is for the Nexus products to be used for converged networks by implementing Fibre Channel over Ethernet over its converged switching fabric. The Nexus uses a specific interface called the *unified port* to support Fibre Channel, FCoE, and classic Ethernet.

The converged fabric supports the required QOS implementations and management features required for FCoE to operate over an Ethernet fabric that can (and will) drop frames, something storage systems are not very tolerant of.

Storage convergence is supported on a limited subset of the complete Nexus products. The 5600 series supports FCoE with unified ports, and the 7000 series has line cards that also support FCoE.

The Nexus 5600 Series SAN Offerings

By implementing the Nexus 5600 into the cloud data center, you are able to converge Fibre Channel, classic Ethernet, and Fibre Channel over Ethernet in the same unified platform. The convergence advantages are many and include savings on power, cabling, rack density, and devices to manage.

The Nexus 5000 gives you a great way to migrate to 10 Gigabit Ethernet, unifying your storage and data networking. What could be better than having Fibre Channel and Ethernet in the same box?

In traditional data centers, a port was either a SAN Fibre Channel port or Ethernet. Cisco introduced the *unified port (UP)* that allows a port to be configured for either Ethernet or Fibre Channel. This allows for flexibility in port densities and enables greater convergence between the storage and data networks. The universal port is configured in the 5600 and after a reload is configured for either Fibre Channel or Ethernet, so thought must be given to the number of Fibre Channel ports required during the initial install to save you from having to perform a disruptive reload in production to change the personalities of the universal ports.

The 5600 comes in the following models:

Nexus 5672UP

- 1/10/40G Ethernet switch in a 1 rack unit form factor
- Wire-speed forwarding performance for up to 48 1/10Gbps Ethernet ports
- 24 unified ports that support both Fibre Channel and classical Ethernet
- Fibre Channel support for 2Gbps, 4Gbps, 8Gbps, and 16Gbps interface speeds
- 10Gbps FCoE capable on all ports
- Six 40Gbps Ethernet ports with FCoE support
- Buffer support for SAN extensions of up to 16 kilometers at 16Gbps
- Two redundant, hot-swappable power supplies (1+1)
- Hot-swappable fans with 2+1 redundancy

Figure 11.9 shows a front-panel view of the Nexus 5672UP.

FIGURE 11.9 Nexus 5672UP

Nexus 56128P

- 1/10/40Gbps Ethernet switch in a 2 rack unit form factor
- Wire-speed frame forwarding, up to 96 1/10Gbps Ethernet ports
- Two expansion slots for generic expansion modules (GEM)
- 48 fixed unified ports that support both Fibre Channel and classical Ethernet
- Eight 40Gbps Ethernet ports with FCoE support
- Fibre Channel support for 2Gbps, 4Gbps, 8Gbps, and 16Gbps interface speeds
- 10Gbps FCoE capable on all ports
- Buffer support for SAN extensions of up to 16 kilometers at 16Gbps
- Four redundant, hot-swappable power supplies (3+1)
- Four hot-swappable fans with 3+1 redundancy

Figure 11.10 shows a front-panel view of the Nexus 56123P.

FIGURE 11.10   Nexus 56128P

Courtesy of Cisco Systems, Inc. Unauthorized use not permitted.

The Nexus 7000 Series SAN Offerings

The Nexus 7000 series can be deployed as a cloud aggregation or core layer switch. It is important to note that the Nexus 7k is an Ethernet switching product that also supports Fibre Channel over Ethernet for converged networking. While it does not have the extensive SAN feature set of the MDS products, the 7000 series is used in converged networking installations as an interconnect between the converged network and Fibre Channel–based SAN if the cloud storage is FC–based. The NX-OS SAN support is designed for FCoE converged networking with a gateway to the SAN by utilizing Nexus to MDS SAN interconnections. The interconnects in the cloud data center are usually implemented by mapping the Nexus 7000 FCoE interface to an FC VSAN in the MDS.

To enable FCoE in the 7k, either 32 or 48-port line cards need to be installed into an available slot in the chassis. The two line cards that support FCoE are currently the 32-port 1/10Gbps Ethernet F1 line card with SFP and SFP+ inserts or the 48-port 1/10 Gbps Ethernet F2 line card also with SFP and SFP+ inserts.

To enable FCoE capability, a license is required to activate the feature set in NX-OS. One license will be required for each line card.

The FCoE feature set in the 7k lines supports VSANs, zoning, and fabric logins (FLOGI).

The UCS Fabric Interconnects

The Unified Computing System (UCS) was introduced in Chapter 5, and we mentioned that one of the many features of UCS was its ability to merge LAN and SAN traffic into a unified, or *converged*, switching fabric. In addition to the UCS B-series blade-server chassis and C-series of rack server products, there is the UCS 6300 fabric interconnect modules that provide the converged switching fabric.

The fabric interconnects feature high-performance, line-rate switchports.

The newer 6300 models support lossless 10 and 40 Gigabit Ethernet interfaces; Fibre Channel over Ethernet; and 4Gbps, 8Gbps, and 16Gbps Fibre Channel. Let's take a look at the current models available in the UCS fabric interconnect lineup.

UCS 6332 and 6332-UP Fabric Interconnects

- Up to 32 fixed 40Gbps Ethernet and FCoE ports
- 16 1/10 Gbps, Ethernet, FCoE, or Fibre Channel ports
- Throughput of 2.56Tbps
- Support for 410Gbps breakout cables

Figure 11.11 shows a front-panel view of the UCS 6332 fabric interconnect.

FIGURE 11.11   UCS 6332 fabric interconnect

UCS 6324 Fabric Interconnect

- Inserts into the UCS 5108 Blade chassis
- Referred to as the UCS mini
- Four 1/10Gbps Ethernet, FCoE, Fibre Channel ports
- Fibre Channel interfaces with speeds of 2Gbps, 4Gbps, and 8Gbps
- One 40Gbps scalability port
- Port-to-port latency in a microsecond

Figure 11.12 shows a front-panel view of the UCS-mini 6324 fabric interconnect.

FIGURE 11.12   UCS 6324 fabric interconnect

The Nexus 9000 Family

The Nexus 9000 products focus on the data center and the cloud and offer high-speed interfaces ranging up to 100Gb. Chapter 6 covered the Nexus 9000 series in detail and will not be revisited here. Since it is a data center product, it supports FCoE traffic and a full feature set for converged networks. However, at the time of this writing, there is no native Fibre Channel support for the Nexus 9000 family of products.

The UCS Invicta (Whiptail) Family

In 2013 Cisco completed the purchase of *Whiptail* to complement its successful UCS line of server products. The Whiptail purchase resulted in the Cisco *Invicta* line of SSD storage array products. The UCS series was gaining market share against the existing server vendors, and with the rapid growth, there was a demand for a complete product offering. With the addition of storage products to the UCS line of servers, Cisco could offer a more complete product line with internally developed products. Now, in addition to integrated networking and compute that has been with the UCS line from its introduction, storage was added and managed under the same UCS manager application for a complete UCS hyper-converged server, storage, and networking offering.

The decision to acquire Whiptail was based on the desire to offer all flash storage arrays in the UCS form factor and to control the product development cycles internally instead of leveraging existing storage partnerships. The engineering teams would go on to integrate the Invicta products into the UCS line at both the hardware and the UCS director management software levels.

The Invicta C3124SA SSD storage appliance was a single-chassis, Fibre Channel or iSCSI-connected storage appliance that was released by Cisco as part of the Unified Computing System offerings, as illustrated in Figure 11.13. The Invicta appliance was based on the UCS C-series rack server platform and supported 64TB of effective storage capacity and around 250,000 input/output operations per second (IOPS) with a throughput of 1.9Gbps. Either Fibre Channel or Ethernet-based iSCSI interfaces connected the device to the UCS domain and offered block-level storage.

FIGURE 11.13   Cisco Invicta C3124SA flash storage appliance

A scaling system and storage blade to the UCS systems rounded out the Invicta products. The array supported up to 30 appliances and up to 2 petabytes of solid-state drive storage capacity and 4 million IOPS.

There was a great deal of engineering challenges to overcome to be able to integrate the Invicta storage system into the UCS product line with a full list of desired features. Eventually Cisco put a stop ship on all Invicta products. In mid-2015 Cisco made the decision to withdraw the Invicta products' line from the marketplace. Today all of the Invicta offerings are end-of-life and no longer sold by Cisco. However, on the CCNA blueprint for the CLDFND 210-451 exam, there are currently exam objectives for the Invicta products. With the need to completely cover the entire blueprint in this book, we are including this short section on the Invicta release and its withdrawal from the marketplace.

Summary

In this chapter, we focused almost exclusively on product families and the individual products that are currently shipping from Cisco in each family.

You learned that MDS is the primary storage product family. The MDS models range from the small and medium business requirements that are included in the MDS 9100 and 9200 lines. For large enterprise and cloud-scale data centers, the chassis-based MDS 9700 was covered in this chapter.

We then reviewed the Nexus family of switches. Since most models were covered earlier in the book and this chapter is exclusive to storage, we covered the Nexus offerings for both converged and storage networking. We also introduced the Nexus 9000 family of data center products with a focus on their storage and convergence capabilities.

Finally, we ended the chapter with an introduction to the Whiptail acquisition by Cisco and the resulting Invicta products that were ultimately removed from the market. You should be familiar with the Invicta products since the Invicta products remain on the CCNA blueprint for the CLDFND 210-451 exam.

Exam Essentials

Know what the Multilayer Director Switch (MDS) is.   The MDS series is the Cisco product family of storage networking switches and is primarily based on the Fibre Channel protocol. There is a complete family of MDS SAN switches ranging from small, fixed-configuration edge switches to large chassis-based core switches for enterprise and data center deployments.

Understand the products in the MDS lineup.   While the Understanding Cisco Cloud Fundamentals exam is not heavily focused on storage, it is important to know where the MDS products are best suited for operations. The 9100 series is a fixed-configuration SAN switch for small SAN networks or edge switching. Know that the 9200 series is designed for medium to large enterprise and cloud operations, has a full feature set, and offers modular interface options. The 9300 has a larger interface count in fixed-configuration form factors with a complete feature set. The large chassis-based MDS switch line is the MDS 9300 series and is for large enterprise and cloud installations. The 9300 is fully redundant and has a wide range of interface cards for high-density cloud deployments.

Understand the storage options available in the Nexus product line.   The Nexus 5600 series offers both FCoE and Fibre Channel options for converged networking. The universal ports on the 5600 allow for software configuration to be either Fibre Channel or Ethernet. The UPs get configured at the initial installation since a reboot is required and disruptive. Then you can insert either Fibre Channel or Ethernet SFP optics in the slot and configure the port as desired.

The Nexus 7000 series is the large chassis-based data center switching system and has limited storage networking with converged fabrics that support iSCSI and FCoE but has no native Fibre Channel interfaces.

Understand the storage networking capabilities of the Nexus 9000.   The Nexus 9000 series is a newer product line and offers high-speed 40Gbps and 100Gbps interfaces. The storage options are limited to Ethernet as there are no Fibre Channel options in this product line.

Know that the UCS 6300 fabric extenders offer a converged fabric.   The UCS 6300 fabric extenders are used to interconnect and manage the UCS B-series and C-series of servers. They also act as the core switching fabric for the USC server systems. One of the outstanding benefits of the UCS offering is that the storage and data networks are merged into a converged fabric that is a function of the UCS fabric interconnect products.

Read the product descriptions in this chapter.   Take the time to read about all the product families in this chapter. While it is not necessary to know all of the specifications for all of the different models, it is important to know how they are different from each other and what their intended use is.

Have a basic understanding of the Whiptail/Invicta products.   While the Whiptail acquisition led to the end of life of the Invicta line of SSD storage arrays, it is still in the Understanding Cisco Cloud Fundamentals exam blueprint. It is suggested that you have a basic understanding that the Invicta product is an SSD storage array that was to be part of the UCS family and is connected to the SAN using either the Fibre Channel or iSCSI protocol.

Written Lab

Fill in the blanks for the questions provided in the written lab. You can find the answers to the written labs in Appendix B.

1. The Cisco line of dedicated storage area networking switches is known as the _____ _____ _____.

2. The _____ product line supports converged networking.

3. The Nexus _____ series supports native Fibre Channel.

4. Converged fabrics require _____ _____ _____ to be configured to prevent the loss of storage frames.

5. The Nexus _____ can be configured for Fibre Channel or Ethernet connections.

6. The MDS _____ is designed for large-scale SAN implementations.

7. The UCS _____ is also referred to as the UCS mini.

8. Fibre Channel speeds in the Nexus products range from 2 to ___ Gbps.

9. Invicta SAN storage arrays connect to the network using both _____ ____ and _____ protocols.

10. The _____ line is for large-scale, high-speed cloud and data center LAN and SAN networking.

Review Questions

The following questions are designed to test your understanding of this chapter's material. You can find the answers to the questions in Appendix A. For more information on how to obtain additional questions, please see this book's Introduction.

1. What is the operating system used in the MDS line of SAN switches?

    A. ISR-OS

    B. IOS

    C. NX-OS

    D. SAN-OS

2. Which Cisco products support both storage and Ethernet networking on the same platform? (Choose two.)

    A. Catalyst

    B. UCS FI

    C. ISR

    D. Nexus

3. The Nexus operating system was adopted from which product family?

    A. Catalyst

    B. MDS

    C. ISR

    D. Invicta

4. What is a Cisco semimodular MDS switch that supports iSCSI, FCIP, and FICON protocols?

    A. 5696

    B. 9222i

    C. 9513

    D. 7010

5. What is a Cisco chassis-based SAN switch for large cloud deployments?

    A. 9148

    B. 9718

    C. 9513

    D. 7010

6. What is a Cisco chassis-based switch for core and aggregation switching in large cloud and data center deployments?

    A. 3124SA

    B. 5696

    C. 9513

    D. 7010

7. Name the Cisco storage array product in the UCS family.

    A. C3124SA

    B. 5632

    C. 6324

    D. 7010

8. Which storage switches are often used for SAN extensions? (Choose two.)

    A. 9100

    B. 9200

    C. 9300

    D. 9700

9. Which storage switches are designed for top-of-rack and end-of-row cloud configurations?

    A. 9100

    B. 9200

    C. 9300

    D. 9700

10. This product family offers high availability, a complete feature set, hot-swappable supervisors, power supplies, and fan trays for core SAN configurations.

    A. 9100

    B. 9200

    C. 9300

    D. 9700

11. MDS to MDS interconnections are referred to as what?

    A. ISL

    B. Trunking

    C. SNMP

    D. Fibre Channel

    E. EtherChannel

12. What Cisco converged network products offer in-service upgrade options? (Choose all that apply.)

A. 56128

B. 9706

C. 7009

D. C3124SA

13. Invicta appliances support which types of SAN network protocols? (Choose two.)

A. FICON

B. iSCSI

C. FCIP

D. FC

14. What storage switch is a fixed-configuration SAN switch designed for medium-size cloud deployments and supports 48 to 96 Fibre Channel connections?

A. 9148

B. 9208

C. 9396S

D. 9796

15. What storage switch is a fixed-configuration SAN switch designed for small cloud deployments?

A. 9148

B. 9208

C. 9396S

D. 9796

16. What application can be used to configure an MDS SAN network?

A. APIC

B. DCNM

C. UCSM

D. ISE

17. What protocol is commonly used to connect an MDS SAN switch to an IBM mainframe?

A. FC

B. FCoE

C. iSCSI

D. FICON

18. What is the operating system used in the Nexus line of data center switches?

    A. ISR-OS

    B. IOS

    C. NX-OS

    D. SAN-OS

19. All MDS switches support what type of virtualization?

    A. VLAN

    B. RSTP

    C. OTV

    D. VSAN

    E. VDC

20. What port types are used for monitoring on an MDS series switch? (Choose two.)

    A. ERN+

    B. RSTP+

    C. SPAN

    D. ERSPAN

    E. VACL

Chapter

12

Integrated Cloud Infrastructure Offerings

THE FOLLOWING UNDERSTANDING CISCO CLOUD FUNDAMENTALS CLDFND (210-451) EXAM OBJECTIVES ARE COVERED IN THIS CHAPTER:

✓ **5.6   Describe various integrated infrastructures**

- 5.6.a FlexPod (NetApp)

- 5.6.b Vblock (VCE)

- 5.6.c VSPEX (EMC)

- 5.6.d OpenBlock (Red Hat)

Integrated Infrastructure Overview

This chapter concludes the portion of this book that covers the Understanding Cloud Fundamentals 210-451 CLDFND exam. The CLDFND exam expects the candidate to understand and describe the various integrated offerings available as well as the underlying concepts. In this chapter, you'll learn about the various integrated infrastructure offerings and what led to the design of each.

Before you jump into the integrated infrastructure, let's take a closer look at what led to these offerings in the data center. Figure 12.1 shows the spread-out design of the early data center.

FIGURE 12.1 Early data center infrastructure

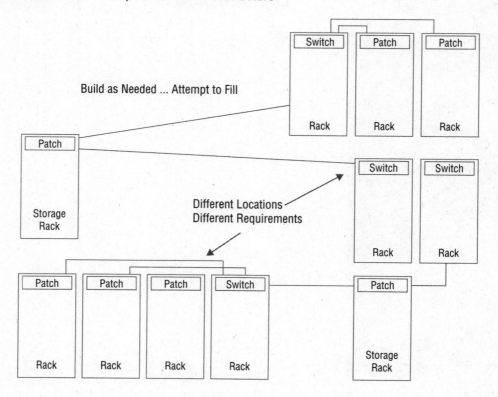

Looking at this design, a few things stick out:

Mixed Infrastructure   Each row or area could be a completely different design. The drawing represents different areas on the data center floor.

Networking   Various design methods are employed here including end-of-row, mid-row, and top-of-rack designs.

Storage   In a separate area, patch panels connect the racks to external disk storage.

Cabling   This design leads to cable plant nightmares. When deploying in one area, you might find that the nearest storage rack is out of capacity.

As the data center grows and projects spin up, the architecture in Figure 12.1 is extremely hard to keep up with. The design is broken up into larger areas, but the equipment is spread out and uneven depending on what areas needed to be interconnected at the time. This can lead to guessing what will be needed in the future and guessing about where to locate the racks in the data center. As an example, predeploying a row of SAN storage arrays before there are servers to consume them leads to a suboptimal data center layout. What if an area runs out of power or there aren't enough servers left to consume the storage available? This leads to both underuse and overuse of resources.

The shortcomings of the past data center design as shown in Figure 12.1 led to organizations creating their own custom rack design standards. One of these is referred to as a *pool of devices* (POD); this is also known as a *point of delivery*. A POD can be described as a grouping of common infrastructure such as network, computing, storage, and application components that deliver a network service or application. The POD is a homogenous structure, making it easy to repeat and scale because its components are known and can be easily replicated.

A POD usually consists of all or several of these components:

- Servers
- Network switches
- Network routers
- Network services, such as firewalls and load balancers
- Storage appliances
- Patch panels
- Application software
- UPS and PDUs for rack power
- Anything else needed to support the application

The POD concept brought sanity to the otherwise random deployments seen in early data center builds and referenced in Figure 12.1. Application teams get together with business partners, architects, and facilities, and design a POD model that fits their application or use case. Each design is likely to be unique with decision points such as the following:

- Type of storage (external or internal)
- Cabling requirements (Twinax, Ethernet, fiber, and more)

- CPU requirements
- Memory requirements
- Other custom requirements

On first look, you may wonder why things such as cabling matter. To the facilities and the application teams, cabling might play a large role. Different types of cabling mean different types of power usage and latency. The same goes for storage and CPU. Once the requirements are built, the POD design is done and repeated as needed. Some common POD footprints are virtualized infrastructure, virtualized desktop, big data, Oracle, SAP, and more. The POD design usually contains a segment of storage, network, and servers. See Figure 12.2 to better understand this concept. Some PODs may be a few racks. Some may be a single rack and need a few cross connections. The choice is entirely up to the application team.

FIGURE 12.2   POD design

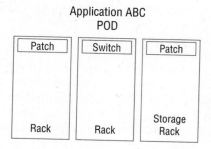

Using the POD design alleviates a lot of the issues you saw in Figure 12.1. If an infrastructure team can build multiple designs for applications, the designs can be standardized and repeated throughout the application's life. As mentioned, if an organization decides on several types of pods for its various applications and use cases, this model scales well. Since the design is repeatable, the power, cooling, and physical requirements can be planned appropriately. The data center then scales in POD units instead of random groupings of equipment, as was discussed earlier and shown in Figure 12.1. See how this is addressed in Figure 12.3.

Now that you've seen the POD design, you can realize that it is a bit analogous to a consumer creating a customer-built computer. For whatever reason, the consumer's needs aren't met by off-the-shelf prepackaged models; they may need special graphics or power, for example. They may need a custom motherboard for more component support. Or in some cases, they may just like building their own. The reasons are many!

There are a few drawbacks to this approach, however. If the consumer buys individual components and pieces together their own system, where does support come from? We'll talk about these items in the next section. This is a primary reason why the industry has moved on to more hyperconverged solutions.

FIGURE 12.3   POD growth design

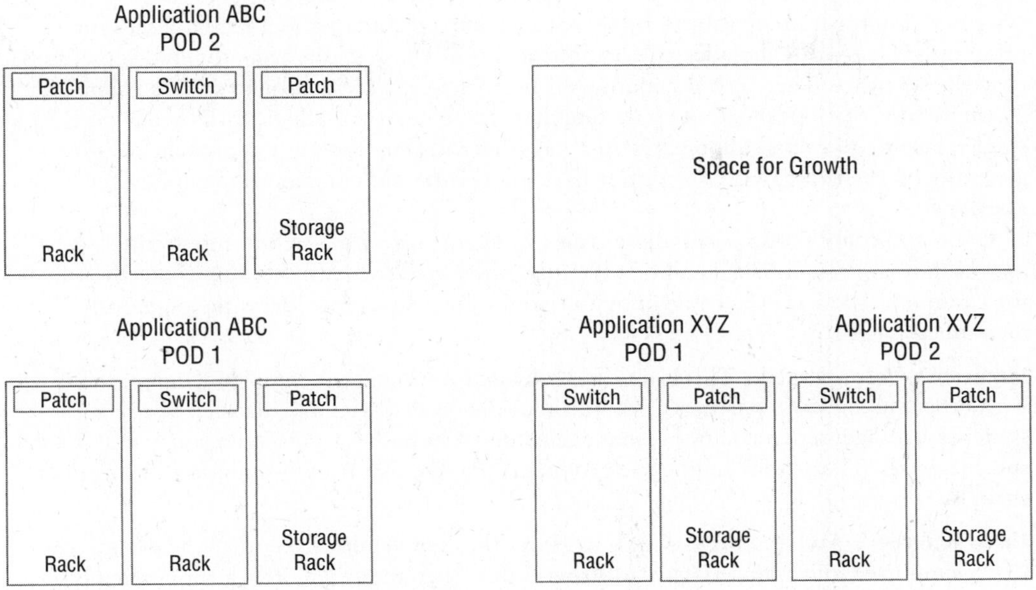

Application ABC
POD 2

Patch	Switch	Patch
Rack	Rack	Storage Rack

Space for Growth

Application ABC
POD 1

Patch	Switch	Patch
Rack	Rack	Storage Rack

Application XYZ
POD 1

Switch	Patch
Rack	Storage Rack

Application XYZ
POD 2

Switch	Patch
Rack	Storage Rack

Integrated Infrastructures and Cisco Reference Designs

Enterprise and cloud data centers have a lot to gain by building custom PODs. They can customize everything to their exact needs, using the network, server, storage, and infrastructure components that fit their specific requirements. Not every operation is up for this, though, mainly because of the planning and time it takes to address such a model for their application needs. This is not a trivial task to engineer correctly.

The unique needs of each application may require different parts and vendors to facilitate the POD design. In the end, the support model could be countless vendors each supporting a subsection of the complete solution that invites the classic finger-pointing routine that we all know and love. You may encounter situations where the vendor's hardware or software isn't supported in the model you've deployed or isn't certified to run with a certain vendor. There may be driver, feature set, versioning, or other interoperability issues. These are issues an enterprise usually won't have time to deal with.

Going back to the personal computer model example at retail stores, the similarities in support are easily seen. You can go into a large retail store and buy a brand-name desktop or laptop computer with everything included. In that model, you would expect the company that sold you the hardware to have verified that the components that make up the system all interoperate by subjecting them to a complete and ongoing quality assurance program. This usually includes all components inside the desktop or laptop and sometimes even the software. There is a premium paid for this, as it's an integrated solution supported by the vendor that put together your computer. To some, it is well worth it by having a single place to go to for support. Others may prefer the custom-built approach, but they're generally on their own with support or have many different companies to contact for assistance.

Cisco and other vendors saw these issues and came up with a tighter integration approach to address it. We'll call this the *integrated infrastructure* because that's the way the exam refers to it. Cisco came up with two different ways to address the previously mentioned issues:

Integrated, Prepackaged   This is a Cisco-provided solution that completely integrates with other vendors and partners. This includes the needed components such as network switches, storage, servers, cabling, management software, basic configurations, and other specific needs. The vendor selling the product is the one that usually supports the product entirely.

Cisco Reference Architectures   Cisco works with other vendors to ensure the design is Cisco supported and tested. The vendors work together and often offer a support model that uses one or more vendors. This helps with the finger-pointing support issue of custom components.

We'll discuss the reference architectures in the next short section. You'll find on Cisco's website examples of reference architectures for VMware, especially in desktop virtualization, Citrix, and others. The goal for these was to be a starting point when you're building your custom POD but need a little bit of help to get off the ground through white papers and design guides.

Cisco took this a step further and created the *Cisco Validated Design (CVD)*. Cisco's section on validated design says the following:

> Cisco Validated Designs (CVDs) provide the foundation for systems design based on common use cases or current engineering system priorities. They incorporate a broad set of technologies, features, and applications to address customer needs.

Cisco uses its CVD program to put its stamp of approval on common projects such as desktop virtualization, big data applications, and more. Cisco includes two different type of design guides to assist customers.

Technology Design Guides   These provide detail about validated products and software for a specific technology. They also include best-practice information.

Solution Design Guides   These are probably what is most referenced when CVD is brought up, as these guides also include third-party integration. They are a combination of the technology guide with added emphasis on integrating and building an entire solution.

The technology guide is usually a shorter guide but it for still offers valuable help with building a solution from the ground up. Cisco works on both guides to provide customers with known validated solutions. You can find test case scenarios, the hardware that was used, and planning information for purchasing. Usually included are diagrams and configuration guides for the solution, including the information for third-party vendors as well.

The reference architecture and validated designs can assist customers with designing integrated solutions, which is what we'll discuss for the rest of this chapter. Cisco worked with various partners to offer integrated solutions that could be purchased as a POD. A customer in this case still has some options for customization, but that mostly relates to the size of the POD and processing power.

FlexPod (NetApp)

FlexPod, from Cisco and Network Appliance, is the first integrated solution we'll discuss. *FlexPod* is a single-rack solution that integrates all the required equipment needed for a specific application. The networking, server, and storage hardware are all included. The PODs are predesigned and include best-practice architectures using the Cisco Unified Computing System (UCS), Nexus switches, and the NetApp Fabric-Attached Storage (FAS) product line.

FlexPod Overview

Some of the FlexPod applications include the VMware virtualization POD, XenDesktop for virtualized desktop, a private cloud, Oracle Real Application Cluster (RAC), ACI, Docker containers, and many more.

FlexPod comes in three platforms.

FlexPod Datacenter   Custom built for massively scalable virtual data center infrastructure. This is suited for virtual desktop environments, public and private clouds, and server virtualization.

FlexPod Express   A compact converged infrastructure platform that is targeted for edge and remote branch use cases.

FlexPod Select   Designed especially for high-performance applications and big data such as Oracle RAC.

FlexPod Components

Table 12.1 lists some of the example components you will find in various FlexPod Datacenter offerings today.

TABLE 12.1 Example FlexPod Datacenter deployments

Solution	Server/Compute	Network	Storage
VMware vSphere 6.0	Cisco UCS 6300/6200 Series Interconnect, UCS 5108 B-Series chassis, UCS C220 M-4 C-Series	Cisco Nexus 9372PX switches, Cisco 1110-X, Cisco Nexus 1000v	NetApp All Flash AFF8040 storage controllers, DS2246 disk shelves with SSD
Docker Enterprise Edition for container management	Cisco UCS 6248UP interconnects, UCS 5108 B-Series chassis, 10 UCS B200 M-4 servers, 2204XP fabric extenders	Cisco Nexus 93180-YC	NetApp All Flash AFF8040 storage controllers, disk shelves with SSD
Infrastructure automation with UCS-Mini	Cisco Cloud Services Platform 2100, Cisco UCS Mini, UCS B-Series M4, UCS-Director	Cisco Nexus 9372PX switches	NetApp FAS 2552

There are many other Datacenter offerings such as Microsoft SharePoint, Microsoft Private Cloud, Citrix XenDesktop, and more. You can find these online on both the Network Appliance and Cisco websites.

The FlexPod Express model is an offering for Microsoft Hyper-V and VMware vSphere environments. It is offered in small, medium, and large configurations. Table 12.2 outlines the options.

TABLE 12.2 Example FlexPod Express deployments

Solution	Server/Compute	Network	Storage
Express Small	Two Cisco UCS C220 M4 stand-alone servers	Cisco Nexus 3048 1G switches	NetApp FAS2520 storage controllers
Express Medium	Four Cisco UCS C220 M4 stand-alone servers	Cisco Nexus 3048 1G switches	NetApp FAS2520 storage controllers
Express Large	Four Cisco UCS C220 M4 stand-alone servers	Cisco Nexus 3524 10G switches	NetApp FAS2552 storage controllers

The FlexPod Select offering is dedicated to specialized offerings, often in the big data or database area. Two of the common ones are Oracle RAC and Hadoop. Table 12.3 shows the most recent example of an Oracle RAC FlexPod.

TABLE 12.3   Example FlexPod select deployments

Solution	Server/Compute	Network	Storage
High-Performance Oracle RAC	Two Cisco B-series 5108 Chassis, 4 B-series servers in each, UCS 6200 inter-connects	Two Cisco Nexus 5548UP switches	Four NetApp EF560 arrays, 24 400G SSD drives

So, what about the support model with FlexPod? The primary vendors here from the hardware perspective are Cisco and Network Appliance. What happens is you receive unified support from both vendors. If there is an issue with the Cisco side of hardware, the customer can contact Cisco. Then Cisco will work with Network Appliance, if needed, to resolve the issue. The same is true for NetApp; if a NetApp issue is suspected, the customer can first contact NetApp support, and then they will work with Cisco if, needed, on the customer's behalf. What you get in the end is unified support and an integrated solution to meet your application needs.

Vblock (Dell, EMC, VCE)

Vblock is the next converged infrastructure solution we'll address. Vblock is a joint venture by Dell EMC and Cisco started in 2011. The company they created is called *Virtual Computing Environment (VCE)* and partners with VMware and Intel. While FlexPod is an integrated infrastructure that largely focuses on reference architecture for how to build your FlexPod, with Vblock you can buy the entire rack and have VCE ship it to your data center, ready to go. This is where the primary difference starts. VCE started out as one of the first vendors to sell a completely prepackaged and integrated solution. The fact that VCE is a company that partners with the other providers changes the support model as well. In this case, you're supported by a single entity, which is VCE. This business model offers tremendous value to VCE's customers and has been a successful joint venture for the companies that created VCE.

Vblock Overview

Vblock systems from VCE come in prebuilt configurations with multiple models to choose from. In this case, you have EMC storage but still use Cisco networking for the hardware switching. Since VMware is an original joint partner (and now part of Dell EMC), other hypervisors aren't supported because VMware is the primary hypervisor. This doesn't mean you can't install your own later. You could, but you wouldn't get any support from VCE for it—and you might start the finger-pointing game again.

There are both VxBlock and Vblock systems offered by VCE. We'll focus on the Vblock offerings because they are identical save for a few software networking changes. VxBlock changes some of the integrated offerings such as using a VMware distributed switch instead of Cisco Nexus 1000v and using ACI instead of NSX. Other than that, the hardware is the same.

Vblock Components

Vblock sells in a format called *system blocks*. Unlike FlexPod, the build isn't based around a certain application requirement. Instead, the Vblock architecture is chosen based on your requirements. Some consumers may see this as detrimental, as it's rigid and fixed. Other consumers might appreciate the all-in-one aspect of it.

All Vblock racks use Cisco UCS compute hardware, Cisco hardware switches, and EMC for storage. Take a look at Table 12.4 to see the various components and sizing Vblock options, which are current as of this writing according to EMC's website.

TABLE 12.4   Vblock offerings and options

Vblock System	240	340	350	540	740
Compute	Cisco UCS 220 M4 Cisco UCS VIC 1227	Cisco UCS Server Chassis Cisco UCS B-series Blade Servers Cisco UCS 2204XP/2208XP Series Fabric Extenders Cisco UCS 6246/6296UP Fabric Interconnects Cisco USC Virtual Interface Card 1227, 1240, 1280, 1340 and 1380 (540 also supports the 1387)			
Network	Cisco Nexus 5548UP Nexus 1000V Cisco ACI	Nexus 9396 Nexus 5548UP Nexus 5596UP Nexus 3172TO Nexus 1000v Cisco MDS 9148S ACI	Nexus 9396 Nexus 93180YC-EX Nexus 3172TQ Nexus 1000v ACI MDS 9148S or 9396S or 9706	Nexus 9396 Nexus 93180YC-EX Nexus 3172TO Nexus 9332PQ Nexus 1000v ACI MDS 9148S or 9396S or 9706	Same except no 9332PQ
Dell EMC Storage	VNX 5200	VNX 5400, 5600, 5800, 7600, 8000	Unity 300F through 600F (flash or hybrid)	XtremeIO 1,2,4,6, or 8 X-Brick Cluster	VMAX 250F/ FX, 450F/FX, and 850F/FX (all flash) VMAX 100K, 200K, and 400K (hybrid)

One of the unique features of Vblock is the extension rack that gives you the ability to extend beyond your initial rack of gear. You have a few options here, but they mainly are for compute or storage extensions.

Vblock has an independent set of management software and hardware as well. It is referred to as *Vblock AMP* (which stands for Advanced Management POD). The components are self-contained and provide out-of-band management for the entire Vblock. The AMP is delivered with a specific set of installed management software that contains everything you need to run the Vblock.

Some of the components you might find in AMP 2.0 are as follows:

- Microsoft Windows Server 2008/2012

- VMware vSphere Enterprise Plus

- VMware vSphere Hypervisor ESXi

- VMware Single Sign-On (SSO) Service

- VMware vSphere Platform Services Controller

- VMware vSphere Web Client Service and vSphere Client

- VMware vSphere Inventory Service

- VMware vCenter Server, Database, and Update Manager

- VMware Distributed Switch or Cisco Nexus 1000v

- PowerPath/VE Electronic License Management Server (LMS)

- Secure Remote Support

- Array management modules such as ExtremeIO Management Server

- Cisco Prime Data Center Network Manager and Device Manager

There are other options as well, and they are constantly changing, upgrading, and expanding the list of products and features. As mentioned, one of the biggest benefits of vBlock is the single point of contact and cross-vendor collaboration. vBlock also comes completely integrated and wired, ready to roll into your data center and be used. This contrasts from the other reference architectures that you may need to build on.

VSPEX (Dell, EMC)

VSPEX is an offering from Dell and EMC that is based on a reference architecture. It is similar to FlexPod and allows multiple design options. It could be inferred that the VSPEX offering was in response to the notion that Vblock was too rigid. Whereas Vblock requires specific hardware providers, VSPEX is more flexible. Cisco and Brocade can be used for networking options, for example. There are more vendor options, but the exam will obviously not cover any non-Cisco options. VSPEX even markets itself as a hybrid of do-it-yourself and integrated solutions.

The support model for VSPEX is via EMC. EMC will support VSPEX solutions, taking advantage of collaborative support effort with the included vendors. If you're thinking back to FlexPod, it's a similar model. Through the Cisco reference designs, Cisco released several VSPEX builds. Table 12.5 shows a few examples of this.

TABLE 12.5   VSPEX options from Cisco

Solution	Server/Compute	Network	Storage
VMware vSphere 5.5 for 1000 VMs	Two Cisco UCS 6248UP interconnects and B- or C-series M4 UCS servers (B200 and C220)	Cisco Nexus 9396PX, Cisco MDS 9148S, and Cisco Nexus 1000v	EMC VNX 5400, 5600, and 5800
VMware vSphere Horizon 5.3 for 2000 Desktops	Two Cisco UCS 6248UP Interconnects, two 5108 Blade Chassis with two 2204XP and 14 UCS B200 M3 Blade Servers	Cisco Nexus 5548UP	EMC VNX5600
Microsoft Private Cloud Fast Track 4.0	Two Cisco UCS 6248UP Interconnects, one 5108 Blade Chassis with two 2208XP and eight UCS B200 M4 Blade Servers	Cisco Nexus 9396PX	EMC VNX 5x00, 7800, and 8000

It should be noted that most of the VSPEX references haven't been updated in quite a while. This is likely because of the industry trending to more hyperconverged solutions. Both FlexPod and VSPEX are more "build it yourself" but offer a tested and validated design. An added benefit of VSPEX is that EMC supports it.

OpenBlock (Red Hat)

Cisco UCS Integrated Infrastructure for Red Hat OpenStack Platform (known informally as *OpenBlock*) is the solution for an integrated private cloud via OpenStack. According to the Cisco design guides, these are some of the goals with OpenBlock:

- Reduce complexity and risk of OpenStack deployment
- Maintain flexibility in your cloud and private cloud environment
- Reduce operating costs

OpenStack itself is a massively scalable open source private cloud architecture. Since it's open source, support is usually an issue. This is where Red Hat offers OpenStack tailored to enterprise needs with support built in. Cisco joined forces with Red Hat to provide an integrated solution that is scalable, reliable, and secure.

This is another reference architecture, supported both by Red Hat and Cisco validated designs. In this case, Cisco Support takes the lead call for support needs.

Table 12.6 shows an example of the main hardware and software components.

TABLE 12.6   VSPEX options from Cisco

Solution	Server/Compute	Network	Storage
OpenBlock	Two Cisco UCS 6248UP interconnects and B200 M4 UCS servers with Red Hat OpenStack Platform 7	Two Cisco Nexus 9372PX and Cisco Nexus 1000v	Red Hat Ceph Storage and C240 UCS servers for Ceph nodes

As mentioned earlier, the industry is trending toward a hyperconverged infrastructure. While not covered on the exam as of now, it's worth noting. A hyperconverged infrastructure is an all-in-one rack unit or chassis platform. This means the storage isn't external; it's usually internal. The compute, storage, and software are all in one fixed device.

Summary

In this chapter, we went through an overview of early data center infrastructure and how integrated infrastructure evolved. We then discussed popular integrated solutions that Cisco has participated in. Vblock, FlexPod, and OpenBlock are the bigger solutions that Cisco has been part of. We also explained the reference design architecture and how that fits into the model of integrated infrastructure.

This is the portion of the book that covers the CCNA Cisco Cloud Administration (CLDFND) 210-451 exam. Next chapter starts the coverage of the Cisco Cloud Fundamentals (CLDADM) 210-455 exam.

Exam Essentials

Understand what a POD is and how it refers to units of compute.   Know the history of infrastructure before integrated designs were introduced. Be ready to explain integrated and converged infrastructure.

Know how the growth model of PODs works.   Know how the integrated infrastructure works, and be able to explain the benefits of each. Make sure you study the partnerships Cisco has with integrated infrastructure vendors.

Know the differences between reference architectures and more rigid integrated infrastructures. Have a basic understanding of the components that make up the larger solutions Cisco partners with.

Written Lab

Fill in the blanks for the questions provided in the written lab. You can find the answers to the written labs in Appendix B.

1. Which term is used to describe a set of guidelines a consumer can follow to build a vendor solution? _____ _____

2. _____ _____ _____ is a Cisco term describing proven architecture that Cisco has tested and used.

3. A _____ is a unit of compute that is built for an application purpose. It can be one or more racks.

4. _____ is the informal name describing the collaboration between Red Hat and Cisco using OpenStack.

5. All Cisco integrated solutions use _____ for the compute portion.

6. Datacenter is one of the terms also used to describe what integrated offering? _____

7. NetApp and Cisco partnered together to offer _____.

8. VCE is a company formed initially by Cisco _____ and _____.

9. The Nexus _____ is often included in integrated infrastructure for virtual switching.

10. VSPEX is a reference architecture from which company? _____

Review Questions

The following questions are designed to test your understanding of this chapter's material. You can find the answers to the questions in Appendix A. For more information on how to obtain additional questions, please see this book's Introduction.

1. Which of the following is a FlexPod offering?
   A. Large
   B. Hyper
   C. Quick
   D. Express

2. What storage is part of the VSPEX reference?
   A. Brocade
   B. Cisco
   C. NetApp
   D. Dell/EMC

3. What is a unit of compute and infrastructure that is designed for a specific reason?
   A. ROW
   B. Rack
   C. POD
   D. Farm

4. What is a valid Vblock offering?
   A. 50
   B. 235
   C. 350
   D. 776

5. What hypervisor is allowed in Vblock?
   A. VMware
   B. VMware and HyperV
   C. HyperV
   D. OpenStack

6. Ceph storage is a component of what offering?
   A. OpenBlock or UCS integrated infrastructure for OpenStack
   B. FlexPod
   C. VSPEX
   D. Vblock
   E. ACI

7. NetApp is a partner in which offering?
   - **A.** VSPEX
   - **B.** Vblock
   - **C.** OpenBlock
   - **D.** FlexPod

8. AMP is a term referring to the management portion of what integrated solution?
   - **A.** FlexPod
   - **B.** Vblock
   - **C.** VSPEX
   - **D.** OpenBlock

9. Which of the following options closely resembles a FlexPod offering?
   - **A.** Select
   - **B.** Pristine
   - **C.** Legacy
   - **D.** Precision
   - **E.** Tracker
   - **F.** OAMP

10. What integrated offering is least like a reference architecture?
    - **A.** FlexPod
    - **B.** VSPEX
    - **C.** Vblock
    - **D.** FlexRack

11. FlexPod Select would be good for which offering?
    - **A.** OpenStack
    - **B.** Exchange
    - **C.** Hadoop
    - **D.** Office365

12. Which is a UCS chassis commonly offered for several integrated infrastructures?
    - **A.** Cisco Nexus 1000v
    - **B.** Cisco Nexus 9322
    - **C.** Cisco UCS B-series
    - **D.** Cisco Nexus 3036

13. What is one of OpenBlock's goals?

   A. Reduced operating costs

   B. Speed of cabling

   C. Custom support GUI

   D. Reduced power expense

14. Dell/EMC is the primary support for which reference architecture?

   A. FlexPod

   B. VSPEX

   C. Vblock

   D. OpenBlock

15. FlexPod Express primarily focuses on which hypervisor? (Choose all that apply.)

   A. Xen

   B. KVM

   C. Hyper-V

   D. VMware

16. Which integrated offering started as a separate company?

   A. FlexPod

   B. OpenBlock

   C. VBlock

   D. CVD

17. Which offering best represents a collaborative support model?

   A. Vblock

   B. CDP

   C. Next

   D. FlexPod

18. ACI can be integrated with which offering from the factory? (Choose the best option.)

   A. FlexPod

   B. Vblock

   C. VSPEX

   D. OpenBlock

19. Dell/EMC storage can be offered in which integrated solution? (Choose the best answer.)

  A. VSPEX

  B. Vblock

  C. FlexPod

  D. Nexus

20. Which Cisco switch series is often used in integrations? (Choose the best answer.)

  A. Nexus 7000

  B. Catalyst 6500

  C. Catalyst 2900

  D. Nexus 9000

Chapter

13

Configuring Roles and Profiles

THE FOLLOWING UNDERSTANDING CISCO CLOUD ADMINISTRATION CLDADM (210-455) EXAM OBJECTIVES ARE COVERED IN THIS CHAPTER:

✓ **1.1   Configure users/groups and role-based access control in the portal, including basic troubleshooting**

- 1.1.a Describe default roles

- 1.1.b Configure new user with single role

- 1.1.c Describe multirole user profiles

- 1.1.d Configure a user profile

CLDFND Exam 210-455 Overview

This chapter begins the second section of the *CCNA Cloud Study Guide* and is focused on preparing you for the second of the two exams required to become a certified CCNA Cloud professional. In the first section, you learned about cloud types and deployment models, virtualization, storage, converged networks, and more. This allowed you to gain a foundational understanding of cloud computing. The second exam has a greater focus on cloud operations and how to manage and run the day-to-day tasks that a certified CCNA Cloud professional will be responsible for when working in the field.

For the rest of the book, we will focus primarily on the Cisco ONE Enterprise Cloud suite of applications since the CLDADM 210-455 exam tests on the applications that make up the Cisco ONE product family. The following are the applications that are included in Cisco ONE:

- UCS Director
- Prime Service Catalog
- Intercloud Fabric for Business
- Virtual Application Cloud Segmentation

We will also cover the Cisco Intelligent Automation for the Cloud at a high level.

An Introduction to Cisco Cloud Administration

Cisco offers a complete suite of cloud management applications that cover all aspects of operations in a hybrid, public, community, or private cloud environment. The CCNA CLDFND 210-455 exam has a heavy focus on cloud administration using the Cisco ONE family of management applications. With the Cisco ONE centralized and integrated suite of software, maintaining cloud operations can be optimized.

You will learn about the various Cisco cloud management software products throughout the rest of this study guide and will be introduced to the Prime Service Catalog, which is a self-service portal to order cloud services and acts as a "storefront" for IT and cloud services. You will also be introduced to *UCS Director* (*UCSD*), which provides integrated infrastructure management for cloud services such as services automation, compute, storage, networking, billing, and much more. The Cisco Intercloud Fabric for Business offers hybrid cloud management and interconnection services, and the Virtual Application Container Services (VACS) is used to secure applications by applying segmentation and offers streamlined provisioning of containers and interoperability between clouds.

UCS Director

In the Cisco ONE Enterprise Cloud suite of applications, the core automation application is UCS Director, or more frequently called UCSD, which was developed to provide automation in the cloud. In traditional data centers today, operations are maintained by separate administrative groups that include servers, operating systems, storage, networking, security, and often virtualization. These separate groups must work together but at the same time perform their duties apart from one another to operate a modern enterprise data center. As we have discussed throughout this book, this is very time-consuming, error-prone, and inefficient. This separation of duties into discrete operational groups is sometimes called a *silo*, which means each group performs a specialized duty, and there may not be very efficient communications, hand-offs, support, and troubleshooting when the groups are operating in their own world, or silo. The silo structure creates a long deployment timeline that has been overcome using automation in the cloud with applications such as UCS Director. When you remove the manual processes and implement UCSD, productivity increases, much of the complexity is removed to do replicated processes offered by UCSD, operations are more consistent, and, best of all, the IT staff is freed up to work on more interesting projects!

The UCS Director is the application that provides on-demand delivery, cloud automation, end-to-end management, and support of the cloud infrastructure and complete management of your company's cloud life cycle. The end result is that deployments are much faster than the traditional silo structure of enterprise operations. UCSD automation processes takes the hardware and software configuration tasks and converts them to programmable modules. These modules are then used to create a workflow that is automated. By using the workflow approach, complete projects can be automated across all of the functional areas of the cloud operations. UCSD uses an object approach, as compared to the script-based architecture, with a graphical design interface (scripting support is available if desired, though). With more than 2,000 tasks included in the UCSD release, the broad base of preconfigured objects allows for fast deployment times. The tool also includes support for versioning and allows conditionals and process loops. The Cisco APIC ACI controller integrates with UCSD and provides support for tenants, bridge domains, endpoint groups, contracts, L4-7 services, router peering, and VMM domains.

UCSD can discover and provide mapping of your infrastructure because workflows are defined to facilitate timely deployments that are mapped to company operational standards, policies, and procedures. UCSD is not specific to Cisco products; it can operate in a multivendor deployment. Since all environments are multivendor, this is a critical requirement.

UCSD comes prepackaged with more than 2,000 workflows that are configured to allow for quick automation, orchestration, and deployment of common IT and cloud operational tasks. UCSD can, without APIC integration, automate and manage firewalls, servers, load balancers, virtual machines, storage, networking, and many other services by replacing manual processes with automation.

The UCS Director comprised different software modules that include an Infrastructure portal for self-service for ordering IT services and resources from a "catalog" of packaged offerings. Think of this as a menu in a restaurant. The cloud administrators package offerings into a menu and publish them online in the *services catalog*. This "menu" is where the cloud customers order their desired services. Catalogs keep services and offerings uniform, which prevents a sprawl of products to support if the offerings were not structured in a services catalog. The services offered in the catalog can be pretested and configured and can be determined to meet all corporate governance and regulatory requirements.

There is a section in UCSD dedicated to infrastructure orchestration, which defines the workflow that provisions the services ordered from the service catalog. If there are any resource limitations or constraints, another UCSD module dynamically monitors and remediates any capacity limitations. UCSD includes a monitoring application that allows for chargeback billing and resource accounting. UCSD offers the standard administration and management capabilities for cloud operations, which includes reporting modules for all aspects of your cloud consumption with reports in either graphical or spreadsheet formats. Cisco has published an open automation software development kit and sample code for developers to integrate applications with UCSD. Finally, UCSD is far from being a stand-alone application and allows for integration to many other applications.

Configure Users/Groups and Role-Based Access Control in the Portal, Including Basic Troubleshooting

This next section will focus on the exam objectives of managing users and roles. Now that you have a basic understanding of the UCD Director, you will learn how to create roles, groups, and users using the application. It is important to note that UCSD supports external directory systems such as Active Directory from Microsoft. The exam will only focus on its own local data and not that of any external directories.

The UCSD portal is where users are created to access all the features of the Cisco ONE cloud ecosystem. These include administrative roles, rights to the catalog to order services, and many other capabilities that will be introduced throughout the rest of this book.

When a user is created, the user can either be assigned a role or be placed in a group of users, and then the group will be assigned a role. The application allows you to create groups to meet your needs, and while there are 11 default roles, you can create additional roles as needed. Additional roles can be created or modified with the rights granted in the Group and Systems Administrator accounts.

Default Roles in UCS Director

The management of user accounts is performed using the UCS Director converged infrastructure management application. The UCSD *user profiles* utilize *role-based access control*

(*RBAC*) that is defined as a method of allowing or restricting user access to network services based on the user's role or location in the organization. The RBAC role grants users privileges when a user is assigned to the role. Additionally, a user can be assigned to a group, such as computing administrators, and then that user group can be assigned to a role. It is important to understand that privileges are assigned to the roles, and the users are granted rights by being a member of a role. Users do not get assigned rights directly; user rights are inherited by being a member of a role.

The UCSD user and role management architecture allows the cloud administrator great flexibility in designing access rights for any conceivable use case. Users can be granted the proper permissions for any needs they may require, such as to order services, monitor, manage, create reports, and administer billing or accounting functions in addition to any custom-created profiles.

UCS Director ships with predefined or default user roles that reduce deployment times. UCS Director can support up to 48 defined roles. There are 11 preconfigured roles that are included in the application.

All Policy Administrator   Manages policies and service request operations (Table 13.1)

TABLE 13.1   All Policy Administrator role

Operations Permissions	Read Permission	Write Permission
Approver Service Request	Yes	Yes
Assign VM to vDC	No	Yes
Budgeting	Yes	No
Catalogs	Yes	No
Chargeback	Yes	No
Cloudsense Assessment reports	Yes	No
Cloudsense Reports	Yes	No
Computing Policy	Yes	Yes
Create Service Request	No	Yes
CS Shared Assessments	No	No
CS Shared Reports	No	No
Deployment Policy	No	Yes

TABLE 13.1   All Policy Administrator role *(continued)*

Operations Permissions	Read Permission	Write Permission
Discovery	Yes	No
End-User Chargeback	No	No
Group Service Request	Yes	Yes
Group Users	Yes	No
Mobile Access Settings	No	No
Network Policy	Yes	Yes
Open Automation Modules	No	No
Orchestration	Yes	Yes
Physical Computing	Yes	Yes
Physical Network	Yes	Yes
Physical Storage	Yes	Yes
Remote VM Access	No	No
Resource Accounting	Yes	No
Resource Groups	No	No
Resource Limit Report	Yes	No
Service Delivery	Yes	Yes
Storage Policy	Yes	Yes
System Admin	Yes	No
Tag Library	No	No
UCSD Cluster	No	No
Users and Groups	Yes	No
vDC	Yes	No

Operations Permissions	Read Permission	Write Permission
Virtual Accounts	Yes	No
Virtual Computing	Yes	No
Virtual Network	Yes	No
Virtual Storage	Yes	No
VM Label	No	Yes
Write Resource Accounting	No	No

Billing Administrator   Manages accounting and billing operations (Table 13.2)

TABLE 13.2   Billing Administrator role

Operations Permissions	Read Permission	Write Permission
Approver Service Request	No	No
Assign VM to vDC	No	No
Budgeting	Yes	Yes
Catalogs	No	No
Chargeback	Yes	No
Cloudsense Assessment reports	Yes	Yes
Cloudsense Reports	Yes	Yes
Computing Policy	No	No
Create Service Request	No	No
CS Shared Assessments	No	No
CS Shared Reports	No	No
Deployment Policy	No	No

TABLE 13.2   Billing Administrator role *(continued)*

Operations Permissions	Read Permission	Write Permission
Discovery	Yes	No
End-User Chargeback	No	No
Group Service Request	Yes	No
Group Users	No	No
Mobile Access Settings	No	No
Network Policy	No	No
Open Automation Modules	No	No
Orchestration	No	No
Physical Computing	No	No
Physical Network	No	No
Physical Storage	No	No
Remote VM Access	No	No
Resource Accounting	Yes	No
Resource Groups	No	No
Resource Limit Report	Yes	No
Service Delivery	No	No
Storage Policy	No	No
System Admin	No	No
Tag Library	No	No
UCSD Cluster	No	No
Users and Groups	No	No
vDC	No	No

Operations Permissions	Read Permission	Write Permission
Virtual Accounts	No	No
Virtual Computing	No	No
Virtual Network	No	No
Virtual Storage	No	No
VM Label	No	No
Write Resource Accounting	No	Yes

Computing Administrator   Manages compute-related operations (Table 13.3)

TABLE 13.3   Computing Administrator role

Operations Permissions	Read Permission	Write Permission
Approver Service Request	Yes	Yes
Assign VM to vDC	No	No
Budgeting	Yes	No
Catalogs	Yes	No
Chargeback	Yes	No
Cloudsense Assessment reports	Yes	No
Cloudsense Reports	Yes	No
Computing Policy	Yes	Yes
Create Service Request	Yes	No
CS Shared Assessments	No	No
CS Shared Reports	No	No
Deployment Policy	Yes	No

TABLE 13.3 Computing Administrator role *(continued)*

Operations Permissions	Read Permission	Write Permission
Discovery	Yes	No
End-User Chargeback	No	No
Group Service Request	Yes	No
Group Users	Yes	No
Mobile Access Settings	No	No
Network Policy	Yes	No
Open Automation Modules	No	No
Orchestration	Yes	Yes
Physical Computing	Yes	Yes
Physical Network	Yes	No
Physical Storage	Yes	No
Remote VM Access	No	No
Resource Accounting	Yes	No
Resource Groups	Yes	Yes
Resource Limit Report	Yes	No
Service Delivery	Yes	No
Storage Policy	Yes	No
System Admin	Yes	No
Tag Library	Yes	Yes
UCSD Cluster	No	No
Users and Groups	Yes	No
vDC	Yes	No

Operations Permissions	Read Permission	Write Permission
Virtual Accounts	Yes	No
Virtual Computing	Yes	No
Virtual Network	Yes	No
Virtual Storage	Yes	No
VM Label	No	Yes
Write Resource Accounting	No	No

Group Administrator   Is an end user with the privilege of adding users (Table 13.4)

TABLE 13.4   Group Administrator role

Operations Permissions	Read Permission	Write Permission
Approver Service Request	Yes	Yes
Assign VM to vDC	No	No
Budgeting	No	No
Catalogs	Yes	No
Chargeback	Yes	No
Cloudsense Assessment	No	No
Cloudsense Reports	Yes	Yes
Computing Policy	No	No
Create Service Request	No	Yes
CS Shared Assessments	No	No
CS Shared Reports	Yes	Yes
Deployment Policy	No	No
Discovery	No	No

TABLE 13.4   Group Administrator role *(continued)*

Operations Permissions	Read Permission	Write Permission
End-User Chargeback	Yes	No
Group Service Request	Yes	Yes
Group Users	Yes	Yes
Mobile Access Settings	No	No
Network Policy	No	No
Open Automation Modules	No	No
Orchestration	No	No
Physical Computing	No	No
Physical Network	No	No
Physical Storage	No	No
Remote VM Access	No	No
Reports	No	No
Resource Accounting	Yes	No
Resource Groups	No	No
Resource Limit Report	Yes	No
Service Delivery	No	No
Storage Policy	No	No
System Admin	No	No
Tag Library	No	No
UCSD Cluster	No	No
Users and Groups	No	No
vDC	Yes	No

Operations Permissions	Read Permission	Write Permission
Virtual Accounts	No	No
Virtual Computing	Yes	Yes
Virtual Network	No	No
Virtual Storage	No	No
VM Label	No	Yes
Write Resource Accounting	No	No

IS Administrator   Administers policy, orchestration, storage, and other IT operations (Table 13.5)

TABLE 13.5   IS Administrator role

Operations Permissions	Read Permission	Write Permission
Approver Service Request	Yes	Yes
Assign VM to vDC	No	Yes
Budgeting	Yes	No
Catalogs	Yes	Yes
Chargeback	Yes	No
Cloudsense Assessment Reports	No	No
Cloudsense Reports	No	No
Computing Policy	Yes	No
Create Service Request	Yes	No
CS Shared Assessments	No	No
CS Shared Reports	No	No
Deployment Policy	Yes	No

TABLE 13.5 IS Administrator role *(continued)*

Operations Permissions	Read Permission	Write Permission
Discovery	No	No
End-User Chargeback	No	No
Group Service Request	Yes	No
Group Users	Yes	No
Mobile Access Settings	No	No
Network Policy	Yes	Yes
Open Automation Modules	No	No
Orchestration	Yes	Yes
Physical Computing	Yes	No
Physical Network	Yes	No
Physical Storage	Yes	No
Remote VM Access	No	No
Resource Accounting	Yes	No
Resource Groups	Yes	Yes
Resource Limit Report	Yes	No
Service Delivery	Yes	No
Storage Policy	Yes	Yes
System Admin	Yes	No
Tag Library	Yes	Yes
UCSD Cluster	No	No
Users and Groups	Yes	No
vDC	Yes	No

Operations Permissions	Read Permission	Write Permission
Virtual Accounts	Yes	No
Virtual Computing	Yes	No
Virtual Network	Yes	No
Virtual Storage	Yes	No
VM Label	No	Yes
Write Resource Accounting	No	No

MSP Administrator   Manages service provider administration (Table 13.6)

TABLE 13.6   MSP Administrator role

Operations Permissions	Read Permission	Write Permission
Virtual Computing	No	Yes
VM Label	No	Yes
Assign VM to vDC	No	No
VirtualStorage	No	No
VirtualNetwork	No	No
Physical Computing	No	No
Physical Storage	No	No
Physical Network	No	No
Group Service Request	Yes	Yes
Create Service Request	No	Yes
Approver ServiceRequest	Yes	Yes
Budgeting	Yes	Yes

TABLE 13.6   MSP Administrator role *(continued)*

Operations Permissions	Read Permission	Write Permission
Resource Accounting	Yes	No
Chargeback	Yes	No
System Admin	No	No
Users and Groups	No	No
Virtual Accounts	No	No
Catalogs	Yes	No
vDC	Yes	No
Computing Policy	No	No
Storage Policy	No	No
Managing Users and Groups	No	No
All Policy Admin	No	No
Permissions Operations Deployment Policy	No	No
Network Policy	No	No
Service Delivery	No	No
Resource Limit Report	Yes	No
Group Users	Yes	Yes
Cloudsense Reports	No	No
Cloudsense Assessment Reports	No	No
Orchestration	No	No
Discovery	No	No
Open Automation Modules	No	No

Operations Permissions	Read Permission	Write Permission
CS Shared Reports	Yes	No
CS Shared Assessments	No	No
Remote VM Access	No	No
Mobile Access Settings	No	No
End-User Chargeback	Yes	No
Write Resource Accounting	No	No
UCSD Cluster	No	No
Resource Groups	No	No
Tag Library	No	No

Network Administrator   Manages networking operations (Table 13.7)

TABLE 13.7   Network Administrator role

Operations Permissions	Read Permission	Write Permission
Virtual Computing	Yes	No
VM Label	No	Yes
Assign VM to vDC	No	No
Virtual Storage	Yes	No
Virtual Network	Yes	No
Physical Computing	Yes	No
Physical Storage	Yes	No
Physical Network	Yes	Yes
Group Service Request	Yes	No

TABLE 13.7   Network Administrator role *(continued)*

Operations Permissions	Read Permission	Write Permission
Create Service Request	Yes	No
Approver Service Request	Yes	Yes
Budgeting	Yes	No
Resource Accounting	Yes	No
Chargeback	Yes	No
System Admin	Yes	No
Users and Groups	Yes	No
Virtual Accounts	Yes	No
Catalogs	Yes	No
vDC	Yes	No
Computing Policy	Yes	No
Storage Policy	Yes	No
Deployment Policy	Yes	No
Network Policy	Yes	Yes
Service Delivery	Yes	No
Resource Limit Report	Yes	No
Group Users	Yes	No
Cloudsense Reports	Yes	No
Cloudsense Assessment	Yes	Yes
Orchestration	Yes	Yes
Discovery	Yes	No

Operations Permissions	Read Permission	Write Permission
Open Automation Modules	No	No
CS Shared Reports	No	No
CS Shared Assessments	No	No
Remote VM Access	No	No
Mobile Access Settings	No	No
End-User Chargeback	No	No
Write Resource Accounting	No	No
UCSD Cluster	No	No
Resource Groups	Yes	Yes
Tag Library	Yes	Yes

Operator   Manages cloud operations (Table 13.8)

TABLE 13.8   Operator role

Operations Permissions	Read Permission	Write Permission
Approver Service Request	Yes	Yes
Assign VM to vDC	No	Yes
Budgeting	Yes	No
Catalogs	Yes	No
Chargeback	Yes	No
Cloudsense Assessment	Yes	No
Cloudsense Reports	Yes	No
Computing Policy	Yes	No

TABLE 13.8   Operator role *(continued)*

Operations Permissions	Read Permission	Write Permission
Create Service Request	No	Yes
CS Shared Assessments	No	No
CS Shared Reports	No	No
Deployment Policy	Yes	No
Discovery	No	No
End-User Chargeback	No	No
Group Service Request	Yes	Yes
Group Users	Yes	No
Mobile Access Settings	No	No
Network Policy	Yes	No
Open Automation Modules	No	No
Orchestration	No	No
Physical Computing	Yes	No
Physical Network	Yes	No
Physical Storage	Yes	No
Remote VM Access	No	No
Resource Accounting	Yes	No
Resource Groups	No	No
Resource Limit Report	Yes	No
Service Delivery	Yes	No
Storage Policy	Yes	No

Operations Permissions	Read Permission	Write Permission
System Admin	Yes	No
Tag Library	No	No
UCSD Cluster	No	No
Users and Groups	Yes	No
vDC	Yes	No
Virtual Accounts	Yes	No
Virtual Computing	Yes	No
Virtual Network	Yes	No
Virtual Storage	Yes	No
VM Label	No	Yes
Write Resource Accounting	No	No

Services End User   Allows only for viewing and use of the self-service portal (Table 13.9)

TABLE 13.9   Service End-User role

Operations Permissions	Read Permission	Write permission
Approver Service Request	Yes	Yes
Assign VM to vDC	No	No
Budgeting	No	No
Catalogs	Yes	No
Chargeback	Yes	No
Cloudsense Assessment	No	No
Cloudsense Reports	Yes	No

TABLE 13.9   Service End-User role *(continued)*

Operations Permissions	Read Permission	Write permission
Computing Policy	No	No
Create Service Request	No	Yes
CS Shared Assessments	No	No
CS Shared Reports	Yes	No
Deployment Policy	No	No
Discovery	No	No
End-User Chargeback	Yes	No
Group Service Request	Yes	Yes
Group Users	No	No
Mobile Access Settings	No	No
Network Policy	No	No
Open Automation Modules	No	No
Orchestration	No	No
Physical Computing	Yes	No
Physical Network	No	No
Physical Storage	Yes	No
Remote VM Access	No	No
Resource Accounting	Yes	No
Resource Groups	No	No
Resource Limit Report	Yes	No
Service Delivery	No	No
Storage Policy	No	No

Operations Permissions	Read Permission	Write permission
System Admin	No	No
Tag Library	No	No
UCSD Cluster	No	No
Users and Groups	No	No
vDC	Yes	No
Virtual Accounts	No	No
Virtual Computing	Yes	Yes
Virtual Network	Yes	No
Virtual Storage	No	No
VM Label	No	Yes
Write Resource Accounting	No	No

Storage Administrator Manages storage operations (Table 13.10)

TABLE 13.10 Storage Administrator role

Operations Permissions	Read Permission	Write Permission
Approver Service Request	Yes	Yes
Assign VM to vDC	No	No
Budgeting	Yes	No
Catalogs	Yes	No
Chargeback	Yes	No
Cloudsense Assessment	Yes	Yes
Cloudsense Reports	Yes	No
Computing Policy	Yes	No

TABLE 13.10   Storage Administrator role *(continued)*

Operations Permissions	Read Permission	Write Permission
Create Service Request	Yes	No
CS Shared Assessments	No	No
CS Shared Reports	No	No
Deployment Policy	Yes	No
Discovery	Yes	No
End-User Chargeback	No	No
Group Service Request	Yes	No
Group Users	Yes	No
Mobile Access Settings	No	No
Network Policy	Yes	No
Open Automation Modules	No	No
Orchestration	Yes	Yes
Physical Computing	Yes	No
Physical Network	Yes	No
Physical Storage	Yes	Yes
Remote VM Access	No	No
Resource Accounting	Yes	No
Resource Groups	Yes	Yes
Resource Limit Report	Yes	No
Service Delivery	Yes	No
Storage Policy	Yes	Yes

Operations Permissions	Read Permission	Write Permission
System Admin	Yes	No
Tag Library	Yes	Yes
UCSD Cluster	No	No
Users and Groups	Yes	No
vDC	Yes	No
Virtual Accounts	Yes	No
Virtual Computing	Yes	No
Virtual Network	Yes	No
Virtual Storage	Yes	No
VM Label	No	Yes
Write Resource Accounting	No	No

Systems Administrator   UCS Director systems operations, superuser account (Table 13.11)

TABLE 13.11   System Administrator role

Operations Permissions	Read Permission	Write Permission
Virtual Computing	Yes	Yes
VM Label	Yes	Yes
Assign VM to vDC	Yes	Yes
VirtualStorage	Yes	Yes
VirtualNetwork	Yes	Yes
Physical Computing	Yes	Yes
Physical Storage	Yes	Yes
Physical Network	Yes	Yes

TABLE 13.11 System Administrator role *(continued)*

Operations Permissions	Read Permission	Write Permission
Group Service Request	Yes	Yes
Create Service Request	Yes	Yes
Approver ServiceRequest	Yes	Yes
Budgeting	Yes	Yes
Resource Accounting	Yes	Yes
Chargeback	Yes	Yes
System Admin	Yes	Yes
Users and Groups	Yes	Yes
Virtual Accounts	Yes	Yes
Catalogs	Yes	Yes
vDC	Yes	Yes
Computing Policy	Yes	Yes
Storage Policy	Yes	Yes
Managing Users and Groups	Yes	Yes
All Policy Admin	Yes	Yes
Permissions Operations Deployment Policy	Yes	Yes
Network Policy	Yes	Yes
Service Delivery	Yes	Yes
Resource LimitReport	Yes	Yes
Group Users	Yes	Yes

Operations Permissions	Read Permission	Write Permission
Cloudsense Reports	Yes	Yes
Cloudsense Assessment Reports	Yes	Yes
Orchestration	Yes	Yes
Discovery	Yes	Yes
Open Automation Modules	Yes	Yes
CS Shared Reports	Yes	Yes
CS Shared Assessments	Yes	Yes
Remote VM Access	Yes	Yes
Mobile Access Settings	Yes	Yes
End-User Chargeback	Yes	Yes
Write Resource Accounting	Yes	Yes
UCSD Cluster	Yes	Yes
Resource Groups	Yes	Yes
Tag Library	Yes	Yes

RBAC privileges are defined as what you are able to see and do inside of the UCS Director application based on your assigned roles and the privileges granted to that role. This defines the menu systems presented to the user. For example, the systems administrator will have access to the systems administration menu system, and the storage administrator would not be presented with this menu option. Within each role, the permissions can be customized to include basic file permissions such as read-only, write, and read-write.

Roles are stand alone in nature, which is to say they cannot be embedded or placed inside of another role.

It is a recommended practice that when creating a new role to copy an existing default role and using that as a template to make changes, it is not advised that you make any changes to the default roles. With a total of 48 roles available, there should be ample capacity to create new roles instead of modifying the defaults.

Creating and Managing Users

In this section, you will learn to create and manage users in UCSD. As you learned, UCSD users either can be locally created in the application or can access an external user database such as Active Directory. We will focus exclusively on creating local users.

Creating a New User with a Single Role

In this section, you will learn how to create a new user in UCS Director and assign that user to a role. This is a basic administrator function, and all users must have an account and belong to a role to use the applications included in UCS Director.

Perform the following steps to create a new user in UCS Director:

1. Log into UCS Director with an account that has administrative privileges.
2. In the top-center drop-down menu, select Administration and then Users And Groups. The Users And Groups screen will appear.
3. Click the Users tab (from the top menu, second from the left).
4. Click the Add User icon near the top of the screen, and the Add User pop-up dialog box will appear.
5. Select the role for the user using the drop-down menu at the top.
6. Select a login name.
7. Enter and confirm the user password.
8. In the User Contact Email field, input the user's e-mail address.
9. The remaining fields are optional, but it is always a good idea to complete these. Enter the user's first and last name and the phone number. The Address field can be used for any notes or comments.
10. To complete the process, click the + Add icon at the bottom of the dialog box, and you will be returned to the main Users And Groups screen. This completes the steps for creating a user locally in UCS Director.

Creating Local Groups

This section demonstrates how to create a *user group* using UCS Director. Just as it sounds, groups are created for each specific function you may require, and then users are placed in a group. This allows for ease of administration since groups can be assigned roles. When a new user is added to a group, the user can inherit the role assigned to the group.

Perform the following steps to create a new group in UCS Director:

1. Log into UCS Director with an account that has administrative privileges.
2. In the top-center drop-down menu, select Administration and then Users And Groups. The Users And Groups screen will appear, and you will be on the User Groups screen by default; otherwise, select the top-left tab labeled User Groups.
3. Click the +Add icon near the top of the screen, and the Edit Group pop-up dialog box will appear.

4. Add a descriptive name of your choice for the new group.

5. Enter the group's primary e-mail address (used for group updates and messages). All other fields are optional and include the description, code, cost center, first and last names, phone number, address, and group share policy.

6. To complete the process, click the Save icon at the bottom of the dialog box, and you will be returned to the main Users And Groups menu. This completes the steps for creating a group locally in UCS Director.

Notice that the group is saved as a local group. If UCSD were connected to a directory service such as Active Directory from Microsoft, it would appear as an external group.

Creating Multirole Access User Profiles

What if a user needs to be in more than one role? That is actually a common requirement, and it is often appropriate to assign a user to multiple *access profiles*. For example, an individual may require the management rights in the network administrator's role to perform networking operations and also have duties as an operator. This is accomplished with multirole access profiles. Access profiles allow the user to access the resources you grant to them. UCSD allows a user to belong to multiple profiles to accomplish this requirement.

Configuring User Profiles

To create a user access profile, perform the following steps using UCSD:

1. Log into UCS Director with an account that has administrative privileges.

2. In the top-center drop-down menu, select Administration and then Users And Groups.

3. The Users And Groups screen will appear, and you will be on the User Groups screen by default; select the Login User tab.

4. Choose a user from the list.

5. Click Manage Profiles.

6. In the Manage Profile window, click + Add.

7. The Add Entry To Access Profiles dialog box will appear; complete the following fields:

> **Name:** The profile name
>
> **Description:** A descriptive name for the profile
>
> **Type:** This is a drop-down list. Select the role type.
>
> **Customer Organizations:** Select the organization this profile will belong to.
>
> **Show Resources From All Other Groups The User Has Access:** This is a checkbox that allows the user to be able to access all the resources in the selected groups.
>
> **Shared Groups:** Click Select to choose the groups the user profile belongs to. The user will then have access to all the rights associated with the groups you selected.

8. Click Submit.

If a user has multiple profiles, the profile required can be selected when logging into UCSD. When presented with the login dialog box, enter your username in the following format:

Username: access profile name

For example, you'd enter todd: SANAdmin and then enter your password to authenticate and gain access to that specific profile.

Summary

The second section of this certification guide begins with this chapter on Cisco cloud administration and creating users and roles. The rest of the chapters in the guide will prepare you for the CLDADM 210-455 exam. To get started on that journey, we began with covering the objective related to configuring user role-based access control in the Cisco ONE management framework.

Prior to covering these objectives, you were introduced to the management applications where the users and roles are defined. You learned about the Cisco ONE family of cloud operation applications that will be a focus of the CLDFND exam. The UCS Director was introduced as the central management application in the Cisco ONE suite. UCSD is where users and roles are defined, and you learned about the many modules included and its role in the cloud ecosystem.

With the fundamentals of UCS Director covered, you learned that here are 48 user roles that can be defined of which there are 11 default or preconfigured roles.

While it is not required for the exam to know the hundreds of objects rights that are in the roles, it is important to understand that roles determine rights to perform actions in the cloud and that these rights are defined in the role profiles. The default roles are All Policy Admin, Billing Admin, Computing Admin, Group Admin, IS Admin, MSP Admin, Network Admin, Operator, Service End User, Storage Admin, and the superuser role of System Administrator. The System account can be thought of as the root account for UCS Director. New roles can be defined by the system administrator as required. It is suggested that an existing role be copied and modified to create new roles but to never modify the default role permissions without creating a new role. Users are granted these rights by being members of the roles.

You then learned how to create single role users using the UCSD application. The steps to fill out the required and optional fields were outlined.

Next the steps to create user groups were explained. By creating groups for specific functions and operations, the users can be placed in these groups, and then the group will be assigned to the role that eases management for large user communities.

Finally, we ended the chapter by introducing the multirole access user profile that allows users to belong to more than one role.

Exam Essentials

Understand the role of UCS Director in creating profiles for users, groups, and roles. UCSD contains the depository for users, groups, and roles. These objects can be created either locally in the application or accessed from external directories. When users log into UCSD, they will inherit the appropriate roles assigned to their accounts.

Know how to create local users using UCS Director. Review the process to create a local user in UCSD using the graphical interface. External users accessed via directory services are beyond the scope of the exam.

Understand what local groups are in UCS Director. Local groups are rights assigned to users to access and perform defined roles in UCSD.

Understand the steps required to create a local group using the GUI in UCSD. Groups are created for each specific function you may require, and then users are placed in a group. This allows for ease of administration since groups can be assigned roles. When a new user is added to a group, the user can inherit the role assigned to the group.

Know how to create a new user in a single role. Using the UCSD user administration configuration dialog, know the steps required to create a local user account.

Understand what multirole access user profiles are. The multirole access user profile allows a user to belong to more than one role and is defined in UCSD administrator users and groups.

Written Lab

Fill in the blanks for the questions provided in the written lab. You can find the answers to the written labs in Appendix B.

1. UCS Director can support up to _____ roles with _____ predefined.

2. _____ _____ _____ _____ is the method to allow users access to defined roles in an organization.

3. In UCSD, _____ are assigned to _____.

4. Users can be placed into _____ that are then assigned roles.

5. The _____ _____ account allows for full control of UCSD.

6. If the user is created in the UCSD users and roles application, it is considered to be _____.

7. A user can belong to more than one role by creating _____ _____ _____ profiles.

8. To create a new user, go to the _____ tab and select _____ _____ _____.

9. Object read-write access is defined in the _____ configuration area.

10. The _____ _____ _____ allows you to view and use the self-service portal.

Review Questions

The following questions are designed to test your understanding of this chapter's material. You can find the answers to the questions in Appendix A. For more information on how to obtain additional questions, please see this book's Introduction.

1. What allows a user to belong to more than one role?

    A. Multirole systems admin

    B. MSP groups

    C. Multirole access user profiles

    D. Group role catalog

2. If a user is created in UCSD, what are they considered to be?

    A. Admin

    B. Local

    C. AD

    D. LDAP

3. A user can be placed into what container for responsibility grouping?

    A. Roles

    B. Groups

    C. MSP

    D. IT administrators

4. What role allows orchestration to be defined between initiators and targets?

    A. IT Admins

    B. Storage Administrators

    C. Network Administrators

    D. Global Admins

5. What role allows read-write access to all role-based objects?

    A. IT admins

    B. System Administrator

    C. All Policy Administrators

    D. Global Admins

6. Each user account can belong to how many roles?

    A. Single

    B. Multi

    C. 4

    D. 11

7. The UC Director default roles offer what advantages? (Choose two.)

   A. Quick deployment times

   B. Read-write access

   C. Service catalog definitions

   D. Are predefined default roles for ease of use

8. Which of the following is the primary application to define users for Cisco cloud administration?

   A. Prime Services

   B. Cisco ONE

   C. UCS Director

   D. Intercloud Fabric for Business

9. UCSD supports specifically Cisco cloud, storage, compute, and networking products.

   A. True

   B. False

10. Name two roles that allow for role creation.

   A. All policy

   B. System admin

   C. Group admin

   D. MSP admin

11. A user can belong to more than one profile.

   A. True

   B. False

12. What of the following are created for each specific function in UCSD?

   A. User groups

   B. User accounts

   C. Service catalogs

   D. Local groups

13. A user can be assigned to multiple user profiles for what reasons? (Choose two.)

   A. Requires system admin rights

   B. Requires multirole access

   C. Needs additional service catalog rights

   D. The user performs several different functions in the organization.

14. What is optional information when creating a single role user in UCSD? (Choose three.)

    A. Address

    B. Phone number

    C. First and last names

    D. Username

    E. E-mail address

15. What process is required to log into a secondary role in UCSD?

    A. Log in as username profile_name.

    B. No separate login is required; rights are automatically assigned.

    C. Single-sign on supports all roles.

    D. Log in as username/profile_name.

16. What are optional fields when creating a user group? (Choose three.)

    A. Group Name

    B. E-mail Address

    C. Cost Center

    D. Phone Number

    E. Group Share Policy

17. Users are assigned to what to gain access to services?

    A. Service catalogs

    B. Roles

    C. RBAC

    D. Access profiles

18. Which UCSD role acts as the superuser account?

    A. All Access Administrators

    B. All Policy Administrators

    C. Systems Administrator

    D. Operator

19. Which UCSD default role is used to allow an end user to add users?

    A. All Access Administrators

    B. Group Administrator

    C. Systems Administrator

    D. Operator

20. Groups can be created in which two locations?

    A. Local data based

    B. SQL database

    C. Directory services

    D. Service catalog

Chapter

14

Virtual Machine Operations

THE FOLLOWING UNDERSTANDING CISCO CLOUD ADMINISTRATION CLDADM (210-455) EXAM OBJECTIVES ARE COVERED IN THIS CHAPTER:

✓ **1.2   Perform virtual machine operations**

- 1.2.a Configure live migrations of VMs from host to host

- 1.2.b Edit VM

- 1.2.c Configure VM snapshots

- 1.2.d Describe reverting a VM to a snapshot

This chapter introduces virtual machine concepts that you'll explore in depth later, primarily in the "Cisco ONE Enterprise Cloud Suite" section of this chapter as it pertains to VM operations. As we've previously discussed the use of virtualization has picked up in the enterprise. You'll still find applications running on bare-metal servers, but virtualization has largely won over in the data center. With virtualization, the VM server count has grown much more rapidly than new physical server deployments.

Increasingly, enterprises are not standardized on a single hypervisor vendor as much as they were at the beginning of the virtualization phase. Enterprises are largely adopting a muli-hypservisor strategy as well as implementing both on-premise and public cloud deployment models to avoid vendor lock-in issues. The multivendor hypervisor approach leads to several issues for operation and management that businesses need solved.

Cisco addresses the multi-hypervisor data center by offering the following:

- Solutions for increasing the speed of business, leveraging compute resources in hybrid and public clouds where hypervisors might be different

- Customer expectations of on-demand service consumption (Service Catalog)

- Need for a consistent infrastructure delivery approach

- Solutions that will accommodate both current and next-generation architectures

In this chapter, we'll focus on basic VM operations. We'll also discuss the *Cisco UCS Director* and *Cisco Prime Service Catalog* components as they relate to VM operations. Throughout the rest of this guide, we'll explore other features of both suites.

VM Operations

One of the areas covered on the exam is basic VM operation. You're required to understand and explain some of the fundamental tasks an administrator would use on-premise or in the cloud. These tasks are usually deployed from a VM manager. UCS Director and vCenter are two examples that can work together to provide these functions.

For editing a VM or VM template, the following items are examples of what you would define for your enterprise needs. The following list is a small set of examples; there are many more.

- OS type
- Virtual NICs

- Data store type and size
- Host/cluster to run on
- Number of vCPUs
- Amount of memory allocated

Some benefits of virtualized machines are the abilities to create clones, use *snapshots*, and use *live migrations* to move your machines. Let's discuss the ability to migrate machines first, one of the most useful features that comes with virtualized infrastructures.

VMware popularized this feature with its vMotion technology and is probably the most thought of product when VM migrations are discussed. It is not specific to VMware, though, as other hypervisors support the same features in their technology. Live migration enables virtual machines to move freely between compatible servers with zero downtime. The active memory and execution state of the VM is sent between the source and destination hosts until a sync is achieved. The source and destination hosts must also be able to see the shared storage target that the VM uses. This is a simplified high-level explanation of the process; each vendor may achieve things slightly differently, but the end effect is still the same.

There are several different types of migrations, listed here:

Host Migration   This is the process of changing the host that supports and runs the current VM to another host. This can be done live or cold. *Cold* refers to when the VM is in a powered-off state. An example might be moving a VM from a host in one rack to another rack in a nearby availability zone.

Storage Migration   This is the process of changing the storage that the VM host uses. The VM stays on the current host, but the storage it points to moves to a new storage area. One use case might be moving the VM's backend storage to a higher-capacity and better-performing array. This should also have the capability of live or cold, depending on your VM vendor.

Both Host and Storage Migration   This is usually done when a VM is powered off, but each vendor may differ in implementations and capabilities. This isn't a live migration, but it fits with the other types and should be a concept you understand. In this case, the VM is shut down, and everything is changed from storage to the host the VM runs on.

As you begin to understand the concept of a live migration, you can see why it is one of the most compelling features of virtualized machines. There are many use cases. Imagine you need to perform maintenance on a rack of hosts running VMs. In the virtualized world, you can migrate all the VMs to a temporary home while you work on the hosts. Another popular example consists of disaster recovery and availability zones. Being able to move your machines freely around your infrastructure enables a multitude of possibilities.

The next areas of VM operations you'll look at are *snapshots* and *clones*. Snapshots are restore points created from a certain state of the VM at a point in time. For example, after you've installed your operating system and all available patches, you create a snapshot. This one might be referred to as your *master snapshot*. If something catastrophic goes wrong, you can always fall back to this state. For example, say new patches were rolled out that rendered the server inoperable for whatever reason. The operations center looks at the server and deems the patches are the issue. It may be simple to roll the patches back, but it may not be. If your known state was saved in a snapshot, you could merely revert to the snapshot state. This would roll back the VM to how it was when it was first installed.

Of course, the original install state isn't the only state you might save. You might save states over time so that you can always revert to a recent state. This enables operations and engineering to focus on deployments and operations while knowing they have a back-out state if it comes to that.

The last area of operations covered lightly on the exam is the use of clones. Cloning and snapshot are almost the same, but they are used for different purposes. While snapshots are used for a state in time for a specific VM, cloning is a copy of how the VM was built and can be used to build other VMs. You might clone a VM for large rollouts, the self-service catalog, and more. Cloning essentially saves you time if you are deploying many copies of the same virtual machine. In the next section, we'll talk about the Cisco products that can automate and use these features from a GUI interface.

Cisco ONE Enterprise Cloud Suite

The Cisco ONE Enterprise Cloud Suite is a set of products released by Cisco as a package meant to automate, maintain, and deploy your infrastructure. We'll describe some of the basics of the suite and how VM operations and automation are achieved with the products.

Some of the goals of Cloud Suite are as follows:

- Increasing the speed of application development and deployment

- Creating on-demand service consumption

- Using a service catalog for easy deployment

- Managing both private and hybrid environments

- Through Cisco UCS Director, automating and using *orchestration* with the various tasks of virtual machines. Some of the features are as follows:

  - UCS Director has muli-hypservisor support. UCS Director supports VMware ESXI, Microsoft Hyper-V, and Red Hat KVM.

  - A self-service catalog is included to aid on-demand ordering.

  - Network management and on-demand provisioning are a large part of UCS Director, including VM operations, VLANs, ACLs, and more.

  - Orchestration is included with built-in tasks and APIs to design workflows for IT end users.

- Through Cisco Prime Services Catalog, using embedded control and governance that sits on top of the Enterprise Cloud Suite. Some of the features offered are as follows:

  - A high level of control with a built-in policy-based approval process

  - A central service catalog

- Life-cycle management
- Financial and demand management
- Dashboards to establish user entitlement

UCS Director and VM Operations

UCS Director is one of the main offerings of the Enterprise Cloud Suite. As mentioned, its goal is to offer ease of use in orchestration and deployment. IT deployment has been a manual effort for some time and comes with its set of drawbacks, such as length of time to deploy and the potential for human error. UCS Director solves this with automation, orchestration, and a service catalog. This offers administrators, systems, and network engineers a more drag-and-drop deployment model. UCS Director offers many services, but we will focus here on the CCNA Cloud exam topics that relate to VM operations.

The operations we previously discussed can also be used in UCS Director through templates and policies. Here are other features: VM administration, powering on and off a VM, using VM snapshots, adding VNICs, managing port groups, and more.

- Browsing the catalog and ordering from preset *workflows* such as different hypervisors
- Customizing VM options such as vCPU, memory, storage, and more
- Performing live migrations of a VM from host to host

UCS Director is built around workflow and automation for the IT engineer. But what is a workflow in the VM management space? Applications usually require several steps. Simply put, a workflow is the process of taking a set of IT tasks and automating them into a workflow from start to finish. An example of this is creating a new network VLAN. You might define the following steps to request a new network:

1. Create an IP network for a new VLAN that's known or assign one.
2. Get administrator approval from the network team.
   a. If layer 3 support is required create subtasks for HSRP, SVI, and more.
3. Add a VLAN where needed on core and access trunks.
4. Add a VLAN where needed on virtual switch and assign to the VM.

The previous list is a highly condensed example, but it illustrates the concept of workflows and automation. Using self-service portals and workflows, an IT organization could automate the creation and approval of a new network from start to finish.

In the next few sections, we'll take a closer look at the policies that govern UCS Director. You can download and install a trial version of UCSD because Cisco offers an evaluation license to try it for yourself or for your business. For the test, you'll only need to know the basics of some administration and operations, so a trial version, while nice to have, is not required. However, it is recommended that for studying purposes, you create your own environment if possible to become knowledgeable with the product.

We'll walk you through a couple of examples of what this looks like. When you first start UCS Director, there are a few easy setup options you can use to get started. Figure 14.1 shows this.

FIGURE 14.1   Cisco UCS Director

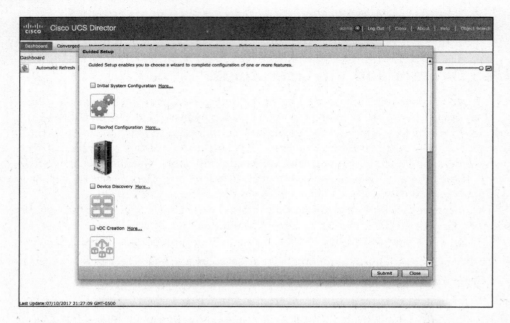

After you've set up the basics of UCS Director, you need to discover devices and connect it to a hypervisor to work with. To do this, follow these steps:

1. Navigate to Administration and select Virtual Accounts (Figure 14.2).

FIGURE 14.2   UCS Director: Virtual Accounts

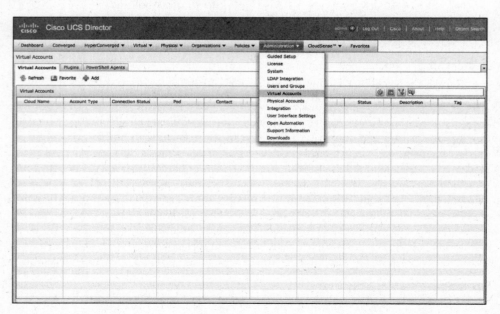

2. On the Virtual Accounts tab, select Add and you'll see the screen shown in Figure 14.3.

FIGURE 14.3   UCS Director: Adding virtual accounts

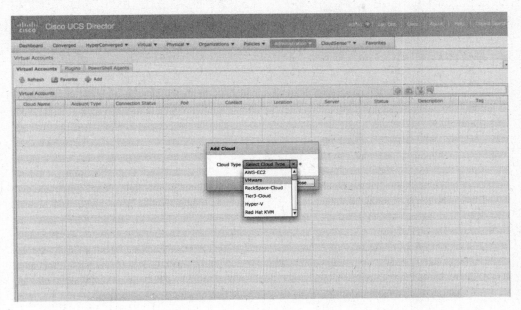

You'll notice in Figure 14.3 that several hypervisors are supported, as previously mentioned. These are shown in the Select Cloud Type list. For this brief overview, we'll look at the VMware options. VMware has the most out-of-the-box integration with UCS Director.

3. Select VMware, and you're presented with the screen in Figure 14.4.

You'll see several fields here that need to be filled out. The asterisks indicate fields that are required. You can complete the following items:

Cloud Name   The cloud name known by UCS Director. Choose a name that makes sense here as this name will be referred to for all reports and statistics.

Server Address   The vCenter server address

Use Credential Policy   This is a checkbox. If you choose this option, you can use a credential policy instead of filling out the server information manually.

Server User ID   The vCenter server username

Server Password   The vCenter server password

Server Access URL   The URL for server access

Server Access Port   The vCenter server port number

VMware Datacenter   The data center name of the vCenter account

FIGURE 14.4   UCS Director: VMware hypervisor

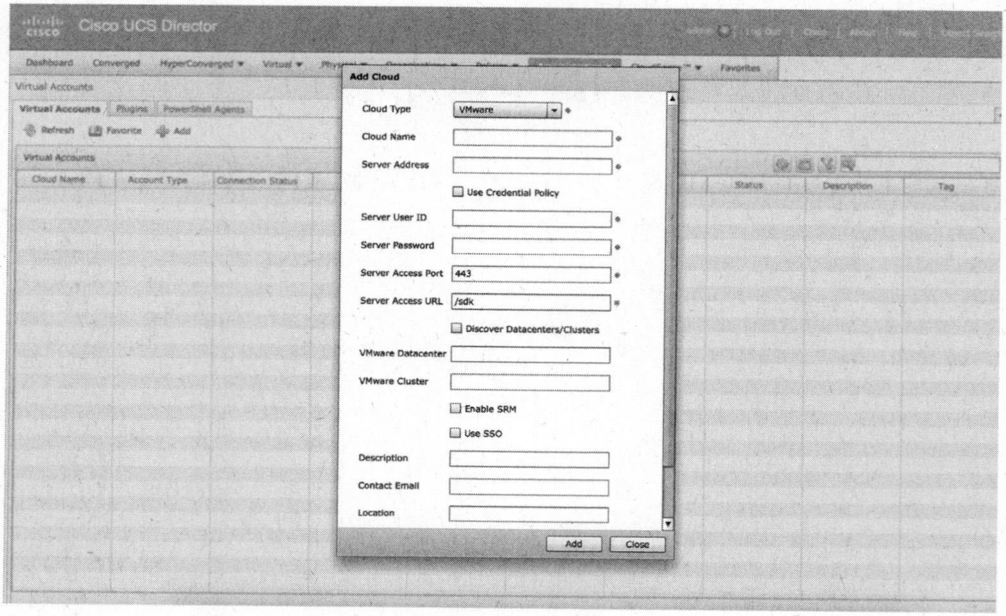

VMware Cluster   The name of the VMware cluster. You can use this field to manage a specific POD resource. Leave it blank if you want to manage the entire vCenter account with UCS Director.

Description   Informational field for description

Contact Email   Administrator e-mail for contact

Location   Location field for tracking later if you use multiple areas

You can repeat this process to add other hypervisors such as Red Hat KVM or Microsoft Hyper-V. After that, you might be thinking about what's next for operating VMs with UCS Director. One of the unique features of UCS Director is the ability to add *policies*. This is an end-user portal where VMs can be provisioned from a pool of resources that are predefined by your administrators. Cisco UCS Director requires that you set up the following policies before you can provision VMs. They are listed here, and you can see them under Policies in Figure 14.5.

Computing   These are policies that determine the compute resources that can be used. This can be vCPUs, memory, and other compute requirements.

Storage   The storage policy defines resources such as the minimum capacity, latency, and other settings. UCS Director supports VM provisioning with multiple disks or multiple data stores.

Network   The network policy controls network settings such as DHCP or static IP, VLAN, and vNIC settings.

System   The system policy defines templates, time zones, OS-specific information, and more.

After the accounts are set up, you can create end-user portals that allow administrators to deploy and manage resources. Like the policies mentioned, UCS Director allows you to control end-user self-service as well. You have the ability to customize policies for different PODs and life cycles. For example, you might have a DMZ POD and a Production POD. Each POD might require different abilities. The DMZ POD might be considered a security risk as it faces the Internet. Similar concerns could be for the Production POD as well. These are some examples of the policies you can create for self-service VM:

- VM Power Management
  - Power On
  - Power Off
  - Suspend
  - Reboot
  - Shutdown Guest
- VM Resizing
- VM Snapshot management
- VM Disk Management
- VM Clone Management

There are other options as well. See Figure 14.5 and follow these steps to get to the end-user self-service policies:

1. Choose Policies and then Virtual/Hypervisor Policies.
2. Choose Service Delivery.

FIGURE 14.5 UCS Director: Policies menu

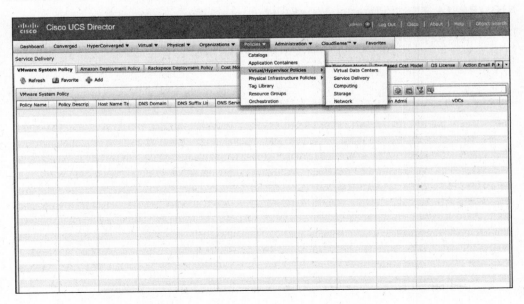

3. Use the middle tab section and scroll until you find the end-user self-service policies, as shown in Figure 14.6.

FIGURE 14.6 UCS Director: the end-user self-service policies

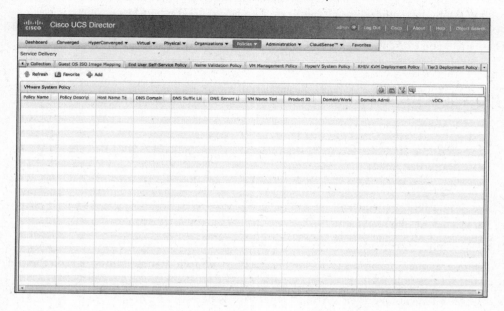

4. Click the Add icon, and again you're presented with cloud type. For this example, pick VMware again (Figure 14.7).

FIGURE 14.7 UCS Director: VMware end-user policies

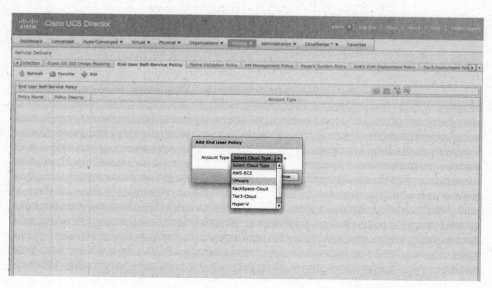

5. See Figure 14.8, where we selected a few options related to power state and clone management. Scroll down to see even more options.

FIGURE 14.8   UCS Director: End User Policy window for VMware

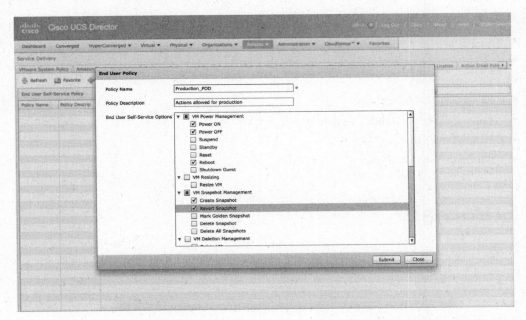

Using the end-user policies allows you to create custom controls for your operational needs. Users can operate within defined limits, and the business can ensure certain operations aren't allowed in various environments.

Prime Service Catalog

In this section of this chapter, we'll briefly focus on the Prime Service Catalog. There is overlap between the two tools, and they can serve entirely different purposes.

Here's a quick comparison between the tools:

UCS Director   UCS Director is more focused on the IT and engineering sides of operations. It can still be used for common tasks and ordering VMs. Workflows can't be built, and policies can be applied to keep end users in bounds with enterprise policy.

Prime Service Catalog   The Prime Service Catalog is a more polished look and all about the end-user experience with the service catalog. The Prime Service Catalog isn't built around intense IT tasks like UCS Director is. However, the two can link together, which we'll explain next.

UCS Director and the Prime Service Catalog both have built-in functions to connect to each other easily. As mentioned, the Prime Service Catalog is a more polished tool and uses HTML5 panes and a streamlined graphical web interface. Prime can do several of the things UCS Director can do, but not all. Some of the common actions for VMs include the following:

- Cloning VMs
- Creating VM disks
- Creating and deleting VM snapshots
- Adding and deleting VNICs
- Resetting VMs
- Reverting VM snapshots
- Putting VMs on standby and suspending VMs
- Powering off and on VMs
- Shutting down VM guests

Summary

In this chapter, we discussed UCS Director's virtual machine operations and briefly discussed how it relates to the Prime Service Catalog. Operational workflows were covered, and examples of how to connect hypervisors to UCS Director were explored. Finally, we discussed the differences between the Prime Service Catalog and UCS Director and where you'd choose to use each tool.

Exam Essentials

Understand the operations that UCS Director can assist with in an organization.   Know the various features of UCSD as they relate to virtual machine operations, such as the ability to perform live migrations, the ability to edit VMs, and the ability to create and revert snapshots.

Know which hypervisors are supported by UCSD.   UCSD currently supports VMware, HyperV, and KVM.

Explain the difference between the Prime Service Catalog and UCS Director.   The Prime Service Catalog is primarily an end-user tool for self-service, and UCSD is an IT engineering–focused tool. The difference is in the presentation. Prime has a polished GUI meant for end customer use, whereas UCSD fits more with IT engineers.

Written Lab

Fill in the blanks for the questions provided in the written lab. You can find the answers to the written labs in Appendix B.

1. _____ _____ is an enterprise cloud suite of multiple products that are geared toward automation and orchestration with private and public cloud infrastructures.

2. List three on premise hypervisors are supported by UCS Director:

    1 _____

    2 _____

    3 _____

3. _____ _____ _____ _____ sits "on top" of the Cisco ONE Cloud Suite and connects to other products within the suite.

4. _____ _____ _____ can be used in UCS Director to define limitations and accepted operations in administrating VMs in the enterprise.

5. _____ _____ is a module in UCS Director that allows users to browse and select items for deployment.

6. The ____ ____ ____ module in UCS Director emphasizes HTML5 at its core for the GUI.

7. The ____ policy in UCS Director defines time zones.

8. The cloud type and cloud name in UCS Director refer to the _____.

9. UCS Director manages the public, hybrid and ____ cloud environments.

10. The ____ ____ ____ manages system life cycles.

Review Questions

The following questions are designed to test your understanding of this chapter's material. You can find the answers to the questions in Appendix A. For more information on how to obtain additional questions, please see this book's Introduction.

1. From the following list, which hypervisor is not supported by UCS Director?

   A. Red Hat KVM

   B. Microsoft Hyper-V

   C. VMware

   D. OpenStack

2. The Prime Service Catalog is primarily for:

   A. Managers

   B. Engineers

   C. Developers

   D. End users

3. What can be used in UCS Director to limit what users can do with VM operations?

   A. Service policies

   B. End-user self-service policies

   C. ACLS

   D. TACACS

4. What policies must be set up before you can provision VMs in UCS Director?

   A. Network, compute, system, storage

   B. Virtual, storage, system, compute

   C. System, bare-metal, virtual, storage

   D. End-user policies

5. A self-service catalog is provided by which of the following? (Choose two.)

   A. UCS Director

   B. Prime Service Catalog

   C. Enterprise Cloud Manager

   D. Hyper-V

6. The Cisco Prime Service Catalog is based on:

   A. Java

   B. Python

   C. HTML5

   D. GO

7. Powering on a VM is a service provided by which of the following? (Choose two.)

    A. UCS Director

    B. Prime Service Catalog

    C. Cloud configuration portal

    D. Enterprise Cloud Manager

8. Which product provides dashboards to establish user entitlement?

    A. Cisco Prime Service Catalog

    B. Cisco cloud management portal

    C. UCS Director

    D. None of the above

9. What hypervisor has the most out-of-the-box integration built in to UCS Director?

    A. VMware

    B. Prime Service Catalog

    C. AWS

    D. Hyper-V

10. What policy encompasses DHCP settings among others in UCS Director?

    A. Services

    B. Network

    C. DNS

    D. Enterprise Cloud Manager

11. Life-cycle management is a focus of:

    A. UCS Director

    B. Prime Service Catalog

    C. Cisco cloud management portal

    D. VMware

12. Which product focuses on built-in policy-based approvals?

    A. UCS Director

    B. Prime Service Catalog

    C. Cisco cloud management portal

    D. Xen

13. What policy deals with the latency and capacity of storage on UCS Director?

    A. Multistorage

    B. Storage

    C. Data store

    D. Enterprise Cloud Manager

14. Memory is part of which policy in UCS Director?

   A. Computing

   B. Services

   C. Computing

   D. RAM

15. UCS Director sits where in relation to Prime Service Catalog?

   A. They are complementary; both work together.

   B. Below the Prime Service Catalog, feeding the Prime Service Catalog service data and information

   C. Above the Prime Service Catalog, passing down information

   D. Nowhere. They don't directly integrate.

16. What product is better suited for financial and demand management?

   A. UCS Director

   B. Prime Service Catalog

   C. Nexus OS

   D. ESXi

17. Which hypervisor is supported by UCS Director?

   A. OpenStack

   B. Fusion

   C. Red Hat KVM

   D. Xen

18. UCS Director provides an experience primarily geared toward which of the following?

   A. Directors

   B. IT engineering and automation

   C. End users

   D. Project managers

19. Which product integrates out of the box with third-party network gear?

   A. UCS Director

   B. Prime Service Catalog

   C. Cisco cloud management portal

   D. None of the above

20. Which product is meant more for end-user self-service?

   A. UCS Director

   B. Prime Service Catalog

   C. Cisco cloud management portal

   D. VMware ESXi

Chapter

15

Virtual Application Containers

THE FOLLOWING UNDERSTANDING CISCO CLOUD ADMINISTRATION CLDADM (210-455) EXAM OBJECTIVES ARE COVERED IN THIS CHAPTER:

✓ **1.3 Deploy virtual app containers**

- 1.3.a Provide basic support and troubleshoot app container with firewall, networking, and load balancer

Understanding and Deploying Virtual Application Containers

In this chapter, you will be introduced to *Virtual Application Container Segmentation (VACS)* services and learn how to create and manage them using the Cisco UCS Director application. A *virtual application container (VAC)* is defined as a logical construct composed of one or more network tiers that contain either virtualized or physical compute resources in a secured private network in a cloud data center that can be ordered, managed, and removed as a single entity.

Each application container is a group of virtual machines or bare-metal servers that contains a private internal network that is controlled by you and not the cloud service provider. The container is protected by security services that you define and manage. UCS Director allows you to create and manage container templates that can be stored, replicated, and offered in a catalog as a preconfigured option. UCS Director allows you to quickly deploy a complete container in the cloud and automatically configures all devices in the VACS service.

A good analogy to help you understand virtual application containers is to think of each VAC as the city or town you live in. The application container would be your city, with each IP subnet being a postal code. Routes can be thought of as roads, and if there are gates on the roads, those are like network access control lists. Servers and services in the container are like buildings, and security groups are much like a security guard in each building.

When migrating to a public, community, or hybrid cloud, security is always a primary concern. The hesitation to run your operations in the "wild west" is certainly understandable, and cloud service providers have taken many steps to make the transition safe, secure, reliable, and easy to manage. One common approach is to emulate your own personal data center inside the public, hybrid, and community cloud models.

What if you could cut out a section of the cloud that is exclusively for your own internal use? You would then have total control over the configuration, security, and management of this personal public cloud. This is what virtual application container services provide customers. VACS provides a secure environment in the cloud that is completely isolated from other users and services. You configure how all the devices in the container interact with each other and also the outside world. Traffic entering and exiting the container are under your complete control. You define all virtual machines, storage options, and network services such as load balancing, DNS, subnetting, and firewall security rules in the container that you obtain from the cloud service provider. There is an almost endless array of services and options offered by the leading public cloud providers today that allow you to design and implement advanced containers quickly and at a reasonable cost.

Before going too far into the world of virtual application containers, you should know that the term *containers* has multiple, and completely different, definitions in the cloud computing industry. You see, *containers* is also a popular term for virtual compute resources that are isolated at the application level instead of at the server level with the traditional hypervisor model. In this context, a single operating system runs many applications that are isolated from each other even though they run on the same operating system instance. Another way of saying this is that containers are an alternative to the standard virtual machine deployments that run multiple virtualized isolated applications at the server operating system level. Examples and frameworks of containers on the market include Kubernetes, Docker, Lambda, and LXC. So, when you hear the term *container*, you will need to determine which definition is applicable.

There are also several different names given to creating a virtual private cloud. Cisco uses VACS, as covered in this chapter. The cloud offerings from Google and Amazon prefer to use the term *virtual private cloud*, or *VPC* for short. If you hear VPC, know that it is the same as VACS.

What Are Virtual Application Container Segmentation Services?

Cisco Virtual Application Container Segmentation services provide cloud segmentation services.

A VACS container provides a secure microsegmentation architecture that allows you to create a "private cloud inside of a public cloud." You can provision VACS to have limited secure ingress and egress points, and then inside you can configure multiple zones and subnets for your deployed applications. Special services such as load balancing, firewalls, and applications such as databases can also be placed in your container.

The Cisco VACS framework consists of the following applications:

- Automated provisioning and orchestration with the UCS Director

- Load balancing with HA Proxy

- Routing and edge firewall services with Cisco CSR 1000 V and Cisco ASAv

- Zone-based firewalls with Cisco Virtual Security Gateway

- Virtual fabric services with the Cisco Nexus 1000v platform for distributed firewalls

VACS features include unified licensing support and life-cycle management. The data throughput into and out of a VACS is up to 10Gb per second with full layer 3 routing supported.

Provisioning a complete compute block from the ground up can take a considerable amount of time, effort, and money in the enterprise. With VACS, configuration wizards are provided to assist with the creation of your application environment. Wizards help create your virtual networks and all of the security requirements between the segments. When the design template is completed, it can be published in the Cisco Prime Services Catalog for user and customer consumption. Containers ordered off of the Prime catalog menu allow for complete application-specific computing systems to be predesigned, standardized, and ready for repeated deployments. With cloud orchestration services, deployments can be live in just a few minutes as compared to many months when using the traditional enterprise data center business model.

The requirements to deploy VACS include the following:

- Virtual Switch Update Manager (VSUM) application

- Nexus 1000 V virtual switch module

- Cisco Prime Network Services Controller

- UCS Director application with support for VACS

VACS creates a logical data center that allows you to deploy all of your cloud-based assets into a private container where all services inside can be interconnected. This logically isolated section of the cloud is for your exclusive use where you can launch applications in a network that you define. Containers are easily customized for network and security configurations to meet your own needs and requirements.

VACS allows you to create a public-facing subnet for your web servers that have access to the Internet, and then you place your backend systems such as databases or application servers in a private subnet with no Internet access. Granular user access control policies, access control lists, and firewall policies can be created at interconnection points and services in the container.

You can leverage multiple layers of security, including zone-based firewall support, to help control access to the container and services in each subnet. The router allows for standard Cisco access control lists to be defined for network-based security. The VACS design allows for much better security over your cloud resources than the traditional cloud offerings of the past.

Using Virtual Application Containers

VLAN access control lists (VACLs) offer the advantage of a reference design that can be quickly deployed in the cloud.

VACL services are often prepackaged based on approved designs. Each application model can be engineered by your organization to meet all corporate governance requirements, governmental compliance laws, performance, security, storage, and network access requirements. All of these requirements can be included in a reference design that is then offered as a supported service to your end users. This allows for ongoing support to be more streamlined since all designs are approved designs that have been prepackaged.

Application container templates are created to allow for easy replication of VACS containers. These templates can serve as a reference design and can also be cloned and modified to create containers with different requirements.

The following elements are created and defined when working with templates:

- Virtual account (cloud)
- Network configuration information
- Virtual machine configuration details
- Security information for the container
- Gateway router policy (This is optional.)
- Any options for services and end-user needs

Deploying Containers

The Cisco UCS Director application introduced in Chapter 13 is your primary management application to create and deploy virtual application containers in the intercloud. The VACS management area in UCS Director allows users to create, deploy, and manage groups of cloud services, such as virtual machines that are grouped into a single logical management entity. Each container can be designed for multiple tiers of applications as is commonly found in public cloud designs. UCS Director allows you to create a virtual data center that you have complete control over. Even though you are using the shared resources of a cloud data center, containers allow you to isolate your operations from the other cloud consumers.

There are different container types offered based on different use cases. UCS Director offers the following container types:

- Application Centric Infrastructure Controller (APIC), used for Cisco ACI APIC deployments
- Fabric, used in Dynamic Fabric Automation (DFA) networks
- Fenced virtual containers, for use with virtual machines and the most common of the container types
- Virtual application container service, specific to UCS Director VACS application subsystem deployments with the VACS modules installed in UCS Director

After a virtual application container has been deployed, the UCS Director application allows for the addition and deletion of objects inside the container. As such, container configurations are not static and can evolve based on user requirements, allowing you to make modifications to containers even after they have been deployed and are live.

Supporting and Troubleshooting Virtual App Containers

The container administrator has management control over the containers to perform different operations such as the ability to add virtual machines as required. Templates can be deleted, cloned, and modified to allow new containers to be defined based on newly created templates.

Firewalls

There are a range of firewall options to choose from when creating a container, such as the virtualized *Cisco Application Security Appliance (ASAv)*. After the container has been deployed, you can add and modify firewall policies as required to support your ongoing operations through the UCS Director management portal.

Networking

VACS support includes all of the advanced capabilities of the Cisco CSR 1000v router, which has all of the software features as the hardware-based CSR series. Full layer 3 routing support is a requirement to route traffic inside and to and from the container. Network-based access control lists can also be implemented in the CSR 1000v.

The management portal supports ERSPAN, which is a method of tapping into a data flow and attaching network test equipment such as analyzers to the VACS for troubleshooting.

Load Balancers

UCS Director implements the load balancer offering from F5 Systems in the fenced virtual application container. F5 is a leading server load balancing vendor that offers virtualized versions of its hardware-based products. Server load balancing allows for the distribution of traffic across multiple virtual servers and allows for high availability, resiliency, scalability, and the efficient utilization of server resources.

UCS Director defines the load balancing algorithm policies such as sending incoming connection requests to a pool of servers via round robin, least connections, fastest response, or weighted preferences.

UCS Director allows you to create and manage all F5 operations in the container including the following:

- Allocation of resources
- Network provisioning
- VM provisioning
- Resync container
- Container gateway configuration
- F5 load balancer–specific configurations

Once the F5 firewall has been deployed in a container, the network administrator can use all the management tools provided by F5 to manage the load balancer. The topics of configuration, management, and support of F5 load balancers are beyond the scope of the CCNA cloud exam and this book.

Power Management

Power management in the VACS can be controlled by the administrator as well. When a container is powered off, all configuration information and interconnections are maintained and restored when the container power is restored.

Monitoring

Each container creates its own set of log files and can provide custom reports for maintenance, benchmark analysis, billing, and many other uses. The UCSD management portal can be used to monitor your deployed VACS.

Summary

In this chapter, you learned about VACS and that the services are used to create a virtual private cloud in a public or shared computing environment.

Containers have two definitions in the industry; for virtual application containers, containers are the complete set of application, compute, storage, networking, and security services in one isolated package that you have administrative control over. You learned that the Cisco UCS Director management application is used to create the containers.

VACS templates can be created that allow for a standardized offering to be published in the Prime Services Catalog for customers to order and deploy. Templates of containers are created for ease of use and replications; a template can be created, cloned, and modified to offer new container designs.

The primary container types in UCS Director are Application Policy Infrastructure Controller (APIC) that is used for Cisco Application Centric Infrastructure ACI APIC deployments, Fabric used in Dynamic Fabric Automation (DFA) networks, fenced virtual containers that are the most common in that they support virtual machines types, and also VACS services that are specific to UCS Director.

When VACS templates are defined, there are many elements that are created and defined, including a virtual cloud account, network configuration information, VM configuration details, security information for the container, gateway router policies, and other options for services and end-user needs.

To create and deploy a VACS service, the following modules are required: the virtual switch update manager application, the Nexus 1000 V Virtual Switch Module, the Cisco Prime Network Services Controller, and the UCS Director application with support for VACS.

Finally, you learned about supporting and troubleshooting options for containers that included firewalls, networking, load balancers, power management, and monitoring.

Exam Essentials

Know that the most common container type is the fenced container that allows VMs to be defined in them. The other UCS Director container types are APIC, Dynamic Fabric Automation (DFA), and standard VACS services created with the UCSD VACS software plug-in module.

Be able to list the applications that are used to create a virtual application container. The Cisco applications that are used in the VACS framework are the UCS Director, load balancing VMs, the CSR 1000V virtual router, zone-based firewalls such as the ASAv and the Cisco Virtual Security Gateway, and the virtual fabric services provided by the Nexus 1000v platform.

Understand the defined elements needed when creating a container. The configuration elements needed when creating a VACS service include a virtual account, the network configuration information, the virtual machine configuration details, the security information, the router gateway policy, and any additional options for services and end-user needs.

Written Lab

Fill in the blanks for the questions provided in the written lab. You can find the answers to the written labs in Appendix B.

1. The virtualized load balancer in a fenced VACS is developed by _____.

2. A _____ container includes virtual machines.

3. Preconfigured containers that are approved for reuse are published in the _____ _____ _____ for end-user access and deployment.

4. A _____ container can be created for ACI deployments.

5. VACS emulates a _____ cloud in the public cloud.

6. _____ _____ _____ are the VACS container type that supports DFA networks.

7. The UCS Director _____ _____ feature allows VMs to be cycled without losing the current configuration.

8. The UCS Director _____ feature allows the creation of log files, benchmarking analysis, maintenance reporting, billing features, and many other options.

9. It is a common VACS design to configure web servers to be _____ _____ with public IP addresses and be referenced by the DNS system.

10. What UCS Director container type supports Cisco automating networking operations?

Review Questions

The following questions are designed to test your understanding of this chapter's material. You can find the answers to the questions in Appendix A. For more information on how to obtain additional questions, please see this book's Introduction.

1. VACS eliminates the need for transparent isolation between cloud consumers.
   - **A.** True
   - **B.** False

2. Containers are designed to be accessible by all users of a public cloud.
   - **A.** True
   - **B.** False

3. VACS prepackaged designs are offered using which application feature?
   - **A.** UCSD
   - **B.** APIC
   - **C.** Templates
   - **D.** Playbooks

4. What is Cisco's cloud offering that allows for a logical construct for private deployments in a public cloud?
   - **A.** VPC
   - **B.** VACS
   - **C.** APIC
   - **D.** UCSD

5. VACS emulates what type of cloud offering?
   - **A.** Hybrid
   - **B.** Public
   - **C.** Private
   - **D.** Community

6. VACS layer 2 switching services are provided by which Cisco product?
   - **A.** UCSD
   - **B.** APIC
   - **C.** VSM 1000v
   - **D.** CSR 1000v

7. What are elements that are configured when creating a VACS template? (Choose three.)

    A. VM configurations

    B. Security configurations

    C. User confederations

    D. Network configuration

    E. Schema tables and columns

8. VACS lifecycle management support is included within which Cisco intercloud management application?

    A. VSUM

    B. CUCM

    C. APIC

    D. UCSD

9. Unified licensing support is provided by which Cisco product?

    A. CULM plug-in

    B. APIC

    C. UCSD

    D. F5 ULAM

10. Approved containers are published for public use and deployment using which Cisco service?

    A. UCS storefront

    B. HEAT

    C. Prime Services Catalog

    D. Cisco user portal

11. What is the status of virtual machines when a container is powered off?

    A. All service configurations are deleted.

    B. VMs are removed from the container.

    C. Storage volumes connected to the root of VMs are flushed.

    D. All configurations are maintained, and the VMs can be powered up at a later time.

12. What Cisco products are required when creating a container? (Choose three.)

    A. APIC

    B. Intercloud Director

    C. UCS Manager

    D. Nexus 1000v VSM

    E. Prime services catalog controller

    F. VSUM

13. The fenced virtual application controller includes a load balancer from which vendor?

    A. Citrix

    B. Cisco

    C. Juniper

    D. F5

14. What Cisco firewall product is available for VACS?

    A. NetScaler

    B. Local Director

    C. ASAv

    D. Alteon

    E. Arrowpoint

15. UCS Director supports which fenced firewall solution? (Choose three.)

    A. Linux

    B. Palo Alto

    C. F5

    D. ASAv

    E. Virtual Security Gateway

16. UCS Director supports the addition and deletion of VMs after the container has been deployed.

    A. True

    B. False

17. UCS Director supports the following container types? (Choose five.)

    A. APIC

    B. Lambda

    C. Kubernetes

    D. LXE

    E. Fabric

    F. VACS

    G. Fenced virtual

    H. Virtual security

18. A container cannot be modified after deployment without first disabling all components.

    A. True

    B. False

19. Virtual application containers eliminate the microsegmentation requirements.

    A. True

    B. False

20. ACLs can be applied to interfaces on which product?

    A. UCSD

    B. APIC

    C. CSR 1000v

    D. VACS

Chapter 16

Intercloud Chargeback Model

THE FOLLOWING UNDERSTANDING CISCO CLOUD ADMINISTRATION CLDADM (210-455) EXAM OBJECTIVES ARE COVERED IN THIS CHAPTER:

✓ **2.0 Chargeback and Billing Reports**

✓ **2.1 Describe the chargeback model**

- 2.1.a Describe chargeback features
- 2.1.b Describe budget policy
- 2.1.c Describe cost models
- 2.1.d Describe adding a cost model to a tenant

Understanding the Chargeback Model

In this chapter, you will continue to explore cloud management applications offered by Cisco. Specifically, Cisco offers an application called the *Chargeback module* that is a *plug-in application* for the UCS Director cloud management application. This module provides you with a granular view of the costs associated with your virtual deployment in the cloud. The Chargeback module allows you to assign costs to units of your cloud deployment and then to measure the consumption of these units so you have accurate reporting and billing information. Data is measured and collected on VMs, and then the system calculates and reports the costs of each associated VM.

Chargeback features are often used for corporate governance where policies are created based on cloud resources that are consumed. With the utility paradigm of cloud computing, a method to define, track, and charge for the pay-as-you-go business model is required, and the Chargeback module for UCS Director offers this capability. The resource consumption is tracked, and charges are based on the profiles configured in the Chargeback module and can be applied to individual users or groups of users. Invoices can be generated based on a wide range of metrics that allow for billing based on cloud service consumption as defined by your organization.

Chargeback Features

The Chargeback module offers a wide range of options to allow flexibility to match the application to your specific business requirements. The module allows for fixed-cost billing of consumed resources; it also accommodates any one-time costs that may be incurred. You can allocate cloud costs between multiple organizations or combine any of these options to suit the needs of the organization.

Cost modeling and templates are included in the Chargeback module; you can use them as is or customize them for your specific requirements. These cost models can be assigned to virtual machines or other services that are managed in the intercloud.

Extensive reporting capabilities are available that allow the operator to generate a wide variety of reports on costs, usage, and comparisons between objects. There is flexibility in generating the report outputs that allow for export to common file formats such as PDF,

CSV, and XLS. There is also a neat feature that generates ongoing reports called Top 5. These reports show the top five highest VM charges, CPU costs, memory costs, and storage costs.

The Chargeback module also includes a web-based dashboard that presents the VM information and chargeback data in real time. This feature is customizable with the use of graphical widgets that monitor and analyze events that are then presented in a consolidated dashboard view in your web browser.

Chargeback Budget Policy

The *budget policy* feature allows a group or complete organization to be attached to a policy that collects and provides usage data and billing reports. The budget policy is the accounting mechanism in the Chargeback module.

In UCS Director with the Chargeback module installed, do the following to create a chargeback policy:

1. Select Administration ➤ Users And Groups from the top menu bar.

2. Click the User Groups tab.

3. Choose the group to apply the policy to and then click Budget Policy.

4. The dialog box for the budget policy will open, and the following fields will need to be filled out:

    a. **Enable Budget Watch.** When this box is selected, the group's budget usage of the group is monitored. If this is not selected, then budget entries for this group are discarded.

    b. **Enable Allow Over Budget.** When this box is selected, the members of the group can exceed the assigned budget parameters. However, if you choose to assign a hard limit to usage, you can deselect this box, which will have the effect of halting all resource requests until a new budget is assigned by the operations staff.

5. When those steps are completed, click Save and exit.

Cost Models

Cost models are where you will create the costs of virtual resources and assign a value per unit consumed. Virtual resources include many different objects including CPU, RAM, networking, and storage units. By associating costs to each unit, you can use them as building blocks for the chargeback calculations. Costs are allocated to each unit to allow for maximum flexibility in creating a chargeback structure that is effective for any requirement.

To determine the cost of each individual virtual machine, the UCS Director Chargeback module determines the total units that are assigned to each VM and what the cost associated to each unit is. The module will poll, or *query*, the VM frequently to collect granular VM resource usage information. With the collected data from the VM, costs can be calculated for billing and reporting.

In addition to ongoing operational costs, additional costs can be defined and associated to a policy such as if the VM is being used in the cost to provision a VM. If you allow VMs to be reserved for future use, you can assign a cost to that as well. All of these objects and their values can be used to determine the cost associated with operating a VM.

You must define cost models in the chargeback application to specify what objects you want to include and what the associated cost of each unit will be.

To create a cost model, you use the UCS Director Chargeback module, and the steps to complete are as follows:

1. From the graphical interface, select Policies ➤ Virtual/Hypervisor Policies ➤ Service Delivery.

2. Select the Cost Model tab and click Add (+) to create a new policy.

3. The Cost Model dialog box appears.

    a. In the Cost Model Name box, enter the name of the cost model per your choice.

    b. In the Cost Model Description box, enter a short description of your cost model.

    c. In the Cost Model Type drop-down listing, select the type of cost model. Standard indicates a linear cost model, and Advanced indicates a package or script-based cost model.

4. In the Charge Duration drop-down list, select the time interval to measure VM usage. The options are as Hourly, Daily, Weekly, Monthly, and Yearly. These total the costs based on the time window selected. In the Virtual Machine Cost Parameters option section, select Fixed Costs in local currency, one-time or up-front cost, which is usually the cost charged to provision and deploy the VM.

5. Define the hourly cost of both inactive and active VMs.

6. Use the CPU Charge drop-down list to apply costs based on either the CPU's gigahertz speed or the number of cores. In this section, you can also define the charge for a reserved CPU and base the charge on the processor speed or the number of cores. The reserved cost is in addition to the VM cost parameters.

   To assign a cost based on actual CPU usage, use the Used CPU Cost field, which is based on the gigahertz speed of the CPU used per hour.

7. Use the Provisioned Memory Cost box to set the RAM/memory charged in gigabytes per hour. There are also Reserved Memory and Used options just as there are for CPUs; these are also charged in gigabytes-per-hour increments.

8. Define networking charges. The Received Network Data Cost box is the amount of ingress data that is also measured in gigabytes per hour. Ingress or egress data is charged in the same manner.

9. Set storage costs. Committed Storage Cost is the storage cost per gigabytes per hour. Uncommitted Storage is unused but available or provisioned storage that is also charged by gigabytes per hour.

10. The Tag Based Costs options are beyond the scope of the exam. These options allow you to select a tag-based model. Do so if you desire.

11. Use the Physical Server Cost Parameters options to define the currency desired. Next define the up-front or one-time cost for deployment of the server, the costs per CPU based on select metrics of either speed or number of cores, the cost per hour per unit, and the percentage utilization that is provisioned in the VM.

12. Set the Blade Server Costs parameters, such as whether a UCS B-series is a full- or half-slot server.

13. When completed, click Add (+) to save the cost model.

Chargeback Reporting

In this section, we will go over the process required to configure and generate the reports based on the collected data from the chargeback application.

The Chargeback module allows you to generate *chargeback reporting* on cloud usage and associated costs. The charges are based on the items you have defined. These resources include a wide variety of cloud computing objects and include used and unused resources.

Reports are generated based on your organization's requirements and can include summaries for the current month, the previous month's usage, and the cost details of individual objects such as usage of CPU, memory, network, or storage resources. The reporting output can be displayed in summaries, tab-based reports, and special widgets via the web-based dashboard. Since the chargeback summary data is stored in daily and monthly buckets, granular reports shorter than one week are not possible; the application offers only weekly and monthly reports.

1. To create a monthly resource accounting report, log into UCS Director and from the menu bar select Organization ➤ Chargeback.

2. On the left side of the GUI, select either a group or virtual data center (VDC).

3. Select the Resource Accounting tab.

The table created is the chargeback report for the group or VDC that you selected earlier.

To export the report, do the following:

1. Log into UCS Director and from the menu bar select Organization ➤ Chargeback.

2. On the left side of the GUI, select either a group or a virtual data center (VDC).

3. Select the Resource Accounting tab.

4. Select Export Report on the right side of the toolbar, and the Export dialog box will open.

5. Using the drop-down list, you can select the file format of the report; this can be PDF, XLS, or CSV.

6. Click Generate Report.

When the report is generated, you are offered the option to download the document.

Summary

In this chapter, you learned about chargeback systems that enable accounting and billing information for cloud-based resource usage. The Chargeback module is the monitoring and billing application that is a software plug-in module to UCS Director. Chargeback enables organizations to create pay-as-you-go billing models based on cloud resource usage and to generate reporting and billing based on usage.

The Chargeback model is accomplished by creating cost models that assign a value to various resources such as CPU, RAM, networking, and storage units. These values are used to create chargeback budget policies that define the costs to users or groups when consuming cloud resources such as virtual machines.

The Chargeback module polls the individual virtual machines for usage-based data that is then used to create billing and reporting data for each VM. All billing and reporting information is collected using the Chargeback module.

You can create policies based on a wide range of selectable options. These polices are assigned to users and groups and compared against data collected from the VMs. Quotas can be defined to create a hard stop of the resources consumed when reached. There are options to allow for the continuation of resource usage beyond the defined quotas and reported to the billing and reporting system of the Chargeback software module.

The chapter also showed you how to create budget policies, cost modules, and reports.

Exam Essentials

Know the chargeback application details.   The Chargeback module is a software module that plugs into UCS Director and allows you to define billing and reporting parameters.

Understand the chargeback model.   The chargeback model is based on object usage over time. You use the Chargeback module to define the billing and reporting criteria specific to your needs. Objects consist of units in CPU, memory, storage, networking, and others that are assigned a cost and then applied to users or groups. The application polls the VMs to collect the defined usage data that is used to create reports and billing information.

Know the export file types.   Export file types include CSV, PDF, and XLS data formats.

Know the components of the chargeback model.   The budget policy allows a group or an organization to be attached to a policy that collects and provides usage data and billing reports. Cost models are where the charges associated with a VM are defined. Charges can be based on many object types including the memory, CPU, storage, or network capacity consumed.

Understand the reporting function of the chargeback system.   The application polls VM objects for the data defined in the chargeback budget policy and places the collected values into data buckets with either daily or weekly buckets. Reports can be run against the collected data and output as a web-based dashboard, or documents can be created in various formats. The collected object usage data is compared with quotas in the policy and the costs associated in the cost models to generate bill reports.

Written Lab

Fill in the blanks for the questions provided in the written lab. You can find the answers to the written labs in Appendix B.

1. The _____ _____ is an application plug-in to UCS Director that allows for reporting and billing of cloud resource usage.

2. The _____ _____ feature of the Chargeback module can provide a hard limit on the usage of a resource that limits a user or group to not go beyond the assigned cost value.

3. A _____ displays customizable current chargeback data in a web-based format.

4. The _____ _____ feature allows a group or complete organization to be attached to a policy that collects and provides usage data and billing reports.

5. _____ _____ are where you will create the costs of virtual resources and assign a value per unit consumed.

6. The Chargeback module will poll, or query, each _____ _____ frequently to collect granular resource usage information. The collected data is used to calculate billing and reporting information.

7. To create a monthly chargeback report, log into UCS Director and from the menu bar select the _____ _____ tab.

8. Chargeback costs can be based on recurring and _____ _____ metrics.

9. The Chargeback module associates _____ to _____.

10. CPU cost metrics can be applied to either _____ or _____.

Review Questions

The following questions are designed to test your understanding of this chapter's material. You can find the answers to the questions in Appendix A. For more information on how to obtain additional questions, please see this book's Introduction.

1. Chargeback summary reports can include which of the following objects? (Choose four.)

   A. CPU resources consumed

   B. VSAN ACLs

   C. VxLAN

   D. RAM

   E. Network ingress

   F. Unused VM resources

   G. SaaS

2. To allow for a hard limit when a policy's budget threshold is reached, which checkbox needs to be deselected?

   A. Object locking

   B. Autoscaling

   C. Budget Watch

   D. Quota policing

3. Chargeback reports can be generated for which intervals? (Choose two.)

   A. Hourly

   B. Daily

   C. Weekly

   D. Monthly

4. The UCS Director Chargeback module supports which two options? (Choose two.)

   A. Cost replications

   B. Dashboard

   C. Cloning

   D. Cost templates

5. Chargeback reports can be exported to which data format? (Choose three.)

   A. XLS

   B. JSON

   C. PDF

   D. CSV

   E. XML

6. Which metrics can be selected to calculate costs using the UCS Director cost model? (Choose all that apply.)

   A. IaaS reservations

   B. CPU speed in gigahertz

   C. Memory used

   D. Number of CPU cores

   E. I/O operations

   F. Reserved blades

   G. One-time, up-front, fixed cost

7. What Chargeback module feature restricts organizations to usage only inside of a budget?

   A. Budget policy

   B. Chargeback policy

   C. Budget container policies

   D. VACS

8. The chargeback dashboard is a real-time web-based output that can be customized with the use of what?

   A. APIs

   B. Widgets

   C. PDF

   D. XML

9. What chargeback definition is used to assign the costs of virtual resources and assign a value per unit consumed?

   A. UCD accounting

   B. Cost models

   C. Budget policy

   D. Resource accounting

10. Which hardware systems can be included in a cost model?

   A. Fabric interconnects

   B. UCS B-series

   C. Netscaler

   D. CSR 1000v

11. Summary data is stored in what two bucket types? (Choose two.)

   A. Hourly

   B. Daily

   C. Weekly

   D. Monthly

12. VM usage can be charged only if it is active.

   A. True

   B. False

13. To allow continued usage of a VM after the budget quota has been reached, which check-box needs to be selected in the budget policy configuration?

   A. Quota Policing

   B. Budget Watch

   C. Autoscaling

   D. Object Locking

14. Which cost model option allows for the definition of resource interval measurements of VM usage?

   A. Charge Interval

   B. Charge duration

   C. VM charge metric

   D. Resource accounting

15. Storage costs can be based on which metrics? (Choose two.)

   A. Logical Unit Numbers

   B. Gigabytes per hour

   C. VSAN

   D. Uncommitted storage

16. Dollar values are associated with objects in the chargeback application with the use of which of the following?

   A. Budget policy

   B. UCS Director

   C. Cost models

   D. Cisco Prime

17. Chargeback data is collected by polling which individual systems?

   A. Hypervisors

   B. VMs

   C. Pooled resources

   D. VACS

18. The chargeback reporting feature has built-in reporting for the top five charges for which objects? (Choose four.)

   A. CPU

   B. VMs

    C. SAN

    D. Memory

    E. CMDB

    F. Storage

19. Cloud charges are calculated by assigning a cost to each defined what?

    A. VM

    B. Unit

    C. CPU

    D. Server

20. Provisioned memory costs are associated with which of the following? (Choose three.)

    A. Gigabyte per second

    B. Gigabyte per hour

    C. Reserved

    D. Memory used

    E. RAM pool consumption

    F. Elasticity

Chapter

17

Cloud Reporting Systems

THE FOLLOWING UNDERSTANDING CISCO CLOUD ADMINISTRATION CLDADM (210-455) EXAM OBJECTIVES ARE COVERED IN THIS CHAPTER:

✓ **2.2   Generate various reports for virtual and physical accounts**

- 2.2.a Execute billing reports

- 2.2.b Execute a system utilization reporting

- 2.2.c Execute a snapshot report

Cloud Reporting Systems

This chapter focuses on reporting and chargeback, specifically with UCS Director. As any infrastructure in the cloud or on-site is used and scaled, monitoring and usage become increasingly necessary. This is especially true with self-service tools, as end users generate virtual infrastructure quickly. This information is beneficial not only to the cloud administrators but to the end users of the infrastructure. In addition to reporting, billing is one of the most important aspects of cloud services whether they are managed locally or off-site.

These tools are usually available with the self-service portals to charge users for the resources they use. These could be items such as hard disk usage, bandwidth usage, CPU, and RAM per machine. Most of these reports will be useful to organizations that sell services to end users or customers. Some organizations may charge internal fees to themselves for reporting and billing as well. We'll look at the basic reporting information first and tie it in later in the chapter to chargebacks.

UCS Director Reporting

There are many different types of reports available from UCS Director. A variety of metrics are tracked that can give insight into how the infrastructure is performing. One of the most common report types are *cloud infrastructure reports*. These reports give snapshots into how the infrastructure is performing, both physically and virtually. The data given is based on the most recent pulling interval, so it's not necessarily in real time. Some of the types of reports are as follows:

- Tabular reports that list information for host nodes and new and deleted VMs
- Bar and pie graph charts and comparisons. Examples are VMs that are active versus inactive VMs.
- Map reports that display system information in the form of heat maps and color-coded maps
- Top-five reports that focus on things such as highest VMs per host, greatest CPU usage, memory, and more
- Reports that can be exported in PDF, CSV, and XLS formats

Physical Network Reports

For a physical network, multiple general reports can be generated. Each report has its own tab that allows you to drill down to network devices that you want to monitor. You can access these from the Physical ➤ Network menu in UCS Director. You'll need to choose the default POD if it's unassigned. The basic general reports offered for network devices are as follows:

- VTP status of the devices
- Port profiles
- Layer 2 neighbors via CDP and LLDP
- VLAN and private VLAN
- Host network details
- VM network details
- Virtual storage area networks

There are also detail reports for the network infrastructure available. You'll find these for different device types under View Details on the Managed Network Elements tab. Examples of such devices are the 1000v, Nexus 5000, 7000, 9000, and MDS 9000 series. UCS Director also supports a 9300 switch. For example, you might have the following available detailed reports:

- Configurations
- Licenses
- Modules
- VPC information
- Features
- Mac address table
- QOS information

The preceding list includes examples, as each device might have more reporting information accessible to the administrator. The detailed reports are in addition to the general reports. You can search through some of the fields as well, such as the MAC address table report. As listed earlier, this report is built on information received from CDP and LLDP relative to the switch and is useful in identifying devices connected to the physical network. It's important to note that not only do these reports list valuable information such as configuration changes, they are accessed via the menu items. For example, you can enable and disable ports on the switch from the menu.

You can export the network inventory reports by doing the following in UCS Director:

1. Choose Physical ➤ Network in the upper menu.
2. On the Network page, choose the appropriate POD.
3. Click a report you'd like to export.

4. Click Export Report.

5. Choose a desired format from the Select Report Format drop-down and then click Generate Report.

6. The report will generate, and then you can click Download.

UCS Compute Reports

When a POD is added in UCS Director, UCS Director discovers and collects the inventory of that POD. You're able to view the status of the components along with the summary reports. You can monitor UCS Manager components throughout the UCS domain, including the following items:

- Organizations
- UCS domains
- Global and local service profiles
- VSANs
- VLANs
- Discovered servers
- FEX, chassis, and more

You can view the majority of these items by navigating to the following area in UCS Director:

1. Choose Physical ➤ Compute in the upper menu.

2. On the Compute page, expand Multi-Domain Managers.

3. On the Compute page, click UCS Central Account.

4. Click View Details under UCS Central Account or All UCS Domains.

5. From the More Actions drop-down list, you can choose More Reports.

6. Choose the report you'd like to view.

As with the network reports, many of these reports allow direct interaction and configuration, expanding the ability to configure the organization from a centralized location.

Application Centric Infrastructure Reporting

We've discussed Cisco Application Centric Infrastructure (ACI) that was introduced previously in this book. Cisco ACI is good for the private cloud and for orchestration within the data center; see Chapter 6 for a review. The ACI fabric can include a significant number of physical switches and servers. One particular addition to the ACI fabric was management. SDN promised the control plane and data center separation, and ACI delivered on that concept. All ACI changes are managed through the central APIC controller.

The APIC pairs well with UCS Director and includes integrated functionality. While the scope of configuring ACI via UCS Director is outside the scope of the exam objectives, the ability to report on it is not. UCS Director offers many reporting abilities for the ACI including the following:

- Fabric nodes

- Fabric chassis, slots, interfaces, and more

- Fabric memberships

- Physical domains

- Tenant health

- EPG health

- Application health

- Nodes health

- Access port health

- Fabric port health

- Line card health

- CDP and LLDP policies

- Tenants (To view more details about a tenant and overall reports, you can find it under View Details after choosing a tenant.)

- Summary (overall tenant)

- Application profiles, networks, bridge domains, contracts, EPGs, routing protocols, and more

The preceding list is not comprehensive. There are any more reports, integration, and quick-view screens you can use with UCS Director and APIC. You can view the list by navigating to the following area in UCS Director:

1. Choose Physical ➤ Network in the upper menu.

2. On the left side, choose Multi-Domain Managers.

3. Expand AIC Accounts and click the APIC account configured.

4. You should now see a screen of tabs and reports to view about specific segments of the APIC infrastructure, including the reports mentioned earlier.

CloudSense Analytics

We've been discussing the basic reports in UCS Director. The reports do have some limitations such as scope and history. The issue with history is that there is no ability to view trending information. Also, the basic reports aren't in real time, but they aren't historical either. The polling interval is indeed configurable, but it's only a current snapshot of what the environment is like. What if you wanted to see something from last week or earlier? In addition to trending and real time, the basic UCS Director reports do not offer any ability to combine multiple sets of data. This could be as simple as a report of all network switches that have a certain license applied or a certain feature. But you wouldn't be able to get a report that combined both. Finally, there isn't really a trending report or data set to plan for growth.

CloudSense Analytics solves these problems in a several ways. CloudSense Analytics allows data to be used from several areas and can report on it in a consolidated view. This can't be done with the traditional reports. CloudSense Analytics can also give reports on real-time capacity and trending. CloudSense Analytics displays the data asked for at that time, making it a true real-time data set returned. It can also be used for *billing reports*, which ties in with the chargeback module discussed next. Forecasting and trending are also available, solving the history problem and the planning issues.

As of version 6.5, the following reports are available from CloudSense Analytics in UCS Director:

- Billing Report for a Customer
- EMC Storage Inventory Report
- Cisco C880M4 Inventory Report
- Group Infrastructure Inventory Report
- Hyper-V Cloud Utilization Summary Report
- IBM Storwize Inventory Report
- NetApp Storage Inventory Report
- NetApp Storage Savings Per Group Report
- NetApp Storage Savings Report
- Network Impact Assessment Report
- Organizational Usage of Virtual Computing Infrastructure Report
- PNSC Account Summary Report
- Physical Infrastructure Inventory Report for a Group
- Service Request Statistics
- Service Request Statistics Per Group
- Storage Dedupe Status Report
- Storage Inventory Report for a Group
- Thin Provisioned Space Report
- UCS Data Center Inventory Report
- VM Activity Report By Group
- VM Performance Summary Report
- VMware Cloud Utilization Summary Report
- VMware Host Performance Summary Report
- Virtual Infrastructure and Assets Report

To get started with CloudSense Analytics reports in the GUI, do the following:

1. Choose CloudSense ➤ Reports in the upper menu.
2. On the left side, choose the report you want.
3. Click Generate Report.
4. In the Generate Report box, you'll complete these fields:

    -   **Context:** This is a drop-down list. Choose the report that you want to generate.
    -   **Report Label:** Provide a label so you can distinguish reports that are run from each other.

5. Click Submit.

You can also run an *assessment* under CloudSense. Assessments are all about the current health of the virtual infrastructure running VMware with vCenter. The assessment can even list compliance with what is in use for physical servers compared to the VMware hardware compatibility list. An assessment is easy to run because it is only for the virtual infrastructure. Do the following:

1. Choose CloudSense ➤ Assessments in the upper menu.
2. Click Virtual Infrastructure Assessment Report.
3. Click Generate Report.

The report is then generated in HTML or PDF format.

The last area on the CloudSense tab is the *Report Builder* area. This is the area where you can build your own custom reports and also where the biggest benefit is gained for trending analysis. You specify the context, the type of report you want to see, and the duration for the data samples. You can set up these reports as templates to build others as well, cloning them and using them later. You can access the Report Builder by following these steps in the UCS Director GUI:

1. Choose CloudSense ➤ Report Builder in the upper menu.
2. Click Add Template.
3. Fill in the fields Name and Description and expand the entries on the Report item.
4. For the report context, you can choose from the following:

    -   VDC
    -   Cloud
    -   Physical Account
    -   Multi-Domain Manager
    -   Global and Global Admin

5. After setting your context, you'll be provided with a variety of reports to choose from as well as the duration for trends. Hourly, daily, weekly, and monthly are available depending upon the type of report.

UCS Director Chargeback

Chargeback and billing are functions UCS Director can provide. Most enterprise or cloud organizations will use these features in some way. Let's first look at some terms you'll hear about as we discuss chargebacks. There is a difference in how the chargeback reports are used in each organization. The method to get the report does not change, but the way the report is used differs. Billing reports can be used for *chargeback* and *showback* depending on how the IT organization runs. In general, most use cases are end customers being sold services by a provider company. This is the traditional method and can equate to selling cloud services, hosting, and more. This scenario falls into the chargeback model.

There is another model for chargeback, and it's used even if the IT organization doesn't have end customers. Companies that fall into this model need a way to track or charge for their internal services. For example, a large network of banks requires a significant amount of data and processing. The IT for that organization would have to be covered by the company itself. It's in this model they need to determine how that is paid for. In the chargeback model, the costs might be known and assumed. Each department might charge the other for the use of resources. The server team may charge the application team for the compute and resources they use. This may seem strange, especially as it's the same company charging itself for use of equipment. However, there are reasons to do this; one of the main ones is keeping track of the services and equipment used.

Showback is closely related to chargeback, in that everything from the previous paragraph could apply, except the actual exchange of money. In the absence of external customers paying for compute and network usage, the business may still want a way to track costs. In this scenario, the term *showback* refers to showing the business what is being spent on the varying efforts. It builds in accountability for project teams and management to see what is being spent and consumed from IT. It is also easy to switch to a chargeback model because the reporting isn't any different; only the way it's used is different.

After your organization has determined how it will proceed with charging, the next step is deciding what to actually charge for. Briefly, some of the most common charges in the cloud model are the following:

- Physical server lease, VM usage, and billing
- CPUs used
- Storage used per server
- Network data transmitted in/out

Chargeback Module

The chargeback module of UCS Director gives visibility into everything mentioned earlier. Metering data for the virtual infrastructure is collected at frequent intervals for accurate collection. *Cost models* can be defined and assigned to various departments, teams, customers, and more. Cisco defines the following features of the chargeback modules:

Flexibility   This is the ability to provide fixed costs, one-time costs, usage costs, allocation costs, and a combination of these based on the business requirements.

Cost Models   These are models that can be assigned to VMs and infrastructure. They can be templated for quick reuse later.

Reporting   There are PDF, Excel, and CSV reports that can be generated for you to view. Summary and comparison reports of costs and resource usage can be generated.

Top 5   This monitors the cost for the top five reports in an organization or group. This could be the CPU, memory, storage, network, or VM cost.

Dashboard   The dashboard monitors the VM and chargeback information in real time.

The cost model defines the unit cost of virtual and physical compute, storage, and network equipment. The cost of a resource is understood by the units that are assigned to it in the VM or physical resource. For example, the unit for a CPU could be per hour. The unit for network equipment could be measured per gigabyte in and out per hour. In addition to units, one-time costs can be defined. These could be items such as startup, migration, and more. A *budget policy* can tie in with the cost model. The budget policy lets you watch group costs and ensure overages are allowed. Examples might be disallowing a customer to spin up more VMs if they're over budget.

Let's briefly look at where the cost model is in UCS Director and how it's set up. In this example, you'll look at the VM/hypervisor policy for a cost model. You can set up a VM cost model by doing the following:

1. Choose Policies ➤ Virtual/Hypervisor Policies ➤ Service Deliver in the upper menu.

2. Click Cost Model and then Add.

3. Fill in the cost model name and description.

4. Choose the cost model type.

   - The Standard type uses a linear cost model.

   - The Advanced type uses a package- or script-based cost model.

   - The Advanced type is for nonlinear cost models and advanced scripting costs.

5. Set the charge duration. Hourly, daily, weekly, monthly, and yearly are options.

6. Select the virtual machine cost parameters. There are many choices here, with the ability to make a cost model per hour or per core CPU, network transmitted data, and storage usage.

The storage cost model and network cost models are included in the VM/hypervisor policy, as referenced earlier. Each has its own set of customizations that you can use for your organization's needs, and cost models are reusable.

The cost model feeds directly into the *chargeback reports*. The reports allow you to view data based on the cost model type. The chargeback is a calculated item and can be shown to the user in the form of reports, graphical reports, tabular reports like worksheets, and more. The reporting is meant to show your organization how much it's paying for resources, used and unused. Using this reporting will allow the business to optimize resource usage and overall cost. The chargeback reporting shows only daily and monthly intervals. If you need hourly reports, you'll have to find it elsewhere such as the Report Builder discussed earlier for CloudSense. UCS Director offers the following types of chargeback reports:

- Viewing reports
    - Current month summary (the current month for VM, network, CPU, storage, and other related costs)
    - Previous month summary
    - Monthly resource accounting details (the resource accounting for CPU and memory statistics)
    - VM resource accounting and chargeback (charged at the VM level for resources and VM usage)
- Export reports
    - Monthly resource accounting details (These reports can be exported as tables.)
    - VM and VM resource accounting (These can be exported as tables.)
    - VM chargeback (chargeback reports that can be exported as tables)

Summary

In this chapter, we discussed UCS Director reporting and analytics. We showed how to access these reports and how they can be used to monitor the infrastructure. We then discussed the varying methods of chargeback that UCS Director offers. Via the chargeback module, tight control can be used to charge end users or internal customers and report on those metrics. The chargeback versus showback differences were discussed including how they relate to charging via UCS Director.

Exam Essentials

Understand what the infrastructure reports can provide.   Know when to use the basic UCS Director reports. Know UCS Director's shortcomings and differences from the other methods previously described, especially when dealing with trend or real-time data.

Understand what CloudSense Analytics can offer.   Know the differences between the base UCS Director reports and what CloudSense Analytics can offer. The trending ability, real-time data, and custom options set the two apart. Know that the 210-455 exam may not differentiate between specific types of reports, as both CloudSense Analytics and base reports are types of reports.

Understand how chargeback works.   Be able to explain the differences between chargebacks and showbacks. Know how the cost model relates to the chargeback module of UCS Director. Understand some of the basic reporting and how charging can be accomplished.

Written Lab

Fill in the blanks for the questions provided in the written lab. You can find the answers to the written labs in Appendix B.

1.   To generate a billing report use the _____ _____.

2.   Which type of reporting offered by UCS Director shows a snapshot of the current state of the data set?

3.   The _____ model can be used directly with the chargeback module and its reporting capabilities.

4.   The _____ _____ reporting module in UCS Director offers trend and historical information.

5.   A _____ _____ prepared for a customer can list charges as well as usage.

6.   The _____ method uses the same billing data and reports but isn't expected to receive money for usage.

7.   The _____ _____ reporting module can provide forecasting scenarios for the infrastructure.

8.   An assessment report can assess the _____ _____.

9.   A billing policy would let a customer go over their _____ _____.

10.   The _____ _____ module offers a top 5 report matrix.

Review Questions

The following questions are designed to test your understanding of this chapter's material. You can find the answers to the questions in Correct Appendix A. For more information on how to obtain additional questions, please see this book's Introduction.

1. What report type offers trending and history in UCS Director?
   A. Cloud Analytics
   B. Infrastructure reports
   C. Java reports
   D. System-level reports

2. Which item can be used for UCS Director cost models? (Choose all that apply.)
   A. Network bandwidth used
   B. Amount of storage consumed
   C. Physical rack space used
   D. Heat index of equipment

3. What type of report can run a health check on the virtual infrastructure?
   A. Service policies
   B. Virtual infrastructure report
   C. ACL list
   D. Hypervisor policy

4. What chargeback model doesn't actually accept money?
   A. Showback
   B. Friend of friend policy
   C. Variable charge
   D. Future charge policy

5. Where would you find a tenant health policy report?
   A. Application report
   B. Prime report
   C. Application Centric Infrastructure reporting
   D. Hyper-V

6. Which reporting type gives a snapshot of the current time the report is run?

   A. Infrastructure reports

   B. CloudSense Analytics report

   C. Application reports

   D. Custom reports

7. What type of report uses heat maps and color-coded reports?

   A. UCS Director imaging

   B. Prime Service Catalog

   C. Map reports

   D. VMware CPU report

8. What would prevent a user or group from going over a spend limit?

   A. Budget policy

   B. Cisco cloud management portal

   C. Cloud Analytics advanced reports

   D. None of the above

9. CloudSense Analytics reports can be generated as which file type? (Choose all that apply.)

   A. HTML

   B. XML

   C. PDF

   D. XDF

10. Which of the following are features of the UCS Director chargeback module? (Choose all that apply.)

   A. Top five reports

   B. Dashboard

   C. Integrated testing

   D. Enterprise cloud peering

11. An organization that charges for the services used by customers or internal users is using what type of model?

   A. Showback

   B. Chargeback

   C. Variable cost

   D. Chargeit

12. Which of the following is a UCS Director network infrastructure basic report? (Choose all that apply.)

  A. VM network details

  B. Layer 2 neighbors

  C. Cisco cloud management report

  D. MAC address report

13. Which of the following is *not* a metric used for the cost model in the chargeback module?

  A. Fixed cost

  B. CPU count

  C. Memory used

  D. Power usage

14. Where can you generate a billing report for a customer?

  A. General Reports

  B. CloudSense Analytics

  C. Application Reports

  D. Multi-Domain Manager

15. Which report type does not offer trending?

  A. CloudSense Analytics reports

  B. Infrastructure reports

  C. Prime reports

  D. IM reports

16. Which reports are based on the cost model type?

  A. Chargeback reports

  B. Prime reports

  C. CloudSense Analytics reports

  D. Infrastructure reports

17. Which is a detailed report from the network infrastructure?

  A. VTP status of devices

  B. VM network details

  C. VLAN

  D. VPC information

18. Which type of reporting can combine metrics and stats from multiple areas?

   A. Infrastructure reports

   B. CloudSense Analytics reports

   C. End reporting

   D. None of the above

19. What can be used to build a custom report and specify the duration of data samples?

   A. Report Builder

   B. Infrastructure reports

   C. Generic reports

   D. Basic reports

20. What can verify physical servers with the VMware hardware compatibility list?

   A. CloudSense Analytics

   B. Infrastructure report

   C. Assessment report

   D. Chargeback module

Chapter

18

UCS Director Service Catalogs

THE FOLLOWING UNDERSTANDING CISCO CLOUD ADMINISTRATION CLDADM (210-455) EXAM OBJECTIVES ARE COVERED IN THIS CHAPTER:

✓ **3.0   Cloud Provisioning**

✓ **3.1   Describe predefined Cisco UCS Director–based services within the Cisco Prime Service Catalog**

- 3.1.a Describe the configuration of service names and icons

- 3.1.b Describe order permissions

    - 3.1.b (i) RBAC

Cloud Provisioning with Service Catalogs

This chapter and the next focus on cloud provisioning and the service catalogs that are used with UCS Director and Prime Service Catalog. End users and customers use service catalogs to order services and workflows. Services can be as simple as bare-metal servers or more advanced such as three-tier applications and templates. The service catalogs from UCS Director are the foundation for supporting the end-user portal via Prime Service Catalog. The look and feel of the end-user portal created in Prime Service Catalog helps you provide a professional portal experience for your users. (Note that UCS Director does include a simplified end-user portal in case your organization has not yet deployed Prime Service Catalog or you do not need the more advanced features and offerings it provides.)

In this chapter, I'll discuss the UCS Director catalogs and types. I'll also cover the end-user portal that UCS Director provides.

In the next chapter, I'll go into detail about Prime Service Catalog.

UCS Director Catalogs

Several different types of service catalogs can be used within UCS Director, and each team in an enterprise may use different ones. For example, the server engineering team needs will vary from the storage team's needs. These are predefined catalogs that can self-provision virtual servers or bare-metal machines.

The following catalog types are available by default:

- Standard
- Advanced
- Service container
- Bare metal
- VDI

Your standard catalog offerings may differ based on the UCS Director software releases. In the following sections, we'll cover the most recent versions here and how they relate to managing catalogs for your end users.

Standard Catalog

The *standard catalog* is the basic offering for end-user virtual machine ordering. Most of the projects that run in today's data centers include virtual machines. Your end users will likely be using this type of catalog the most. The standard catalog provides an easy-to-use front end to order machines for your end users. It can be customized based on templates and policies you configure as well, such as who can see certain catalogs.

You can create new standard catalogs from the UCS Director GUI by selecting Policies ➤ Catalogs. When you create a standard catalog, you'll choose the source image or the ISO for the VM to be built. UCS Director supports many different types of private clouds and VMs within the standard offering.

As of this writing, the standard catalog supports the following hypervisors:

- VMware vSphere
- Microsoft SCVMM for Hyper-V
- Red Hat KVM

UCS Director supports all of the operating systems compatible with the preceding list. Different templates are used for each vendor, and they are not interchangeable without conversion. I'll walk you through how to add a standard catalog and explain the relevance of each item and how it relates to the overall service catalog.

To get started, select Policies ➤ Catalogs in the GUI. Then follow these steps:

1. Choose the Catalog tab and click Add (+).

2. On this screen, you choose the type of catalog to create. Here, choose Standard and hit Submit.

3. You'll see the Add Catalog dialog with several options to fill in, as shown in Figure 18.1.

FIGURE 18.1   Cisco UCS Director: Add Catalog dialog

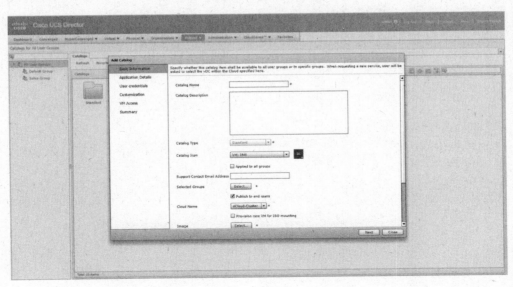

These are the fields you'll see:

- *Catalog Name*: Here you can give the catalog a name that your end users will see. Choose wisely; once you pick the name, you can't modify it. You'll have to make a new catalog to change the name.

- *Catalog Description*: This is a description for your catalog.

- *Catalog Type*: Notice that this option is grayed out; you already picked this option when you selected Standard.

- *Catalog Icon*: You can choose from a list of predefined icons to associate with the catalog item. This is what users will see when they go to click a catalog icon.

- *Support Contact Email Address*: This is the e-mail address of support contacts.

- *Selected Groups*: Use the Select button to select groups from the Select Items dialog box. The selected groups can use the catalog to provision new VMs.

- *Publish To End Users*: This is selected by default. If for some reason you don't want your end users to view this catalog, you can deselect this box. Then no one but the administrator can see this item for ordering.

- *Cloud Name*: Choose the cloud with the image for VM provisioning.

- *Image*: Choose the image type such as Windows, Linux, or any other templates your setup uses.

- *Windows License Pool*: This option only appears for Windows images for dealing with license pools and Windows activations and is not shown in the figure.

4. Click Next; you'll arrive at the Application Details pane, as shown in Figure 18.2.

FIGURE 18.2 Add Catalog dialog: Application Details pane

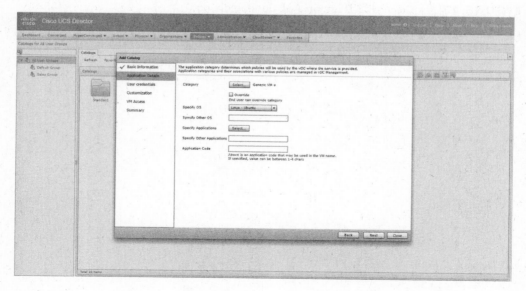

On the Application Details pane, you will see these options:

- *Category*: Figure 18.3 shows an example of the dialog that appears when you click Select. This is where you can apply different VDC policies to VMs within the same VDC. If this option isn't used, UCS Director will assume that the VM is generic.

- *Override*: Select this box if you desire the end user to override the selected category while provisioning the VM.

- *Specify OS/Specify Other OS*: This is for setting the type of OS installed on the VM when it is provisioned.

- *Specify Applications/Specify Other Applications*: This displays a checkbox of specific applications from the catalog that can be installed during provisioning, such as Apache, MySQL, or others.

- *Application Code*: This is for a code used in the VM name. An example might be W2K8 for Windows Server 2008. You can then use this name in templates and policies.

FIGURE 18.3   Add Catalog dialog: Application Details pane, Category option

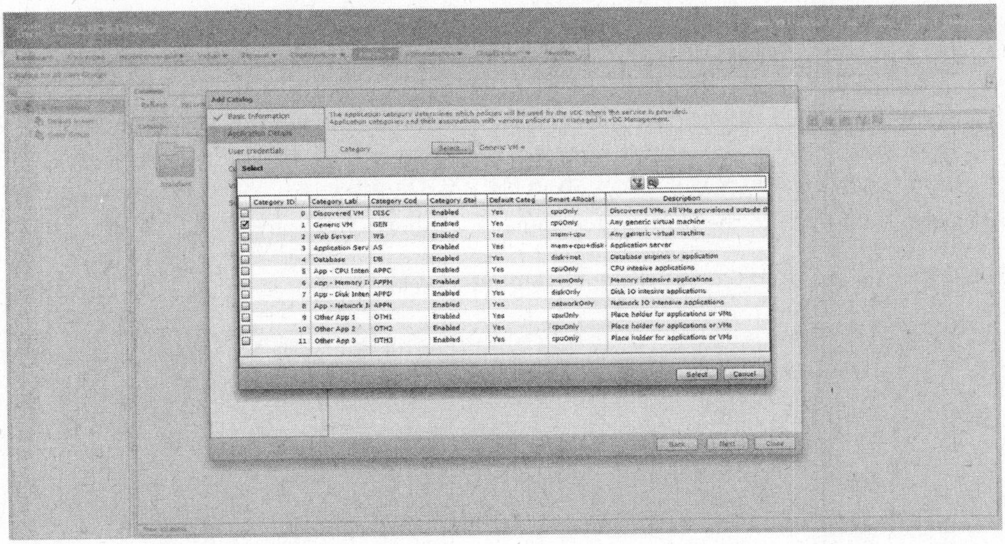

5. Click Next to go to the User Credentials pane, as shown in Figure 18.4.

FIGURE 18.4 Add Catalog dialog: User Credentials pane

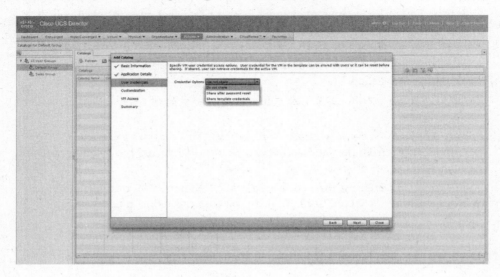

There are only three options here: Do Not Share, Share After Password Reset, and Share Template Credentials. Choose one of the latter two if you don't have another service to authenticate the users, such as LDAP. If you already have a service to authenticate users, you could choose the Do Not Share option because their accounts could already be set up to log in. When shared, the password will be available through a VM action called Access VM Credentials in the USCD portal.

6. Click Next to go to the Customization pane, as shown in Figure 18.5.

FIGURE 18.5 Add Catalog dialog: Customization pane

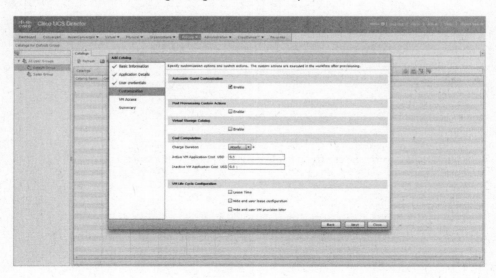

- *Automatic Guest Customization*: This lets UCS Director use the customization features of the hypervisor to configure DNS, network, and guest OS properties. If you don't select this, customization will have to be configured later.

- *Post Provisioning Custom Actions*: Select this box, and new workflows show up that you can choose after the VM is provisioned. This allows you to run certain tasks after the VM is built. The workflow drop-down list appears only if you select this option.

- *Virtual Storage Catalog*: Select the Enable box to select storage entries from the virtual storage catalog.

- *Cost Computation*: This area offers a quick way to apply some lease options and charge options to VMs. This is an easy option to choose if you haven't used the more robust chargeback features covered in Chapter 16. The chargeback features previously covered offer far more control than this Lease option, but you can use either.

- *VM Life Cycle Configuration*: These options allow you to define a lease time or prevent users from editing lease times or provisioning VMs later.

7. Click Next to go to the final VM Access pane, as shown in Figure 18.6.

FIGURE 18.6   Add Catalog dialog: VM Access pane

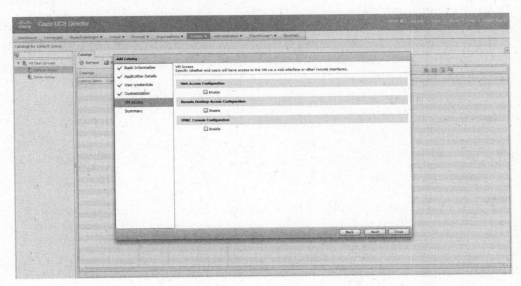

The options here let you choose what type of access UCS Director can provide to users for newly created VMs. You can use Web Access, Remote Desktop, or the VM Remote Console service provided by vSphere.

The final page after clicking Next shows you a summary of all the options chosen. Here you can go back and edit them or click Submit to build your standard catalog.

Advanced Catalog

The *advanced catalog* is a bit of a misnomer in the way it's named. You would think that it simply adds on to the standard catalog with advanced features. In reality, the advanced catalog is easier to deploy than the standard catalog. A standard catalog is used to create a new VM with a limited set of options. There are post-creation jobs that can be run under application details, but the options end there. What if you wanted to do something outside the bounds of just a VM turn up? You could use the built-in integration with ACI, for example, to turn up VMs, add them to an endpoint group, and edit firewall rules all within an orderable catalog item. The possibilities are endless, especially when creating your own custom workflows.

Let's look at the front end of the advanced catalog, as shown in Figure 18.7.

FIGURE 18.7   Cisco UCS Director: advanced catalog

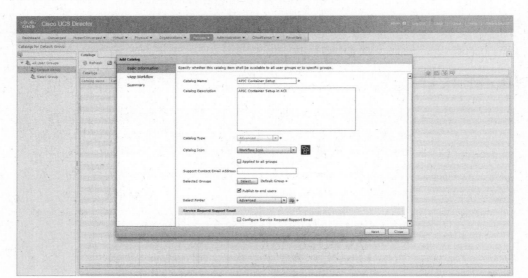

We won't go through all the fields here because they're similar to the previous fields for standard catalogs. However, notice that there are very few options. There are only three panes in this dialog, and one of them is for the summary. This is because you've already built the workflow or are using a predefined one. Clicking Next on the Basic Information pane brings you to the next page where you can choose your workflow by clicking Select, as shown in Figure 18.8. UCS Director includes many predefined workflows for you to get started. Yours may be different than shown here depending on the version of UCS Director that you have. You can also create your own workflow, as discussed.

FIGURE 18.8   Advanced catalog creation: clicking Select on the vApp Workflow pane

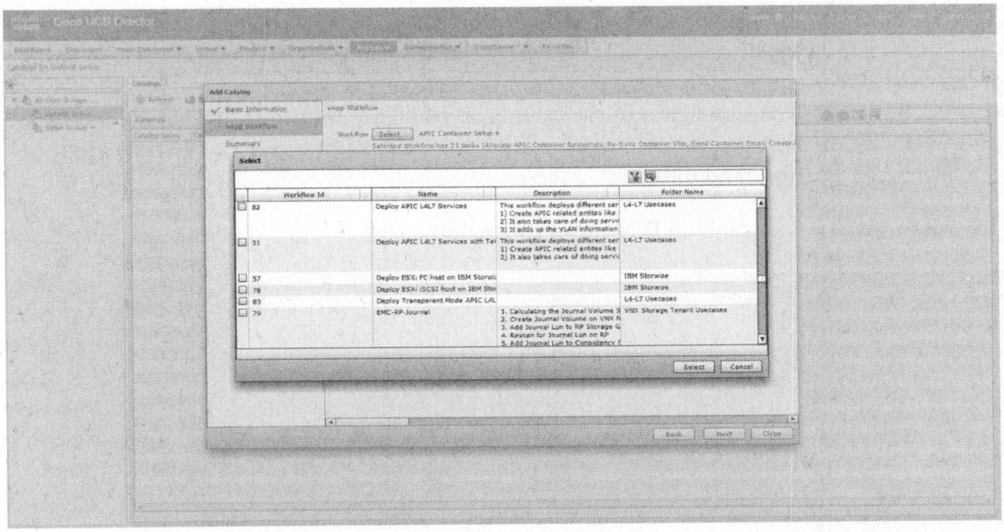

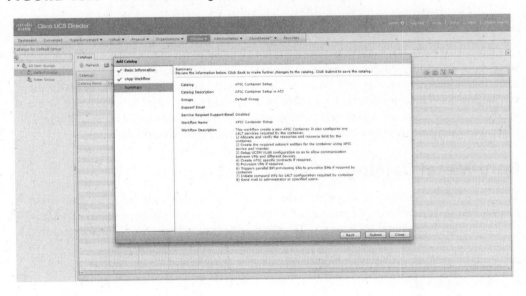

You can see the power of advanced workflows by creating orderable items for your end users that follow a detailed list of orchestration instructions. The standard catalog can spin up VMs, but the advanced catalog can do almost anything you've programmed the workflows and orchestration to do. Figure 18.9 shows the final summary screen.

FIGURE 18.9   Advanced catalog creation: Summary pane

Service Container Catalog

The *service container catalog* deals with the three-tiered container Cisco Virtual Application Cloud Segmentation (VACS) that we've discussed in previous chapters. The service container catalog allows you to combine physical and virtual offerings.

Select Policies ➤ Catalog again in the GUI, and you'll see the Add Catalog dialog for a service container catalog, as shown in Figure 18.10. The example here is the typical grouping of web, application, and database servers.

FIGURE 18.10 Cisco UCS Director: service container

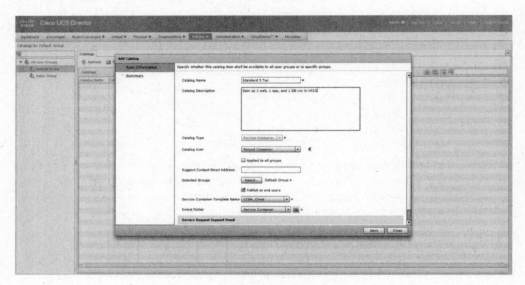

Here we've chosen a basic three-tier template called CCNA_Cloud. This spins up simple web, database, and application server containers. These templates can be configured by selecting Policies ➤ Application Containers in the GUI, and you can read more about them in Chapter 15. These containers have security and load balancing policies and can be managed as a single resource. Using this catalog lets your end users order custom containers that you've defined as templates. The customizations are entirely up to you.

Bare-Metal Catalog

The exam doesn't go into detail on the *bare-metal catalog*, but it's good to have an understanding of the differences. As you would suspect by the name, the bare-metal catalog is for provisioning a bare-metal UCS server. To create a bare-metal workflow, you are required to perform the following set of tasks:

- Create the bare-metal provisioning wrapper.
- Select a UCS server.

- Create a UCS server profile from a template.
- Associate the UCS service profile.
- Set up a PXE boot with BMA selection.
- Power on the UCS server.
- Monitor the PXE boot.
- Modify the UCS service profile boot policy.
- Power on the UCS server.
- Assign the UCS server to group.

VDI Catalog

Previous versions of UCS Director also had a Virtual Desktop Infrastructure (VDI) catalog. Depending on the version you're using, yours may not. You can use the VDI catalog to deploy virtual desktop environments managed via Citrix. It is not within the scope of the exam, so it is not covered here.

UCS Director End-User Portal

We've been discussing the catalogs in UCS Director and items for orchestration and automation, but where do you go after you've set them up?In the case of UCS Director, you can use the built-in *end-user portal* to quickly fulfill those needs. To use the portal, you need to be a user configured with an access level of Service End-User. Based on the administration setup, you can perform one or more of the following tasks:

- Provision virtual machines, application-specific infrastructure, and bare-metal servers.
- Manage, create, and review service requests.
- Upload and deploy OVF templates.
- Create reports to monitor your virtual and physical assets.
- Approve service requests to provision infrastructure.

The *landing page* opens when you log in to the portal, as shown in Figure 18.11. Recent UCS Director upgrades have a classic view and a newer view. I'll focus on the classic view since that is what is covered on the exam.

FIGURE 18.11   Cisco UCS Director: end-user portal

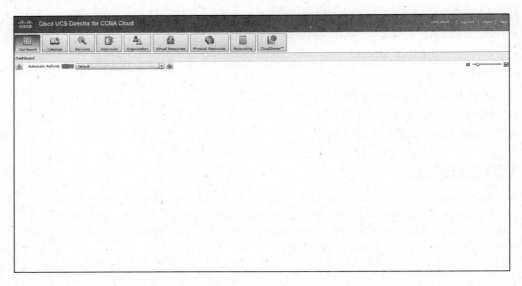

You'll see the following buttons when the landing page appears:

- *Dashboard*: If enabled, this can add one or more summary reports to your landing page. It is not enabled by default, and you'll have to create reports to add to the landing page.

- *Catalogs*: Here you can provision infrastructure using the catalogs discussed previously in this chapter.

- *Services*: With this button you can create service requests to provision VMs, services, and applications.

- *Approvals*: This is where the end user can go to manage pending, approved, and rejected service requests.

- *Organization*: Clicking this button provides a summary of resources, their limits, and OS usage for a group of users or a single user.

- *Virtual Resources*: Clicking this button provides a summary of virtual resources and reports.

- *Physical Resources*: Clicking this button provides a summary of physical resources and reports.

- *Accounting*: Clicking this button lists chargeback reports and gives more detailed accounting reports.

- *CloudSense*: Clicking this button gives you access to the CloudSense reports.

Most users will start by clicking Catalogs and submitting service requests. Clicking Catalogs takes you to a page where the requests are presented with all the orderable workflows and catalogs, as shown in Figure 18.12.

FIGURE 18.12   End-user portal: Catalogs page

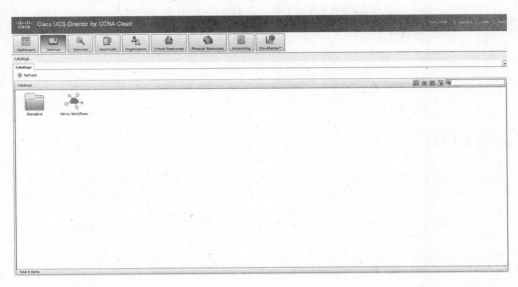

Depending on what you have configured, this screen might be jam-packed full of catalogs that you created in the previous chapter. In this example, there is only a workflow and the standard catalog. Clicking the standard catalog leads you to the VMs that can be spun up, as shown in Figure 18.13.

FIGURE 18.13   End-user portal: catalog selection page

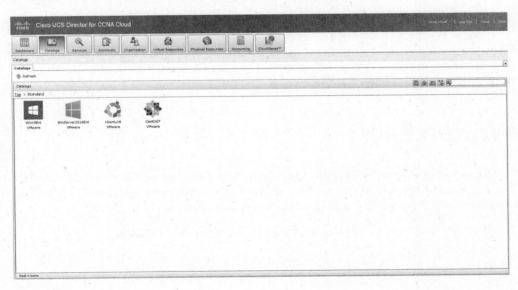

The exam doesn't go much further into detail about the UCS Director end-user portal, but you need to understand what it is and how it compares with Prime Service Catalog. The UCS Director end-user portal is something that can be used when you don't have Prime Service Catalog installed or you simply need something quick.

If you're really looking for a more polished look, Prime Service Catalog will offer that. In the next chapter, we'll cover the templates, workflows, and catalog integration differences between the two.

Summary

In this chapter, we discussed UCS Director catalogs. We covered the four different types of catalogs and the differences between them. We then showed examples of how some of them could be used for end users and your organization.

We rounded out the chapter by briefly showing the UCS Director end-user portal. This needs to be understood in order to contrast it to Prime Service Catalog, which we'll cover in the next chapter.

Exam Essentials

Understand what UCS Director catalogs do.   Know the difference between the types of catalogs and what they offer. Be able to explain the difference between standard and advanced. Remember that advanced deals with workflows and offers a lot of customization. Standard catalogs revolve around turning up VMs. Know that the service container catalog can turn up three-tier application container services.

Understand what the UCS Director end-user portal can do.   Know the benefits of the UCS Director end-user portal. The portal is meant to be used as a quick catalog for end users in the absence of Prime Service Catalog, which is a more polished solution.

Written Lab

The following questions are designed to test your understanding of this chapter's material. You can find the answers to the questions in Appendix B. For more information on how to obtain additional questions, please see this book's Introduction.

1. What are the four types of catalogs offered by default by UCS Director?

    A. _____

    B. _____

    C. _____

    D. _____

2. The _____ catalog is used for basic KVM needs.

3. The _____ catalog is used in conjunction with custom workflows and predefined workflows.

4. The UCS end-user portal is not meant to be the final solution for end-user catalog needs. True/False?

5. The _____ _____ catalog is used to provision physical systems.

6. If you were using a three-tiered container template, the _____ _____ _____ is used in UCS Director for user ordering.

7. The advanced catalog has more options than the standard catalog. True/False?

8. The landing page is a page for which part of UCS Director?

9. What feature can be used for UCS Director to autoconfigure DNS and network settings, among other options, for a VM?

10. What features use a pool to deal with OS licenses for Microsoft?

Review Questions

The following questions are designed to test your understanding of this chapter's material. You can find the answers to the questions in Appendix A. For more information on how to obtain additional questions, please see this book's Introduction.

1. When you use the end-user portal of UCS Director, what page do you start on?

   A. Default

   B. Administration

   C. Landing page

   D. Intro page

2. Which hypervisors are supported by UCS Director? (Choose all that apply.)

   A. Xen

   B. KVM

   C. Hyper-V

   D. VMware

3. The service container catalog deals with what container template?

   A. VACS

   B. VMware

   C. ACL list

   D. Hypervisor policy

4. What integrates with UCS Director to build a more polished end-user experience?

   A. vCenter

   B. Prime Service Catalog

   C. HTML Director

   D. Charge Reports

5. Which step is a requirement for the bare-metal workflow?

   A. Develop a server

   B. Power on the UCS server

   C. Start the application

   D. Set up Hyper-V

6. Which catalog uses custom and predefined workflows?

   A. Infrastructure reports

   B. Bare metal

   C. Standard

   D. Advanced

7. New catalogs can be created under what section of UCS Director?

   A. Security

   B. Policies

   C. Map Reports

   D. Settings

8. What can post-provisioning custom actions be used for?

   A. Budget reconciliation

   B. Running custom workflows before the VM is built

   C. Running custom workflows after the VM is built

   D. None of the above

9. Which feature offers stripped-down options for chargeback?

   A. Lease options

   B. Rental time

   C. Billing module

   D. Rent agreement

10. What feature of UCS Director is meant to be used with a service catalog if you don't have Prime Service Catalog?

   A. Top 5 reports

   B. Dashboard

   C. Integrated testing

   D. End-user portal

11. Which catalog is meant just to quickly deal with VMs and their ordering?

   A. Standard

   B. Bare metal

   C. Variable

   D. Advanced

12. Where could a customer upload and deploy OVFs?

   A. VM network details

   B. Layer 2 portal

   C. End-user portal

   D. Billing area

13. Which catalog could be used to create orderable Cisco ACI functions such as VMs and firewall policies to the fabric?

   A. Fixed page

   B. Advanced catalog

   C. Bare-metal catalog

   D. Power user area

14. What code can be used to name VMs for reuse in templates and policies?

   A. Application code

   B. VM code

   C. Service code

   D. Multi-Domain Manager

15. What catalog offers the combination of multiple virtual and physical resources combined?

   A. Service container catalog

   B. Bare-metal catalog

   C. Standard catalog

   D. Server catalog

16. What option controls whether end users see your catalog?

   A. Chargeback Reports

   B. Publish To End Users

   C. CloudSense Reports

   D. Infrastructure Publishing

17. The bare-metal catalog can be used only for which of the following?

   A. Physical servers

   B. Virtual and physical servers

   C. Virtual servers

   D. KVM servers

18. Which type of user credential options in the standard catalog is a valid password-sharing choice?

   A. Share Via Portal

   B. Share After Password Reset

   C. Share Before Power On

   D. None of the above

19. What feature relates to the image users see when they order items?

   A. Catalog icon

   B. Custom image

   C. User icon

   D. Basic reports

20. Where can you manage, create, and review service requests?

   A. CloudSense

   B. Infrastructure portal

   C. End-user portal

   D. Chargeback portal

Chapter

19

Cisco Prime Service Catalog Templates and Provisioning

THE FOLLOWING UNDERSTANDING CISCO CLOUD ADMINISTRATION CLDADM (210-455) EXAM OBJECTIVES ARE COVERED IN THIS CHAPTER:

✓ **3.0 Cloud Provisioning**

✓ **3.1 Describe predefined Cisco UCS Director-based services within the Cisco Prime Service Catalog**

- 3.1.a Describe the configuration of service names and icons

- 3.1.b Describe order permissions

- 3.1.c Describe template formats

✓ **3.2 Describe provisioning verification**

- 3.2.a Describe how to place an order for a service from the Cisco Prime Service Catalog as an end user

- 3.2.b Verify that provisioning is done correctly

- 3.2.c Access VMs and applications that have been provisioned

✓ **3.3 Deploy preconfigured templates and make minor changes to the service catalog offerings that do not affect workflows or services**

Prime Service Catalog Introduction

This chapter will focus on Prime Service Catalog and integration with UCS Director and on the templates Prime Service Catalog provides. As explained in the previous chapter, *Prime Service Catalog (PSC)* makes it easy for to order services and create service catalogs. UCS Director standard and advanced catalogs can be imported and spun up as orderable services. As you'll see in this chapter, there are many templates and predefined settings to assist you in building your portal. Prime Service Catalog is meant to be your one tool for order and life-cycle management with embedded control and governance. These are some of the features:

- Policy-based controls and approvals
- Billing and financial management with pricing, quota, and lease management
- Service life-cycle management and tracking
- *Role-based access control (RBAC)* and user entitlement

The goal of Prime Service Catalog is to ensure that all users across the enterprise, whether they be end users, application developers, programmers, or IT professionals, have access to a unified portal. This portal gives them full visibility into their orderable products and life cycles, along with built-in tracking for resource management. Let's look at some of the pieces that make up Prime Service Catalog, starting with the front end.

Prime Service Catalog Showcase

The *showcase* is what everyone sees as they first log in, as shown in Figure 19.1. This may also be referred to as the *service catalog home page*. It's the front page to guide you to features and provide easy access to some common services.

FIGURE 19.1   Cisco PSC: the showcase

Each of the sections you see can be customized and linked to *categories* of your choosing, which I'll discuss in the next section. The following sections are customizable:

- **Top (left and center):** This section contains the general information and images. It doesn't have services or categories associated with it to display them. This can be your company welcome image, web links, and more.

- **Middle (left and right):** This section is for categories and subcategories.

- **Bottom (left, middle, and right):** This section is for displaying categories and their list of services.

- **Browse Categories:** Shown on the upper left, this a drop-down menu that you can use to browse categories.

Figure 19.2 shows the drop-down list found under Service Designer where all of the previously mentioned elements can be customized.

Categories

Categories are for organizing services for ordering purposes and displaying on the front page, the showcase. Essentially, categories enable customers to find a service that meets their requirements. The category model is completely user defined. A single service can be assigned with multiple categories. The *Service Designer* module assists with creating categories, as shown in Figure 19.3. There are many things you can do in the designer, including create your own custom descriptions, names, and images. You'll want to pick what is most relevant to your end users, and you have a lot of flexibility in how these categories are presented.

FIGURE 19.2   Customizing the showcase

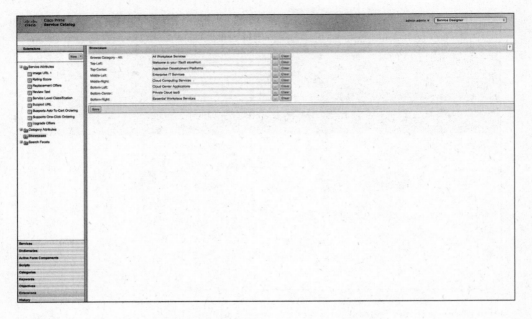

FIGURE 19.3   Cisco PSC: categories

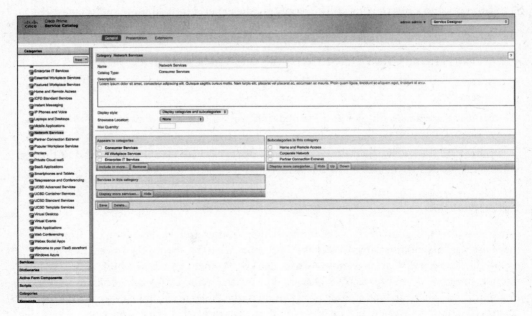

Figure 19.3 is just an example; there are many prebuilt categories for you to modify out of the box. The designer has a presentation page to add custom images, the category location, and custom HTML. You can see an example of this in Figure 19.4.

FIGURE 19.4 Cisco PSC: categories and presentation

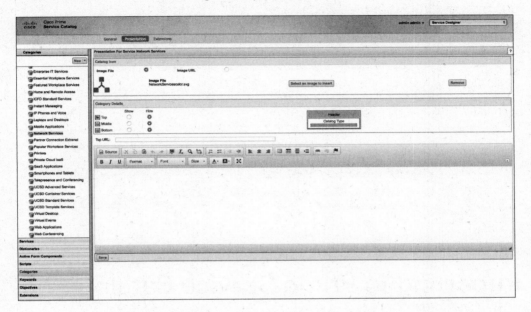

I'll return to categories when I show how services are ordered. Keeping your services in logical categories will greatly benefit your end users when it comes time to finding an orderable service.

Services

Prime Service Catalog *services* are the actual objects that do things. Referencing Figure 19.3, you'll see that the categories are an organizational structure that hold services. Figure 19.5 shows one of the service windows from the BYOD category.

Prime Service Catalog has an extremely powerful service designer that can deliver just about anything your organization may need. The first CCNA cloud exam, CLDFND 210-451, doesn't go into Prime Service Catalog deeply, so we won't cover it at length here, but you need to understand the difference between Prime Service Catalog services and the UCS Director catalogs. As previously discussed, Prime Service Catalog works directly with UCS Director and can import catalog and services right from UCS Director. I'll discuss this in later sections and show how to work with the integrations.

FIGURE 19.5 Cisco PSC: BYOD services

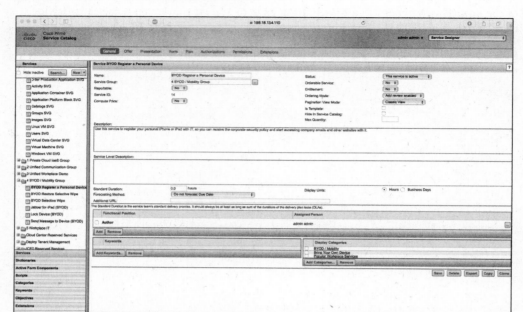

Importing to Prime Service Catalog

Now we'll move on to showing how to integrate UCS Director into Prime Service Catalog. You can use the built-in workflows and catalogs from UCS Director to populate orderable services in Prime Service Catalog. Here's how to do it:

1. Log in to Prime Service Catalog and click the upper-right corner menu icon to find the advanced service configurations and integrations, as shown in Figure 19.6.

2. Click Integrations, and you should see Figure 19.7.

3. Choose the UCS Director Integration and then fill out the fields for your UCS Director instances. The Identifier field is used within Prime Service Catalog to refer to separate external connections, as there can be more than one. You can choose HTTP/HTTPS here and also copy your root CA certificate for UCS Director. If you don't copy the certificate, you can optionally skip the validation step. Figure 19.8 shows the integration fields.

4. After you've filled out your fields and clicked Next, you can navigate up to Manage Integration and click Test Connectivity.

FIGURE 19.6 Cisco PSC: integrations

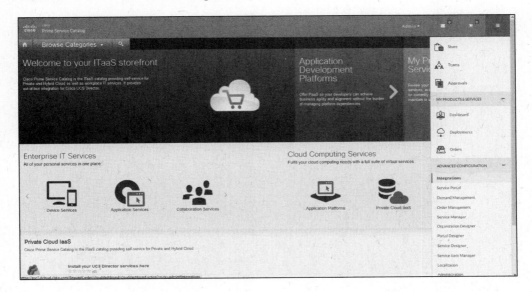

FIGURE 19.7 Cisco PSC: new integration

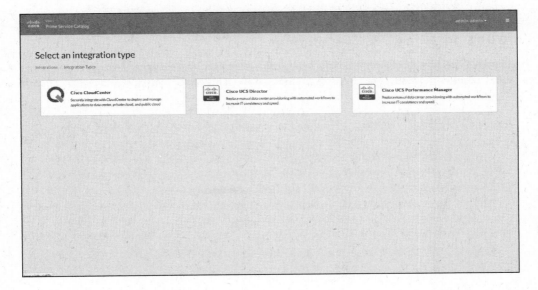

FIGURE 19.8   Cisco PSC: integration fields

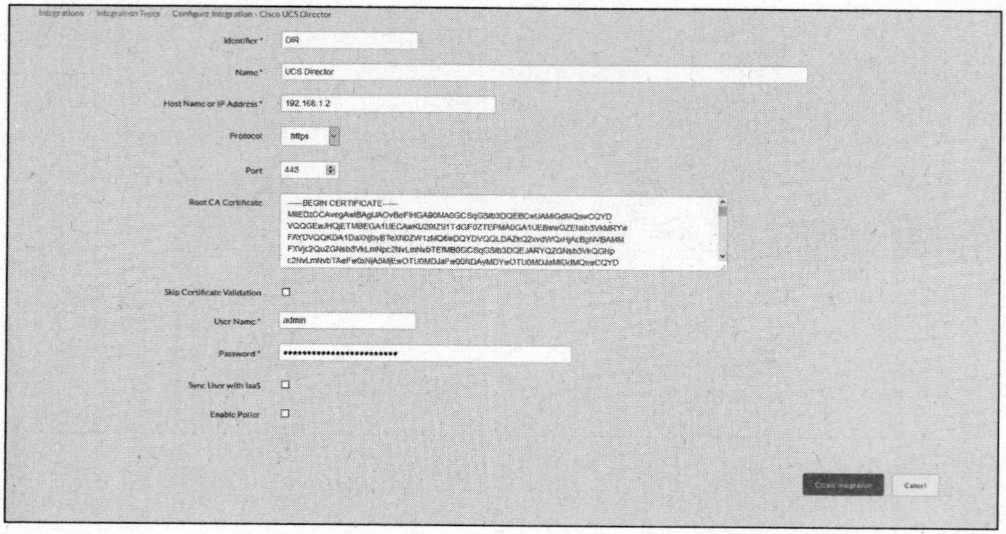

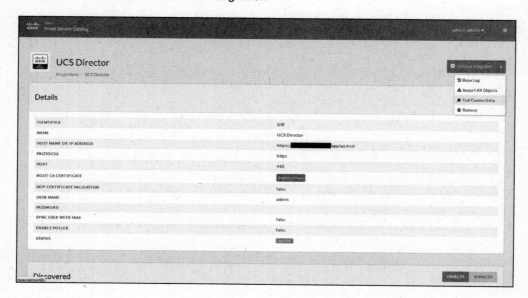

5. After your connectivity test passes, you can import all the objects. This button is right above the test button shown in Figure 19.9. This may take some time depending on how many objects you have.

FIGURE 19.9   Cisco PSC: test integration

6. After discovery has finished, you can scroll down and see the imported objects and services from UCS Director. Note that the identifier field is the name used in Figure 19.8. This can be useful to determine where an object was imported from, so name your fields appropriately.

As you can see in Figure 19.10, we imported several standard catalog VMs from UCS Director. There are even more objects that can be scrolled through depending on what is currently configured in your UCS Director version. My instance has many workflows and other objects, as shown in Figure 19.11.

FIGURE 19.10   Cisco PSC: imported services

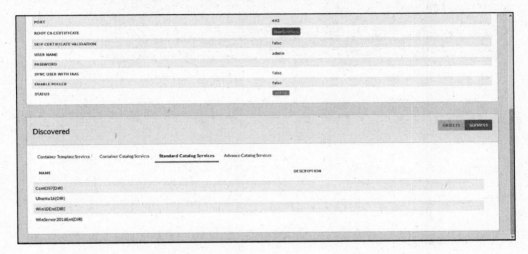

FIGURE 19.11   Cisco PSC: imported workflows

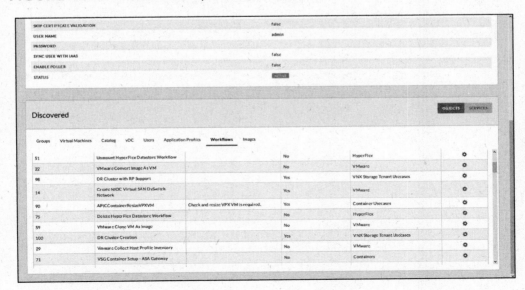

7. The next step is to enable the UCS Director agent and scheduler. You can find the agent under Advanced ➢ Service Link on the main page, as shown in Figure 19.12.

FIGURE 19.12   Cisco PSC: Service Link

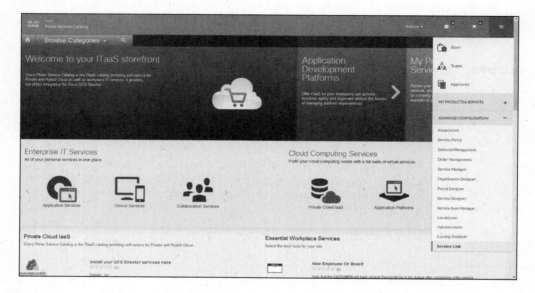

8. Click Control Agents, choose the UCSD agent, and start it, as shown in Figure 19.13.

FIGURE 19.13   Cisco PSC: UCSDAgent

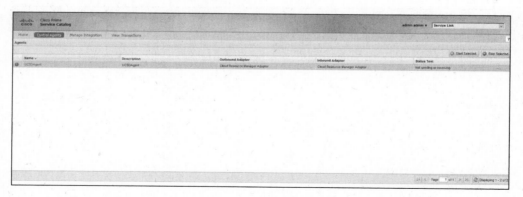

9. Using the drop-down menu in the upper-right corner, select Administration, as displayed in Figure 19.14, and then click Settings in the upper bar.

FIGURE 19.14   Cisco PSC: Administration

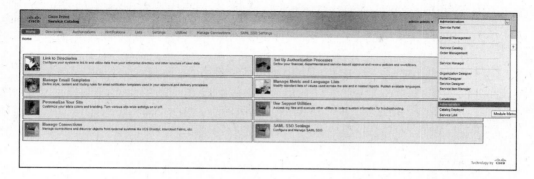

10. Under Common you'll find the UCSD scheduler that is set to Off by default. Toggle it On and click Update at the bottom of the page.

You've now imported all the catalogs and workflows from UCS Director into Prime Service Catalog. They've also been added to your front store, which can be customized to your needs. You'll want to do this because the default icons and names may not be easily understandable by end users and customers. You can see this in the Service Designer module, as shown in Figure 19.15.

FIGURE 19.15   Cisco PSC: Services Designer

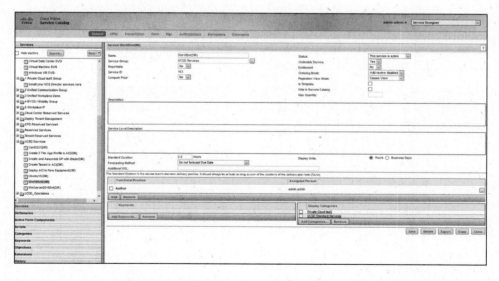

Notice the "DIR" identifier again in the name. That's the short name I used on import. You can change this name to something that has more meaning to your end users. The icon is also blank, so you can click the Presentation tab to change it. There are a lot of built-in images for you to choose, and you can also import your own or point to a URL of an image, as shown in Figure 19.16.

FIGURE 19.16 Cisco PSC: Presentation options

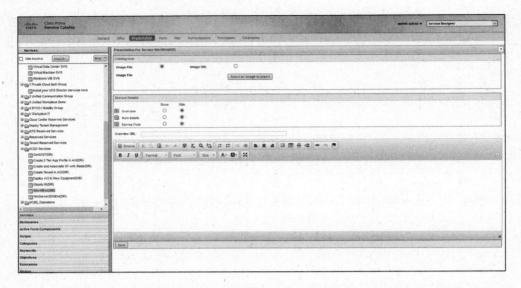

Figure 19.17 shows the permissions page. These permissions are inherited from the import, and you may not have to do anything if the permissions were set up correctly for your needs in UCS Director. Prime Service Catalog contains several customizations to adjust security in its own RBAC settings. There are many things that are customizable in the service and portal designer that you can explore. I won't cover them here because they're beyond the scope of the CCNA CLDADM exam.

FIGURE 19.17 Cisco PSC: service permissions

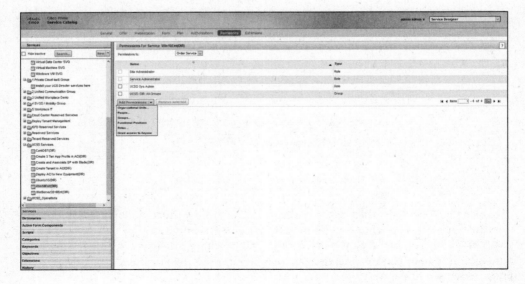

Ordering from Prime Service Catalog

Now let's put all of this together with how you'd order from the catalog. Remember, when designing your catalog and front end that the goal should be ease of use for your customers. Prime Service Catalog will help you achieve that. The showcase, as explained in the beginning of the chapter, is the first page that end users will see as they log in. Often a shortcut will be here for quick services, and you have full control over how that looks. But what if a user is just browsing?

Finding Services

This is where the categories come into play, as discussed earlier. Look at Figure 19.18 and the Browse Categories shortcut on the showcase.

FIGURE 19.18   Cisco PSC: Browse Categories

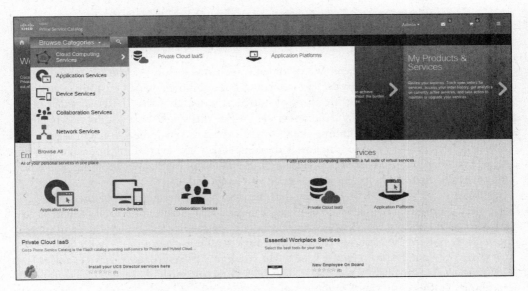

Your end users can use this to browse all of your predefined categories. You have control over this in the service designer. You can bind your services to any category you choose or define your own category with custom icons for your company. In this case, we am showing the standard, out-of-the-box categories. Click Private Cloud IaaS to see the screen in Figure 19.19.

FIGURE 19.19   Cisco PSC: Private Cloud IaaS category

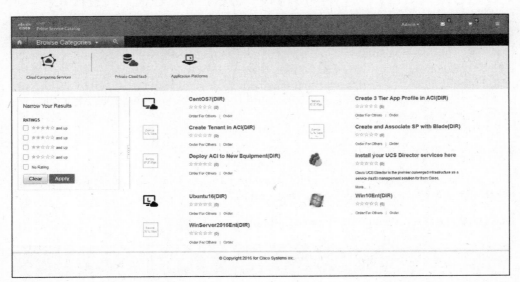

You'll notice a few things here. We've added some icons to some of the services and not others. This makes it obvious what services stand out and how you can customize yours to your needs. There is one important thing to notice here, which is the "DIR" shortcut in the name from the imported UCS Director services. While this might be a good name for the administrator, it might make finding the service hard for the customer. You can see services here easily because the Browse Categories shortcut shows you everything bound to that category. If you had hundreds of services, though, it would not be that easy to find. You could continue ordering from here, but let's assume you can't find it.

Looking at Figure 19.20, you can see that the search icon is right next to the Browse Categories drop-down menu. Some users might prefer this method of search. You need to again be careful of how you design your services and names to make it easy for end users to find services. Figure 19.21 shows the results from a search for *windows*.

You see only one result in Figure 19.21, but you know there are more services out there for Windows. The problem is the name. The UCS Director imported services have abbreviated names. In this case, the *Win* name refers to Windows. When you search for that abbreviation, you see different results, as shown in Figure 19.22.

This should highlight again the need for clear service names. When search and browsing aren't enough, you can also stick services directly on the showcase front page. In my example catalog, scrolling down shows the Private Cloud IaaS services. If a user was trying to locate a service in that category, they could browse to it, search for it, or see it on the front of the showcase. All of this is entirely up to you, the administrator.

FIGURE 19.20   Cisco PSC: search

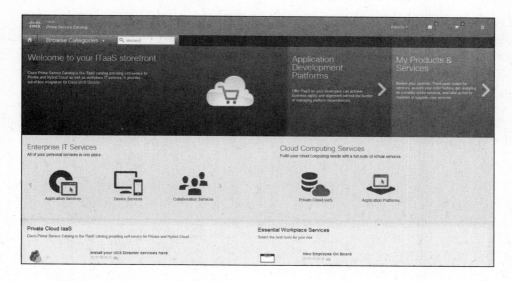

FIGURE 19.21   Cisco PSC: search results

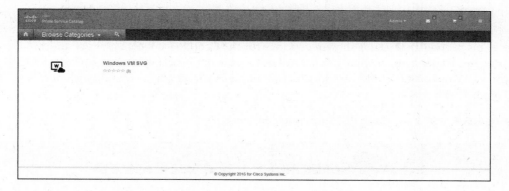

FIGURE 19.22   Cisco PSC: search continued

Ordering and Monitoring

Let's walk through an order now. There are several places to order services, as previously discussed. The Browse Categories area, search results, and front page of the showcase are the most common. Clicking Order on any of the available services will bring you to a screen with options, as shown in Figure 19.23.

FIGURE 19.23   Cisco PSC: CentOS7 Ordering

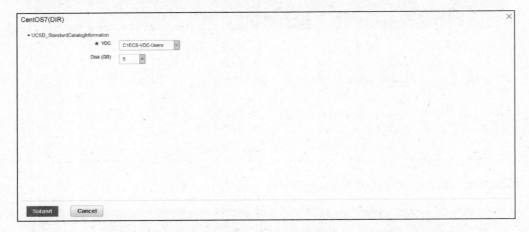

This particular screen is showing options for the CentOS7 imported service from UCS Director. Depending on what you defined as tunable options, they'll show up here. Picking the VDC and disk size and then hitting Submit takes you to a final screen, as shown in Figure 19.24.

FIGURE 19.24   Cisco PSC: ordering continued

Under My Products & Services in the upper-right menu, you can click Orders to see the status of your services. This is particularly useful if you've ordered a large number of services. In this example, there are a couple here, as shown in Figure 19.25.

FIGURE 19.25 Cisco PSC: two services ordered

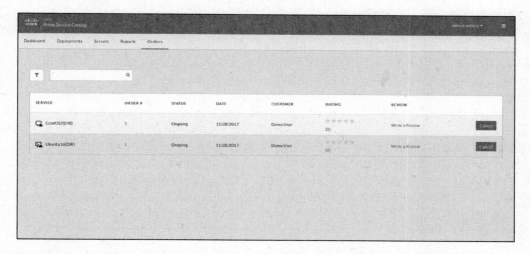

This example showed an immediate order after hitting Submit. As the administrator, you can specify the use of a *shopping cart* in the order mode of the service designer. This would typically be used with services that are grouped together and ordered together after all the options are chosen. You can see this option selected in Figure 19.25.

FIGURE 19.26 Cisco PSC: order mode

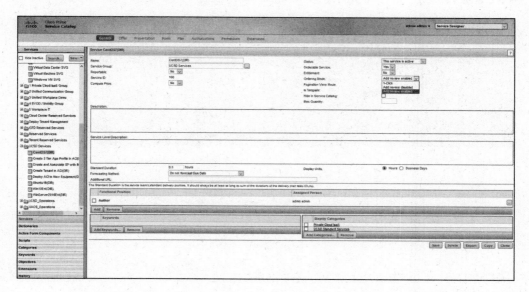

Changing the mode to Add Review Enabled, as shown in Figure 19.26, changes how the imported CentOS service is ordered. Now when a user selects this, they will add it to a cart and can check out later after ordering other items. Figure 19.27 shows the difference.

FIGURE 19.27   Cisco PSC: adding to a cart

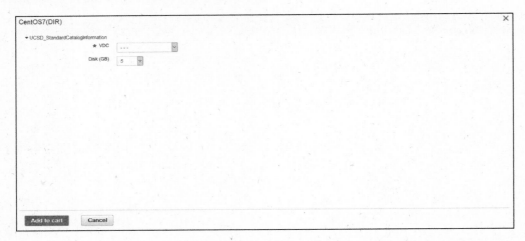

After the submission or checkout process, your order will be built, and you will be notified when it is finished. One of the places to look for the status is the *notifications menu.* This is right next to the shopping cart, as shown in Figure 19.28. You'll notice the indicators in the upper left corner indicating letting the user know that there are currently three notifications. In this case, they're for the status that the orders are building.

FIGURE 19.28   Cisco PSC: notifications

Accessing and Managing Services

After ordering and using the system, you'll want to know where your dashboard is. On the front page of Prime Service Catalog (or showcase), the far-right side of the screen has a link to My Products & Services. Clicking it shows a dashboard where your end users can keep track of their open orders, charges, servers, and services, as shown in Figure 19.29.

FIGURE 19.29   Cisco PSC: dashboard

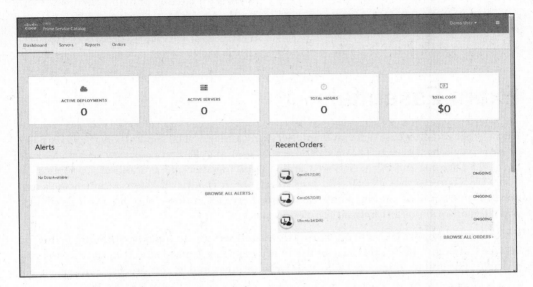

As shown in Figure 19.29, you will be able to see several statistics. Most notably, you'll see the recent orders, charges, and the number of servers you have deployed. For this example, my orders are still in progress. If you were to click the server's section, you could access several options to manage your servers. The various options available on the Servers tab are as follows:

- **Create VM Disk:** This creates another disk for the selected VM.

- **Clone VM:** This creates a similar VM.

- **Create and Delete VM Snapshot:** This creates or deletes an existing snapshot.

- **Reset VM:** This reboots the selected VM.

- **Revert VM Snapshot:** This chooses a snapshot to revert the VM to.

- **Standby VM:** Using this option, the processes are stopped, but virtual devices will remain connected.

- **Suspend VM:** This stops all processes and turns off the VM temporarily.

You can also view resource reports for virtual data centers and reports for cost and service usage. These items aren't covered in depth on the exam, but it's important to know that they're there.

Summary

In this chapter, we discussed Prime Service Catalog and its ability to offer a storefront-like service for your end users. We covered the showcase, categories, and how to find and order services. You learned that Prime Service Catalog is extremely flexible, and nearly everything can be configured with the brand of your company.

We also went through how to import the UCS Director catalog and how permissions are inherited with workflows and services. Finally, you learned how to access and manage your orders and resources via the user dashboard. In the next chapter, you'll explore some more components of the Prime Service Catalog suite.

Exam Essentials

Know what the showcase is for in Prime Service Catalog.   The showcase is the front page or entryway into the services catalog for an end user. It's the first page they see. Understand that UCS Director and Prime Service Catalog work together and as stand-alone applications. UCS Director has its own end-user storefront. It is not as highly customizable as the one in Prime Service Catalog. Know that Prime Service Catalog is the choice for flexibility and customization of a storefront for cloud services.

Know how to import UCS Director workflows and services to quickly configure Prime Service Catalog.   The goal is ease of use in getting a customized storefront up as soon as possible. The ability to import UCS Director workflows makes this process quicker.

Understand how categories relate to Prime Service Catalog and how they're displayed on the front page.   Categories are the basic unit for holding services and orderable items and are highly customizable from icon images to permissions and how they're invoked.

Know how basic ordering works and the difference between checkout and simple one-click ordering when hitting Submit.   Understand how to monitor the order process and where to find your dashboard to check on orders and provisioned services.

Written Lab

The following questions are designed to test your understanding of this chapter's material. You can find the answers to the questions in Appendix B. For more information on how to obtain additional questions, please see this book's Introduction.

1.   The front page of the Prime Service Catalog is also referred to as _____ _____.

2.   The _____ _____ is used within Prime Service Catalog to refer to separate external connections.

3. _____ _____ _____ _____ is where an end user can find dashboards and the status of ongoing orders.

4. Importing from UCS Director can be found in the section called _____.

5. _____ is the term described for organizing services for ordering.

6. The _____ will assist you in creating categories and services.

7. Reset VM is something you could do from what section?

8. The service icon can be customized for orderable services. True/False?

9. Top-Left and Top-Center is a naming convention referring to what part of Prime Service Catalog?

10. Where would a user see an indicator of current order issues or action items?

Review Questions

The following questions are designed to test your understanding of this chapter's material. You can find the answers to the questions in Appendix A. For more information on how to obtain additional questions, please see this book's Introduction.

1. What is an organizational unit in Prime Service Catalog?
   A. Showcase
   B. Service icon
   C. Categories
   D. Intro page

2. Which are sections of the front page of Prime Service Catalog? (Choose all that apply.)
   A. Bottom-Left
   B. Shopping cart
   C. Browse Categories
   D. Bar

3. What automation platform integrates with Prime Service Catalog?
   A. UCS Director
   B. VMware
   C. KVM
   D. Universal hypervisor

4. What can be done from the Servers menu portal? (Choose all that apply.)
   A. Create a VM snapshot.
   B. Chargeback a team.
   C. Suspend a VM.
   D. Clone a VM.

5. What part of the front page could a user use to find a named service?
   A. Search
   B. Top-Left
   C. Start Application
   D. Shopping cart

6. Where can you find reports on open orders and charges?
   A. Infrastructure Reports
   B. The showcase
   C. My Products & Services
   D. Advanced Reports

7. To change what category a service appears in, you would use what?

   A. Presentation

   B. Policies

   C. Map reports

   D. Settings

8. A service icon image can be loaded from which of the following?

   A. A URL location

   B. The shopping cart

   C. A custom container

   D. None of the above

9. Where would you look to see what services you are about to order?

   A. Review page

   B. Shopping cart

   C. Billing module

   D. Rent agreement

10. You can set service permissions from where in Prime Services Catalog?

   A. Service designer

   B. Dashboard

   C. Presentation

   D. End-user portal

11. When integrating with UCS Director, how must the root CA must be configured? (Choose all that apply.)

   A. Skip validation and not be used

   B. Used, imported

   C. Variable

   D. None of the above

12. Where can you change a service from being an immediate order to just going in the shopping cart?

   A. Ordering mode in the service designer

   B. Presentation in Services

   C. Order Type in General

   D. Billing Type in Presentation

13. What is the Identifier field used for in an integration?

   A. A nickname for reference

   B. For automation

   C. For service design

   D. For the showcase

14. Browse Categories is part of what?

   A. The showcase

   B. The service designer

   C. The portal designer

   D. Multi-Domain Manager

15. Cloning a VM could be done from where in Prime Service Catalog as an end user?

   A. Service container catalog

   B. Operations area

   C. Standard area

   D. Server area under My Products & Services

16. Browse Categories lets you do what?

   A. Browse through all services under a category.

   B. Publish to end users.

   C. Report on services.

   D. Order infrastructure services.

17. Integrations under the main menu let you do what? (Choose all that apply.)

   A. Integrate with VMware.

   B. Integrate with UCS Director.

   C. Integrate with KVM.

   D. Integrate with UCS Performance Manager.

18. Where would a user be told of a pending order in the showcase?

   A. Portal menu

   B. Service portal

   C. Notifications menu

   D. None of the above

19. How many customizable areas are on the showcase?

   A. 5

   B. 3

   C. 7

   D. 8

20. The identifier field during integration is required and configured during what part of integration?

   A. Configured on import from UCS Director

   B. Never, it is not needed after import editors discretion.

   C. Configured on Export from UCS Director

   D. None of the above

Chapter

20

Cisco Prime Service Catalog Components

THE FOLLOWING UNDERSTANDING CISCO CLOUD ADMINISTRATION CLDADM (210-455) EXAM OBJECTIVES ARE COVERED IN THIS CHAPTER:

✓ **4.1 Identify the components of Cisco Prime Service Catalog**

- ■ 4.1.a End-user store front
- ■ 4.1.b Stack designer
- ■ 4.1.c Heat orchestration

✓ **4.2 Describe the components of Cisco UCS Director**

- ■ 4.2.a Describe infrastructure management and monitoring
- ■ 4.2.b Describe orchestration
- ■ 4.2.c Describe the portal
- ■ 4.2.d Describe the Bare Metal Agent

✓ **4.3 Describe Cisco UCS Performance Manager**

- ■ 4.3.a Describe capacity planning
- ■ 4.3.b Describe bandwidth monitoring
- ■ 4.3.c Describe how host groups facilitate dynamic monitoring

✓ **4.4 Describe the components of Cisco IAC**

- ■ 4.4.a Describe Cisco Process Orchestrator
- ■ 4.4.b Describe Cisco Prime Service Catalog
- ■ 4.4.c Describe Cisco Server Provisioner

Prime Service Catalog Components

This chapter will focus on some of the individual components for the Prime Service Catalog we haven't discussed yet, as well as Cisco IAC and UCS Director. We'll also review some component items that may have been lightly covered elsewhere. We'll mention that for clarity, so you can review those items as you see fit.

Cisco Intelligent Automation for Cloud

The majority of the chapters have revolved around Cisco ONE Enterprise Cloud Suite and its components. There is another closely related suite of products that Cisco offers as well, called *Cisco Intelligent Automation for Cloud (CIAC)*. Cisco IAC is a management and automation suite for private, public, and hybrid compute clouds. Cisco IAC like the Cisco One suite is built around self-service and end users utilizing a service portal to track and order content. The Cisco IAC is deployed as a solution that contains preconfigured catalog services, service forms, portal pages, portlets, integration adapters, and automation processes.

If you're wondering what the difference between the products are, there isn't much except the integration both provide to other products. Cisco One Enterprise Suite has a certain list of products it integrates with without much support for things out of that list. Cisco IAC allows for more complex integrations and can support more third-party solutions integrated with IAC then Cisco One can. This is primarily through the Cisco Process Orchestrator, described below.

The Cisco IAC solution includes two products:

- *Cisco Prime Service Catalog:* Performing the duties of the end-user catalog, just as the One Enterprise Suite. Besides this chapter, more information on Prime Service catalog is covered in Chapters 18 and 19 as well.

- *Cisco Process Orchestrator (CPO):* The provisioning, automation and integration platform. The CPO is for automating IT processes in complex environments.

The CPO includes automation packs to deliver best practices and the packs are programmable through third-party partners, services, and end users. The pre-packaged automation packs are one of the strengths of the CPO. It's through these packs that CPO can support nearly any IT service your business uses. Other features of the CPO as defined by Cisco include:

- Workspace for administrators, operators, and developers to manage services and create them

- With hundreds of prebuilt workflows, alignment to IT standards is achieved including the IT Information Library (ITIL), Common Information Model (CIM), and the Topology and Orchestration Specification for Cloud Applications (TOSCA).

- Extensive reporting is built in, including ROI and auditing.

There was a third component, *Cisco Server Provisioner*. This component provided initial configuration and automation of servers. It also relied on PXE boot for initial installs of servers. It is very similar to the *UCS Bare Metal Agent*, which we will discuss briefly later in the chapter. The Cisco Server Provisioner is deprecated and no longer sold; however, the exam blueprint still references it. You'll need to understand what it did for the test.

Prime Service Catalog Components

We've talked about Prime Service Catalog extensively in Chapters 18 and 19, including UCS Director and Prime Service Catalog themselves. We covered the *end-user storefront* and portal in both chapters, and it's important that you can differentiate between the two. The UCS Director portal usually isn't referred to as a storefront, but as an *End User portal*. The UCS Director portal is a stripped-down basic portal meant for use when you don't have a Prime Service Catalog offering. There are a few components of both we have yet to discuss, and we'll cover them in the remainder of this chapter.

The *Stack Designer* of Prime Service Catalog lets you build application stacks. They can be designed as a template and published as services for the Prime Service Catalog storefront. This lets users design Product as Service applications using the designer. Application stacks and services are built by adding components to infrastructure containers. These components can be services, databases, and more. There are predefined out-of-the-box applications for use, such as SharePoint, Java EE Server, HAProxy, Docker, and other applications.

When a user orders an application stack or template, the Orchestration components provision the needed infrastructure from UCS Director and *Puppet* provisioned applications in the containers provided from UCS Director. Puppet is a popular open source configuration management tool. Puppet uses a modeling language built on the Ruby programing language. Puppet is designed to manage Linux and Microsoft Windows systems in a declarative fashion. Puppet runs in a master client relationship, with clients being referred to as agents. Many Cisco switches and routers support puppet and have agents built-in, including many NX-OS series switches. Prime Service Catalog does not include a full puppet environment, but it does include a master to talk with other puppet environments for automation and stack design.

As mentioned above, there are also orchestration components to assist in automating the build of an application stack. The orchestration components of Stack Designer consist of the following items:

- *OpenStack Keystone Server:* Handles identity management

- *RabbitMQ Server:* Responsible for sending service requests from Prime Service Catalog to the orchestrator service

- *Orchestration service with embedded Heat Orchestration Engine:* Another OpenStack project to help cloud administrators model cloud applications in a text file

The RabbitMQ server is an open source messaging platform that allows applications to exchange messages between other applications and servers. The message platform helps the orchestration and automation layer reliably exchange messages quickly. The protocol used to do this in RabbitMQ is the *Advanced Message Queuing Protocol,* or *AMQP.* Prime Service Catalog includes this in the software for orchestration components that support RabbitMQ. The test doesn't go into detail about RabbitMQ, but it's important you understand that it's part of the orchestration of stack designer.

Heat Orchestration is the service used along with Keynote and RabbitMQ as mentioned above. Heat is also from OpenStack and it assists in orchestrating application model templates built with the Stack Designer. The Heat Orchestration Template engine is also referred to as *HOT* for short. HOT templates are often (but not always) written in the YAML format which stands for Yet Another Markup Language. The stack is what Heat is orchestrating. The stack is a collection of resources, mainly VMs and their configurations. A *heat template* defines the resources that make up the stack. There are four separate sections to the heat template:

- **Resources:** These are configuration details of your stack. These objects are created or modified when the template is executed. Resources could be VMs, Security Groups, IP Addresses, Volumes, and more.

- **Properties:** Variables within the template or placeholders to prompt for input to the user

- **Parameters:** These are the actual Properties value above that must be passed when running the Heat Template.

- **Output:** This is the data passed back to the user or Prime Service Catalog after the template finishes.

Cisco UCS Director Orchestration and Automation

Cisco UCS Director works with the Cisco ONE Enterprise Cloud Suite and also directly integrates with Prime Service Catalog. UCS Director is built with automation and *orchestration* in mind. We previously covered the ONE suite in Chapter 14 and UCS Director content in Chapters 13 through 15 if you'd like to review further. In the next few sections we'll talk about some of the aspects of UCSD we haven't covered in detail yet. As a brief overview, UCS Director has the following features:

- UCS Director can support multiple hypervisors including VMware ESXi, Microsoft Hyper-V, and Red Hat KVM.

- A self-service catalog and portal are included to aid on-demand ordering. Remember that this can be used when you don't have Prime Service Catalog. UCSD however does integrate with Prime Service Catalog offering a more robust catalog and portal.

- Network management and on-demand provisioning is a large part of UCS Director, including VM operations, VLANs, ACLs, and more.

- Orchestration is included with built-in tasks and APIs to design *workflows* for IT end users. Workflows are the aide to how orchestration is built. Workflows are a series of *tasks* arranged to automate operations.

- UCS Director Bare Metal Agent: Separate virtual appliance to automate bare-metal installs

For the exams blueprint on automation and orchestration, we'll take a look at the workflows, templates and Bare Metal Agent.

Cisco UCS Director Bare Metal Agent

The Bare Metal Agent (BMA) is a virtual appliance that is installed separately. UCS Director with the Bare Metal Agent automates the process of the *Pre-Boot Execution Environment (PXE)* installing operating systems on bare-metal servers or virtual machines. UCS Director supports only one Bare Metal Agent in versions previous to 5.2. The Bare Metal Agent provides the following services:

- DHCP

- HTTP

- TFTP

- Image storage for operating systems to install on the end agent

- The actual PXE boot service

The exam doesn't cover the actual install of the Bare Metal Agent, but you add it under Administration ➤ Physical Accounts on the UCS Director Portal. You'll see the Bare Metal Agents tab to click on, as shown in Figure 20.1.

After that, you can click Add with the plus sign and you'll be presented with a window of information to put in. The following values are required:

- Account Name

- Management/PXE Address

- Login ID

- Password

- Database Address

FIGURE 20.1   Cisco UCSD – Bare Metal Agent

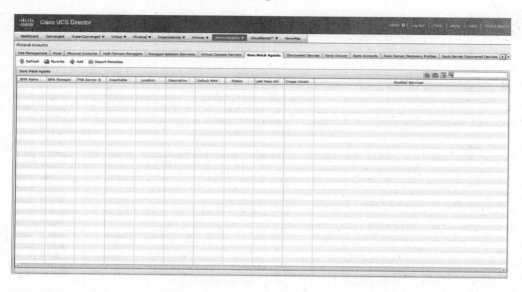

FIGURE 20.2   Cisco UCSD – Bare Metal Agent Add

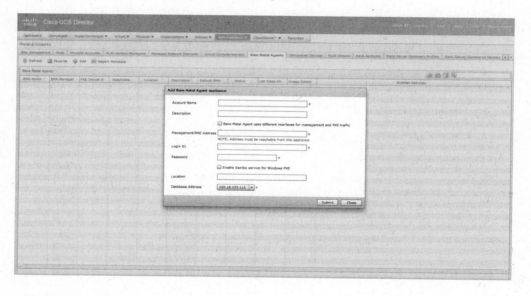

The agent will be accessible via the normal UCS Director console and will integrate directly with it, which is the Database Address you would fill out in Figure 20.1. Simply put, all configuration work done with the Agent is done via the normal UCS Director GUI. The Agent functions as an extension once it is installed and connected. Cisco provides a few guidelines you need to be aware of.

For network reachability, Cisco requires the following:

- The UCS Director Bare Metal Agent must be able to reach UCS Director over your network infrastructure.
- The same goes for UCS Director; it must be able to reach the Bare Metal Agent over the network.
- The bare metal servers must be on the same network as the UCS Director Bare Metal Agent.

If you use DHCP, the server must also be located in the same PXE VLAN as the Cisco UCS Director Bare Metal Agent. You can access the Bare Metal agent via SSH if needed, and can start and stop services. The majority of the work will be done via the UCS Director though, and you can integrate the Bare Metal Agent into your workflows for hosts. The following is a list of how the PXE process would occur:

1. An administrator would create a PXE boot request in the UCS Director portal. The server MAC address, hostname, IP information, and OS Type are fields that you would fill out.

2. When a host is plugged into the network that is configured to PXE boot, it will generate a DHCP request.

3. The Bare Metal Agent will hear this and respond with the IP information you created in the PXE boot request.

4. The Bare Metal Agent will also provide the next-server information for PXE boot along with the TFTP location on where to get the operating system to boot.

5. PXE boot starts and the image is transferred directly from the Bare Metal Agent or from another location the Bare Metal Agent offered in the response.

Cisco UCS Director Workflows, Orchestration, and Automation

As we discussed at the beginning of this chapter, Orchestration and Automation are two of the main use cases for UCS Director. The biggest piece that fits these together are the Orchestration workflow, or simply just workflows. The workflow function of UCS Director allows you to join multiple *tasks* together. Each task performs one action. You can join these tasks together so that the input of one task is the output of a previous task. This is where the workflow concept comes from. You can build a workflow to automate processes such as VM creation, bare-metal server setup, network setup, compute options, and many others.

The UCS Director ships with hundreds of predefined tasks. When you can't locate a task that fits your needs, you can create a custom task. Some of the predefined tasks are as simple as SSH commands. Using that task, you could build a workflow to automate connecting to a server and running a command. To navigate in UCS Director to where the workflow and tasks are, go to Policies-➢ Orchestration. You can see this by looking at Figure 20.3.

FIGURE 20.3 Cisco UCSD – Orchestration Workflows

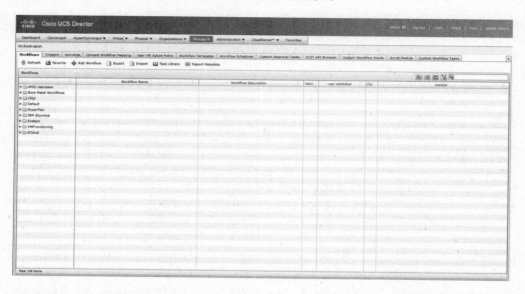

UCS Director makes workflow construction easy by incorporating a *Workflow Designer* that has drag and drop functionality. Remember that tasks can feed into each other, taking outputs from other tasks. See Figure 20.4 to see the drag and drop functionality. This is dragging from the predefined tasks mentioned above, in this case the SSH command.

FIGURE 20.4 Cisco UCSD – Workflow Designer

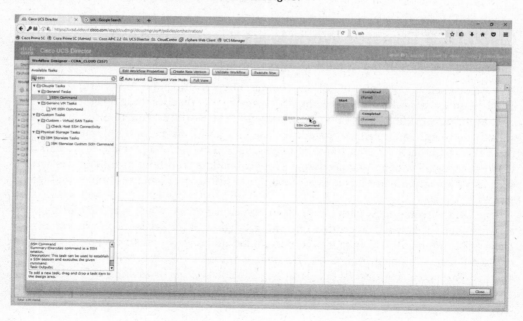

Notice the start and completed in the designer. The tasks are input between these sections. Look at a complete workflow on Figure 20.5.

FIGURE 20.5   Cisco UCSD – Workflow Edit

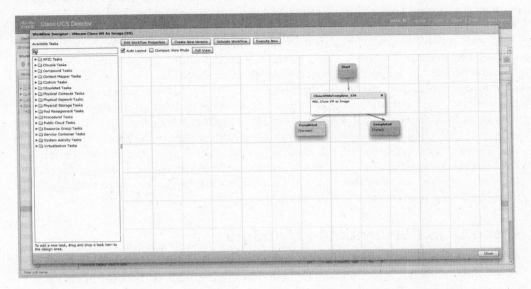

The example here is simple, but you should begin to understand the power that you control with custom workflows and tasks. You can also add conditional processing to workflows and loops, including conditional statements and IF ELSE statements. There are other ways to trigger the workflow though, which brings in more automation and reaction based on monitored events.

Triggers can be defined on a set of conditions. When the trigger is activated based on the condition, it can execute a workflow. The trigger can be defined as two types:

- *Stateful:* The last trigger state is recorded and kept. The workflow is executed when there is a change in the trigger state. When the trigger conditions are met, the state is Active. If they are not met, it is Clear. You can define workflows to be executed for both sides of Clear and Active. The trigger state can be checked at a defined frequency.

- *Stateless:* The trigger executes anytime the conditions are met, at a frequency you can define.

Activities are another way you can create conditional workflows based on a simple task. An example of this might be an overall workflow that builds a VM. But what if that VM is Linux or Windows? The tasks would be different based on what is being built. An activity could hold the task that is associated to one or more workflows. When a user supplies the appropriate input, the activity can then determine which workflow to follow.

UCS Director also includes an *approval* process for workflows that can be used in your organization. Most organizations would use this for approval from cross teams, a last check to make sure a team can order something or build infrastructure. Managers would be a common approver. In some cases, workflows may be considered dangerous depending on who runs them. Approvals may be used there to make sure anyone doesn't shut down infrastructure or cause outages.

Workflows also have a *rollback* feature that can be used. You would do this to remove virtual infrastructure created in error, or stuck flows that didn't complete fully. Rollbacks function because each task consists of two scripts. One script does the work you programmed it to do, while the other simply reverses the task. When a task is run, the instructions are executed in the order the workflow has them defined. When the rollback is called on a workflow, the task rollback script reverses the order of the instructions. Tasks are atomic in UCS Director, a single action that can include inputs and outputs. This means that you can't break up tasks into smaller objects, as the task is treated as a whole unit. This has further implications on rollback capabilities. You can rollback a workflow starting with any task, but you cannot partially rollback a task itself. The whole task has to be rolled back as it is a complete unit of instruction.

Cisco UCS Performance Manager

In this final section and the next chapter, we'll discuss the last items of the exam blueprint. Monitoring, visibility, capacity planning, and overall operations will consist of the next section and chapter. There are several Cisco products that cover the One Enterprise Cloud suite for this area. The first item we'll briefly introduce is the *Cisco UCS Performance Manager*.

Cisco UCS Performance Manager has two versions that can be deployed. The express version is more lightweight, and doesn't do the rest of the infrastructure. The versions are listed below:

- *UCS Performance Manager Express:* The express version only covers the physical and virtual compute side. What this means is no storage, switches, and the rest of the infrastructure. It is only compute VMs and physical servers.

- *UCS Performance Manager:* The full version covers the physical and virtual compute like express but also adds in storage arrays, fabric, and network gear. For the rest of this chapter and the next, we'll be covering the full version.

Cisco UCS Performance Manager is a stand-alone management application, usually deployed as a virtual appliance on VMware. It offers performance, monitoring, and capacity planning reports and information across the entire infrastructure of Cisco ONE Enterprise Cloud suite. One of the major benefits to Performance Manager is the unification of multiple areas of infrastructure for reporting. Different teams in the IT organization may use different tools, each without insight to another team's tool. UCS Performance Manager was meant to solve that issue by offering a wide view into all of the infrastructure whether that be compute, network, or storage. Some of the features of UCS Performance Manager are as follows:

- One tool for monitoring performance and management of the infrastructure, eliminating the need for many conflicting tools
- Real time views into bandwidth usage. Detailed reports about storage, network and compute bandwidth
- Capacity management and forecasted capacity based on trends
- Provides northbound APIs for integration with other systems and automation
- *Application groups* to dynamically link components together to be monitored. This allows correlation and understanding between an application's infrastructure and how it impacts the application. An example could be switches, storage, and servers that make up a group for an application.

Figure 20.6 shows the front page of the UCS Performance Manager. In the next chapter, we'll dive deeper into the portals and monitoring of UCS Performance Manager as well as other reporting and services in the Cisco One Enterprise Cloud suite.

FIGURE 20.6   Cisco UCS Performance Manager

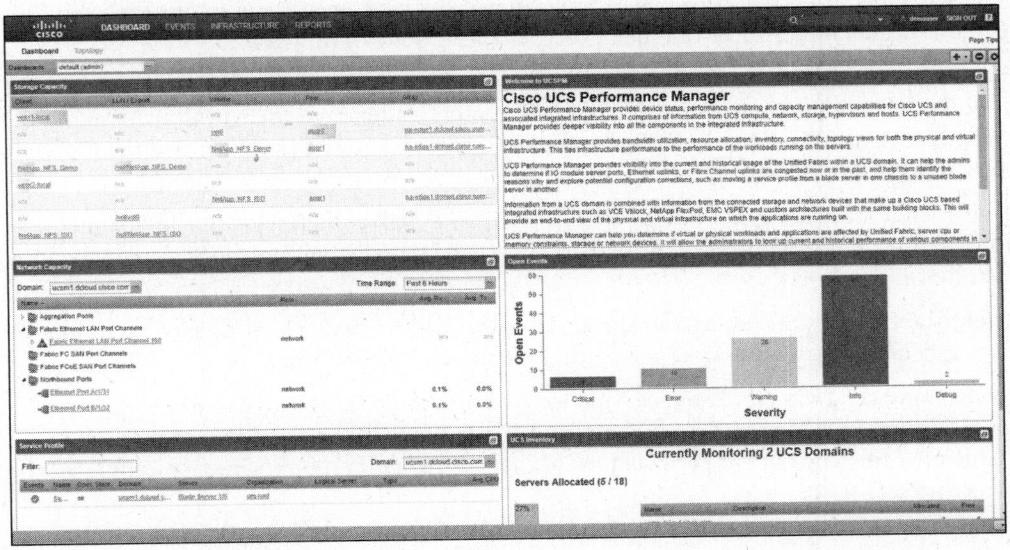

Summary

In this chapter, we discussed the Prime Service Catalog and its many components. We also covered the Cisco IAC, which is a similar offering to Prime Service Catalog. You learned about the differences between the two, particularly the integration components and how they differ with third party interaction.

We also reviewed UCS Director and the Prime Service Catalog storefronts and how they differ. We covered the stack designer and heat orchestration of UCS director and how that works with stack designer to build application stacks.

The UCS Bare Metal Agent was covered and its capabilities explained, and how the agent would automate install and boot up for bare-metal and virtual servers.

UCS Director workflows were discussed along with how they are used to automate the infrastructure. We covered the workflow designer and it's drag and drop capabilities as well as how the workflow can be built. Triggers and activities were introduced and how they contribute to the overall automation of the infrastructure.

Finally, we introduced the UCS Performance manager and some of its basic concepts. In the next chapter, we'll look more into UCS Performance manager and the overall monitoring of the infrastructure as well as reporting and services.

Exam Essentials

Know what the difference is between Prime Service Catalog and Cisco IAC.   One of the main concepts to remember is the integration efforts of both. The Cisco IAC offers more complex integration with third party environments. This comes down to one tool, the Cisco Process Orchestrator offered in the Cisco IAC suite of products.

Know how UCS Director Orchestrates and Automates.   One of the main orchestration tools is the workflow functionality in UCS Director. Understand the workflow designer and the pieces that make it work. Know how the triggers and activities can extend the functionality of workflows and offer greater automation.

Know what Stack Designer is used for.   Understand and explain what Stack Designer does for creating application stacks. Be able to explain heat orchestration and the components that make it up.

Understand the UCS Bare Metal Agent.   Know what the Bare Metal Agent is used for and how it helps provision physical and virtual servers for PXE booting.

Understand the UCS Performance Manager.   You should be able to explain what the UCS Performance Manager is and how it assists in the monitoring of the infrastructure. Remember that the goal of Performance Manager is to unify monitoring of multiple infrastructure sets.

Written Lab

The following questions are designed to test your understanding of this chapter's material. You can find the answers to the questions in Appendix B. For more information on how to obtain additional questions, please see this book's Introduction.

1. The PXE Bare Metal Agent includes a _____ _____ to assign a client an IP Address.

2. The _____ designer is used to help build automation flows in a drag and drop area for UCS Director.

3. The Cisco _____ Orchestrator is part of the IAC suite that enables integration with various third party vendors.

4. Application stacks can be built using the _____ _____ in UCS Director.

5. Workflows have a _____ feature to undo a failed workflow.

6. The Cisco _____ Provisioner was a third component of IAC that provided PXE services.

7. OpenStack _____ handles identity management.

8. Workflows are a series of _____ grouped together to provide automation.

9. A bare-metal server can boot with assistance from _____, which provides network and OS configuration amongst other items.

10. The End-User _____ is the portal in Prime Service Catalog that users see to order services from.

Review Questions

The following questions are designed to test your understanding of this chapter's material. You can find the answers to the questions in Appendix A. For more information on how to obtain additional questions, please see this book's Introduction.

1. What are grouped together to make up a workflow?

   A. Bullet points

   B. Service Icon

   C. Tasks

   D. Service Chains

2. Which are part of Cisco IAC? (Choose all that apply.)

   A. Cisco Process Orchestrator

   B. Cisco Prime Service Catalog

   C. Cisco PIX

   D. UNIX

3. What assists in the building of application containers and stacks?

   A. Prime Service Catalog

   B. Stack Designer

   C. KVM

   D. Workflow Designer

4. What allows workflows to be conditional and trigger different branches in workflow designer?

   A. Tasks

   B. Charges

   C. Activities

   D. Templates

5. What can be used to stop a workflow for someone to inspect it before it continues?

   A. Search

   B. Approvals

   C. Start Application

   D. Start Workflow

6. Which of the follow are some of the protocols that can be used to transfer an OS in PXE? (Choose all that apply.)

   A. HTTP

   B. DHCP

   C. TFTP

   D. SNMP

7. What can be used to execute a workflow automatically?

   A. Presentation

   B. Triggers

   C. Keys

   D. Settings

8. From the below, what items are types of triggers? (Choose all that apply.)

   A. Soft

   B. Solid

   C. Stateless

   D. Stateful

9. What links component groups together in UCS Performance Manager?

   A. Review page

   B. Application Groups

   C. Application module

   D. Performance Groups

10. What are features of UCS Performance Manager? (Choose all that Apply.)

   A. Northbound APIs

   B. Capacity Management

   C. Presentation

   D. End-User portal

11. When a workflow reaches an error, what feature can be used to undo it?

   A. Rollback

   B. Used, imported

   C. Variable

   D. None of the above

12. What helps cloud administrators model cloud applications in a text file?

   A. UCS Director Orchestrator

   B. Presentation Engine

   C. Heat Orchestration Engine

   D. Service Engine

13. What is responsible for sending service requests from Prime Service Catalog to the orchestrator service?

   A. UNIX Server

   B. RabbitMQ Server

   C. Service Designer

   D. Service Engine

14. What handles identity management in Stack Designer?

   A. Keystone Server

   B. The service designer

   C. The portal designer

   D. Multi-Domain Manager

15. What is written in often written in YAML for templates in Stack Designer?

   A. Heat Orchestration Templates (HOT)

   B. Operations templates (OTT)

   C. Standard templates

   D. J templates

16. What is a collection of resources, VMs, and their configurations in Prime Service Catalog?

   A. Stack

   B. Host list

   C. Host group

   D. Infrastructure Services Ordering

17. What is meant to replace several tools by providing a unified reporting ability across infrastructure?

   A. Windows Manager

   B. UCS Operations Manager

   C. Cisco Services Engine

   D. UCS Performance Manager

18. What protocol is used in RabbitMQ for exchange of messages?

   A. SNMP

   B. HTTPS

   C. AMQP

   D. None of the above

19. What is used to provision applications and servers in Stack Designer and is a popular open source configuration management server?

   A. Puppet

   B. Chef

   C. NetQ

   D. NetIQ

20. What is a smaller version of UCS Performance Manager?

   A. UCS Performance Manager tiny

   B. UCS Performance Manager small

   C. UCS Performance Manager express

   D. None of the above

Chapter

21

Cloud Monitoring and Remediation

**THE FOLLOWING UNDERSTANDING
CISCO CLOUD ADMINISTRATION
CLDADM (210-455) EXAM OBJECTIVES
ARE COVERED IN THIS CHAPTER:**

✓ **4.5   Perform cloud monitoring using Cisco Prime Service
  Catalog, Cisco UCS Director, Cisco Prime infrastructure**

  ▪ 4.5.a Describe fault monitoring

  ▪ 4.5.b Describe performance monitoring

  ▪ 4.5.c Describe monitoring of provisioning outcomes

✓ **4.6   Create monitoring Dashboards**

  ▪ 4.6.a Configure custom Dashboards

  ▪ 4.6.b Configure threshold settings

✓ **5.1   Configure serviceability options**

  ▪ 5.1.a Configure syslog

  ▪ 5.1.b Configure NTP

  ▪ 5.1.c Configure DNS

  ▪ 5.1.d Configure DHCP

  ▪ 5.1.e Configure SMTP

✓ **5.2   Interpret Logs for root cause analysis**

  ▪ 5.2.a Analyze fault logs

  ▪ 5.2.b Analyze admin logs

  ▪ 5.2.c Analyze application logs

✓ **5.3   Configure backups**

  ▪ 5.3.a Configure database backup

  ▪ 5.3.b Configure database restore

Cloud Monitoring

This final chapter will focus on monitoring and logging for your cloud operations. The Cisco ONE Enterprise Cloud Suite comes with several products for this, as well as some stand-alone applications outside of the suite. Some of these were already discussed in previous chapters in relation to their automation and deployment capabilities. This chapter will also cover serviceability options as well as logging and backups as they pertain to the exam.

Cisco UCS Performance Manager and Capacity Management

UCS Performance Manager is meant to be a centralized performance tool for multiple teams. It is designed to give the network, system, storage, and operation teams a common place to get reporting and statistics on the Unified Computing System environment. Chapter 20 covered UCS Performance Manager briefly; you learned about its initial requirements and how it's ordered. In this section, you'll learn about some of the monitoring tools UCS Performance Manager gives you.

On the main login screen, click Topology to the right of the Dashboard. This will give you a quick snapshot of all the UCS domains that UCS Performance Manager is connected to. You'll see a few gauges on the side such as Overall Ethernet Bandwidth Utilization and Connected Bandwidth Utilization, as shown in Figure 21.1.

Notice the map of the infrastructure that can be zoomed in and out. This map is also clickable and allows you to drill down to device statistics, events, and faults. Figure 21.2 shows an example of double-clicking Chassis 3 in the map.

FIGURE 21.1   Cisco UCS Performance Manager: Topology screen

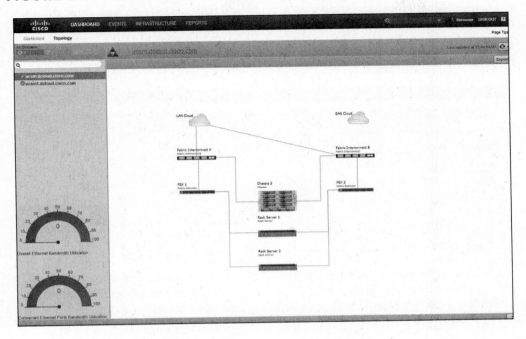

FIGURE 21.2   Cisco UCS Performance Manager: drilling down

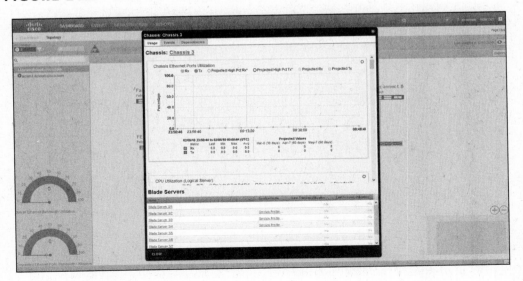

Not only can you monitor the immediate usage of a server from the pop-up window, but you can drill down into events and look at faults and issues. Now let's look at monitoring the infrastructure as a whole. Click Infrastructure on the top menu bar to get to the screen shown in Figure 21.3.

FIGURE 21.3   Cisco UCS Performance Manager: Infrastructure screen

Looking at the main infrastructure view in Figure 21.3, you'll see the left pane has selections for Network, Storage, vSphere, and more. Clicking any object in this area allows you to drill further down. Clicking Server and then choosing an app server brings you to Figure 21.4.

FIGURE 21.4   Cisco UCS Performance Manager: server drill-down

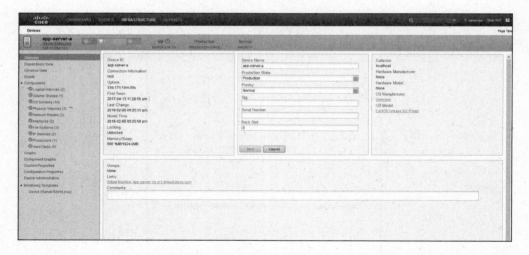

Notice all of the views and items you can click. UCS Performance Manager gives you an array of options to monitor and track individual components down to the routes on the server, bandwidth usage, CPU usage, and more. Click Graphs to see the screen in

Figure 21.5, which shows only one server at a time. UCS Performance Manager has statistics and options for all of your infrastructure, network, storage, and compute systems.

FIGURE 21.5 Cisco UCS Performance Manager: server graphs

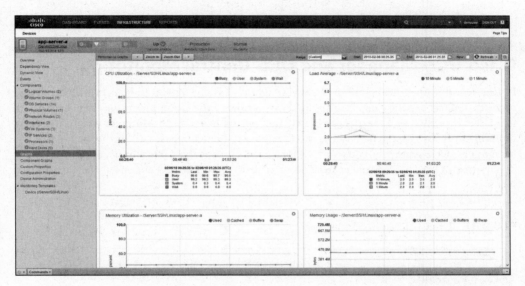

UCS Performance Manager also offers extensive reporting options. If you click Reports in the top menu of Performance Manager, you'll see a list on the left of the screen for different categories of reports. There are many predefined reports that can be selected and exported to file formats such as CSV and PDF. Keep in mind that your reports may vary depending on whether you have the full version of Performance Manager or the Express version. The top menu items are as follows:

- *Cisco UCS Capacity Reports*: This section is for capacity management and gives a large number of reports for usage such as CPU, memory, bandwidth, overall port utilization, storage capacity, and more.

- *Cisco UCS Reports*: These are reports for free memory slots and hardware inventory per managed UCS domain.

- *Enterprise Reports*: These are reports on how many devices are being managed, how many data points have been collected, user group members, and more.

- *Monitoring Capabilities Reports*: These reports list all of the installed templates so you can understand the types of infrastructure that can be monitored. A brief description is included with each template.

- *Performance Reports*: Different from capacity reporting, these are the performance reports for usage in general for CPU, memory, interface, threshold, and device availability.

- *System Reports*: These reports list non-UCS servers that are being monitored but are not part of the current license. You have the option to update your license to enable monitoring on them.

- *vSphere*: This area includes vSphere-specific reporting such as clusters, data stores, hosts, LUNs, VMs, and more.

Cisco UCS Manager and UCS Central Monitoring

In this section, you'll learn about UCS Manager and UCS Central in respect to their monitoring and capacity capabilities as they pertain to the exam blueprint. You'll see the infrastructure such as Ethernet, physical, and virtual hosts. UCS Manager acts as a server-domain controller and provides a virtual chassis that encompasses all of the UCS devices it manages. UCS Manager runs as an application on the fabric interconnect of the UCS deployment. One UCS Manager instance can scale up to 20 UCS chassis at the time of this writing.

Figure 21.6 shows the screen you're presented with when you first open UCS Manager.

FIGURE 21.6   Cisco UCS Manager

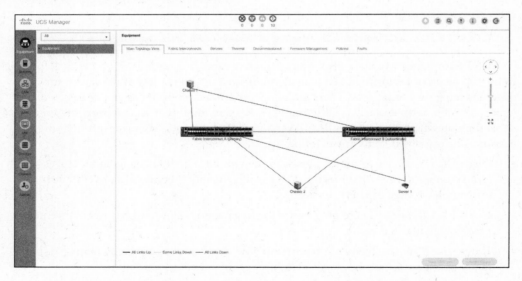

Depending on the version you have installed, your start screen may differ slightly. As you can see from Figure 21.6, you can start at the Main Topology View tab, which shows an overview of the servers and network fabric. From this screen, you can navigate to several areas to monitor and administrate your hosts and network ports. UCS Manager has several screens where you can capture this information. Clicking Fabric Interconnects in the upper menu and expanding the options brings you to the screen shown in Figure 21.7.

FIGURE 21.7   Cisco UCS Manager: Fabric Interconnects tab

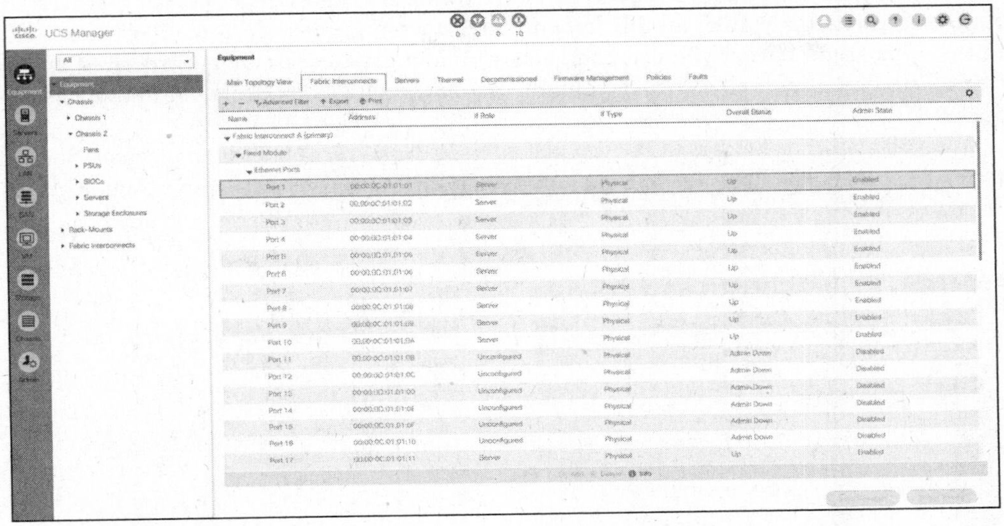

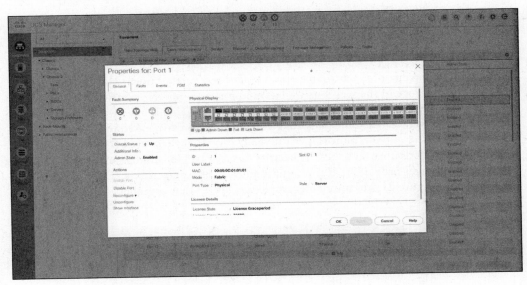

The information presented here can tell you the role of the port, its admin state, and its overall status. Further, you can double-click any of these ports to be presented with more information about the individual network port. As an example, double-clicking Port 1 shows the screen in Figure 21.8.

FIGURE 21.8   Cisco UCS Manager: port properties pop-up

In the individual network port pop-up window, you can see a number of points to gather information and even perform some actions. The lower-left corner features actions that let you enable, disable, reconfigure, unconfigure, and show interface stats. In the upper-right corner you can click Statistics and get a breakdown of received and transmitted bytes as well as packets, jumbo frames, multicast packets, and broadcast packets.

You can also click Servers in the top menu to see the servers under management. Stats shown here include CPU cores, memory, and overall status. You can see an example of this in Figure 21.9.

FIGURE 21.9 Cisco UCS Manager: Servers tab

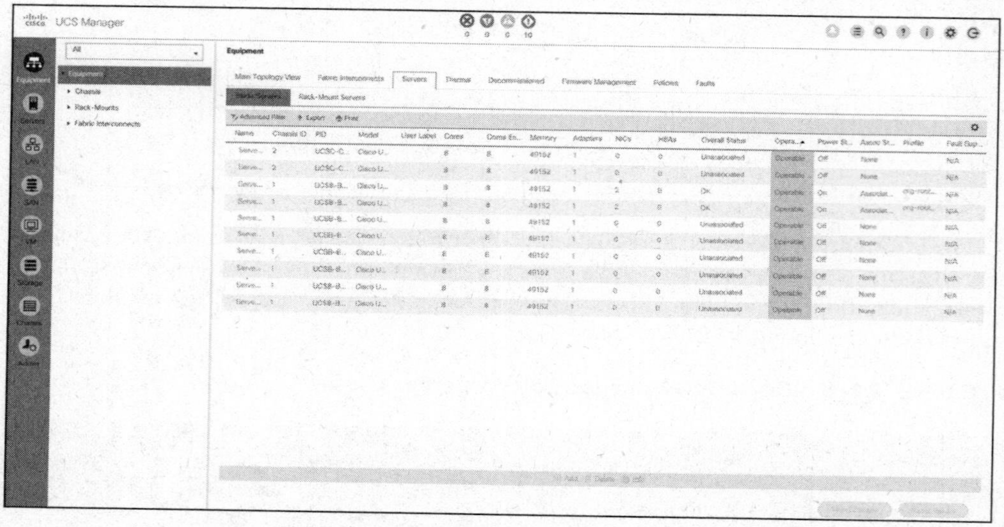

Double-clicking any of the available servers takes you further inward to monitor and view the performance of the server as well as administer common operational tasks. You can see faults, events, virtual server stats, and much more. This is one of the many places where you can monitor real-time performance and basic statistics of your inventory. An important note here about monitoring is the realization that these are all environmental statistics and performance statistics. They aren't usage stats for billing customers or end users. UCS Manager provides real-time environmental and performance stats of your infrastructure. Figure 21.10 shows an example of a server that was clicked to review even more details.

FIGURE 21.10   Cisco UCS Manager: individual server

As with the screen shown earlier in Figure 21.8, you can drill down to individual adapters and NICs of the server and gather statistics on packet rate, bandwidth, errors, and more. Figures 21.11 and 21.12 show selecting Adapters and then the pop-up screen you'd receive if you double-click Adapter 1.

FIGURE 21.11   Cisco UCS Manager: Adapters tab

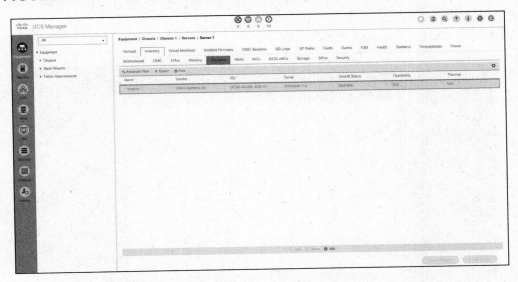

FIGURE 21.12   Cisco UCS Manager: adapter 1 properties

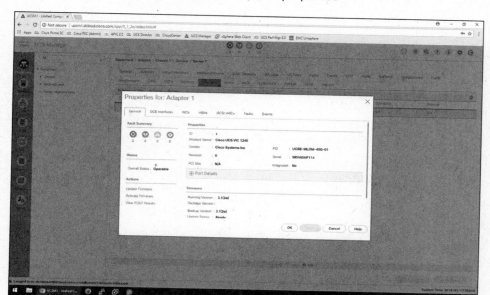

As you can see in Figure 21.12, you can still go further and look at individual NICs, HBAs, iSCSI vNICs, faults, events, DCE interfaces, and general stats. Click the NIC section to see another pop-up that shows you general Ethernet stats as well as the chart section that can plot the performance. Again, as mentioned, this isn't meant as a long-term performance trending tool. UCS Performance Manager has much better options for trend statistics. You can see an example of the NIC pop-up in Figure 21.13.

FIGURE 21.13   Cisco UCS Manager: NICs

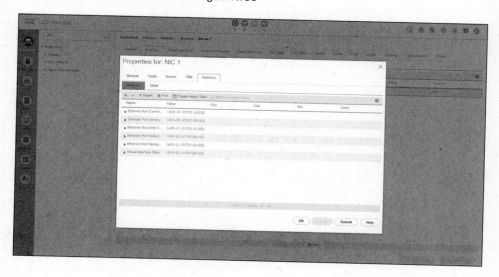

UCS Central is another tool for monitoring the infrastructure, especially on a global scale. As mentioned, UCS Manager scales to only 20 UCS chassis. UCS Central does not replace UCS Manager, which is a tool for a single UCS domain. Instead, it is geared toward grouping together multiple UCS domains to view and manage through a single pane of glass. UCS Central is a virtual appliance that scales to 10,000 total endpoints.

The interface is similar to UCS Manager and provides some of the same statistics and reporting on bandwidth, but at the UCS domain level, to see what the top talker might be in the domain. This is the large benefit of UCS Central that UCS Manager cannot fulfill. UCS Central allows a centralized inventory and health status for all your UCS components across the entire infrastructure, globally.

Cisco UCS Director Capacity Management and Monitoring

UCS Director also has extensive reporting capabilities and capacity management. *CloudSense* reporting is one of the more customizable and powerful reporting tools within UCS Director. CloudSense reports allow data to be used from several areas and reports it in a consolidated view. CloudSense reports can also give reports on real-time capacity and trending.

As of UCS Director 6.5, the following reports are available from CloudSense:

- Billing Report for a Customer
- EMC Storage Inventory Report
- Cisco C880M4 Inventory Report
- EMC Storage Inventory Report
- Group Infrastructure Inventory Report
- Hyper V Cloud Utilization Summary Report
- IBM Storwize Inventory Report
- NetApp Storage Inventory Report
- NetApp Storage Savings Per Group Report
- NetApp Storage Savings Report
- Network Impact Assessment Report
- Organizational Usage of Virtual Computing Infrastructure Report
- PNSC Account Summary Report
- Physical Infrastructure Inventory Report for a Group
- Service Request Statistics
- Service Request Statistics Per Group
- Storage Dedupe Status Report
- Storage Inventory Report for a Group
- Thin Provisioned Space Report
- UCS Data Center Inventory Report
- VM Activity Report By Group

- VM Performance Summary Report
- VMware Cloud Utilization Summary Report
- VMware Host Performance Summary Report
- Virtual Infrastructure and Assets Report

To get started with CloudSense analytics reports, do the following in the GUI:

1. Choose CloudSense ➢ Reports in the upper menu.

2. On the left side, choose the report you want.

3. Click Generate Report.

4. In the Generate Report box, you'll complete these fields:

   - *Context*: This is a drop-down list. Choose the report that you want to generate.

   - *Report Label*: Provide a label so you can distinguish reports that are run from each other.

5. Click Submit.

There are many reports you can run, all customizable and with a large historical data set. Figure 21.14 shows an example of the VMware Host Node Performance report.

FIGURE 21.14 Cisco UCS Director: CloudSense report

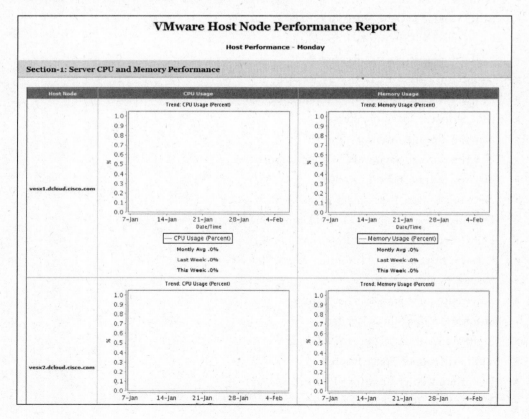

You can also run an assessment under CloudSense. Assessments are all about the current health of the virtual infrastructure running VMware with vCenter. An assessment is easy to run because it is only for the virtual infrastructure. Running this report will show you faults and hardware compatibility information. Do the following:

1. Choose CloudSense ➢ Assessments in the upper menu.

2. Click Virtual Infrastructure Assessment Report.

3. Click Generate Report.

The report is then generated in HTML or PDF format. You can see an example in Figure 21.15. In this case, there are a few minor faults, and it even lets you know that the underlying hardware you're using isn't technically compatible.

FIGURE 21.15   Cisco UCS Director: CloudSense assessments

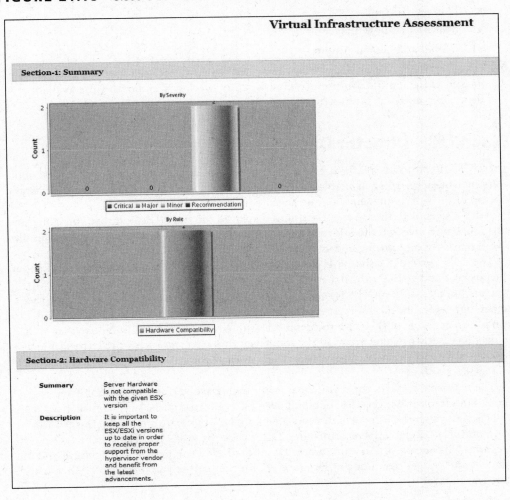

The last feature of CloudSense to mention is Report Builder. This is the area where you can build your own custom reports and also where the biggest benefit is gained for trending analysis and capacity. You can set up these reports as templates to build others as well, cloning them and using them later. You can access the Report Builder by following these steps in the UCS Director GUI:

1. Choose CloudSense ➤ Report Builder in the upper menu.

2. Click Add Template.

3. Fill in the fields Name and Description and expand the entries on the Report item.

4. For the report context, you can choose from the following:

   ▪ VDC

   ▪ Cloud

   ▪ Physical Account

   ▪ Multi-Domain Manager

   ▪ Global and Global Admin

5. After setting your context, you'll be provided with a variety of reports to choose from as well as the duration for trends. Hourly, daily, weekly, and monthly are available depending upon the type of report.

Cisco UCS Director Dashboards

The *UCS Director Dashboard* is a powerful feature for displaying quick information about your environment. You can enable the Dashboard by clicking your profile or username at the top of the screen and enabling the Dashboard on the Dashboard tab.

After it's enabled, there are a few things displayed for you by default, but you can customize it to give you the information that's useful to you. You can even set up multiple Dashboards for monitoring and switch between them on the Dashboard tab.

The UCS Director Dashboards consist of groups of *widgets* that can display data about the physical and virtual infrastructure. The Dashboard also has the ability to export its widgets in PDF, CSV, or XLS format. You can resize the widgets on the screen with the upper-right sidebar and can even maximize the widgets to full-screen for a better look. You can see an example of this with the default Dashboard in Figure 21.16. Notice that each widget has a down-facing arrow at the top. Click this arrow to access the Expand View or Export Report submenu. In the upper-right corner, you can increase or decrease all the widget sizes at once.

The real benefit starts when you create your own Dashboards and switch between them. Hundreds of widgets are found all over UCS Director in the summary sections as you click through the infrastructure. As an example, let's create a network Dashboard for monitoring. Referring back to Figure 21.16, click the green plus sign next to the word *Default*. This allows you to name a new Dashboard. You can even set autorefresh and its interval and widget size. Look at Figure 21.17 for the pop-up you'll receive when you add a new Dashboard.

FIGURE 21.16   Cisco UCS Director: default Dashboard

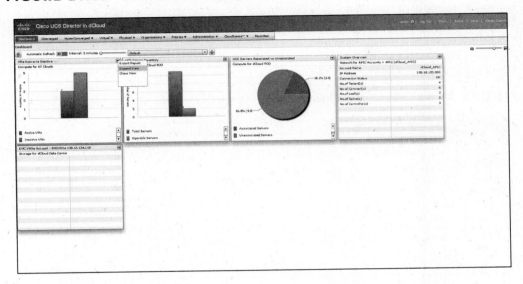

FIGURE 21.17   Cisco UCS Director: new Dashboard

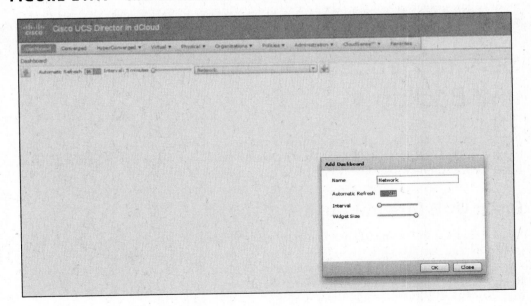

Now you need to add some things to the Dashboard so it's not blank. Simply navigating to any major area will land you on the summary screen with widgets for that section. For this example, select Virtual ➤ Network. Depending on what you have running in the virtual network, you'll see a summary of a few widgets. Pick the ones you want by clicking in the upper-right corner of each widget. This will reveal the ability to add to your Dashboard, as shown in Figure 21.18.

FIGURE 21.18   Cisco UCS Director: adding to the Dashboard

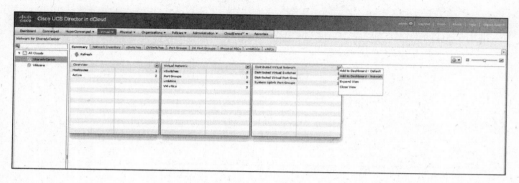

As you can see, you can create many Dashboards for an organization and its end users to monitor infrastructure quickly. The Dashboard feature is a powerful feature for monitoring within UCS Director.

Service Request Monitoring, Logs, and Backup

In this section, you'll take a brief look at service request monitoring. You'll also look at logs to view in UCS Director and Prime Service Catalog and how to back up the platform databases for recovery efforts.

Cisco UCS Director Logs

Service request monitoring in UCS Director is beneficial to all users. As the cloud administrator or end user, you'll want to have a grasp of how service requests have completed or failed. You can see the status of service requests by navigating to Organizations ➤ Service Requests in the UCS Director GUI. From this location, you'll be able to see all the requests that aren't archived. The requests can be in one of four states:

- **Complete:** Completed request, successful. You can click to get more details, and you can archive the request to move it to the archived tab.

- **In Progress:** Still in the building state. You can click here to activate a pop-up to see logs and the current state of where the service request is at.

- **Submitted:** The immediate state right after submission. It won't stay here for long, and it is running background processes to kick off the build where it will be moved to in progress.
- **Failed:** A failed service request. Clicking here will activate a pop-up with logs and data to go through to see where the service request failed.

Figure 21.19 shows an example of the service request screen.

FIGURE 21.19   Cisco UCS Director: service request monitoring

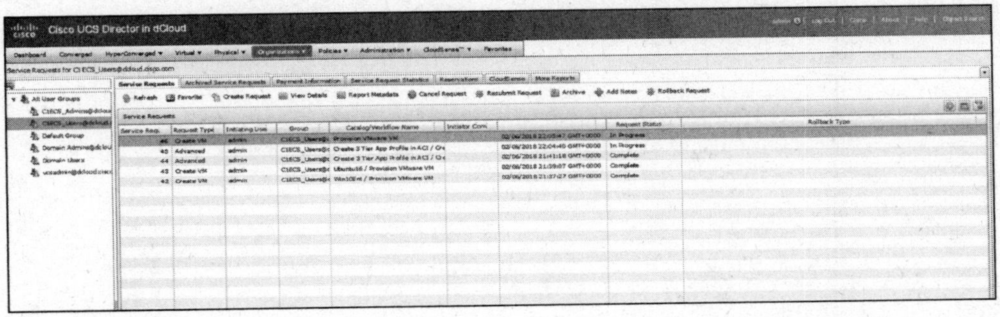

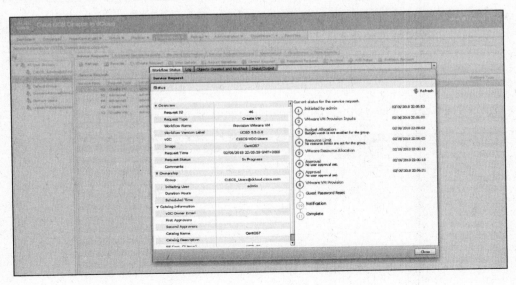

As you can see in Figure 21.19, some are in progress, and some have completed. Those that have completed can be moved to the Archived tab by simply clicking Archive in the toolbar. Double-click one of the in-progress runs, and you can begin to see how far you can follow and monitor service requests, as shown in Figure 21.20.

FIGURE 21.20   Cisco UCS Director: service request in progress

You can see in Figure 21.20 that you're still in the middle of provisioning and have a few steps left. The monitoring here is extremely beneficial to end users and administrators to follow along with their service requests, especially when one fails. Notice that there is a Log tab as well. The log is very long, but an example of it is in Figure 21.21. The log will give you detailed line items of exactly what is happening and what steps are being taken.

FIGURE 21.21 Cisco UCS Director: service request logs

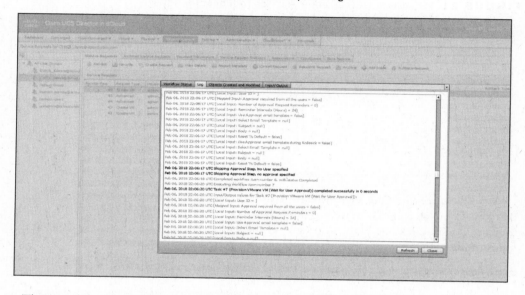

There is also a Service Request Statistics tab; you can see it by looking at Figure 21.22. The tab is right next to Payment Information. This tab is a good place to get a quick summary of what's going on and the past service requests. It groups together the workflows so you can see an aggregate of how many failed requests or succeeded, invoiced, and cancelled requests there are. In this case, there are a few in progress.

FIGURE 21.22 Cisco UCS Director: service request statistics

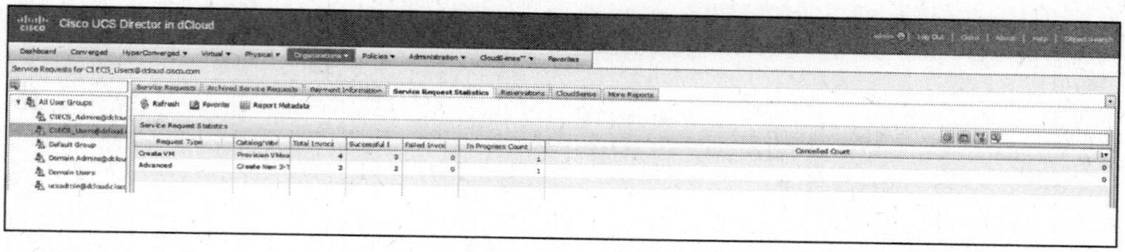

Next you'll look at some of the logs that are offered by UCS Director and Prime Service Catalog. You may use these logs for troubleshooting certain system problems, failures, or even debugging scenarios. The likelihood of you using the debugging sections is rare unless they're needed for advanced troubleshooting with Cisco TAC Support. In the UCS Director portal, you can navigate to Administration ➤ Support Information, as shown in Figure 21.23. You can then click the Support Information drop-down, as shown in Figure 21.24.

FIGURE 21.23   Cisco UCS Director: Support Information menu item

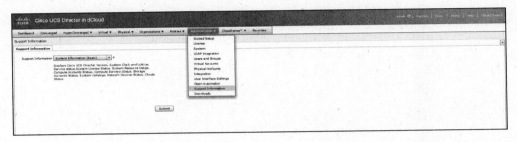

FIGURE 21.24   Cisco UCS Director: Support Information drop-down

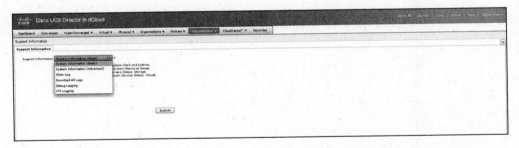

From the drop-down options you can see that you can look at system information, view logs, and even download the logs. The log will give you info on the system uptime, processes running, licensing, network information, and more. Figure 21.25 shows a small snapshot of the basic log.

FIGURE 21.25   Cisco UCS Director: system information log

```
Cisco UCS Director[6.0.1.1] System Information

**************************************************************
                 System Clock and Uptime
**************************************************************
Software Clock
Wed Feb  7 00:56:25 UTC 2018

Hardware Clock
Wed Feb  7 00:56:23 2018  -0.125721 seconds

Uptime
 00:56:26 up 3 days,  6:12,  0 users,  load average: 0.06, 0.02, 0.00

**************************************************************
                  Services Status
**************************************************************
Service         State     PID       %CPU %MEM    tELAPSED #Threads
-------------   -------   --------   ----------------------------------
broker          UP        3146       0.2  1.5  3-06:12:13 33
controller      UP        3321       0.0  1.3  3-06:11:27 72
eventmgr        UP        3479       0.1  6.1  3-06:10:43 85
idaccessmgr     UP        3624       0.2  5.9  3-06:10:37 85
inframgr        UP        3769       3.5 31.5  3-06:10:31 360
websock         UP        3850       0.0  0.0  3-06:10:25 1
tomcat          UP        3919       0.1 11.6  3-06:10:19 49
flashpolicyd    UP        3954       0.0  0.0  3-06:10:03 1
mysqld          UP        2709       2.9 11.0  3-06:12:29 176

Database        IP Address        State    Client           Connections
-------------   -------------     -------  -------------    ------------
infradb         127.0.0.1         UP       localhost           25

Disk            Size      Used    Available    %Use     Usage
-------------   -------   ------- -------------------   -------------
/dev/sda3       97G       35G     57G          39%      NORMAL
/dev/sda1       194M      36M     148M         20%      NORMAL
--------------------------------------------------------------
Database Service Status
Database        IP Address        State    Client           Connections
-------------   -------------     -------  -------------    ------------
infradb         127.0.0.1         UP       localhost           25

--------------------------------------------------------------


**************************************************************
                 System License Status
**************************************************************
[
License:Production Base,
Remarks:,
Licensed_Limit:1,
Available:-1,
Used:1,
```

The Show Log menu item is where you'll find all the logs you can look at. It isn't obvious by looking at it, but when you click it, you'll see a new drop-down list of several options, as shown in Figure 21.26.

FIGURE 21.26   Cisco UCS Director: Show Log menu item

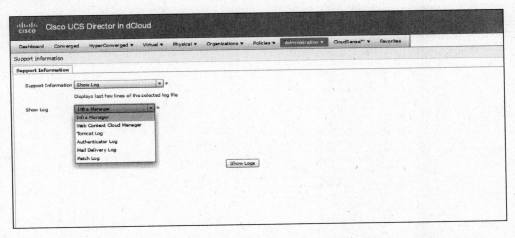

The following are the logs for downloading and viewing, as shown in Figure 21.26:

- **Infra Manager:** This log has information on system tasks and service orders that are executed as well as the overall automation services. This log can also be looked at via the shell when you have a system issue with the portal.

- **Web Context Cloud Manager:** This log's resources are accessed by users who are configured via the web portal or the API.

- **Tomcat Log:** This log offers details on the Tomcat server that is responsible for executing all the Java programs that make the GUI and portals run.

- **Authenticator Log:** This log provides details about local and LDAP authentication for when a user logs in or makes API calls.

- **Mail Delivery Log:** This log provides details on errors and issues with mail delivery for alerts and other mail-related processes such as workflow notifications.

- **Patch Log:** As its name suggests, this log has information on any updates or patches applied to UCS Director.

You can also view the Infra Manager logs from the shell console. This is the place where you can still perform system functions in case the portal has issues. You can do many things from the shell console of UCS Director. You'll have to SSH to the UCS Director server with the appropriate credentials, and you can see the list of commands available in Figure 21.17.

Notice option 18 has the ability to tail the Infra Manager logs, which are exactly the logs you'd want to see if there were major system problems. Figure 21.28 shows an example of this.

FIGURE 21.27   Cisco UCS Director: shell console

```
                        Cisco UCS Director Shell Menu
        Node:Standalone | Version:6.0.1.1 | UpTime:  01:50:44 up 3 days,  7:07

            1)  Change ShellAdmin Password
            2)  Display Services Status
            3)  Stop Services
            4)  Start Services
            5)  Stop Database
            6)  Start Database
            7)  Backup Database
            8)  Restore Database
            9)  Time Sync
            10) Ping Hostname/IP Address
            11) Show Version
            12) Generate Self-Signed Certificate and Certificate Signing Request
            13) Import CA/Self-Signed Certificate
            14) Configure Network Interface
            15) Display Network Details
            16) Enable Database for Cisco UCS Director Baremetal Agent
            17) Add Cisco UCS Director Baremetal Agent Hostname/IP
            18) Tail Inframgr Logs
            19) Apply Patch
            20) Shutdown Appliance
            21) Reboot Appliance
            22) Manage Root Access
            23) Login as Root
            24) Configure Multi Node Setup (Advanced Deployment)
            25) Clean-up Patch Files
            26) Collect logs from a Node
            27) Collect Diagnostics
            28) Configure default end user UI type
            29) Quit

            SELECT> ▮
```

FIGURE 21.28   Cisco UCS Director: shell console, Infra Manager logs

```
                Cisco UCS Director Shell Menu
    Node:Standalone | Version:6.0.1.1 | UpTime:  01:52:19 up 3 days,  7:08

        1)  Change ShellAdmin Password
        2)  Display Services Status
        3)  Stop Services
        4)  Start Services
        5)  Stop Database
        6)  Start Database
        7)  Backup Database
        8)  Restore Database
        9)  Time Sync
        10) Ping Hostname/IP Address
        11) Show Version
        12) Generate Self-Signed Certificate and Certificate Signing Request
        13) Import CA/Self-Signed Certificate
        14) Configure Network Interface
        15) Display Network Details
        16) Enable Database for Cisco UCS Director Baremetal Agent
        17) Add Cisco UCS Director Baremetal Agent Hostname/IP
        18) Tail Inframgr Logs
        19) Apply Patch
        20) Shutdown Appliance
        21) Reboot Appliance
        22) Manage Root Access
        23) Login as Root
        24) Configure Multi Node Setup (Advanced Deployment)
        25) Clean-up Patch Files
        26) Collect logs from a Node
        27) Collect Diagnostics
        28) Configure default end user UI type
        29) Quit

    SELECT> 18
    2018-02-07 01:52:31,457 [pool-46-thread-22] INFO  getVms(VMwareVMHandler.java:495) - Collecting VM inventory for the vm [ ubuntu1404-worker ] in the cloud account [VMware ]
    2018-02-07 01:52:31,457 [pool-47-thread-15] INFO  getStatus(SystemTaskStatusProvider.java:193) - Current System task status Deleted PNSC Account Cleanup:In Progress
    2018-02-07 01:52:31,502 [pool-47-thread-15] INFO  executeLocally(SystemTaskExecutor.java:163) - Done executing task. name=Deleted PNSC Account Cleanup; status=OK
    2018-02-07 01:52:31,585 [pool-47-thread-15] INFO  getStatus(SystemTaskStatusProvider.java:193) - Current System task status Deleted PNSC Account Cleanup; status=OK; lastExecuted=1517068351502
    2018-02-07 01:52:31,585 [pool-47-thread-15] INFO  updateStatus(SystemTaskStatusProvider.java:201) - Task: task.Deleted PNSC Account Cleanup changed state to OK
    2018-02-07 01:52:31,579 [pool-46-thread-4] WARN  collectHostNetworkData(VMwareInventoryCollector.java:0962) - Not able to fetch mor value for the pg: Management Network
    2018-02-07 01:52:31,579 [pool-46-thread-4] WARN  collectHostNetworkData(VMwareInventoryCollector.java:0962) - Not able to fetch mor value for the pg: vMotion
    2018-02-07 01:52:31,580 [pool-46-thread-4] WARN  collectHostNetworkData(VMwareInventoryCollector.java:0962) - Not able to fetch mor value for the pg: NAS
    2018-02-07 01:52:31,622 [pool-46-thread-4] INFO  collectHostNetworkData(VMwareInventoryCollector.java:7220) - Finished collecting host network data for host vesx2.dcloud.cisco.com in 43 milliseconds
    2018-02-07 01:52:31,622 [pool-46-thread-4] INFO  populateVMwareHostStorageAdapter(VMwareInventoryCollector.java:3193) - Finished collecting host storage data for host vesx2.dcloud.cisco.com in 18 milliseconds
    2018-02-07 01:52:31,699 [pool-46-thread-4] INFO  getDataStoreInfo(VMwareHostDatastoreHandler.java:616) - Total Datastores for Host vesx2.dcloud.cisco.com: 2
    2018-02-07 01:52:31,732 [pool-46-thread-4] INFO  doInventory(VMwareHostDatastoreHandler.java:171) - after collecting n and dss dCloud-DC VMware
    2018-02-07 01:52:31,797 [pool-46-thread-22] INFO  getVms(VMwareVMHandler.java:495) - Collecting VM inventory for the vm [ centos6-worker ] in the cloud account [VMware ]
    2018-02-07 01:52:31,960 [pool-46-thread-4] INFO  doInventory(VMwareHostDatastoreHandler.java:175) - After persist on it and DSS dCloud-DC VMware
    2018-02-07 01:52:31,961 [pool-46-thread-4] INFO  doInventory(VMwareHostDatastoreHandler.java:178) - end of host and ss handler dCloud-DC VMware
    2018-02-07 01:52:31,961 [pool-46-thread-4] INFO  execute(ConnectorManager.java:286) - Completed Inventory task vmware.hostdatastore VMware
    2018-02-07 01:52:32,038 [pool-46-thread-4] INFO  execute(ConnectorManager.java:292) - Skipping child inventory for-  vmware.hostdatastore VMware
    2018-02-07 01:52:32,094 [pool-46-thread-11] INFO  getDVSwitches(VMwareDVSwitchHandler.java:367) - DVSwitches for VMware dCloud-DC 2
    2018-02-07 01:52:32,120 [pool-46-thread-22] INFO  getVms(VMwareVMHandler.java:495) - Collecting VM inventory for the vm [ UbuntuSvr16 ] in the cloud account [VMware ]
    2018-02-07 01:52:32,126 [pool-46-thread-11] INFO  getDVSwitches(VMwareDVSwitchHandler.java:381) - DVPGs for VMware dCloud-DC 32
    2018-02-07 01:52:32,126 [pool-46-thread-11] INFO  doInventory(VMwareDVSwitchHandler.java:140) - End of dv switch handler VMware dCloud-DC
    2018-02-07 01:52:32,125 [pool-46-thread-11] INFO  execute(ConnectorManager.java:286) - Completed Inventory task vmware.dvswitch VMware
    2018-02-07 01:52:32,259 [pool-46-thread-22] INFO  execute(ConnectorManager.java:292) - Skipping child inventory for-  vmware.dvswitch VMware
    2018-02-07 01:52:32,433 [pool-46-thread-22] INFO  getVms(VMwareVMHandler.java:495) - Collecting VM inventory for the vm [ WinSvr16Ent ] in the cloud account [VMware ]
    2018-02-07 01:52:32,433 [pool-46-thread-22] INFO  getVms(VMwareVMHandler.java:495) - Collecting VM inventory for the vm [ CentOS7 ] in the cloud account [VMware ]
    2018-02-07 01:52:32,588 [pool-46-thread-22] INFO  getVms(VMwareVMHandler.java:495) - Collecting VM inventory for the vm [ Win10Ent ] in the cloud account [VMware ]
```

Cisco Prime Service Catalog Logs

When you log in to the Prime Service Catalog portal, you can navigate to the Utilities section to find the log section. If your landing page is the portal, you'll have to click the upper-right corner menu item and select Advanced Configuration ➤ Administration. You can see this in Figure 21.29.

FIGURE 21.29   Cisco Prime Service Catalog: administration

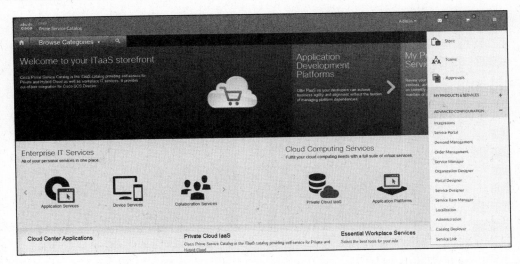

There are only a few logs available via the GUI, but there are several tools, as shown in Figure 21.30. The tools on the tabs are beyond the scope of the exam, but you can see that this is where you'd come to look at basic logs and use tools for troubleshooting. Remember that Prime Service Catalog is an orchestrator and not doing the heavy lifting that UCS Director is doing, which explains the lesser log count.

FIGURE 21.30   Cisco Prime Service Catalog: Utilities tab

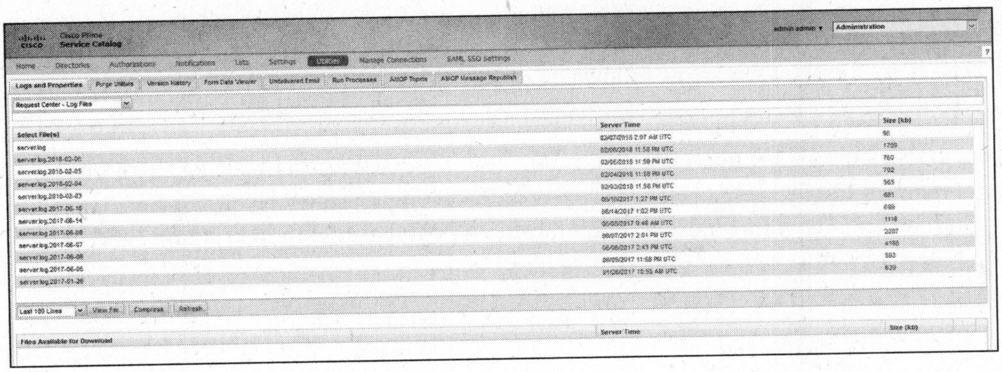

Like UCS Director, Prime Service Catalog also has a shell that can be accessed to view logs and run administrative tasks in case of an issue with the portal. Four types of logs can be accessed from the shell. Figures 21.31 and 21.32 show the menu and logs via the shell.

FIGURE 21.31   Cisco Prime Service Catalog: shell

```
Cisco Prime Service Catalog Shell Menu

Prime Service Catalog Node

Select a number from the menu below

1) Manage Users
2) View Services Status
3) Stop Services
4) Start Services
5) Manage Database
6) Manage Firewall
7) Manage Network Interface
8) Manage SMTP
9) Manage Cluster
10) View Logs
11) System Information & Cisco Support
12) Manage Packages and Patches
13) Login as Root
14) Shutdown Appliance
15) Reboot Appliance
16) Quit

SELECT>
```

FIGURE 21.32   Cisco Prime Service Catalog: shell logs

```
View Logs

1) View Prime Service Catalog Log
2) View Service Link Log
3) View Firstboot Log
--------------------
4) Return to Previous Menu

SELECT> █
```

The three logs you see are as follows:

- **Prime Service Catalog Log:** This is the basic log for the portal and catalog interface.
- **Service Link Log:** This is the integration log to other systems like UCS Director.
- **Firstboot Log:** This log offers information from when Prime was first booted up. This information contains initial configuration and database setup instructions and more that were run.

Backups in UCS Director and Prime Service Catalog

There will be a point where you want to save the database of UCS Director and Prime Service Catalog for backup purposes. This is needed in case of system failure but could also be used to get back to a known good state. Having a copy of the database backup is a good strategy as long as it's stored somewhere safe.

You'll need an FTP account for both cases to save the database to. You'll also have to stop all services before you're allowed to back up the database. All of this is done via the command line. You can't do this via the portal because the database has to actually stop in order for you to copy it. Figure 21.33 shows an example of running this via the UCS Director command line.

FIGURE 21.33   Cisco UCS Director: database backup

```
                    Cisco UCS Director Shell Menu
         Node:Standalone | Version:6.0.1.1 | UpTime:  02:55:33 up 3 days,  8:12

         1)  Change ShellAdmin Password
         2)  Display Services Status
         3)  Stop Services
         4)  Start Services
         5)  Stop Database
         6)  Start Database
         7)  Backup Database
         8)  Restore Database
         9)  Time Sync
        10)  Ping Hostname/IP Address
        11)  Show Version
        12)  Generate Self-Signed Certificate and Certificate Signing Request
        13)  Import CA/Self-Signed Certificate
        14)  Configure Network Interface
        15)  Display Network Details
        16)  Enable Database for Cisco UCS Director Baremetal Agent
        17)  Add Cisco UCS Director Baremetal Agent Hostname/IP
        18)  Tail Inframgr Logs
        19)  Apply Patch
        20)  Shutdown Appliance
        21)  Reboot Appliance
        22)  Manage Root Access
        23)  Login as Root
        24)  Configure Multi Node Setup (Advanced Deployment)
        25)  Clean-up Patch Files
        26)  Collect logs from a Node
        27)  Collect Diagnostics
        28)  Configure default end user UI type
        29)  Quit

        SELECT> 7
        Services will be stopped before Database Backup. Do you want to continue [y/n]? y
        Stopping services...
        Taking local Database backup...
        Backup will Upload file to an FTP server. Provide the necessary access credentials

           FTP Server IP Address: testserver.com
           FTP Server Login: yourlogin
           FTP Server Password:
        BACKUP_DIR=/tmp
        BACKUP_FILE=/tmp/database_backup.tar.gz
        Services are not running.
        Taking backup of inventory database...............
```

You can see option 7 was used, and FTP information was entered. You'll need to use your own FTP credentials. The services are stopped automatically, and a backup of the database was performed. After the backup was taken, it was uploaded to the FTP server. Option 8 allows you to restore the database from backup, in the same fashion. You would enter the FTP information and pull the backup down from off-site. Then the restore process can begin.

Prime Service Catalog, like UCS Director, also backs up its database via the shell command line. You can refer to Figure 21.31. Choosing option 5 would give you the option to back up and restore the Prime Service Catalog database and the orchestration database. The same details apply when using FTP to back up or restore the databases.

An interesting side note is that both appliances are UNIX based, so tools are available to automate and run this backup without using the shell menu. You would need to log in with the root or appropriate account to bypass the shell menu and access the real UNIX command line. There are Cisco guides online for how to do this. Performing it via the real shell is beyond the scope of the exam, but knowing it's a possibility to further automate backups is not.

Cloud Serviceability Options

This section covers the cloud *serviceability* options. Serviceability refers to the installing, monitoring, maintenance, and configuration of computer products in the broadest terms. It also relates to the ability to identify faults and isolate the root cause of issues. The term serviceability is a bit old and refers to on-premise gear and how it is maintained and monitored.

The move to the cloud opened up automation and ease of use, but you still need a collection of tools to maintain, monitor, and troubleshoot issues. The serviceability aspects of cloud can cover many tools, applications, and protocols. Here you'll look at the few that are covered for the exam that you should know.

Syslog

Syslog is a standard for message logging and defined in RFC 5424. If you have configured any network or system device, you more than likely have run across syslog and configured it. Syslog consists of messages logged to detail the health and status of a particular device along with the timestamp of when it was logged. Some of these messages can be simply informational, and some might require more urgent care on their receipt. Syslog on most systems defaults to storing locally and is usually something that can be turned on and off.

Depending on how syslog is set up, the local log file can be difficult to sort through. It can be quite large depending on what is being logged. One of the ways to combat this issue is to log certain levels locally. Syslog uses a *severity field* to indicate the severity of the message. This also means that different messages are assigned to a different severity level. Let's look at the levels here:

- **0 – Emergency:** This means the system is in a panic or unstable state.
- **1 – Alert:** An action needs to be taken immediately.
- **2 – Critical** Critical failures need to be corrected immediately.
- **3 – Error:** An error condition needs to be corrected soon.
- **4 – Warning:** Warning conditions may become errors if not fixed.
- **5 – Notice:** Unusual conditions may require special handling.
- **6 – Informational:** This reports normal behavior and is useful for reporting and measuring.
- **7 – Debug:** This is used for debugging an application or process.

There are also *facility* messages used in syslog. They are numbered from 0 to 23 and map to a value that is supposed to identify the source and category of a message. They are not used the same way from vendor to vendor and are not covered in detail beyond their definition on the exam.

It's up to vendors to assign their messages to severity levels. In your local syslog setup, you may set any of these levels and adjust as needed. If you, for example, set level 5, your local syslog would have all messages from 0 to 5. Syslog treats the logging in this way because 0 is considered the most important, followed by 1, 2, and so on. The benefit here is that you'll always receive the messages that the system considers emergencies. While not always the case, the higher levels generally can receive more messages as they're for informational and debugging reasons. For this fact, you'd set your local syslog accordingly. During times of debugging and troubleshooting, you might adjust the level all the way to 7, which would allow any message to be saved to the local syslog.

While local syslog is easy to set up, it may not be reliable in outage scenarios and may even clear in some scenarios like rebooting your device. A more practical approach is using local logging and remote logging at the same time. Syslog has the built-in ability to send timestamped messages to a central log server capable of receiving them. By default, most implementations will use UDP port 514 to accomplish this. TLS over TCP port 6514 is supported in newer servers and equipment as well.

There are several benefits to setting up a remote log server, one of them being access in times of an outage. The remote log server will likely have syslog messages right up to the time of the incident. The remote log server will also be reachable and available during such incidents, allowing you to ascertain what went wrong on a device by viewing logs. The ability to sort and look through archived logs on the remote syslog server is also a major benefit. The local device may not have the storage capabilities that a dedicated remote log server might have. This would allow teams to store a large history of events and problems, often useful to correlate new problems to previous events.

UCS Director supports sending syslog messages to a remote server. You can find the configuration for this under Administration ➤ Integration on the main portal. You'll have to click the Syslog tab and then select the Enable Syslog Forward box. You'll then be able to configure two syslog servers. Figure 21.34 shows where this is configured in UCS Director.

FIGURE 21.34   Cisco UCS Director syslog

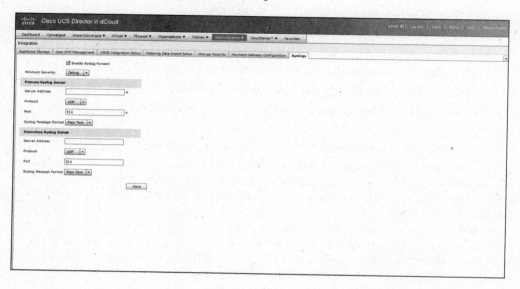

Network Time Protocol

The previous section discussed syslog and its ability to log information locally or remotely with timestamped messages. But how does a logging device ensure its time is accurate? This is one of the many use cases for *Network Time Protocol (NTP)*, a protocol within the IP stack.

NTP uses UDP port number 123 in both directions and operates traditionally in a client-server model. It can also operate in a peer-to-peer relationship where both servers sync with each other. In NTP, synchronization usually refers to the client-server model, and peering refers to the mutual synchronization of devices or server to server.

NTP operates in a hierarchical layered model of time sources. Each layer or level is referred to as a *stratum*. This allows for an organization to scale clock synchronization across a range of devices. The stratum levels are 0 through 15, with 16 being reserved for an unsynchronized clock. Synchronization allows higher stratum level servers to synchronize to lower ones. For example, stratum 3 servers would synchronize with stratum 2 servers. Stratum 2 would synchronize with stratum 1. The lower the stratum, the more accurate the clock is.

Devices on the same stratum level are allowed to mutually peer with each other, but this is not allowed between stratum levels. Peering is allowed between servers at the same stratum level for accuracy and are backed up in case a device loses its downstream synchronization to the next stratum level. A brief explanation of stratum levels follows:

- **Stratum 0:** This is the master clock level and will include very accurate time-keeping devices. This could be GPS, radio, and atomic clocks. Stratum level 0 devices are known as the *reference clock*.

- **Stratum 1:** This level of device synchronizes with the stratum 0 devices within a few microseconds because they are directly connected. Stratum 1 devices may often peer with other stratum 1 devices for sanity check and backup.

- **Stratum 2:** This level consists of devices that are synchronized to stratum 1 servers. Stratum 2 servers will synchronize to multiple stratum 1 servers. They will also peer with other stratum 2 servers to provide backup for devices in the stratum.

- **Stratum 3:** This level is a continuation and will peer with other stratum 3 servers or synchronize to stratum 2 devices. This hierarchy continues all the way to stratum level 15.

UCS Director can be configured to synchronize to an NTP server either from the command line or from the Guided Setup Wizard within the GUI. In the portal, you select Administration ➤ Guided Setup and then click Launch Guided Setup. You can see this in Figure 21.35. You'll then have to check the box for initial system configuration and click Submit. This is shown in Figure 21.36.

FIGURE 21.35 Cisco UCS Director: guided setup

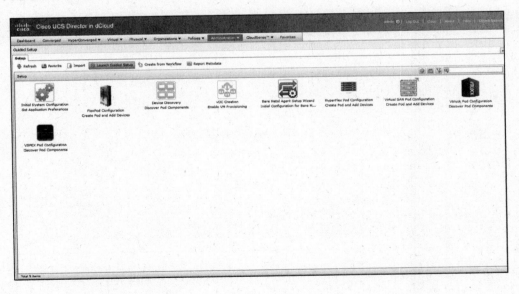

FIGURE 21.36 Cisco UCS Director: initial config

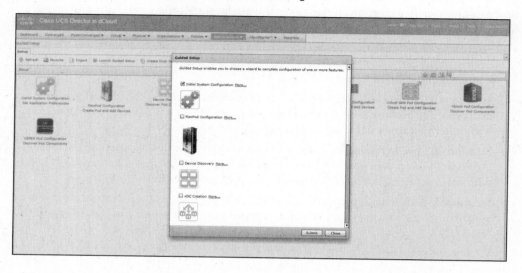

After hitting Submit, you'll be presented with a window of guided setup options to choose from. Here, you can uncheck everything but NTP and click Submit. You can see this in Figure 21.37.

FIGURE 21.37 Cisco UCS Director: guided setup for NTP

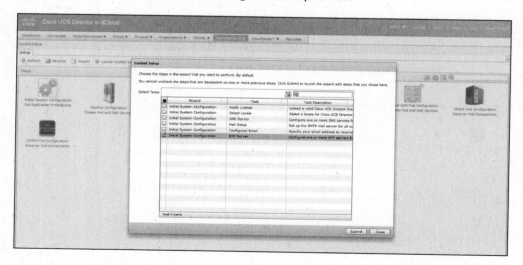

Finally, you'll be presented with an overview that you can read and click Next. Then, you'll be able to add multiple NTP servers. If one is already defined, you'll have to click Modify NTP Servers. You can see this in Figure 21.38.

FIGURE 21.38   Cisco UCS Director: NTP setup

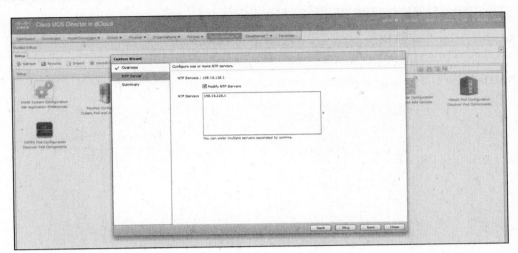

Domain Name System

The *Domain Name System (DNS)* is a protocol within the IP suite of applications just like NTP is. DNS allows normal domain names to resolve to IP addresses. In most cases, networks route traffic to destinations based on what the IP address is. This number can vary and would be hard for individuals to remember. In fact, the Internet would be much harder to navigate if everyone had to remember and bookmark numbers for popular websites. This is where DNS makes life easier. DNS runs on UDP or TCP port 53 and is something most networks will have configured either manually or via DHCP-given settings.

When you enter a domain name like google.com in your web browser, your browser asks a DNS server to translate that name into an IP address. This is the server that you have manually configured, or it would have been automatically configured for you via DHCP. The DNS server will respond with the real IP address of the name, and then your computer will communicate with that server via the IP address. This is a simple example meant to illustrate the concept for the exam, as there are obviously more details involved than this for full communication.

Another benefit of DNS is when moving servers. IP addresses can change, and servers can be retired or relocated to other areas. The DNS name doesn't have to change, just what IP address it points to. This is by far the biggest benefit of DNS as it offers a front door that can stay constant. By simply updating what IP address it points to, the DNS name now points to a different server. The same can be said for load-balanced services.

Like NTP, UCS Director can utilize DNS. The big benefit is the same as the one mentioned. Using DNS allows you to add hostnames instead of IP addresses to services, servers, and more. This allows the IP address to change as well, but the service or server is still bound to the hostname that resolves to the new IP address. The configuration for DNS is located in the same area that NTP was located, the guided setup. DNS can also be configured via the command line or the portal GUI.

In the portal, you navigate to Administration ➤ Guided Setup and then click Launch Guided Setup. You'll check initial system configuration just like you did for NTP and submit. This time you'll uncheck everything and leave DNS checked, as shown in Figure 21.39.

FIGURE 21.39 Cisco UCS Director: DNS guided setup

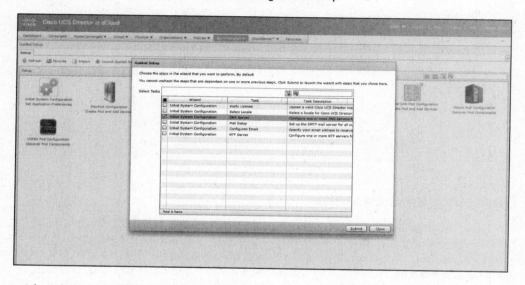

After clicking Submit and moving on, you can change or add the DNS servers of your choice. You'll have to select Modify if you need to change already added servers. Here you'll have to enter the IP address of the DNS servers. This is shown in Figure 21.40.

FIGURE 21.40 Cisco UCS Director: DNS setup

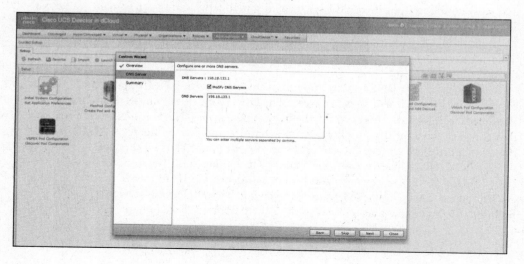

Dynamic Host Configuration Protocol

Dynamic Host Configuration Protocol (DHCP) is another networking protocol just like NTP and DNS. DHCP runs over UDP and uses ports 67 and 68 for communications. The DHCP server listens on port 67, while DHCP clients use a source port of 68 for communication. DHCP clients broadcast to servers asking for network configuration information that the DHCP server responds with.

One of the most well-known examples is simple IP address assignment. If you have a wireless network at your home, your router is likely running a simple DHCP service to provide IP addresses to clients as they join the network. You can manually assign IP addresses to devices, but that doesn't scale and becomes cumbersome when all that a device needs is basic connectivity.

There are other things DHCP can do, such as carry information for PXE and for where to find servers to boot from. This was discussed in Chapter 20 regarding the UCS Director Bare Metal Agent. This is also where the easiest example is seen for DHCP use in UCS Director: PXE builds via the UCS Director Bare Metal Agent. For the exam you'll need to understand the basic request and offer messages between the client and server, so let's walk through those:

1. A DHCP client sends a DHCP discover message from source port 68 to destination port 67 and broadcast address 255.255.255.255.

2. If a DHCP server is on the local network listening, it will hear the broadcast and respond with a DHCP offer giving more configuration details if an IP and such details are available.

3. The DHCP client responds to the offer by sending a DHCP request to the broadcast address asking the DHCP server for the offered IP address and information.

4. The DHCP server receives the request and responds with the final message, the DHCP acknowledgment. This response includes lease duration and any other configuration still left to tell the client.

You might be wondering why the client responds to the offer with a request. Not only does the client respond, it broadcasts the response. This is to serve a few purposes. The first is an acknowledgment that it received the offer and wants to formally request what it was offered. The second is the possibility of more than one DHCP server on the same subnet, which means the client may have received multiple offers. The client picks the fastest response to the discover request packet and sends an offer back as a broadcast to let all other servers hear it. This makes sure other DHCP servers are aware when the client didn't pick their offered IP address so they can be returned to the pool.

As stated previously, the main use case of DHCP for the exam is the UCS Bare Metal Agent and its ability to PXE boot virtual and physical machines. DHCP has many options it can pass in the DHCP offer message. These are the special ones relevant to the exam that make PXE work:

- **DHCP option 66:** This is the TFTP server name or IP address from where the client can ask for a file to be downloaded.

- **DHCP option 67:** This option actually provides the filename to download. Combined with option 66, the client knows the server and filename it should ask for to PXE boot.

Combine these options with the standard IP, subnet mask, and gateway, and a server has enough information to start communicating and boot up via PXE. UCS Director can do this for both virtual and physical workloads.

Simple Mail Transfer Protocol

Anyone using the Internet knows what e-mail is. E-mail is driven by the *Simple Mail Transfer Protocol (SMTP)* to send messages. There are other protocols for receiving messages such as POP and IMAP, but they are unrelated to the exam. SMTP historically has used TCP port 25 to communicate, but that is often now reserved only for mail servers. Most ISPs and mail servers will ask you to connect to their mail server or other mail servers on TCP port 587 or 465.

UCS Director can use e-mail to send alerts and management messages to end users. The alerting aspects can be of use when monitors detect something is wrong or some services that were ordered fail. There are also approval notifications and updates to orders that end users can receive as orders are built. E-mail is a big part of self-service delivery with UCS Director and something you'll have configured.

SMTP can be configured in the initial configuration wizard. You can click Submit and go through the setup options. You can also configure SMTP in a separate location by selecting Administration ➤ System and clicking the Mail Setup tab. You can see this in Figure 21.41.

FIGURE 21.41 Cisco UCS Director: mail setup

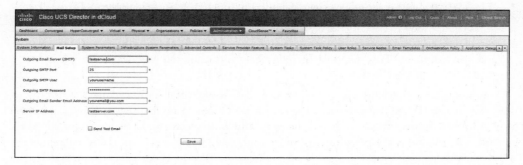

Fill out the fields with your appropriate information. Your e-mail server likely requires a username and password to send e-mail, but some may not. When all the fields are filled out, you can send a test e-mail by selecting the box. When you do, a new box appears to create an e-mail to test with. Assuming you receive the e-mail at your account, you're good to go for UCS Director sending monitoring information and alerts.

Summary

This chapter covered information related to monitoring and logging in the Cisco cloud experience. The chapter discussed UCS Performance Manager and what its use cases are; it's a shared tool meant to be used for performance monitoring among multiple teams.

The chapter then discussed UCS Central and UCS Manager. You looked at their differences and how UCS Central is meant for larger-scale deployment. You learned about the logging and performance monitoring capabilities available in both tools.

The chapter also reviewed the UCS Director Dashboard and widgets as well as its logging options for monitoring performance and issues. The chapter also covered Prime Service Catalog and its logging abilities for troubleshooting and monitoring.

Finally, the chapter covered the serviceability protocols and how they help with monitoring, alerting, and overall operations. NTP was discussed with its time synchronization capabilities. DHCP was covered with regard to using it with PXE and the Bare Metal Agent. SMTP was shown and discussed in its relation to sending alert and notification e-mails. Syslog was also covered with its ability to log alerts and notifications both locally and remote.

Exam Essentials

Know UCS Performance Manager.   Know what UCS Performance Manager is. Understand it's a shared tool and meant to be used by multiple teams. It's an aggregation point for statistics and monitoring of the entire UCS environment. It can monitor network, storage, and compute resources. There are two versions, with the smaller Express version only doing compute.

Understand UCS Central and UCS Manager.   Know what UCS Manager can do for operations and monitoring. Have an understanding of the statistics that can be collected. UCS Central is a larger tool that isn't meant to replace UCS Manager but can complement it in very large domains. UCS Central scales higher than UCS Manager and offers some of the same statistics and reporting but at the entire domain level, where UCS Manager only offers a smaller view into its managed install base.

Know UCS Director monitoring, backup, and Dashboards.   Know what CloudSense reports can offer as well as assessments. Understand what Dashboards can do and how they're customizable for end users to view. Know where to locate logs and know how to back up and recover the database. Understand what a shell is used for.

Know Prime Service Catalog logs and backup.   Know where to locate the logs in the GUI and in the shell. Understand how backups are performed via the shell and how the restore process is done.

Understand serviceability protocols.   Know the protocols discussed and where they fit into the tools used for cloud management and monitoring.

Written Lab

The following questions are designed to test your understanding of this chapter's material. You can find the answers to the questions in Appendix B. For more information on how to obtain additional questions, please see this book's Introduction.

1. The PXE Bare Metal Agent uses the _____ protocol to assign a client an IP address and help it boot.

2. UCS Director _____ is a custom page that can be used for multiple teams and users to monitor their environment.

3. _____ _____ is a management application that works locally with up to 20 chassis.

4. _____ is a protocol used to synchronize time between devices.

5. Backing up the UCS Director database requires logging in to the _____.

6. UCS _____ _____ is a tool meant to be shared by teams to monitor performance.

7. Translating names to IP addresses is handled by the _____ protocol.

8. The _____ log contains log information on updates in UCS Director.

9. ____ _____ is a management application to administer multiple UCS domains outside of the local environment.

10. The _____ protocol is used for mail delivery.

Review Questions

The following questions are designed to test your understanding of this chapter's material. You can find the answers to the questions in Appendix A. For more information on how to obtain additional questions, please see this book's Introduction.

1. What protocol deals with logging?

   A. Syslog

   B. Service logging

   C. Servicing protocol

   D. Service chains

2. What area of the UCS Director allows for widgets?

   A. Dashboard

   B. Service portal

   C. Service screen

   D. Order portal

3. UCS Manager can manage which of the following?

   A. 3 UCS domains

   B. 30 UCS chassis

   C. 20 UCS chassis

   D. 5 UCS domains

4. The shell is required to do what operation in UCS Director?

   A. Back up the database.

   B. Change a service.

   C. Set up syslog.

   D. Set up DNS.

5. A stratum 2 server can peer with what server in NTP?

   A. Stratum 2

   B. Stratum 1

   C. No server

   D. Stratum 3

6. Which of the following in UCS Director makes use of PXE for installing virtual machines?

   A. HTTP Agent

   B. Bare Metal Agent

   C. Order Agent

   D. Dashboard Agent

7. Which options in DHCP are used for PXE? (Choose all that apply.)

   A. 69

   B. 66

   C. 67

   D. 70

8. Which log in UCS Director can also be viewed via the shell in addition to the GUI for troubleshooting system issues?

   A. Soft log

   B. Authenticator log

   C. Infra Manager log

   D. System log

9. Which are valid states found in service request monitoring for a particular request? (Choose all that apply.)

   A. Complete

   B. In Progress

   C. Processing

   D. Error

10. What feature of CloudSense provides a report on the virtual infrastructure, including hardware compatibility?

    A. Assessment

    B. Capacity management

    C. VM report

    D. End User report

11. In syslog, what is meant to identify the source and category of a message and is numbered from 0 to 23?

    A. Facility

    B. Logger field

    C. System variable

    D. None of the above

12. Which of the following are proper alert levels for syslog? (Choose all that apply.)

  A. Emergency

  B. Failure

  C. Warning

  D. Notice

13. Level 7 syslog would often be used for which of the following?

  A. Debugging, rarely

  B. Day-to-day logging

  C. Information Dashboards

  D. Paging for alerts

14. Select the protocol for sending mail.

  A. FTP

  B. IMAP

  C. POP

  D. SMTP

15. What feature of CloudSense allows you to assemble your own reports?

  A. Report Designer

  B. Report Builder

  C. Reporting Tool

  D. Report templates

16. UCS Central can scale to how many endpoints?

  A. 1,000

  B. 5,000

  C. 10,000

  D. As many as UCS Manager

17. Which are valid DHCP messages in an exchange for an IP address? (Choose all that apply.)

  A. DHCP discover

  B. DHCP offer

  C. DHCP re-offer

  D. DHCP OK

18. Which VM reports are available in CloudSense? (Choose all that apply.)

  A. VMware Host Performance Summary report

  B. VMware CPU report

  C. VMware Performance Summary report

  D. VMware Storage report

19. Where would you find good statistics on network, storage, and compute at the same time?

   A. UCS Director

   B. UCS Performance Manager

   C. UCS Central

   D. UCS Manager

20. UCS Performance Manager comes in which versions? (Choose all that apply.)

   A. UCS Performance Manager Large

   B. UCS Performance Manager

   C. UCS Performance Manager Express

   D. UCS Performance Manager Medium

Appendix A

Answers to Review Questions

Chapter 1: Fundamentals of Cloud Computing

1. D. The utility concept of purchasing computing resources enables on-demand access without having to purchase the underlying data center hardware.

2. D. Scale up refers to adding cloud capacity by increasing the capability of a computing resource.

3. B, D. Hypervisors and virtual machines implement virtualized network interface cards and Ethernet switches internally for network communications.

4. C. Hypervisors are virtualization applications that manage virtual machines and manage resource pools for the hosted virtual machines.

5. B. On-demand server service is a key component of a cloud service offering.

6. C. Multitenancy is the term that identifies the sharing of a single application between many cloud customers.

7. A. Data centers must be designed for current and anticipated computing workloads.

8. C. Memory resource pooling allows for the grouping and allocation of RAM.

9. A, C, F. The four main cloud deployment models are community, hybrid, private, and public. On-demand, interexchange, and resilient are not valid cloud deployment models.

10. A, D, E. Common public cloud characteristics include measured or metered service, multitenancy usage, on-demand services resiliency, and ubiquitous access. Tiered service is not valid, and exclusive access is a private cloud attribute.

11. A, C, F. Infrastructure as a Service, Platform as a Service, and Software as a Service are the three primary cloud service models. The Application, Communications, and Security models may be valid but are not considered primary.

12. B, D, F. Common cloud characteristics include metered service, elasticity, and ubiquitous access. While interconnectivity, virtualization, and resource pooling help to enable the cloud, they are not considered to be a cloud characteristic.

13. B. Scale out refers to adding cloud capacity by adding additional virtual machines to spread the workload between a greater number of VMs.

14. B. Storage area networks (SANs) are high-speed storage communication networks that connect servers to remote storage systems.

15. C. The hybrid model is a combination of cloud deployment models.

16. A, C, F. Data center–critical facilities include stable power, cooling systems, and physical security.

17. A. Interexchange providers offer private interconnects between corporate network and the cloud provider.

18. C. Virtualization technology was a key enabler of cloud computing by allowing on-demand computing.

19. B. Public, private, community, and hybrid are common cloud deployment models. Corporate is not considered a cloud deployment model.

20. A, C. To enable redundancy and high availability, cloud providers structure their data centers into regions and availability zones.

Chapter 2: Defining Cloud Service Models

1. B. IaaS or Infrastructure as a Service includes the server operating system with the underlying infrastructure but not any applications running on the server.

2. C. The three primary cloud service models defined by NIST are Infrastructure as a Service, Platform as a Service, and Software as a Service.

3. C. Public cloud service providers offer geographical areas known as regions for proximity to customers.

4. B. Software as a Service is a cloud-based service that includes all underlying infrastructure, the operating systems, and the application.

5. B. An availability zone is a separate and redundant facility in a region that allows for resiliency and failover should another availability zone in the region fail.

6. B, C, D. Infrastructure is the key word in this question and indicates that hardware, such as memory, storage, and CPUs, is included, but higher-level services such as Linux, domain name services, or object brokers are the responsibility of the customer.

7. B. IaaS stands for Infrastructure as a Service. All other answers offered are not valid.

8. C. SaaS or Software as a Service is the NIST service model offering full-stack services up to and including applications such as e-mail and big data.

9. A, C, E. Isolating virtual machine instances is a security step taken in the shared public cloud, VPNs offer encryption services, and firewalls are network-level security devices.

10. A, C. Both enterprise resource planning and analytics are considered applications that are included in the Software as a Service model but not as a Platform as a Service offering.

11. B. IaaS or Infrastructure as a Service is the NIST service model that addresses basic data center infrastructure such as servers, CPUs, memory, routing/switching, and storage.

12. C. PaaS stands for Platform as a Service. All other answers offered are not valid.

13. C. Infrastructure as a Service or IaaS is the most prevalent cloud service model that defines the underlying data center infrastructure operations but does not include any operating systems or applications, which remain the responsibility of the cloud customer.

14. C. SaaS stands for Software as a Service. All other answers offered are not valid.

15. C. IaaS or Infrastructure as a Service offers the basic data center infrastructure and services that are similar to private data centers and are frequently deployed by corporate IT administrators.

16. B. CaaS or Communications as a Service would host IP telephones, videoconferencing, and collaboration. While SaaS and XaaS may also apply, CaaS is more specific. PaaS does not include applications.

17. B. Of the answers offered, only Google Compute Engine is in the PaaS service model category.

18. C. When implementing the Platform as a Service in the cloud, the application software must be provided by the customer.

19. D. With so many service models being offered in the market, XaaS, or Anything as a Service is now a defined service model.

20. B, D, F. Only IaaS, PaaS, and SaaS are primary service models; all others such as CaaS, XaaS, and DRaaS are not the primary service models.

Chapter 3: Understanding Cloud Deployment Models

1. A. The public deployment model is accessed by the general public and hosted in the service provider's data center.

2. C. Cloud bursting is the ability to use cloud services for additional compute capacity on demand.

3. C. Public, private, community, and hybrid are the four primary cloud deployment models defined by NIST.

4. A. The public cloud is shared by many customers across a wide spectrum of businesses.

5. D. Public, hybrid, and community clouds are shared models; the private cloud is exclusive to one company.

6. C. Cloud bursting is the ability to use cloud services for additional compute capacity on demand.

7. B, C. Resource pooling allows for the dynamic allocation and sharing of compute resources such as CPU, memory, storage, and networking.

8. D. Private deployment models are not shared and allow the most end-user control.

9. C. Cloud bursting refers to the ability to access additional compute capacity in a remote cloud data center.

10. A, B, E. U.S. regulations such as Sarbanes-Oxley (SOX), Payment Card Industry Data Security Standard (PCI DSS), and the Health Insurance Portability and Accountability Act (HIPAA) are all natural fits for companies wanting to utilize a specialized community cloud deployment model that allows them to meet regulatory requirements.

11. A. Public cloud deployments follow the pay-as-you-go usage model.

12. C. The service level agreement is a service provider document that details the metrics to be delivered to the customer.

13. A. Private, hybrid, and community clouds are well suited for hosting critical applications. The public clouds are orientated towards mainstream applications.

14. D. A hybrid cloud is the interconnection between two or more cloud deployment models.

15. C, D. Community and private clouds may exist on or off the premises, as outlined in the NIST definitions.

16. B. Public cloud deployments offer scalability and on-demand provisioning and prevent the company from purchasing peak server capacity that sits idle most of the year.

17. B. Public clouds that have provider proprietary implementations may cause vender lock-in and lack of portability to migrate to another cloud provider.

18. B, D, E. Common customer interfaces used to manage a public cloud deployment include the application programmable interface, command-line interface, and browser's graphical interface.

19. B. Of the answers given, elasticity best describes the ability to react to load demands.

20. D. The hybrid model is the interconnection of two or more cloud models.

Chapter 4: Introducing the Cisco Intercloud Solution

1. A, C, E. The Cisco Intercloud Fabric interconnects public, private, and Cisco business partner clouds with a single management portal and secure interconnections.

2. A, D. The Cisco Intercloud Fabric includes a self-service management portal and encrypted interconnections between the private and one or more public clouds.

3. B, D. The Intercloud solution comes in two unique application models that are designed to work together as a complete solution. *Cisco Intercloud for Provider* is for end cloud providers that are part of the Intercloud partner cloud offering. These are your commercial cloud providers that offer consumer services through Intercloud. *Cisco Intercloud for Business* is the traditional model for end consumers and corporations that want to use Cisco Intercloud.

4. F. Intercloud is designed to support all the major public cloud platforms including AWS, Azure, and the Google cloud platform as well as the cloud offerings of Cisco's business partners.

5. A, B, C, F. The Intercloud Fabric Director (ICFD) is a single point of management for end users and IT administrators of hybrid cloud services included with Intercloud Fabric Director including monitoring, user management, service catalog, policy management, VM management, and customized portals.

6. B, D. The Virtual Security Gateway is a virtual appliance based on the Nexus 1000v that uses Cisco Virtual Path (vPath) technology to abstract the forwarding plane, and it allows inline traffic redirection.

7. A, C, D. The Intercloud Fabric Extender, Fabric Director, and Virtual Security Gateway are all components of the Intercloud solution.

8. C. The Intercloud Director is a centralized management portal for hybrid cloud deployments.

9. D. The CSR is an IOS-XE router running as a virtual machine.

10. B. The VSG or virtual security gateway provides edge security and firewall services for the Intercloud Fabric to protect VM-to-VM and VM-to-edge security.

11. B. The Intercloud Fabric Switch (ICS) provides a virtualized layer 2 Ethernet switch for local switching.

12. C. Having layer 2 extensions between cloud data centers is a feature of the Intercloud Secure Extension or ICX application.

13. A, D. The Cisco Intercloud Fabric Extender and private clouds are part of the Intercloud product offering. However, community clouds and resource pools are not.

14. A, C. Cisco Intercloud offers a central management portal, a service catalog, and secure interconnections to public, private, and Cisco partner clouds. Intercloud is not limited to any specific hypervisor system.

15. A, C. The Intercloud Secure Extension's primary function is to interact with the private cloud or on-site switch and to initiate the secure tunnel to the far-end public Intercloud Fabric.

16. A. The Intercloud Secure Extension is the initiator of the secure tunnel, encapsulates Ethernet frames into IP packets, and uses Datagram Transport Layer Security to ensure confidentiality.

17. B. The public cloud VMs run an agent referred to as the *Intercloud Fabric Agent (ICA)*. This agent provides an overlay in the cloud environment that tunnels to the ICS for VM-to-VM communication. Overlay statistics are also collected via the agent and used for monitoring.

18. A. The Cisco Secure Intercloud Fabric Shell is the high-level grouping of all Cisco Intercloud Fabric products.

19. C. Intercloud Fabric for Providers interconnects and communicates directly with Azure and AWS via their own APIs. Any other provider or managed service offering would use Intercloud Fabric for Providers to offer the services to customers.

20. A. The Cisco Intercloud routing services can be integrated with the ICF components or run as a separate VM image that is referred to as CSR and includes features such as inter-VLAN routing, direct network access to virtual machines, network address translation, and edge firewall services.

Chapter 5: The Cisco Unified Computing System

1. C. The USC Manager stores server boot configuration information on the Profiles tab.

2. C. WWNs are a globally unique Fibre Channel address assigned by the host bus adapter manufacturer to uniquely address a Fibre Channel interface in a storage area network.

3. C. XML APIs allow machine-to-machine automation, configuration, and management from third-party vendors.

4. D. UCS Central is the global application that manages and monitors one or more UCS domains.

5. B, C. 6300 series fabric interconnects utilize both 10Gbps and 40Gbps interfaces.

6. A, C, D. The UCS 6300 series fabric interconnects provide a converged data and storage networking fabric, host the UCSM manager, and act as the interconnect point for the UCS 5108 blade server chassis.

7. D. UCS Manager is the Cisco-developed application used to manage multiple UCS domains.

8. B. The UCS Manager application runs on the active/standby model.

9. B. The UCS 5108 chassis can house either four full-width or eight half-width servers.

10. A, B, E. The UCS product line features the convergence of compute, networking, and storage technologies into one integrated and centrally managed family of products.

11. C. The data plane forwarding fabric in the 6300 series fabric interconnects are always in a forwarding mode, or an active/active configuration.

12. B. The UCS family supports a 10Gb converged switching fabric, a design optimized for virtualized environments, centralized management with the UCSM and UCS Central applications that can support configurations profiles and pools, and a wide selection of device input/output options.

13. A. An Ethernet layer 3 switched interface is called a switched virtual interface (SVI).

14. B, C, D. Solid-state drives (SSDs), serial attached storage (SAS), and serial advanced technology attachment (SATA) drives are supported in the C-series product line.

15. B, D. The unified ports in the 6332-16UP fabric interconnect can be configured to support either native Ethernet or Fibre Channel.

16. D. UCSM server profiles are assigned to servers in a 5108 chassis to obtain configuration information.

17. A, B, D, G. UCSM maintains pools of addressing objects that can be dynamically applied to servers in a profile; commonly used pools include UUID, MAC, Mgmt. IP, and WWN.

18. D. UCS Central manages multiple UCS domains using APIs in the UCS Manager application.

19. A, B, E, G. The UCS Manager provides objects to configure the 6300 fabric interconnects. Configurations for VSANs, Uplinks, VLAN identifiers, and quality-of-service configurations are stored in UCSM and applied to the fabric interconnect modules.

20. A, B, D. The primary differences between the B-series and C-series UCS servers are locally connected storage, server, and interface slot density.

Chapter 6: Cisco Data Center Products and Technologies

1. A, B, F, H. Resiliency, availability, flexibility, scalability, and monitoring are key data center networking attributes.

2. A. The Nexus 1000 series is a distributed virtual switch and is a software-only product.

3. C. Fibre Channel storage area networking deployments require a lossless switching fabric.

4. B. The Nexus 2000 series uses FEX technology and acts as a remote line card connected to a 5000 or 7000 series Nexus switch.

5. C. The Nexus 5000 series is the parent switch for FEX technology and supports unified ports for converged networking.

6. B. The data center bridging exchange protocol performs DCB peer discovery, mismatched configuration detection, and peer link configuration.

7. A. Virtual device contexts logically partition a Nexus 7000 series switch into multiple virtual devices that appear to run their own NX-OS and physical interfaces.

8. D. The Nexus 9000 series of data center switches was developed to operate in an application-specific infrastructure environment.

9. D. The Nexus 9000 series of data center switches is designed to support a spine/leaf data center architecture.

10. D. Software Defined Networking (SDN) replaces manual configurations with a centralized SDN controller that is used to automate network deployments.

11. A, D, E. The Cisco three-tier network design consists of the access, aggregation, and core layers.

12. B. Fabric extension (FEX) technology is used to interconnect and control remote Nexus 2000 series switches.

13. D. FabricPath uses the IS-IS routing protocol to provide a loop-free layer 2 switching fabric that allows for resiliency and a loop-free topology that uses all available interconnecting links.

14. B. Overlay Transport Virtualization (OTV) is a Nexus feature that interconnects layer 2 VLANS across a router layer 3 network.

15. D. A virtual port channel enables two Nexus switches to appear as one device when interconnected via a port channel for network resiliency.

16. D. The Nexus 9000 series, and more specifically the 9200 family, offers multirate high-speed interfaces using SFP+ technology.

17. A. Software Defined networking (SDN) replaces manual per-device configuration with a centralized controller that allows for network automation.

18. C. SDN technologies centralize and automate the network control plane.

19. B. The Application Centric Infrastructure is an SND network and switching fabric developed by Cisco that is a centralized control plane interoperating with a distributed Nexus 9000 network.

20. A, C. The northbound SDN interface communicates to configuration controllers and uses using a graphical interface or a published application programmable interface (API).

21. C. The Cisco APIC controller is part of the ACI family and is the central control plane in a Nexus 9000 leaf/spine architecture.

Chapter 7: Server Virtualization in the Cloud

1. C. A hypervisor is software that allows multiple virtual machines to run on a single server hardware platform.

2. B. A Type 1 hypervisor runs directly on the server hardware.

3. B. A Type 2 hypervisor requires an operating system to be installed, and the Type 2 hypervisor runs as an application on the OS.

4. B, D. VirtualBox and KVM are open source hypervisors.

5. B, D. The UUID and MAC address are required to be unique on each server and are changed during the cloning process.

6. A, B, C. A cloned image includes the reference for creating new virtual servers and should include the operating system, service packs, and security configurations.

7. C. A snapshot is a software copy of a virtual machine at a specific moment in time.

8. C. A virtual switch is a virtualized Ethernet switch that runs inside a hypervisor and connects the virtual server's vNICs to the outside Ethernet network.

9. D. Shared resources, rapid deployment, and portability are all benefits of virtualization.

10. C. A virtual network interface card (vNIC) is a software representation of a hardware network interface card that virtual machines load to connect to the outside network.

11. D. Type 1 hypervisors are installed on the computer hardware.

12. D. Orchestration systems are used to provide self-service cloud operations.

13. C. The hypervisor control application for EXSi is vCenter.

14. D. A virtual-to-virtual (V2V) migration is when a virtual machine is migrated from one virtualized server environment to another.

15. B. Storage volumes can be large, and if there is limited network bandwidth to the cloud provider, an online migration may take a long time.

16. B. A live migration over the WAN network to the cloud is referred to as an online migration.

17. A, C, D. Of the answers offered, ESXi, Hyper-V, and KVM are Type 1 hypervisors that are often used in public and private clouds.

18. A, B, C, F. The bare-metal server supports hardware resources such as NICs, HBAs, RAM, and CPUs.

19. B, D. The question is asking for hypervisor products. Of the answers offered, KVM and ESXi are both examples of hypervisors.

20. A. Elasticity is the process of using a pool of computing resources in the cloud to dynamically assign and reclaim resources as needed.

Chapter 8: Infrastructure Virtualization

1. D. There are more than 16.7 million possible identifiers to be used in the VxLAN format.

2. B. vPath is a Cisco-developed protocol that can direct the flow of traffic to virtual appliances.

3. C. Enhanced VxLAN refers to the 1000v's ability to learn hosts as they come online and distribute MAC addresses to other 1000v VTEPs. This reduces flooding in the environment.

4. B. EVPN is an address family of BGP and is used to distribute MAC addresses and IP routes throughout the VxLAN fabric.

5. B, D. The VMware distributed virtual switch and Cisco Nexus 1000v each supports a centralized point of management and does not require host-by-host configuration.

6. B. Virtual switching operates at the hypervisor level.

7. C. The 1000v virtual Ethernet module is a line card that connects to vNIC on a virtual server.

8. A, B, C. Layer 2 connectivity is the prime service of virtual switching. 802.1q trunking and link aggregation control protocol are also supported. DNS is an application, and OSPF is a routing protocol, neither of which is a layer 2 switching function.

9. D. BGP is a routing protocol and not a switching function. The 1000v supports many protocols including TrustSec, Cisco Discovery Protocol, quality of service, and VM Tracker.

10. C. The virtual security gateway executes rules and enforces policy from the Prime Services Controller.

11. B. The cloud services router is a virtualized full-featured Cisco ASR model router with an extensive protocol support list.

12. A. The Netscaler 1000v is a Citrix virtualized application controller that has an extensive feature list including SSL offload and content switching.

13. B. Service chains enable service stitching across the virtual environment by redirecting traffic through multiple virtual services before the end device is reached.

14. C. While D might sound close, SNAT is used to change the source IP address of outgoing packets to something owned by the appliance. An example might be a load balancer. This ensures reply traffic comes back to the load balancer.

15. A, B, C, D. The CSR supports all of these protocols and more, being a fully functional router and security appliance in the virtual world.

16. C. VMtracker connects to vCenter to discover the VMs connected and running on the network equipment.

17. D. While LLDP was true at one point in time, the correct answer here is SPAN. SPAN gives the ability to wire capture traffic as it moves from VM to VM.

18. B. In 1000v terminology, the Ethernet interface is the representation of the physical connection to the real switch as seen from the 1000v's perspective.

19. B. The vmknic is a virtual adapter in the kernel for management, live migrations, IP storage access, and more.

20. C. The best answer is the configuration group. VMware doesn't configure or show individual virtual interfaces that connect to each VM. Instead, port groups are used that are assigned to similar VMs. The most common occurrence is the VM identifier.

Chapter 9: Cloud Storage

1. C. Network-attached storage is available to multiple server systems and clients over a network.

2. D. Direct-connected storage is the most common connection type in this scenario. Fibre Channel is a remote storage protocol, and RAID is a fault tolerance technique.

3. C. Pooling is the logical grouping of storage resources to create logical storage volumes for virtualized systems.

4. C. Tier 3 storage is the correct answer because it is used for low-cost, rarely accessed applications such as data backups.

5. C. The VMware File System was specifically designed for VM storage deployments.

6. D. RAID 6 writes two separate parity stripes across the entire array and supports operations when one or two disks in the array fail.

7. C, D. Microsoft operating systems support both NTFS and FAT.

8. C. Thick provisioning allows for the maximum volume size at deployment time. Thin provisioning uses less than the maximum, and both Tier 1 and Tier 2 are storage models and not provisioning techniques.

9. A, C. Both the Extended File System (EXT) and the UNIX File System (UFS) are common in Linux storage environments.

10. B. Tier 2 storage is less expensive that Tier 1 and is a good solution for many storage requirements such as web, e-mail, and file sharing. Thick and thin are not relevant, and Tier 1 does not meet the requirements of this question because of cost.

11. B, C. The two primary drive designs found in cloud storage systems are spinning and solid state. NTFS and EXT are both file systems.

12. A, B, C. Standardized hardware storage interconnects include ATA, SATA, and SCSI. Block and file are not hardware interconnections.

13. C. Tiering is the process of defining the storage needs of the cloud services consumer and aligning them with the provider's offerings. RAID is a hardware storage family of redundancy types. Multipathing is a redundant SAN technique, and policies are not related to the question.

14. B. RAID groups multiple physical disks together for redundancy and performance. Multipathing is a redundancy SAN design, masking is a LUN access process, and tiering is a storage hierarchy technique.

15. D. RAID 5 allows a drive array to be rebuilt if a single drive in the array fails by recovering the parity data stored across the array. The other offered options do not contain parity data.

16. C. The UNIX File System (UFS) was developed for UNIX but is not commonly found in many Linux operating systems. FAT, VMFS, and ZTS are all file system types but are not common for UNIX or Linux storage file systems.

17. D. Thin provisioning allows for a less than maximum volume size at deployment time and dynamically allocates storage capacity as required.

18. A. Only RAID 0 is the correct answer as the other options offer recovery by writing the same file onto multiple drives, whereas RAID 0 does not.

19. D. RAID 1 is the correct answer as the other options either do not offer recovery or require more than two disks to be deployed.

20. B, C. RAID 1+0 and 0+1 combine the striping of RAID 0 and the mirroring of RAID 1.

Chapter 10: Storage Area Networking

1. C. The host bus adapter (HBA) is a server-based interface card used to connect the server to the storage network.

2. B, C. A converged network combines LAN and SAN traffic onto a single switching fabric. Ethernet is the standard frame type with Fibre Channel being encapsulated into an Ethernet-based protocol.

3. B. Network-attached storage is file-based and relies on common file systems such as NFS for Linux and CIFS for Windows.

4. B, D. iSCSI and FCoE are LAN protocols specifically designed to encapsulate storage traffic for transmission over an Ethernet network.

5. C. The initiator performs disk requests for functions such as read or write operations.

6. D, F. Common Internet File System (CIFS) and Network File System (NFS) are standard file systems used in network-attached storage systems.

7. A. A node port can be an endpoint such as an HBA installed in a server that connects to a SAN switch.

8. A. An HBA would be defined as a node port, and the SAN switch is a fabric port. So, A is correct. This would be an N_port to F_port SAN connection.

9. B. A fabric login process is performed when a storage device initially connects to the SAN switch fabric to register its WWN with the SAN fabric.

10. A. LUN masking is an access control method that can restrict specific initiators' access to defined SAN storage targets.

11. C. The iSCSI protocol encapsulates the SCSI protocol into a TCP/IP Ethernet packet.

12. B. A VSAN logically segments a Fibre Channel SAN switch into multiple logical SANs with each VSAN providing network serveries such as login and initiator to target communications.

13. A, C. Storage arrays and host bus adapters (HBA) are Fibre Channel–based systems that connect to a SAN.

14. D, E, H. Fibre Channel, iSCSI, and FCoE are all block-based storage protocols.

15. A, C, D. SAN permissions allow the cloud administrator to define rights for file operations and access.

16. B, C. A logical unit number (LUN) is a block of storage that can be created over multiple disks and has a unique identification.

17. A, B. Network-attached storage systems are file-based and can have authentication and permissions assigned.

18. A. Fibre Channel over Ethernet (FCoE) encapsulates a Fibre Channel frame into an Ethernet frame so that it can traverse an Ethernet-based switching fabric.

19. C, E. Converged networks rely on the ability to encapsulate Fibre Channel into an Ethernet frame using standards-based options such as iSCSI or FCoE.

20. B. The SAN target, which is most commonly a storage array, receives a SAN operation request from the initiator.

Chapter 11: Cisco Storage Product Families and Offerings

1. D. SAN-OS is the operating system for the MDS product line.

2. B, D. The UCS fabric interconnect and Nexus products support both storage and LAN converged switch fabrics.

3. B. The Nexus operating system is based on the MDS SAN switch operating system.

4. B. The 9222i is a member of the MDS family of SAN switches that supports multiple protocols including iSCSI, FCoE, and FICON.

5. B. The 9718 MDS SAN switch is a chassis-based product for large-scale deployments.

6. D. The Nexus 7000 series of chassis-based switches are designed for data center aggregation and core switching.

7. A. The Nexus Invicta C3124SA offers SSD storage arrays as part of the UCS family.

8. A, B. Both the MDS 9100 and 9200 series products are used for SAN extension deployments.

9. C. The MDS 9300 product family is designed for top-of-rack and end-of-row designs.

10. D. The MDS 9700 products are large-scale high-availability core SAN switches.

11. A. A SAN interswitch link (ISL) interconnects SAN switches.

12. B, C. The MDS 9700 and Nexus 7000 series offer redundant supervisors that enable ISSU support.

13. B, D. The Invicta C3124SA flash storage appliance supports both Fibre Channel and iSCSI communication protocols.

14. C. The MDS 9300 series switches are designed for medium-size deployments and offer both 48 and 96 ports.

15. A. The MDS 9100 series switches are designed for small or edge SAN implementation.

16. B. The Cisco Data Center Network Manager application can be used to configure, monitor, and manage an MDS-based SAN.

17. D. Fibre Connection or FICON is an IBM mainframe storage interconnect.

18. C. NX-OS is the operating system for the Nexus product line and is derived from the SAN-OS MDS operating system.

19. D. Virtual SANs (VSANs) are supported on the complete line of Cisco MDS SAN switches.

20. C, D. Both the local and remote switchport analyzer ports can be used to mirror traffic for monitoring and troubleshooting.

Chapter 12: Integrated Cloud Infrastructure Offerings

1. D. Express is one of the FlexPod offerings, along with Select and Datacenter.

2. D. Dell/EMC is the actual provider of the reference architecture known as VSPEX.

3. C. POD is a term that refers to a group of devices or infrastructure designed for a certain requirement, network service, or application.

4. B. 350 is a valid offering of Vblock, along with 240, 340, 540, and 740 as of this writing.

5. A. Vblock only allows VMware.

6. A. Red Hat OpenStack uses Ceph storage.

7. D. FlexPod is the offering from NetApp and Cisco.

8. B. Vblock AMP or Advanced Management POD refers to the separate management component of Vblock.

9. A. Select is a FlexPod offering, along with Datacenter and Express.

10. C. Vblock is known for being an all-in-one integrated solution. FlexRack isn't a real solution. The others are more reliant on reference architectures.

11. C. FlexPod Select is especially designed for big data and other select applications.

12. C. The Cisco UCS blade or B-series is commonly found in several offerings.

13. A. According to Cisco, one of the goals with OpenBlock is reduced operating costs.

14. B. Dell/EMC offers support for VSPEX reference architectures. The others aren't Dell/EMC or aren't reference architectures.

15. C, D. Express focuses on both Hyper-V and VMware.

16. C. VCE is the collaboration between Dell/EMC and Cisco. It also partners with VMware and Intel.

17. D. Of the options listed, FlexPod works more off a collaboration between Cisco and NetApp. Both vendors work together to troubleshoot. One could call either vendor.

18. B. Vblock has an option to have Cisco's Application Centric Infrastructure (ACI) be installed.

19. B. Of these, Vblock is the correct answer. VSPEX works, but it isn't an integrated solution out of the box; it is a reference architecture.

20. D. Of the options given, the Nexus 9000 series is one of the more often used series in the integrated solutions.

Chapter 13: Configuring Roles and Profiles

1. C. The multirole access user profile capabilities of UCS Director allow a user to perform more than one role.

2. B. A user account created directly in UCSD is considered to be a local account.

3. B. Users with matching job requirements can be placed into groups, and then the group can be assigned a role.

4. B. The Storage Administrator role has storage orchestration rights.

5. B. The System Administrator has complete access to all role-based objects.

6. B. Each user is allowed to belong to multiple roles.

7. A, D. The predefined user roles in UCS Director allow for fast deployments and ease of use.

8. C. The Cisco ONE application that contains local user accounts is the UCS Director (UCSD).

9. B. UCSD supports multivendor environments.

10. B, C. The system administrator and Group admin role have permissions to create additional roles.

11. B. UCSD supports multirole access profiles if a user has more than one requirement that would necessitate a need to belong to more than one group.

12. D. Local groups are created or predefined to support specific user functions in UCSD.

13. B, D. An individual user can be assigned to more than one role based on their requirements in the organization or if they perform more than one role.

14. A, B, C. When creating a single user account in UCS Director, the username and e-mail address are mandatory fields, with address, phone number, and first/last name being optional fields.

15. A. The syntax "username profile_name" is the appropriate login for a user with multiple profiles.

16. C, D, E. Group Name and E-mail Address are mandatory group fields and the rest are optional.

17. B. In UCSD, users are assigned to roles where access is defined.

18. C. The Systems Administrator account is the primary management account in UCS Director.

19. B. The Group Administrator role is intended to allow an end user the right to add end-user accounts.

20. A, C. UCSD supports local user definitions and can access remote directory services.

Chapter 14: Virtual Machine Operations

1. D. UCSD currently supports VMware, Hyper-V, and KVM.

2. D. The Prime Service Catalog is geared toward end users and connects to UCS Director. It is more polished and meant for the end-user experience.

3. B. End-user self-service policies are one of the many ways you can limit what a user can do in UCS Director.

4. A. UCS Director requires network, compute, system, and storage policies to be configured before VMs can be provisioned.

5. A, B. Both the Prime Service Catalog and UCSD provide self-service catalogs.

6. C. The Prime Service Catalog is largely focused on the GUI experience and is written in HTML5.

7. A, B. Both the Prime Service Catalog and UCSD can accomplish this task.

8. A. The Prime Service Catalog has a focus on this.

9. A. VMware has the most workflows and out-of-the-box integration with UCS Director.

10. B. The UCSD network policy controls this.

11. B. While it could be argued that UCSD does some as well, the Prime Service Catalog is more marketed toward this.

12. B. Of all the choices, the Prime Service Catalog is the one that has a focus on this functionality.

13. B. The storage policy is the correct answer in this case.

14. A. The computing policy controls memory.

15. B. The Prime Service Catalog is considered above UCSD in the suite. The Prime Service Catalog is the overall portal when used in conjunction with UCSD.

16. B. The Prime Service Catalog is more suited for this than UCSD. As stated previously, UCSD is primarily an engineering tool. The Prime Service Catalog is meant for reporting, self-service, orchestration, and more. The other answers are an OS and a hypervisor and are not valid answers.

17. C. OpenStack, Fusion, and Xen are not supported. Red Hat is an officially supported hypervisor.

18. B. Don't be fooled by option C. UCSD is primarily meant for the engineers working in IT with automation and orchestration tools. Prime is more polished and meant to look like something end-user customers would use.

19. D. None of the offered options do this, as A and B are focused on Cisco networking and C is not a product.

20. B. The Prime Service Catalog is exactly that—an end user portal. UCS Director offers this too, but it's more for automation and IT users.

Chapter 15: Virtual Application Containers

1. B. One of the primary advantages of deploying containers is the ability to isolate your public cloud architecture into a private grouping of services that you have complete control over.

2. B. Containers are logical private clouds and can be administered and managed by the container administrator.

3. C. Templates are a UCS Director application feature used for defining container resources.

4. B. Virtual Application Container Segmentation services are a logical construct composed of one or more network tiers that contain either virtualized or physical compute resources in a secured private network in a cloud data center that can be ordered, managed, and removed as a single entity.

5. C. A virtual application container emulates a private cloud.

6. C. The Cisco Nexus 1000v virtual switch module is required for layer 2 switching support in a VACS deployment.

7. A, B, D. The following elements are created and defined when working with templates in UCS Director: virtual accounts, network configuration, virtual machine configuration, security information for the container, gateway router policy, and any options for services and end-user needs.

8. D. The Cisco UCS Director application features full life-cycle support for virtual application containers.

9. C. The UCS Director features unified licensing management for VACS deployments.

10. C. Cisco Prime Services Catalog acts as a storefront where end users can obtain approved container configurations.

11. D. All VM configurations are maintained when a container is powered off, and the VM will power up with its configuration when power is restored.

12. D, E, F. Containers require UCSD, 1000v VSM, Prime Services Catalog, and the Virtual Switch Update Manager.

13. D. The fenced container utilizes a virtual load balancer from F5.

14. C. The virtualized version of the Application Security Appliance is used for firewall services in VACS.

15. A, D, E. Firewall applications supported natively in UCS Director include Linux, ASAv, and the Cisco Virtual Security Gateway appliance.

16. A. UCS Director allows containers to be modified after deployment, which would include the addition and deletion of virtual machines inside the VACS.

17. A, E, F, G, H. Containers supported in UCS Director include APIC, fabric, VACS, fenced virtual, and virtual security.

18. B. Deployed containers can be modified when in production.

19. B. Microsegmentation is a benefit of deploying virtual application containers.

20. C. The Cisco CSR 1000v is a full-featured router that supports access control lists for network security.

Chapter 16: Intercloud Chargeback Model

1. A, D, E, F. When creating a chargeback summary report, any cost-based object can be selected including CPU, RAM, network traffic, and unused VM resources.

2. C. The Budget Watch checkbox in the budget policy configuration will provide a hard stop on resource usage when the budget is reached if it is unchecked.

3. C, D. Object usage data is stored in daily buckets, which allows for weekly and monthly reporting.

4. B, D. The Chargeback module supports a dashboard interface and includes chargeback templates. Cost replications and cloning are not valid features.

5. A, C, D. The UCS Director Chargeback module's report generation tools allow output files in XLS, PDF, and CSV formats.

6. B, C, D, G. There is a wide range of cost metrics that can be defined in the Chargeback module including CPU speed or number of cores, the amount of memory consumed, and a one-time deployment of fixed charge.

7. A. The budget policy defined in the Chargeback module can provide a hard limit on a resource that exceeds a budget value of the cost of its usage.

8. B. Widgets are included with the Chargeback application software that can be used to customize the dashboard output.

9. B. Cost models are where you create the costs of resources such as CPU, RAM, memory, storage, and networking and use them as building blocks to create a chargeback policy.

10. B. UCS B-series hardware can be defined in a cost model for resource usage billing and can be defined as either full- or half-slot servers.

11. C, D. Usage data is collected by the Chargeback module and is stored in daily and weekly buckets.

12. B. A VM can be included in a cost model, and charges can be applied for both active and inactive consumption.

13. B. The Budget Watch checkbox in the budget policy configuration enables the use of a resource after its quota has been reached.

14. B. Charge duration is the time interval used to measure VM usage. The options are Hourly, Daily, Weekly, Monthly, or Yearly.

15. B, D. The chargeback cost models for storage include storage traffic as measured in gigabytes per hour and the amount of uncommitted storage. Logical units and VSAN assignments are not valid selections.

16. C. The value associated with objects are created in the cost model definitions. All other options do not pertain to the question.

17. B. The Chargeback module polls VMs to collect predefined objects to collect resource usage and produce billing and reporting services.

18. A, B, D, F. The included top five reports generate the highest cost objects for CPU, VMs, memory, and storage.

19. B. Costs are assigned to each unit when creating a cost model.

20. B, C, D. Cost models for VM memory offer the option to measure data transfer in gigabyte per hour, total RAM reserved, and total RAM used.

Chapter 17: Cloud Reporting Systems

1. A. UCSD cloud analytics offers trending and history. Infrastructure reports do not offer historical information beyond snapshots.

2. A, B. Both network and storage can be used as items in a cost model for UCS Director.

3. B. The Virtual infrastructure report found under Assessments is for a health check of the entire virtual infrastructure.

4. A. The showback model doesn't charge and uses reporting and documents to show what the costs are for using the infrastructure. This way, the costs are still tracked and can be used for reporting purposes. They are generally used when there are no end customers, only internal customers.

5. C. Tenants are part of ACI and have a report available on the ACI Reporting tab of UCS Director.

6. A. UCS Director reporting has basic infrastructure reports. In contrast to CloudSense Analytics, infrastructure reports do not have trend history and are mostly based on current data.

7. C. Map reports use both color coding and heat maps.

8. A. A budget policy can be used to prevent or allow groups from going over a predefined limit for charges.

9. A, C. CloudSense Analytics generates reports in HTML or PDF format.

10. A, B. The UCSD chargeback module has the top-five reports and a dashboard, as well as cost models, overall reporting, and flexibility.

11. B. The chargeback model is the most often thought of example. It is the method of charging for services used and consumed by customers or internal departments.

12. A, B. The VM network details and layer 2 neighbors are two basic reports. The MAC address report is a detailed report.

13. D. Options A, B, and C are all metrics that can be tracked for chargeback. Power is not tracked for the cost model.

14. B. CloudSense Analytics includes a billing report that can be generated.

15. B. The basic infrastructure reports do not offer a historical report.

16. A. The chargeback reports use the cost model and build a report based on the cost model type.

17. D. VPC information is from the detailed section of the basic network infrastructure reports.

18. B. Of the given list, CloudSense Analytics is the one type of reporting that can combine metrics from multiple areas. Infrastructure reports and generic reports do not offer this capability.

19. A. The Report Builder area on the CloudSense tab allows custom reports, including the duration of the metric, such as the last week or day.

20. C. The assessment report can verify this; one of its features is verifying the physical infrastructure based on the VMware hardware compatibility list.

Chapter 18: UCS Director Service Catalogs

1. C. The landing page is the default page when users log into the end-user portal.

2. B, C, D. Red Hat KVM, Microsoft Hyper-V, and VMware are the currently supported hypervisors.

3. A. The Virtual Application Cloud Segmentation template is used to deploy traditional three-tier containers easily.

4. B. Prime Service Catalog is a separate application that can be integrated with UCS Director that adds advanced service catalog capabilities and allows for highly customized catalogs. vCenter is a VMware management product, HTML Director is not a valid product, and charge reports do not apply to the question.

5. B. Powering on the UCS server is a required step of the bare-metal service catalog workflow.

6. D. The advanced catalog is meant to combine and build more advanced functionality than just the standard catalog. This is accomplished using workflows.

7. B. Under Policies ➤ Catalogs is where you'll find the UCS Director catalogs.

8. C. This feature can be used to run workflows after the VM has been built.

9. A. Lease options under customization in the standard catalog offer a quick way to deal with billing, but they are not as robust as the chargeback modules and system used outside of the catalog.

10. D. The end-user portal is a simple portal with UCS Director that is meant to be used if you have nothing else for catalog ordering. Prime Service Catalog is a far better choice for end-user portal building.

11. A. The standard catalog provides a simple way to select and order virtual machines for your end users. It is only for VMs.

12. C. One of the features of the UCS Director end-user portal is the ability to upload and deploy OVFs.

13. B. The advanced catalog offers many predefined workflows and integration into products such as ACI.

14. A. This is for a code that is used in the VM name for VMware. You can then use this name to refer to the object or group of objects in templates and policies.

15. A. The service container catalog offers the ability to combine both physical and virtual resources managed as a single service.

16. B. Publish To End Users is an option that if not selected will make the catalog invisible to end users.

17. A. As apparent by the name, the bare-metal catalog is for deploying and ordering physical servers, not virtual ones.

18. B. Share After Password Reset is one of the three options. The others are Share Template Credentials and Do Not Share.

19. A. The catalog icon is a set of predefined images the user will see when ordering from the end-user portal.

20. C. Creating, managing, and reviewing service requests are functions of the end-user portal.

Chapter 19: Cisco Prime Service Catalog Templates and Provisioning

1. C. Categories are the basic unit to organize and put services into.

2. A, B, C. These are all items you'll find on the front page.

3. A. UCS Director integrates and imports into Prime Service Catalog.

4. A, C, D. The servers menu portal includes VM operations such as creating snapshots, and suspending and cloning Virtual machines.

5. A. The search portion of the front page allows a search across all services available to the end user.

6. C. My Products & Services contain many things for the end user. It's their dashboard and centralized location to gather reports and metrics.

7. A. Under Service Designer ➤ Categories ➤ Presentation, you can define what category your service appears in and what subcategory.

8. A. A URL can be used, and you can also use predefined images or load one from your computer.

9. B. The shopping cart contains all the services that have yet to be ordered. Remember, some services don't use the shopping cart and immediately will be ordered upon hitting Submit.

10. A. You can use the Service Designer's Permissions page to set custom permissions. They can also be inherited through the UCS Director import and further customized.

11. A, B. You can skip the validation and not import the certificate, or you can import it. The choice is yours.

12. A. The ordering mode can change how a service is ordered, meaning whether it goes to the shopping cart or is an immediate order.

13. A. The nickname is the right answer for reference in multiple areas.

14. A. Browse Categories is a drop-down box on the upper left of the showcase, or front page.

15. D. My Products contains the main dashboard for end users, including the ability to manage servers with certain commands under Server.

16. A. If the shortcut on the showcase doesn't exist, either the search tool or the Browse Categories link can help you find what you need.

17. B, D. As of this writing, only three are shown in integrations: UCS Director, Performance Manager, and Cloud Center.

18. C. The notifications icon looks like a mail icon and is in the upper-right corner of the showcase, serving to notify a user of events.

19. D. There are currently eight customizable areas on the showcase.

20. A. Configured on import, the identifier field lets Prime Service Catalog keep track of all integrated external connections.

Chapter 20: Cisco Prime Service Catalog Components

1. C. Tasks are grouped together to build an overall workflow.

2. A, B. Both Cisco Process Orchestrator and Prime are a part of the IAC. Cisco Server Provisioner is too, but has been deprecated as of this writing. You might still see it on the test, so watch out for it.

3. B. Stack Designer, a part of UCS Director, helps you build application stacks and containers.

4. C. Activities allows differing workflows to be triggered on a condition.

5. B. Simply, the approval process in workflow designer can be used to stop a workflow and ask for an approval before it continues.

6. A, C. The supported file transfer protocols for PXE booting are HTTP and TFTP.

7. B. Triggers can be used to watch for a state, and when that state occurs, a workflow is executed.

8. C, D. Stateful and stateless are the two trigger types.

9. B. Component groups in UCSM are linked together in the Application Groups section of the console.

10. A, B. While not all the features, Northbound APIs and Capacity Management are two of the features.

11. A. You can skip the validation and not import the cert, or you can import it. The choice is yours.

12. C. The heat orchestration engine; an OpenStack project does this.

13. B. The RabbitMQ server is responsible for sending requests to the orchestrator service, one of three components for Stack Designer.

14. A. The OpenStack Keystone server handles identity management.

15. A. HOT Templates are often but not always written in YAML.

16. A. The stack in stack designer refers to a collection of resources, mainly VMs and their associated configurations.

17. D. Performance Manager, a tool with a unified view into multiple areas of the infrastructure including networking, storage and compute. It can also do capacity planning.

18. C. AMQP is used in RabbitMQ to exchange messages reliably.

19. A. Puppet is used for building in Stack Designer.

20. C. The UCS Performance Manager is also offered in an express version. The large difference is it only does physical and virtual compute. It does not monitor or report on storage and network items, making it not as capable as the full version.

Chapter 21: Cloud Monitoring and Remediation

1. A. Syslog is the standard for local and remote logging.

2. A. Widgets can be placed on the Dashboard. Widgets are available through multiple summary statistics throughout UCS Director.

3. C. UCS Manager can manage only 1 domain and 20 chassis or less. Any higher would require UCS Central.

4. A. The shell is required because services have to stop for the database to be backed up. This cannot be done from the GUI.

5. A. Servers on the same stratum level are allowed to mutually peer and synchronize in both directions. This is not allowed between other levels.

6. A. The Bare Metal Agent uses PXE and DHCP to assist in configuring newly booted machines both virtual and physical.

7. B, C. Options 66 and 67 are Server Name and Bootfile Name, respectively. Both are used to help the server with where to pull the file from and what the filename is.

8. C. The Infra Manager log can be viewed at the shell when there is a problem with the portal to see system information. The log is also available via the portal.

9. A, B. Of the options listed, Complete and In Progress are both valid. The other states are Submitted and Failure.

10. A. The assessment feature of CloudSense provides a health of the overall virtual infrastructure as well as hardware compatibility.

11. A. The facility is meant to convey the source and category of a message. It has a field of 0 to 23. Its usage heavily varies between vendors.

12. A, C, D. Failure is not a level. Emergency, Warning, and Notice are.

13. A. Level 7 is the highest level and is intended for debugging serious problems. In other words, it produces a lot of messages and is not something that would be turned on routinely.

14. D. SMTP is the standard for sending mail messages between servers.

15. B. Report Builder is the tool under CloudSense that allows you to customize your own reports.

16. C. UCS Central can scale to 10,000 endpoints and multiple UCS domains.

17. A, B. Both discover and offer are valid messages. The final two are not messages in the DHCP spec.

18. A, C. The performance and host performance reports are both available in CloudSense. The others are not reports in CloudSense.

19. B. While some of these answers might yield statistics as asked, the best answer is Performance Manager, which is described exactly as the question states. It is meant as a multidomain tool for statistics and monitoring.

20. B, C. There are only two versions, Express and the normal version, which is simply named UCS Performance Manager. The Express version is smaller and eliminates all but compute statistics and monitoring.

Appendix B

Answers to Written Lab

Chapter 1: Fundamentals of Cloud Computing

1. Infrastructure as a Service, Platform as a Service, Software as a Service

2. Public, Private, Hybrid, and Community

3. Elasticity

4. Resource pooling

5. Multitenancy

Chapter 2: Defining Cloud Service Models

1. Infrastructure as a Service, Platform as a Service, and Software as a Service

2. Platform

3. Amazon Web Service, Google Cloud Services, Microsoft Azure, and Cisco Intercloud

4. Regions and availability zones

5. Infrastructure

Chapter 3: Understanding Cloud Deployment Models

1. Public, private, community, and hybrid

2. Hybrid

3. Service level agreement

4. Public

5. Community

Chapter 4: Introducing the Cisco Intercloud Solution

1. Shadow IT

2. Intercloud Fabric Shell

3. Virtual Security Gateway (VSG)

4. Cloud Services Router (CSR)

5. Intercloud Secure Extension of ICX

Chapter 5: The Cisco Unified Computing System

1. LAN and SAN

2. UCS Central

3. XML API, CLI, or GUI

4. 5108

5. Pools

Chapter 6: Cisco Data Center Products and Technologies

1. Access, aggregation, and core

2. Data center bridging

3. Top of rack

4. Core three

5. 7000

6. Flexible

7. Scalability

8. Unified fabric

9. 5000

10. Overlay transport virtualization

Chapter 7: Server Virtualization in the Cloud

1. ESXi, Hyper-V

2. Virtual, virtual

3. Memory, CPU, storage, network

4. UUID, MAC

5. Portability

6. Type 1

7. VirtualBox, Zen, KVM

8. Snapshot

9. Type 2

10. Offline

Chapter 8: Infrastructure Virtualization

1. Networking services

2. Policy-based routing

3. Virtual Application Container Services

4. Virtual Supervisor Module

5. VxLAN Network Identifier (VNI)

6. vSwitch

7. Cisco Virtual Switch Update Manager

8. Virtual Service Blade

9. EVPN

10. VxLAN Gateway

Chapter 9: Cloud Storage

1. RAID 0+1

2. Thick provisioning

3. Spinning, solid-state

4. VMFS

5. Tiering

6. EXT, UFS

7. Thin provisioning

8. RAID 6

9. RAID 5

10. FAT, NTFS

Chapter 10: Storage Area Networking

1. Converged

2. Network-attached storage

3. Host bus adapter

4. Block

5. World Wide port name

6. Converged network adapter

7. Direct-attached storage

8. File

9. Initiator, target

10. LUN

Chapter 11: Cisco Storage Product Families and Offerings

1. Multilayer director switch

2. Nexus

3. 5600

4. Quality of service

5. 5600

6. 9718

7. 6324

8. 16

9. Fibre Channel, iSCSI

10. 7000

Chapter 12: Integrated Cloud Infrastructure Offerings

1. Reference architecture

2. Cisco Validated Design

3. POD

4. OpenBlock

5. UCS

6. FlexPod

7. FlexPod

8. EMC and VMware

9. 1000v

10. Dell/EMC

Chapter 13: Configuring Roles and Profiles

1. 48 and 11

2. Role-based access control

3. Users, roles

4. Groups

5. System administrator

6. Local

7. Multirole access user

8. Administration, users, and groups

9. Roles

10. Services end user

Chapter 14: Virtual Machine Operations

1. Cisco ONE

2. VMware, Microsoft Hyper-V, Red Hat KVM

3. Cisco Prime Service Catalog

4. End-user policies

5. Service Catalog

6. Prime Service Catalog (as of this writing, UCSD also has an update for HTML5)

7. System

8. Hypervisor

9. Private

10. Prime Services Catalog

Chapter 15: Virtual Application Containers

1. F5

2. Fenced

3. Prime Services Catalog

4. APIC

5. Private

6. Fabric containers

7. Power management

8. Monitoring

9. Public-facing

10. APIC

Chapter 16: Intercloud Chargeback Model

1. Chargeback module

2. Budget policy

3. Dashboard

4. Budget policy

5. Cost models

6. Virtual machine

7. Resource Accounting

8. One-time

9. Costs, units

10. Cores or gigahertz

Chapter 17: Cloud Reporting Systems

1. Cloudsense analytics

2. Infrastructure reporting

3. Cost

4. CloudSense Analytics

5. Billing report

6. Showback

7. CloudSense Analytics

8. Virtual infrastructure

9. Spend limit

10. Chargeback module

Chapter 18: UCS Director Service Catalogs

1. Standard, advanced, service container, and bare metal

2. Standard

3. Advanced

4. True; Prime Service Catalog offers a better end-user portal

5. Bare metal

6. Service container catalog

7. False; actually, the advanced catalog has only a few options, using predefined or custom workflows previously built

8. UCS Director end-user portal

9. Automatic guest customization

10. Windows license pool

Chapter 19: Cisco Prime Service Catalog Templates and Provisioning

1. The showcase
2. Identifier field
3. My Products & Services
4. Integrations
5. Categories
6. Service designer
7. Servers under My Products & Services
8. True; the icon is completely customizable
9. The showcase
10. The notifications menu

Chapter 20: Cisco Prime Service Catalog Components

1. DHCP Server
2. Workflow
3. Process
4. Stack Designer
5. Rollback
6. Server
7. Keystone
8. Tasks
9. PXE
10. Storefront

Chapter 21: Cloud Monitoring and Remediation

1. DHCP

2. Dashboard

3. UCS Manager

4. NTP

5. Shell

6. Performance Manager

7. DNS

8. Patch

9. UCS Central

10. SMTP

Index

T

W

X

Y

Z

Comprehensive Online Learning Environment

Register to gain one year of FREE access to the online interactive learning environment and test bank to help you study for your CCNA Cloud certification exams—included with your purchase of this book!

The online test bank includes the following:

- **Assessment Test** to help you focus your study to specific objectives
- **Chapter Tests** to reinforce what you've learned
- **Practice Exams** to test your knowledge of the material
- **Digital Flashcards** to reinforce your learning and provide last-minute test prep before the exam
- **Searchable Glossary** to define the key terms you'll need to know for the exam

Register and Access the Online Test Bank

To register your book and get access to the online test bank, follow these steps:

1. Go to `bit.ly/SybexTest`.
2. Select your book from the list.
3. Complete the required registration information including answering the security verification proving book ownership. You will be emailed a pin code.
4. Go to `http://www.wiley.com/go/sybextestprep` and find your book on that page and click the "Register or Login" link under your book.
5. If you already have an account at testbanks.wiley.com, login and then click the "Redeem Access Code" button to add your new book with the pin code you received. If you don't have an account already, create a new account and use the PIN code you received.